Praise for *The Chief Diversity Officer*

"*The Chief Diversity Officer* provides an extremely thorough and thoughtful overview of the importance of the evolving role and responsibilities of this position in higher education. This timely volume includes a sophisticated discussion of the structural issues involved in diversity leadership, incorporating both educational theory and practical wisdom and advice. It will be a valuable resource for academic leaders across the country who care about the educational imperatives of diversity in higher education."

—***Jonathan Alger****, President, James Madison University*

"*The Chief Diversity Officer* is a seminal contribution to the post-secondary leadership and campus management literature. The authors successfully bring together disparate literatures on campus diversity, university administration, and systemic change into a well-reasoned, comprehensive, and evidence-based guide for administrators who serve as chief diversity officers; those who supervise and evaluate their results; and scholars interested in extending the discussion. *The Chief Diversity Officer* moves the field of higher education from 'we know it when we see it' toward a canonical base for a campus unit that has become commonplace in the aftermath of Title VI compliance, affirmative action litigation, and campus-based efforts to create an environment that maximizes learning and inquiry. Each chapter offers proven management theories, contextualized insight into the shifting terrain of campus diversity, visual models of applied concepts, and a refreshing optimism on how to grow and maintain diverse campus communities. The names 'Williams' and 'Wade-Golden' must now be added to the required reading lists of both higher education research and practice."

—***M. Christopher Brown II****, President, Alcorn State University, author of* Organization and Governance in Higher Education *and coauthor of* The Case for Affirmative Action on Campus

"*The Chief Diversity Officer* breaks new ground. This much-needed book is based on both the empirical research and the collective experience of the authors effecting transformative change. The wealth of information provided makes clear the imperative for having a chief diversity officer who oversees the quality of the organizational culture. This comprehensive book will benefit anyone interested in leading, engaging, or improving higher education, leaving no excuses for failing to make a difference."

—***Mitchell J. Chang****, Professor of Education and Asian American Studies, University of California, Los Angeles*

"Williams and Wade-Golden build on earlier trailblazing work, the *Primer for College Presidents*, and offer advanced insight into the significance and importance of the CDO role. They demonstrate how the CDO's work embodies integrative, inventive, and pragmatic institutional leadership that is crucial to grappling with contemporary and imminent transformational changes in higher education. This discerning and engaging work offers advanced insight into the significance and importance of the CDO role. The authors demonstrate how the CDO's work embodies integrative, inventive, and pragmatic institutional leadership that is crucial to grappling with contemporary and imminent transformational changes in higher education."

—***Lisa M. Coleman***, *Chief Diversity Officer and Special Assistant to the President, Harvard University*

"If you are interested in chief diversity officers, you have to read this book. It will frame how you think about the definition, design, and realities of the CDO role, whether you are a leader in higher education or the corporate sector. Grounded in research, but written for practitioners and scholars alike, this book provides an excellent road map, telling leaders how to develop high impact CDO roles, lead through relationships and influence, get off to a fast start, and the critical principles for leading change. We've waited too long for the *Chief Diversity Officer* and I'm glad it's finally here, very well done!"

—***Billy Dexter***, *Partner, Global Diversity Services Practice, Heidrick & Struggles*

"For too many years, talented educators assigned roles and responsibilities for achieving access and equity, creating an inclusive climate, contributing to the scholarship around diversity, and preparing students for a diverse and interconnected world, have been handicapped in carrying out their roles effectively because diversity, though publicized as a priority, has not been an area of *strategic importance* in many colleges and universities. This publication is a sophisticated guide on how to position the CDO as a legitimate campus leader, in collaboration with other campus units, and adequately equip him or her to carry out the goals of the chief diversity officer—and in so doing, position the institution for maximum effectiveness."

—***Gwendolyn Jordan Dungy***, *Executive Director Emeritus, NASPA—Student Affairs Administrators in Higher Education*

"As organizations of all kinds look to engage issues of diversity and inclusion, they often think of creating or recasting the CDO role within their respective organizations. Done correctly, the results can be powerful; done incorrectly, and the fallout can be devastating. *The Chief Diversity Officer* carefully lays out the questions that need to be answered and the critical factors to ensure that the person who is going to assume the role is set up for success. Focused on higher education, but relevant across the board, every HR executive, CEO, or board member who is considering the CDO role in their organization should read this book."

—***Dennis Kennedy***, *Founder and CEO, National Diversity Council*

"The first and definitive book on the development and design of chief diversity officer infrastructures, this book offers an unprecedented contribution to the field of strategic diversity leadership. Focused on higher education, but valuable for corporate, non-profit, and government leaders, this book creates an unprecedented balance between theory and practice as the authors offer frameworks, theories, and practical ideas to build, evolve, and optimize the chief diversity officer role across organizational life. It is a classic that will show the way for generations of chief diversity officers, scholars, consultants, and those aspiring to role of chief diversity officer."

—***Christopher Metzler****, Senior Associate Dean for Applied Management Degrees and Associate Dean for Human Resources and Diversity Studies, Georgetown University*

"*The Chief Diversity Officer* provides much needed expertise regarding an increasingly important position across institutions and sectors. Embedded in this essential guide is not only scholarly and administrative excellence, but a passion for nurturing and mentoring students, one of the greatest traits of leadership for anyone in higher education. *The Chief Diversity Officer* provides a beacon that is essential for colleges and universities everywhere.

—***Steven J. Olikara****, University of Wisconsin-Madison Class President 2012, and Founder and President, Millennial Action Project*

"*The Chief Diversity Officer* is the second of two volumes on 'Diversity Leadership.' The excellent first book, *Strategic Diversity Leadership*, provided an organizational perspective on institutional change and transformation. This book, building on the first, focuses more explicitly on, and makes the case for, the emerging role of the chief diversity officer. In this volume the authors provide a rationale for such an office and its role in the organization of a college or university that takes diversity seriously. More importantly they provide guidance in designing, implementing, and integrating a Diversity Office that supports an institution's development of a strategy for, and a culture that values, diversity. This volume is a 'must read' for scholars of organizational behavior in higher education, for executive officers, and for anyone else interested in guiding the development of a strong institutional effort for promoting a culture of diversity."

—***Marvin W. Peterson****, Professor Emeritus, University of Michigan, and Former Director, Center for the Study of Higher and Postsecondary Education*

"*The Chief Diversity Officer* is the first text to provide a comprehensive overview of the development of the CDO role and a clear and detailed analysis of the strategic contributions that the CDO can make to organizational transformation. A must-read for the new or seasoned CDO, *The Chief Diversity Officer* engages the reader with the depth and clarity of its analysis. There are no recycled clichés, but rather a thought-provoking and well-researched treatment of the underpinnings of the various CDO models, their contributions to institutional transformation, along with practical suggestions for the new or seasoned CDO. It is well-balanced and highly readable."

—***Benjamin D. Reese***, *Vice President and Chief Diversity Officer, Duke University/Duke University Health System; and President, National Association of Diversity Officers in Higher Education (NADOHE)*

"With increasing international trade and growing migration of students and workers across country borders, the management of diversity has become a strategic opportunity for all types of organizations. *The Chief Diversity Officer* provides an insightful and pragmatic understanding of how diversity officers can help their organizations unlock the potential of diversity to drive organizational success."

—***Ian O. Williamson***, *Associate Dean, International Relations and Helen Macpherson Smith Chair in Leadership for Social Impact, Melbourne Business School, University of Melbourne*

"A successful diversity plan, which prepares students for global citizenship, can only be achieved when an institution's leadership team is committed and involved. This book is the tool needed by chief financial officers, presidents, and other campus leaders to effectively oversee the creation, development, and success of the CDO role in the academy. The authors have done an amazing job of taking the complex and making it clear, creating a higher education management text that is essential reading for leaders at every level of higher education."

—***John Walda***, *President and CEO, National Association and of College and University Business Officers (NACUBO)*

"Equity and inclusion are the most important values for all American universities in the 21st century. On many campuses these values are embodied in a senior official often carrying the title Chief Diversity Officer. This marvelous book is the first to consider in a comprehensive way the principles, structure, and responsibilities of the offices of the CDO. I recommend the book enthusiastically to all members of the university community: staff, students, faculty, and, especially, senior administrators."

—*Robert J. Birgeneau, Chancellor, University of California, Berkeley*

THE CHIEF DIVERSITY OFFICER

COMPANION VOLUME

STRATEGIC DIVERSITY LEADERSHIP

Activating Change and Transformation in Higher Education

Damon A. Williams

Also available as

THE DIVERSITY LEADERSHIP SET

THE CHIEF DIVERSITY OFFICER

STRATEGY, STRUCTURE, AND CHANGE MANAGEMENT

DAMON A. WILLIAMS
and
KATRINA C. WADE-GOLDEN

Foreword by Mark A. Emmert

Stylus

STERLING, VIRGINIA

Published by Stylus Publishing, LLC
22883 Quicksilver Drive
Sterling, Virginia 20166-2102

Library of Congress Cataloging-in-Publication Data
Williams, Damon A., author.
The chief diversity officer : strategy, structure, and change management / Damon A. Williams and Katrina Wade Golden.—First edition.
pages cm.
Includes bibliographical references and index.
ISBN 978-1-57922-235-2 (cloth : alk. paper)
ISBN 978-1-579 22-817-0 (library networkable e-edition)
ISBN 978-1-57922-818-7 (consumer e-edition)
1. Minority college students—Recruiting—United States. 2. Educational equalization—United States. 3. Universities and colleges—Employees—United States. 4. Organizational change—United States. I. Golden, Katrina Wade, author. II. Title.
LC3731.W52 2013
378.1'9820973—dc23 2012050463

13-digit ISBN: 978-1-57922-235-2 (cloth)
13-digit ISBN: 978-1-57922-817-0 (library networkable e-edition)
13-digit ISBN: 978-1-57922-818-7 (consumer e-edition)

Printed in the United States of America

All first editions printed on acid-free paper that meets the American National Standards Institute Z39-48 Standard.

First Edition, 2013

To the diversity champions
who toil to make our institutions
inclusive and excellent for all.

CONTENTS

FOREWORD

Like most higher education leaders, I have long realized that for universities and colleges to be successful we have to do more than serve the diverse members of our population. Our services need to focus on diversity as a resource that enriches the institutional culture and promotes an understanding of diversity as a critically important element of the communities in which our graduates live and work. As a former university president, and now president of the National Collegiate Athletic Association (NCAA), I have always seen the position of chief diversity officer (CDO) as my retinal partner in pursuing my educational philosophy. As leaders, we should provide our students, faculty, and staff the opportunity to engage in our organizations in a way that is inclusive; for me, this has always been one of the defining performance metrics of success.

At each campus where I have held a leadership position, diversity and inclusion were integral to the university's core values. Making diversity a priority starts at the top. Leaders must firmly champion diversity as part of the core values and the mission of their college or university. Naming an individual to fulfill the CDO role and bringing that individual into the leadership circle states clearly that inclusion is a fundamental priority. But experience shows that while naming a CDO is essential, that act falls short of realizing the potential of the role. It's what follows the appointment that is crucial to the CDO's success and the success of the campus.

The CDO must be established as a critical partner to the president, a partner who is fully engaged as member of the leadership team. The CDO is not only an individual who carries the message but is, more significantly, positioned to work across the campus and with individual leaders at all levels to develop the capacity for success. The purpose is to establish diversity and inclusion as part of ongoing leadership conversations and to stay at the forefront of the minds of those who maintain hiring and decision-making authority. This consistent engagement of the CDO with leadership and consultation is critical. It underscores the need for the CDO to focus on opportunities to expand diversity in meaningful ways and to keep leadership apprised of current diversity and inclusion issues within the campus and broader community. This goes a long way to make certain that diversity is an integral aspect of how the institution characterizes itself. Further, having an engaged CDO ensures that the way in which the organization does its business and holds people accountable reflects its core values. For diversity to be operationalized as a core value, it must be a thread woven through the fabric of the campus.

As leaders of higher education organizations, we have moved well past the moment in our social evolution in which we were compelled to define, describe, and defend diversity as critical to academic success. We get that. Today, what most organizations are moving toward is the examination of how to execute those values on our campuses, and to hold people accountable to our expectations. In this book, Williams and Wade-Golden articulate the key components to the CDO position. They extend our understanding of diversity in practice by outlining the CDO as the foundation of an integrated approach framed within the academic mission. As leaders, it is our responsibility to position the CDOs to create organizational capacity, encourage understanding, and develop a proactive approach to the overall work. By creating such an organizational structure the CDO can be positioned for success—success that can be evidenced by key partnerships across campus and the community. Ultimately, the CDO facilitates the development of diversity as a lens through which goal-setting, action, and measurement of success occurs.

Congratulations to Damon Williams and Katrina Wade-Golden on their book, *The Chief Diversity Officer: Strategy, Structure, and Change Management.* This is an incredibly valuable contribution to both higher education and to our working knowledge of the CDO role and how to position, support, and create an environment in which diversity flourishes as a resource on our campuses.

Mark A. Emmert
President, National Collegiate Athletic Association

ACKNOWLEDGMENTS

A project of this magnitude and scope could not have been undertaken without the support, participation, collaboration, and encouragement of many individuals throughout the journey—our network of care. This book is a reflection of that network, and is the result of many years of research and insightful discussions that have caused us to reexamine some of our assumptions about diversity, multiculturalism, equity, and inclusion in our personal lives, in our professional careers, and in the nation, generally.

Of special significance was the generous and clarifying aid of our editor John Ramsburgh who, with patience and powerful attention to the nuances of writing, provided stellar assistance through multiple drafts of this manuscript. We also thank Dan Chen of Pixedge, who designed the cover and models embedded throughout both books. John and Dan, we look forward to our continuing work together.

Kudos to John von Knorring, publisher of Stylus Publishing, who was eternally patient and supportive as this book dragged into the third and fourth years of writing, and ultimately became two books that complement and extend one another. Your efforts to provide a tier-one publishing platform for diverse ideas make you a powerful leader in the strategic diversity leadership movement. We are thankful to call you a friend and ally in this work.

Special Thanks by Dr. Damon A. Williams

Genuine gratitude goes to my family and friends for their love, support, and sacrifices, during the sustained recesses in developing this work. I appreciate your patience through the long silences and unreturned phone calls, as my nearly every moment was consumed with my leadership responsibilities and dogged desire to produce two books worthy of the investment that each of you have made in me through the years.

I am especially thankful to my wife, Kisha Mitchell Williams, who is a friend, confidante, and BIG THINKER who gave me the time, space, and encouragement to chase the dream of this project. As I said in my dedication to *Strategic Diversity Leadership*, "It begins and ends with you." I love you.

My every success is a reflection of the sacrifices made by my father and mother, Stephen and Melanie Williams, and my grandparents, Melvin and Katherine Williams, Arthur and Marjorie Stephens, and Charles and Mary Fields, who sacrificed so much to ensure that I received the best education possible. A special shout out to my good friend and brother Bryon Williams, who always asked about the status of the project, encouraged me during the valleys, and believed in my potential to reach this summit of the climb. You are a true brother!

This work would not have been possible without my coauthor on *The Chief Diversity Officer*, research partner, and sister—Dr. Katrina C. Wade-Golden. You are an amazing scholar, wonderful mother, wife, sister, and friend to all who know you. I am thankful to have you in my life and look forward to our continuing partnership and collective contributions to this work.

I have been particularly privileged to have a number of mentors and role models who have made powerful contributions to my development through the years. Ronald Taylor, Gerald Gurin, Frank Longstreth, Sallye McKee, John Matlock, Ron Crutcher, Alma Clayton-Pederson, Othello Harris, Cheryl Apprey, Marvin Peterson, Susan Mosley-Howard, Rodney Coates, Lester Monts, Walter Kimbrough, and Charlie Nelms have been particularly strengthening in their vision, support, and role modeling.

To my staff, students, and colleagues at the University of Wisconsin–Madison and the University of Connecticut, I appreciate your investment in this project and understanding of the life that I have chosen to lead as a scholar-administrator-educator. Your genuine concern for the broader mission of diversity, equity, and inclusion is a reflection of the true character and commitment that each of you possess. While too many exist to name—please know that I am eternally grateful for your contributions toward making this work possible.

Special Thanks by Dr. Katrina C. Wade-Golden

I wish to thank my dear friend, brother, and colleague, Dr. Damon A. Williams, whose expertise and passion for this topic served as a catalyst for this effort. It has been an absolute joy to collectively cultivate this project. I look forward to many more years of working together.

I also wish to thank Dr. John Matlock, Dr. Gerald Gurin, Dr. Patricia Gurin, and Dr. Lester Monts, our shared mentors and role models, whose investments in our lives have been invaluable, and whose insights and experiences helped us think through and conceptualize our research.

I have been especially blessed to work in an office that has been at the vanguard of developing and sustaining diverse and enriching experiences for students—the Office of Academic Multicultural Initiatives (OAMI) at the University of Michigan. Thank you for your encouragement and support throughout my time as a student at Michigan, and throughout my professional career.

We owe a special debt of gratitude to all of the respondents in our study who took the time to answer the surveys and participate in the interviews for this project. To them, we say "Thank You."

Finally, I wish to thank my wonderful husband, Roderick Golden, Jr., and our family for their unwavering support, understanding, encouragement, and love—essential elements that allow me to be my best self.

INTRODUCTION

The Chief Diversity Officer: Strategy, Structure, and Change Management

Several considerations are paramount in seeking to create or appoint a chief diversity officer. First and foremost, the president must commit to transformative change and build diversity into the mission, core values, planning, resource allocation, and accountability measures of the institution. With this level of institutional support in place, the CDO strengthens the university's national and global leadership in advancing institutional diversity; maintains a balanced advocacy role between historic considerations of access and equity for students and the expanded portfolio of institutional transformation; establishes and maintains strong, effective collaborative partnerships with peers across the university; and develops partnerships and programs with diverse communities and constituencies across the state and region to respond effectively to their needs.

—Mark Emmert, president of the National Collegiate Athletic Association and former president of the University of Washington

In recent years, the chief diversity officer (CDO) has assumed an increasingly vital role in fostering a more diverse, productive, and inclusive learning and work environment. Over the last decade, dozens of academic institutions—from Harvard University to Grand Valley State University, from Connecticut College to the University of Texas at Austin—have reframed their diversity policies and programs and developed a CDO position. The emergence of the CDO in higher education mirrors trends already taking place among hundreds of entities outside of academia, including IBM in the corporate sector, Major League Baseball in professional sports, the Democratic Party in politics, and the American Cancer Society in philanthropy. All of these organizations have created a CDO position as part of their formal efforts to achieve their diversity goals and, more fundamentally, accomplish their missions.

Whatever the setting, the CDO's responsibilities are daunting. Because the CDO position frequently spans organizational, legal, cultural, political, ethical, and even symbolic boundaries, CDOs must answer a challenging and sometimes controversial set of professional responsibilities. Moreover, because the evolution of the CDO into a dedicated leadership role has been a somewhat recent phenomenon, the position often does not possess the same institutional support and resources that other "C"-level executive positions enjoy. For this reason, we offer this book, not only to describe the challenges that today's CDO must confront, but to provide a detailed analysis of the ways that academic institutions specifically, and other organizations more generally, can empower the CDO position, making it an effective agent for diversity change efforts.

It is no longer the case that colleges and universities can simply give a minority administrator, female faculty member, or leader from the LGBT community the title "Chief Diversity Officer" and call it a day. For academic institutions to maintain their relevance and compete in an increasingly diverse, global marketplace, they must learn to take greater advantage of a resource that they have long taken for granted: their diversity. To fully integrate diversity policies and programs into the curriculum, student enrollment, the hiring and retention of diverse staff and faculty, and the promotion of an inclusive welcoming campus community—to name just a few objectives—requires academic institutions to commit significant financial and institutional resources. If they are serious about capitalizing on the educational, cultural, and economic advantages of a diverse community, they need to treat their diversity efforts in a strategic and professional manner. This book aims to offer a road map for developing the CDO position and empowering it with the institutional, financial, and administrative authority necessary to be effective.

If this book is a road map, the terrain it covers is today's colleges and universities. Indeed, our analysis is intentionally framed to have wide applicability, whether the institution in question is a large public university, a small liberal arts college, a historically Black institution a technical or vocational school, or a community college. Indeed, many of the theoretical frameworks and concrete recommendations offered here may prove useful for individuals and institutions outside of the academy. Whether responding to federal and state regulations, or hoping to take advantage of changing

American demographics, corporations, government organizations, and non-profits have increasingly taken steps to incorporate diversity values into their infrastructures and policies. For organizations with a long history of a CDO, the following chapters should help reinforce existing programs while providing suggestions for new initiatives. For organizations just beginning to consider creating a CDO position, this book offers a detailed description of several adaptable organizational models and explains how to implement them.

Finally, this book is also responding to recent changes in the legal landscape surrounding diversity. The effort by conservative legislatures and judges to undo affirmative action and other policies aimed at achieving the educational benefits of diversity is taking a toll, both on these policies and on broader leaders and how they engage issues of diversity as a strategic priority. If our diversity efforts are going to flourish, they must do so in an increasingly hostile political and judicial climate. Thankfully, a growing body of research is demonstrating conclusively that diverse learning and working environments are more productive, creative, and impactful. In short, diversity confers both an educational and an economic advantage (Cox, 1991; Milem, Chang, & Antonio, 2005; Paige, 2007; R. Thomas, 1991; D. A. Thomas, 2004). In today's world, diversity is no longer simply a question of answering our moral or social obligations; it is a matter of academic and institutional excellence. For too long, diversity has sat on the back burner of American higher education, somehow separate from issues like mission development, curriculum design, fund-raising, and leadership development. This book provides a detailed analysis of the CDO position and lays the groundwork for precisely the kind of transformational leadership that our diverse democracy now requires.

Strategic Diversity Leadership Companion Volumes

Although there is a substantial body of literature focusing on issues like the educational benefits of diversity (e.g., Milem, Chang, & Antonio, 2005), the recruitment and retention of diverse students (e.g., Bowen & Bok, 1998; Coleman & Palmer, 2004), and the challenges of diversifying our faculty ranks (e.g., Smith, Turner, Osei-Kofi, & Richards, 2004), there is a dearth of work focusing on the role of the CDO in higher education. Only recently has the CDO role begun to attract scholarly attention, and researchers are now taking a more rigorous approach to uncovering the roots, rationale, challenges, and responsibilities of a successful CDO (Arnold & Kowalski-Braun, 2011; Leon, 2010; Pittard, 2011; Williams & Wade-Golden, 2007, 2008). Given the changing demographics of higher education, the persistence of social and economic inequalities, and the rise of a knowledge-based, global economy, we can expect the CDO field to expand.

Working from research compiled over several years, and our direct professional experience as experienced diversity professionals, we have sought to make two contributions to this nascent field. The first volume in a two-volume set, *Strategic Diversity Leadership: Activating Change and Transformation in Higher Education*, is written by Damon Williams and establishes the groundwork for understanding diversity efforts in the twenty-first century. This volume begins by laying out the history of and a rationale for diversity before turning to detailed proposals for developing and implementing effective diversity policies, including strategic diversity plans; accountability scorecards; recruitment and retention programs; and leadership, resource, and infrastructure development. The second volume, *The Chief Diversity Officer: Strategy, Structure, and Change Management*, is coauthored by Williams and Katrina Wade-Golden and provides a systematic examination of the CDO role on college and university campuses. Our focus here is to provide systematic guidance on how best to define, design, and deploy the CDO role in higher education. Depending on his or her expertise and interests, the reader may find one volume more relevant than the other. But although we have written them in such a way that each can stand on its own, they do cover different aspects of strategic diversity leadership and ideally should be read together.

As we prepare our students for global citizenship, and confront conservative challenges to the emerging imperatives of diversity in the twenty-first century, we will need to develop a new kind of leadership. Working from our definition of *strategic diversity leadership* as an "artful science," we explore in both volumes a wide range of leadership issues, including the CDO's rank, organizational placement, and responsibilities. Most importantly, because CDOs confront such a wide range of institutional and administrative settings, both volumes explore in detail the *multifaceted* leadership styles that characterize the CDO role.

More than in most executive leadership roles, the authority of the CDO is a function of his or her ability to frame the issues, build relationships, facilitate collaboration, and inspire allies and stakeholders to create change. Although we consistently maintain that institutions need to imbue the CDO position with the formal authority, financial resources, and staff to design and implement robust diversity policies and programs, we also recognize that because of the nuance required of this position, CDOs need to possess a profound understanding of the history and culture of their institutional environments, and a degree of sensitivity and interpersonal skills unmatched by other "C"-level executive roles. In addition, most senior leaders have not fully appreciated that campus diversity efforts need to be fully incorporated into an institution's broader goals and mission. Thus, we emphasize throughout both volumes the advantages of integrating the CDO role into a senior leadership role, with direct access to the president or provost, and granted both access to and command over a broad range of institutional resources.

The Chief Diversity Officer in particular explores ways the CDO can improve the organizational culture and broader campus community's quality of life for all faculty, staff, and students. Because diversity benefits everyone, the entire community has a stake in diversity efforts, and the CDO's role is to enable a multipronged approach that not only leads to concrete and measurable outcomes, but a broad, positive cultural transformation. Although our primary focus is on the CDO in higher education, our research has drawn from and is relevant for corporate, nonprofit, and public sector leaders seeking to implement or improve diversity efforts. Our treatment of organizational design (Chapters 1–4), strategic diversity leadership (Chapters 5–7), and the "First 100 Days" as a new diversity executive (Chapter 8) speaks to a number of different audiences. Chapter 9 concludes the book by offering the first detailed comparison of the CDO role across sectors, applying a framework introduced in Chapter 3, the Chief Diversity Officer Development Framework (CDODF), to an examination of the CDO role in higher education and the corporate sector.

Diversity Goals Pyramid

Over the years, colleges and universities have developed dedicated diversity capabilities designed to (a) achieve access and equity for historically underrepresented groups, (b) create a multicultural and inclusive climate for the entire campus community, (c) enhance domestic and international research and scholarship opportunities around diversity issues, and (d) prepare all students for a diverse and interconnected global society. In our conversation with dozens of campus diversity committees and hundreds of individual leaders, these four goals consistently emerged as foundational to the CDO's overall mission. Figure I.1 presents these four concepts visually in the form of a diversity goals pyramid.

We place these four goals in a pyramid model to provide an accessible visual framework for appreciating the connection between diversity's historic role and its new, contemporary objectives. Access and equity are placed at the top of the model because we believe that every institution's diversity efforts must begin by engaging the historic and ongoing imperative to achieve access and equality for racially and ethnically diverse individuals, women, economically vulnerable communities, and other historically excluded groups. Promoting a diverse student, faculty, and staff community helps create a context in which institutions can take advantage of the educational and cultural benefits of diversity. Indeed, this aspect of the model could also be extended into a conversation of vendor relationships and strategic sourcing, ensuring that minority- and women-owned companies are treated fairly in an institution's procurement process.

As Figure I.1 illustrates, at the center of the model is the need to build a multicultural and inclusive campus climate where every student, staff person, faculty member, and administrator can thrive. This means more than simply mitigating overt acts of discrimination and prejudice; rather, it means creating and promoting a welcoming an inclusive environment. Thus, academic institutions are actively supporting identity-themed organizations and initiatives designed to create an inclusive experience for diverse individuals and groups (Hurtado & Carter, 1997; Patton, 2010; Peterson et al., 1978).

FIGURE I.1
Diversity Goals Pyramid

The creation of a multicultural and inclusive campus community will enhance the institution's potential to build a diverse learning and work environment that accomplishes the two strategic goals at the base of the pyramid: preparing all students for a diverse and global world, and pursuing areas of scholarship and inquiry that will help us to understand issues of diversity across disciplines. Although some administrative leaders have begun talking about the diverse educational needs of all students as part of their institutional diversity agenda, they have not similarly embraced the need to support faculty engaged in ethnic or gender studies, or pursuing scholarship that is critical to understanding our increasingly diverse and multicultural society. We placed both of these goals at the base corners of the pyramid because they are foundational to higher education and its focus on teaching, learning, research, and service. In the twenty-first century, we must fully embrace diversity as a core dimension of the overall mission of higher education, and this imperative needs to find expression as part of a robust and strategic campus diversity agenda.

Understanding the educational and research components of diversity is essential to defining a strategic diversity agenda that goes beyond traditional social justice and historical imperatives. Moreover, by focusing on these two areas, we can strengthen the legal and policy arguments for improving access and equity diversity efforts (Alger, 2009; American Association for the Advancement of Science, 2010; Coleman & Palmer, 2004). In the twenty-first century, the primary rationale for diversity must always flow from a discussion of its educational benefits and the broad societal merits of having a diverse institutional environment. Over the years, even as they have been forced to steer clear of quota systems, colleges and universities have been able to expand diversity programs as they relate to curriculum development, hiring and retention of diverse faculty and staff, funding and prioritization of research projects, and efforts to enhance cocurricular learning and service opportunities.

Because the stakeholders involved in higher education are themselves so diverse and so numerous, the theoretical models and structural frameworks we propose must be correspondingly complex and agile. To make diversity a matter of institutional excellence, the campus diversity agenda must simultaneously expand access and equity, create inclusive environments, and build the institution's academic diversity capabilities. Running along the base of the pyramid are efforts at building "strategic diversity capacity," which are the administrative building blocks of an institution's diversity efforts. They include diversity plans, accountability techniques, scorecards, intergroup relations offices, cultural centers, affirmative action officers, and other capacities designed to support the delivery of the various diversity goals outlined here.

Diversity Initiatives in Higher Education

Although the CDO nomenclature is fairly new in higher education, diversity leadership roles have existed for over 40 years. Indeed, many of the first minority affairs, African American cultural centers, academic bridge programs, and ethnic studies programs were created in the 1960s. Most of these early efforts grew out of the civil rights movement and nationalist social movements (Ogblar 2005). They not only improved the access of minority students to higher education, but also were instrumental to the quality of their experience once they arrived. Some of these programs, however, merely served as window dressing, a chance for colleges and universities to say they were doing something to advance diversity when the overall effect was to relegate diversity efforts to their institutional backwaters. *The Chief Diversity Officer: Strategy, Structure, and Change Management* emerged in part from our frustration with seeing diversity leadership roles that either had atrophied over the years or were too poorly designed and situated to be effective.

Part of the challenge we face is that many senior academic leaders lack the theoretical and organizational tools to move their diversity policies and programs into a higher gear. Appreciating diversity's importance also means understanding the complex historical and cultural setting against which our diversity efforts take place, as well as the overlapping objectives that these efforts seek to fulfill.

To capture the complexity of diversity in higher education, we have created a venn diagram in Figure I.2 that defines broadly three models or frames for understanding diversity efforts in higher education: (a) the Affirmative Action and Equity Model; (b) the Multicultural and Inclusion Diversity Model; and (c) the Learning, Diversity, and Research Model. Each model approaches the diversity issue differently and has its own set of organizational capabilities, including policies, programs, initiatives, and objectives that, although unique, often have areas of overlap and synergy. These models amplify our discussion of Figure I.1 and its presentation of the Diversity Goals Pyramid as each organizational model provides the capabilities

FIGURE I.2
Three Primary Models of Diversity in Higher Education

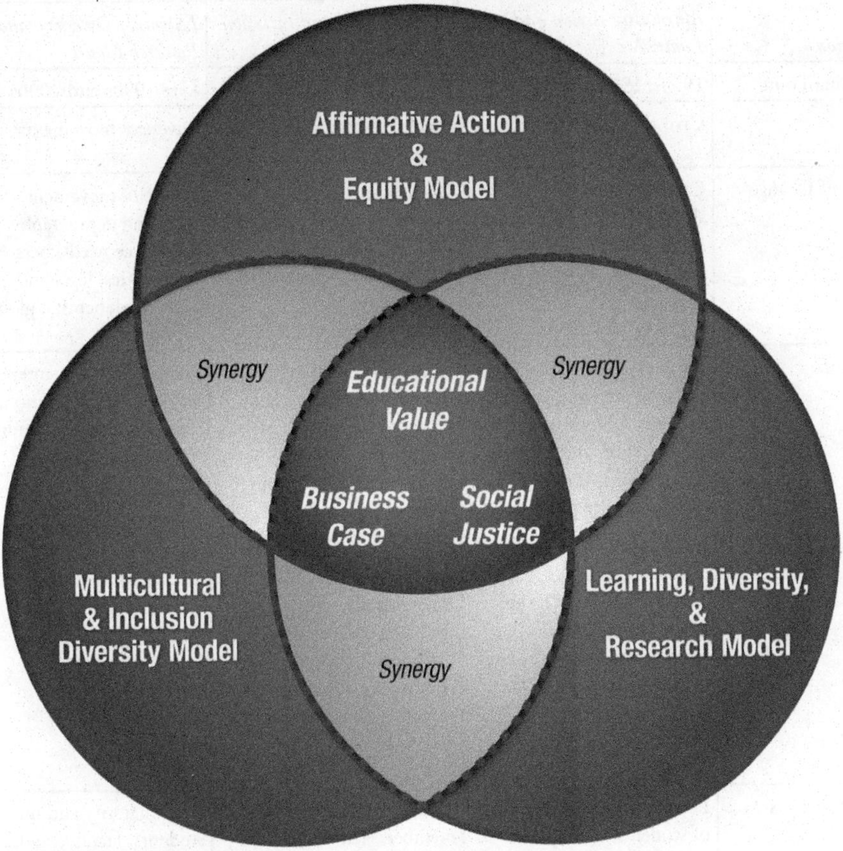

Source: Williams, 2012.

required to help institutions achieve their diversity goals, however they are defined.

Three Organizational Diversity Models in Higher Education

Our conception of the Affirmative Action and Equity Model emerged from the civil rights movement and the watershed political upheavals of the 1950s, 1960s, and 1970s. The model describes college and university diversity efforts to eliminate overt discrimination and increase the demographic representation of federally protected groups of historically underrepresented minorities,

TABLE I.1
Three Models of Organizational Diversity Capabilities in Higher Education

Dimension	*Affirmative Action and Equity Model*	*Multicultural and Inclusion Diversity Model*	*Learning, Diversity, and Research Model*
Launching Point	1950s, 1960s, and 1970s	1960s and 1970s	Late 1990s and 2000s
Locus	Civil rights movement	Black Power and other empowerment movements	Diversity movement
Drivers of Change	Civil rights movement; shifting laws, policies, and social movements	Broader social justice movements, campus social protests, shifting legal policies	Diversity movement, changing demographics, workforce needs, persistent inequalities, legal and political dynamics, global economy
Definition	Focused efforts designed to enhance the compositional diversity of an institution's faculty, staff, and students, and to eliminate discriminatory practices	Institutional efforts designed to nurture and promote the culture of racially and ethnically diverse minorities, women, members of the LGBT community, and diverse social identity groups	Focused agenda centered on infusing diversity into an institution's curriculum and its research priorities
Character	Elimination of exclusionary barriers, remediation, process improvement, and diversity as a positive factor among several used in admissions and hiring decisions	Providing diversity services, fostering community and inclusion on campus, and conducting research and teaching courses in the diversity field	Diversity as a vital component of student learning and faculty research
Target of Efforts	Federally protected groups of students, faculty, and staff	Minorities, LGBT members, faith-based communities, women, and other bounded social identity groups; primarily focused on students, with faculty serving as a secondary target	Both majority and minority students, faculty, staff, and administrators
Primary Organizational Capability	Affirmative action offices, plans, and policy statements; race-conscious admissions and financial aid programs; equal opportunity programs like Upward Bound, Talent Search, etc.	Multicultural affairs offices, minority affairs offices, cultural centers, lactation lounges, reflection/prayer areas, diverse student organizations, diversity affinity organizations for faculty and staff	Centralized diversity requirements; ethnic studies, gender studies, international studies, diversity programs like Intergroup Relations Offices; study abroad and service learning initiatives

women, the disabled, and veterans. Responding to important federal legislation, academic institutions used a confluence of affirmative action and equity offices, policies, and programs to begin redressing the historic exclusion of minority groups from higher education.

Our identification of the Multicultural and Inclusion Diversity Model emerges from our review of the Black Power and other nationalist and identity-themed movements of the 1960s and 1970s. This model looks beyond the strict regulatory and legal setting of the Affirmative Action and Equity Model toward the broad cultural and social shifts that paralleled the civil rights movement, as institutions restructured their institutional capabilities to support the experiences of African Americans and other emerging diverse groups in higher education. The primary goals of the multicultural model are to foster the educational environments that support the experience and success of diverse social groups (Williams & Clowney, 2007). In recent years, the diversity umbrella has expanded to include a broader range of populations, including native populations, persons with disabilities, faith-based communities, members of the LGBT community, veterans, and foreign nationals, among others. Thanks to recent demographic shifts, Asian Americans, people of Middle Eastern decent, members of diverse religious communities, as well as other constituencies are taking their seats at the diversity table. Although focusing explicitly on promoting and protecting the values of multiculturalism, this model also contains a strong social justice rationale, namely that no individual or group should be subject to biased or hostile treatment on the basis of minority status. The Multicultural and Inclusion Diversity Model has helped power the emergence of new capabilities on campus, including multicultural and minority affairs offices, disability offices, ethnic- and gender-specific cultural centers, women's centers, lactation areas, reflection or prayer rooms, historical theme celebrations like LGBT history month, and student organizations.

We posit the Learning, Diversity, and Research Model as a means to demarcate the most recent developments in diversity discourse, namely the growing understanding of diversity's importance to educational outcomes, beginning first with the Supreme Court's 1978 *Bakke* decision. This legal rationale for diversity was later reinforced in the 2003 Supreme Court decisions *Gratz v. Bollinger* and *Grutter v. Bollinger.* The primary goal of the Learning, Diversity, and Research Model is to use diversity as a resource to improve college students' cognitive and relational skills (Gurin, Dey, Hurtado, & Gurin, 2002). Put simply, diversity is a functional resource that can enhance student learning. Accordingly, this model focuses on curricular and cocurricular experiences that connect diversity to a student's academic and leadership development (Gurin et al., 2002). Intergroup relations programs, general education diversity requirements, living learning communities, and study abroad initiatives are just some of the technologies that institutions can deploy to accomplish the diversity goals of this model. If we broadly demarcate the target populations of the three models, the Affirmative Action and Equity Model is oriented toward federally protected groups; the Multicultural and Inclusion Diversity Model focuses on diverse social identity groups; and the Learning, Diversity, and Research Model is aimed toward all students as well as faculty and staff engaged in the research process.

Summary of the Three Models

These three models illustrate how the diversity paradigm has expanded from an initial focus on historically underrepresented groups to encompass the entire institutional community. Over time, institutions have developed a host of diversity policies, practices, offices, and units to accomplish an expanding set of diversity objectives. This expansion is one of the reasons that the CDO role is becoming both more common and more prominent, as presidents and other senior leaders look to maximize resources and coordinate initiatives through a professional CDO. Our outline of these three models establishes the framework for understanding the different types of capabilities that CDOs must consider when coordinating new policies and programs. As in most organizational contexts, the CDO role is emerging interdependently with preexisting roles (Abbott, 1988). CDOs emerge from affirmative action and equal employment opportunity offices, multicultural student development positions, human resources specialists, the faculty ranks (especially those with a diversity research agenda), and administrators in various areas of academic affairs.

It is important to note that many diversity capabilities are not easily mapped into a single model. For example, ethnic and gender studies areas have characteristics of both the Multicultural and Inclusion Diversity and the Learning, Diversity, and Research models. On today's campuses it makes sense to develop hybrid capabilities, blending the three models in ways that address both the legal and regulatory concerns of specific subgroups while also promoting a more inclusive campus community that can take advantage of our increasingly diverse and multicultural society. A multifaceted approach allows academic institutions to highlight the educational benefits of diversity; expand the scholarly understanding of diverse groups; and support a wide variety of student, faculty, and staff constituencies on campus.

Most long-standing campus diversity capabilities are rooted in either the Affirmative Action and Equity or the Multicultural and Inclusion Diversity model. Consequently, there are inherent tensions surrounding what should be the primary focus and work priorities of the CDO. As we discuss in subsequent sections, a well-designed CDO role should engage diversity efforts across all three of these models. Ideally, the CDO is situated at the intersection of a broad range of different capacities, by turns directly supervising various diversity programs, providing leadership in a facilitating role with key allies and committees, and helping to develop and implement long-range policy. Throughout these efforts he or she is establishing accountability and reporting systems that reach simultaneously toward specific efforts on the ground and toward the institution's senior leaders, including the president and provost. Throughout this book, we return to these models in an effort to place the CDO's role at the central hub of an institution's diversity capabilities.

Defining the CDO Role

Chapter 1 dives directly into defining the CDO role, noting that some institutions define the CDO as the highest-ranking diversity administrator, regardless of whether this individual is an assistant dean of student diversity programs or serves more broadly in a diversity, equity, and inclusion role at the vice presidential level. Too often in higher education, issues of rank and role responsibility are ignored, leaving the CDO position without the same institutional and budgetary authority of other "C"-level executive roles that exist in other areas. *The Chief Diversity Officer* works to challenge this tendency, advancing a definition of the CDO that is consistent with the "chief" designation of executive-level leadership reserved for chief executive, academic, financial, and information officers. Hence, we offer the following *grounded* definition of the CDO role:

> Reporting to the president and/or provost, the CDO is an institution's highest-ranking diversity administrator. The position designates an individual who serves in a senior administrative role working toward diversity-themed organizational change as a top priority at the highest levels of leadership and governance. The role is integrative, spans administrative and institutional boundaries, and reflects the CDO's capacity to lead, coordinate, facilitate, enhance, and at times supervise the formal diversity capabilities of the institution in an effort to create an inclusive and academically rewarding environment for all. Within this context, diversity is not merely a demographic goal but a strategic priority that is fundamental to creating

a dynamic educational and work environment that fulfills the teaching, learning, research, and service mission of the institution.

Throughout this book, we consistently argue against a lone-wolf leadership style, emphasizing instead that strategic diversity leadership is a practice of shared responsibility. If the CDO ends up as the only person responsible for diversity efforts, his or her efforts will likely fail and the CDO position will end up serving as little more than a figurehead. To be effective, academic institutions need to make enhancing diversity a strategic priority and tie their efforts to specific outcomes.

Professionalizing the CDO Role

Both *The Chief Diversity Officer* and *Strategic Diversity Leadership,* therefore, are aimed at helping to professionalize the CDO role as a specialized leadership position that rests on a credible body of organizational theory and research. Our goal is not simply to define the CDO role, but to frame it within a broader conversation about how organizations of all kinds are developing their capacity to engage in issues of diversity, equity, and inclusion. In fact, Chapter 5 explores the energies crystallizing around what we refer to as a *strategic diversity leadership movement* and the specific way that professional affinity organizations, credentialing programs, and research are driving the professionalization of the CDO role. During one interview, a longtime CDO at two different Fortune 500 companies told us:

> This role is a profession now and it needs to be respected accordingly. There is an approach, a language, and strategies that need to be put into place if we are going to lead on diversity and inclusion. It is not simply about understanding affirmative action and compliance issues. I have to know the base business for my company and be able to translate this reality to my diversity efforts. My job as CDO is to bring this professionalized approach, so that we can retain great talent, capitalize diverse markets, and create an inclusive culture where the entire company can thrive.

Although we support the general tenor of this leader's perspective, a good amount of territory remains to be traveled if the CDO is to become officially recognized as an established profession in the corporate, higher education, and nonprofit sectors. To cover this remaining distance, it is paramount that our profession establish clear expectations, standards and ethics, and best practices on issues like leadership, jurisdiction, and competency.

A Professionalization Framework

In his article "The Professionalization of Everyone?" H. L. Wilensky (1964) elaborated a series of five steps that characterize the professional development of an organizational role. The first step is the emergence of a durable, paid, full-time activity as an occupation. The second step describes the development of formal education programs, including degree and certification programs offered by academic institutions. Over time a vocation's contents become standardized and a college or university undergraduate or graduate degree becomes a preferred qualification for access to the occupation. The third step is marked by the emergence of professional associations that help formulate standards and regulate access to the occupation, while also representing its members and their interests. In the fourth step, professional associations succeed in creating a formal license associated with the profession's name and area of responsibilities. Practicing the occupation without adequate qualification is ultimately outlawed, further protecting the profession's legitimacy. The fifth and final step is the establishment of a professional ethics code that regulates the conduct of the profession's members, works to eliminate the unqualified, and emphasizes the importance of the service ideal embedded in the work itself.

Higher Education Corporate and Nonprofit CDOs in a Comparative Context

Applying Wilensky's criteria to CDOs illustrates that there is a professional community associated with diversity, but that the CDO role has not yet reached the status of "profession" as defined by the evaluative framework we offer in Table I.2. Even if we do not insist on Wilensky's ordered progression of steps, CDO professional communities do not meet many of the criteria associated with professional associations, whether educational, corporate, or nonprofit in nature.

In Table I.2 we offer a simple scoring rubric demonstrating that with respect to the professionalization of the CDO role, only the "full-time job status" criterion is generally satisfied across CDO ranks. Led by the corporate sector, many companies have developed permanent CDO roles. They are followed by higher education, whereas nonprofit organizations are just beginning to hire CDOs. Yet if we use the more stringent definition of CDO of serving as a profession, one could make the argument that the CDO role has not emerged fully even in the corporate sector. Those strong positions that do exist, whether in the corporate, academic, or nonprofit sector, tend to congregate in large, well-resourced organizations, rather than smaller ones (Dexter, 2010; Diversity Best Practices, 2005; Metzler, 2008).

TABLE I.2
Chief Diversity Officer Professionalization Comparison Matrix

Dimension	*Description*	*Higher Education*	*Corporate*	*Nonprofit*
Full-Time Status	The chief diversity officer designation is a full-time occupation.	✔✔	✔✔✔	✔
Specialized Training	Specialized training anchored in higher education is available to systematically prepare leaders for the role of chief diversity officer.	✔	✔✔	✔
Professional Organization	Professional organizations exist for chief diversity officers to strengthen and define the field as a professional community.	✔✔✔	✔	✔
Defined Territory and Jurisdiction	Chief diversity officers have formally established the right to define their area of specialization and area of responsibility.	✔	✔	✔
Formal Expression of a Professional Code of Ethics	Chief diversity officer professional organizations have established a formal code of ethics to eliminate the unqualified, protect clients, and emphasize the role's service ideal.	✔	✔	✔

Source: Wilensky, 1964.
✔ = Nearly nonexistent within the professional community doing the work
✔✔ = Moderate and growing in prevalence within the professional community doing the work
✔✔✔ = Very strong and robust as a characteristic of the professional community doing the work

That many CDOs do not have a formal education in strategic diversity leadership points to another of the major challenges of the profession: without focused, professional training, many are forced to learn the job on the fly, one of the primary drivers that led us to write this book. For the role to gain legitimacy, the CDO's work responsibilities must be directly linked to a credible body of research. Moreover, the role would benefit from professional development trainings that contain a certification or credentialing dimension. In Chapter 5, we explore the strategic diversity leadership literature as it pertains to diversity planning, recruitment and retention, law, change management, and other relevant areas. The presence of a robust body of credible research and theory around diversity efforts establishes an important foundation for CDOs to build on in their work. However, more structured academic systems—including "strategic diversity leadership" degree programs, majors, minors, and certifications—have yet to fully emerge across the landscape of higher education even as a number of consultants and for-profit companies have begun developing diversity leadership certifications outside of the academy.[1] Colleges and universities must take on the mantle of developing curriculum, certification, and degree programs if the role is to achieve full maturity as a profession. At present, the capabilities in this area are nascent, as only a few seasoned strategic diversity leadership programs exist at a handful of institutions, including Georgetown University, Cornell University, and Cleveland State University. The curriculum at these institutions is more focused toward the corporate community than toward higher education or nonprofit organizations, although some promising efforts are underway.[2] At the same time, their efforts have helped establish precedents that other institutions should be looking to adopt and extend, a point we explore in our discussion of the isomorphic forces driving the strategic diversity leadership movement in Chapter 5.

Our investigations have also revealed that there are no professional CDO organizations that cut across the higher education, corporate, and nonprofit sectors. The most evolved CDO professional organizations are fairly new, and leaders in higher education have created the National Association of Diversity Officers in Higher Education (NADOHE). NADOHE is providing an effective context for professionalizing the role of the CDO, creating individual and institutional memberships, developing state chapters, publishing an academic journal, hosting annual meetings, and inspiring institutions to develop the CDO role in more credible and legitimate ways. We explore the role of the NADOHE in Chapter 5.

Where the professionalization of the CDO faces its greatest challenge is at the fourth stage and the efforts to define and enforce a strict code of qualifications and responsibilities of a "licensed CDO." Indeed, this is the litmus that many fields fail to achieve. For example, it is what distinguishes the legal and psychiatric professions from areas like marketing and human resources. In these examples, the former professions not only enjoy a clearly defined area of expertise, they have received formal legal support that sets clear qualification benchmarks and is regulated by a clear code of ethics. Just as this litmus has never been achieved by marketers and human resources professionals, the strict enforcement of a "license to practice as a CDO" is unlikely to occur.

In higher education, this standard may be particularly difficult to achieve as many college and university leaders have little or no formal training to lead their organizations. This is a reality that departs from the senior leadership ranks of the private sector, where it is common for executive leaders to hold an MBA, in addition to their on-the-ground leadership experiences rising through the ranks. For better or worse, leaders in higher education rarely receive specific training and credentialing to lead in their respective areas as many presidents and provosts hold degrees outside of higher education administration or educational leadership. Indeed, the standard of leadership in higher education is often on-the-job experiences as faculty members and department chairs, illustrating how the very administrative DNA of colleges and universities is inconsistent with the idea of having specifically credentialed leadership roles in all areas of administration, not just in the role of CDO.

Finally, the CDO field lacks a formal code of ethics to regulate behavior and maintain a high level of personal and professional conduct. This code could serve as a benchmark for reviewing and eliminating unqualified CDOs, protecting organizations, and articulating the service ideal that is at the heart of the CDO position's mission. It would require the leadership of NADOHE and others to come together and establish an ethical code and other licensing procedures to fully activate this dimension. We hope this book will contribute to the discussion of the necessary qualities that diversity officers must possess to serve in the CDO role. In Chapters 1 through 4, we examine the key competencies of the CDO role. To establish a formal code of ethics, our "profession" must establish a clear understanding of the CDO's responsibilities and competencies as an organization's CDO.

Designing the CDO Role to Enhance Core Competence

The Chief Diversity Officer seeks to provide the critical insights and theoretical frameworks necessary to empower senior leaders as they design CDO roles at their institutions. For this reason we emphasize the theory and practice of CDO role design in Chapters 1 through 4, applying the organizational design literature to the topic of diversity leadership.

With their boundary-spanning, catalyzing role, CDOs are key to integrating disparate diversity capabilities into a cohesive institutional competency. C. K. Prahalad and Gary Hamel (1994) define core competencies as the ability to integrate various strategies, policies, structures, people, and knowledge around a focused set of goals and outcomes. Core competence is about harmonizing knowledge and capability, organizing work processes, and delivering value to the institution. It is also about blending different areas of expertise in new ways that amount to more than their individual parts. This requires creating vertical and lateral structures so as to interrupt traditional ways of doing business on campus and facilitating new alignments that interface with the office and person of the CDO.

Competence is enhanced and expanded as it is applied and used. For example, if one grant initiative significantly improves the recruitment, retention, and graduation rates of minorities in the science, technology, engineering, and math fields, campus leaders must be able to weave this knowledge into other institutional areas. The CDO can play a critical role in spreading lessons and initiatives across the notoriously decentralized institutional environments that tend to characterize academic institutions. A CDO is important to fostering campus organizational competencies because he or she can help the institution effectively utilize diversity resources already in place. As such, officers should place a premium on alliances and partnerships.

The Chief Diversity Officer Study in Higher Education

This contribution to the emerging field of strategic diversity leadership is informed by an intensive research project that we conducted, "The Chief Diversity Officer Study in Higher Education," and published in *The Chief Diversity Officer: A Primer for Presidential Leadership* (Williams & Wade-Golden, 2008). This study used a mixed methodology consisting of both qualitative and quantitative components designed to provide deep insights into the topic of strategic diversity leadership in the academy.

The qualitative aspect of the study included intensive interviews with more than 100 individuals, numerous site visits, more than 200 hours of audio-recorded data, and the analysis of several thousand pages of internal institutional documents. From these data the authors developed a firmly grounded understanding of various diversity roles and the process of strategic diversity leadership. In our consulting visits with dozens of institutions and through a systematic collection of diversity research found on the Internet, we compiled hundreds of strategic and diversity plans, reports, position papers, websites, and newspaper articles. Table I.3 summarizes these research resources.

The quantitative dimension of the study involved a national survey built from our initial qualitative investigations. The target sample for the project

TABLE I.3
Chief Diversity Officer Study Documents Overview

Dimension	*Description*	*Number*
Diversity Plans	Plans outlining a comprehensive institutional diversity agenda	87
Diversity Reports	Progress reports, updates, annual reports, and other documents illustrating diversity efforts, implementation, campus climate studies, etc.	52
Dedicated Diversity Position Descriptions	Position descriptions outlining the strategy, structure, and goals of a new position dedicated to accomplishing institutional diversity goals	109
Diversity Websites	Websites describing campus diversity units and initiatives	137
Concept Papers for New Positions	Concept papers delineating new diversity positions and units, often with a comparative context	7
Newspaper Articles	Articles announcing new diversity positions, initiatives, responses to institutional crises, challenges, etc.	150
Academic and Strategic Plans	Academic and strategic plans with at least some component focusing on issues of diversity	22

included diversity officers broadly defined at more than 2,500 higher education institutions. Out of 2,513 officers contacted, we received responses from 772 individuals, a 31 percent response rate. We then pursued direct interactions with the most high-ranking diversity administrators, which for the purpose of this book we define as CDOs. These individuals were selected for inclusion on the basis of four criteria: (a) self-classification as a CDO; (b) a direct reporting relationship to their institution's president or provost; (c) institutional rank of either special assistant/senior advisor to the president, vice president/provost/chancellor, associate vice president/provost/chancellor, assistant vice president/provost/chancellor, or dean, reflecting the institutional titles that most frequently populate the "chief" designation nationally; and (d) a diversity element in their title. This query yielded 110 individuals.

This book is also informed by our nearly 40 years of cumulative experience working in CDO divisions and offices. During this time, we have consulted with more than 300 organizations across a wide variety of sectors. This work has centered on helping leaders understand issues of diversity, inclusion, strategic planning for diversity, assessing diversity outcomes, and establishing dedicated diversity infrastructures. Examples of our work include creating a CDO position in higher education; conducting strategic planning for diversity, equity, and inclusion efforts; managing change, conflict, and crisis incidents; conducting survey research to understand the educational implications of diversity; researching organizational climates and cultures; and developing diversity training and executive education programs.

Book Overview

As our title suggests, *The Chief Diversity Officer* centers on the who, what, when, and how of this strategic diversity leadership role in the academy. Rather than prescribing one path for designing the CDO role, this book covers many of the key dimensions and contingencies that senior leaders must consider in developing this position. We then elaborate the process of situating the CDO in such a way that he or she can maximize opportunities, not only to help design and implement effective diversity policies, but to move the entire organizational culture toward a proactive stance with respect to the educational and cultural benefits of diversity.

Informing *The Chief Diversity Officer* is an effort to professionalize the CDO role, articulating the position's competencies, its design and performance, how it is situated within the administrative hierarchy, and the strategies and principles that inform day-to-day efforts. Finally, we place the CDO role in the context of the broader strategic diversity leadership movement in higher education and, in the concluding chapter of this book, in relationship to CDOs operating in the corporate environment.

The overall text of the book is divided into two major sections. Part One (Chapters 1–4) addresses the definition, design, and structure of the CDO role. Part Two (Chapters 5–9) focuses on the role of the CDO in leading change. The last two chapters of this volume, Chapters 8 and 9, are designed to help CDOs get off to a fast start and to understand some of the key similarities, and differences, between CDOs in the academic and corporate worlds. Chapter 9 points toward the most recent developments in our research, as we have sought to demonstrate how CDOs from different professions can learn from each other. The simple fact is, CDOs in academia have a great deal to learn from their colleagues in the corporate world, and vice versa. By collaborating, especially through the development of professional networks and associations, they can disseminate and adapt a broad and evolving body of diversity best practices.

Part One: Defining, Designing, and Optimizing the Role of the Chief Diversity Officer

Beginning with Chapter 1, we discuss the evolution of the CDO role in the academy. Relying on organizational design literature, we examine the CDO role as it has emerged in response to a complex and shifting historical and cultural landscape. Chapter 2 works to further clarify the role of the CDO as an integrative force helping to coordinate, engage, and lead the diversity agenda on college and university campuses as an agent of organizational transformation. The complexities, power base, and challenges associated with leading as a CDO are highlighted using a number of stories and insights from officers.

Chapter 3 presents the CDODF as a tool to aid institutions with the CDO design process. The CDODF emerged from the qualitative data collected during our research, consultations, and site visits to institutions in different stages of diversity development. The framework is built on the foundational concepts of organizational design and argues that structure should follow from the big-picture diversity goals of the institution and its strategic diversity plan. Specific issues addressed by the CDODF include (a) the *strategic diversity platform* of the role, which establishes its mission and priorities; (b) the *vertical diversity structure,* which defines its formal scope of authority and power; (c) the *lateral diversity infrastructure,* which defines its scope of relationships; (d) *change management systems,* which define how CDOs drive and encourage diversity change efforts on campus; and (e) *officer skills, knowledge, background, and abilities,* which are critical to understanding the key characteristics necessary to perform the CDO role. This framework also creates a big-picture research framework for scholars interested in studying CDOs at the organizational or interpersonal level as it was intentionally built as a resource to inspire the exploration of themes and the testing of different organizational frameworks.

Chapter 4 focuses on vertical structure and organizational redesign, which are among the most contested dynamics on college and university campuses. Leveraging the work of Mintzberg (1979) and building from our discussion of the CDODF, we present three archetypes that elaborate possible configurations of the CDO role: the *Collaborative Officer Model*, the *Unit-Based Model*, and the *Portfolio Divisional Model.* Although all the models are characterized by collaborations and lateral relationships consistent with the CDO's integrative role on campus, each one operates from a different power base in terms of staff, supervisory role, reporting relationships, and other dynamics. Chapter 4 also provides a case study of one institution's experience reconfiguring its vertical structure, as well as a framework to help leaders reorganize their diversity infrastructure, a critical strategy for achieving campus diversity goals.

Part Two: The Strategic Diversity Leadership Movement

Part Two of this volume focuses on the role of the CDO as a change leader. We begin with a discussion of the way that the strategic diversity leadership movement has established new energy that is both energizing the emergence of a more professional approach to diversity leadership and setting the stage for more institutions to lead on diversity institutionally. Next, we move into an overview of diversity-themed change management and an in-depth focus on strategies around faculty diversity recruitment and retention, a major challenge that most institutions continue to struggle with.

Chapter 5 discusses a number of different organizational contributors whose efforts are at the forefront of the strategic diversity leadership movement. Working from an institutional perspective, this chapter presents several themes that we term *isomorphic* because, despite their distinct individual characteristics, they follow parallel trajectories and exert a shared influence on the expansion and elevation of the CDO role. These isomorphic forces, which include scholarly research, policy organizations, conferences, and professional bodies, have created a loosely connected network of professionalizing dynamics that are shaping the way diversity is defined and implemented. More specifically, Chapter 5 explains how national diversity affinity groups and associations, higher education policy organizations, diversity management degree and certification areas, and a growing diversity research canon are driving new diversity possibilities. By collaborating with each other, diversity leaders are generating an evidence-based platform to guide their work. The more CDOs can tap into these dynamics, the better they can leverage external energy to drive the internal change discussion.

Chapter 6 provides an overview of strategic diversity leadership, relying heavily on principles and themes first introduced in the companion volume to this book. The chapter begins with a discussion of the several key themes associated with strategic diversity leadership. Principles include the role of senior leaders, development of a coordinated diversity approach across disparate capabilities, diversity planning and implementation, and accountability techniques. From here the discussion moves to a comparison of institutions that have a CDO role with those that do not. Using measurements detailed in our companion volume, we discuss the strategic advantages of having a CDO at an academic institution and how it can positively affect diversity efforts.

Chapter 7 provides a detailed exploration of faculty diversity recruitment and retention issues. We focus specifically on this topic because faculty diversity is one of the consistent challenges facing CDOs. After first providing a brief overview of the challenge, we delve into an overview of legal and statutory theory, as well as promising techniques to increase faculty diversity and enhance retention. This chapter also features a case study that demonstrates how the Rochester Institute of Technology made noticeable improvements in diversifying its faculty.

Chapter 8 provides guidance to help CDOs get off to a great start in their first days and months on the job. Drawing from leadership literature and our own research, we provide a strategic transition framework designed to help CDOs during their first 100 days and beyond. Specific topics include navigating the relationship between the CDO and the president, establishing transition goals, and developing a set of relationships that can prove helpful to developing new policies and programs.

The CDO in Comparative Context

We conclude this book by comparing higher education and corporate CDOs. Drawing from "The Chief Diversity Officer Study in Higher Education" (Williams & Wade-Golden, 2008) and corporate diversity reports and programs, in Chapter 9 we compare officers in academia and the corporate sector. Beginning with a discussion of the history of both roles, we turn our attention to their strategic diversity priorities and ways that each could enhance the effectiveness of the other. Although the institutional and organizational setting obviously differs for each, CDOs in academia and corporate America have much to gain from greater networking and collaboration.

The Big Picture

One of the most rewarding aspects of working on this book was that it allowed us to give voice to the men and women who have long grappled with diversity issues, often in obscurity or in overtly hostile settings. Long before diversity became a matter of strategic interest and educational outcomes, leaders were working to champion the needs and interests of a wide variety of diverse individuals and communities. These leaders made a positive difference, despite an absence of staff, financial resources, and administrative authority. They pursued these efforts even as senior leaders touted diversity as a top priority in glossy brochures and other expensive media campaigns.

This book will help leaders at all levels, investigating the institutional motivations, both proactive and reactive, that led to the creation of the CDO role. Moreover, we present the major barriers to success in the CDO role and consider the knowledge, skills, and competencies associated with effective CDOs. As emphasized in both volumes of this study, commitment and involvement throughout the senior administrative ranks is essential, not just for the success of the CDO, but for the overall health of the strategic diversity plan. It is vital for the president, provost, and other senior leaders to understand, endorse, and empower the CDO, even as he or she works to build effective relationships with all members of the campus community. In the end, we offer insights to senior leaders confronted with decisions about when and how to create, structure, evolve, and staff the CDO role. We also offer this book for those individuals considering or already occupying the CDO role as a way to help them develop and optimize their efforts.

Incorporating and promoting diversity throughout higher education is paramount to our ability to achieve our educational ends. Bringing new students and faculty into an institution that does not respect or reflect diversity compromises their ability to thrive, just as it compromises our ability to achieve our educational and moral mission. In these companion volumes, *diversity* implies a new understanding of difference, one that encompasses race, gender, economic background, ethnicity, sexuality, disability, religion, age, nationality, and veteran status. Our academic institutions are uniquely poised to capitalize on the contributions of these disparate communities and improve the social, economic, and cultural well-being, not just of our colleges and universities, but of American society as a whole. New research is demonstrating the clear positive effects of diversity on improved educational outcomes. If our society is to finally address, and resolve, long-standing discriminatory practices, it will be partly because academic institutions have helped show the way.

Notes

1. For example, the Society for Human Resource Management has created a Diversity and Inclusion Strategic Leadership Program as part of its efforts to create a credentialing

system for CDOs, human resources professionals, and others engaging diversity issues within their organizations. For more information, please visit www.shrm.org/Education/seminar/Pages/diversityinclusion.aspx for an overview of the program. Other examples can be found at the Institute for Diversity Certification at www.diversitycertification.org/about.html, and the Society for Diversity at http://societyfordiversity.org/About_Us.html, to name a few of the non–university-affiliated programs that exist to provide certification opportunities for leaders engaging issues of strategic diversity leadership.

2. At the time of this publication, the American Association of Medical Colleges is developing a new partnership certification program with Associate Dean and Professor Christopher Metzler of the Center for Continuing and Professional Education at the Georgetown University School of Continuing Studies. This program will assist professionals in academic medicine to develop strategic diversity leadership skills and competencies.

PART ONE

DEFINING, DESIGNING, AND OPTIMIZING THE ROLE OF THE CHIEF DIVERSITY OFFICER

1

EMERGENCE, DEFINITION, AND EVOLUTION OF THE CHIEF DIVERSITY OFFICER

> The system-wide task force on diversity found that we could not achieve our strategic positioning goals unless we sustained a genuinely diverse community. With that reality in mind, we are conducting a nationwide search for a new vice president to create and shape effective initiatives and programs in access, educational equity, and diversity.
>
> —Robert H. Bruininks, president, University of Minnesota[1]

In recent years, the chief diversity officer (CDO) has assumed an increasingly vital role in fostering a more diverse and productive learning and work environment. Over the last decade, institutions ranging from Harvard University to the University of Wisconsin–Madison to Connecticut College to the University of Texas at Austin to Tarrant County College and numerous others have developed or reframed the CDO role at their institutions. The emergence of the higher education CDO follows the trend of comparable CDO roles in existence at entities like IBM, the Democratic Party, Major League Baseball, West Point, the American Association of Medical Colleges, General Mills, and the American Cancer Society. All of these organizations have developed CDO roles as part of their formal effort to achieve their diversity goals and more fundamentally accomplish their organizational missions.

In this chapter we discuss the emergence of the CDO role in the academy, starting with a grounded definition of the CDO role before situating this position in a broader discussion of how it can evolve to meet the challenges of our dynamic and changing diversity landscape. Next, we provide several key principles of organizational design to serve as anchors for the chapters that follow. These principles include several techniques that leaders can deploy when attempting to develop or reframe the diversity infrastructures of their institutions. We conclude with a discussion of how poor design can deal a crippling blow to the success of any CDO.

What Is a Chief Diversity Officer?

Consistent with the diversity of the American higher education system, titles for comparable roles often differ across institutions. Hence, presidents and provosts lead some institutions, whereas a chancellor and a vice chancellor for academic affairs lead others. Some may have a vice president for student affairs, and others may have a dean of students, or at smaller institutions, a dean of the college who provides leadership on student life and other student-centered areas on campus. This complexity extends to dedicated diversity leadership roles and poses a major challenge to our efforts to identify CDOs and answer the simple question, "What is a CDO?"

Although the CDO title is standard in the corporate community, where the *chief executive officer, chief financial officer,* and *chief marketing officer* nomenclature is common, the same is not true in higher education, where the language of leading in the *C* or *chief* executive suite of leadership is not nearly so widespread. In fact, in our early higher education research, we found very few leaders for whom "chief diversity officer" was part of their formal administrative title, although many more are now using the CDO designation as the strategic diversity leadership movement gathers momentum. Indeed, one of the most confounding themes that we discovered in our research is that when we asked diversity officers at institutions small or large, who supervise from 1 or 100 staff, and with titles that are high ranking or low, to define their roles, many would respond by saying that they are their institution's CDO.

A General Definition of the Chief Diversity Officer

Speaking with senior administrators, CDOs, executive recruiters, search committee members, and others, we realized that many are struggling to define clearly the CDO role. This misunderstanding has led many institutional leaders to label one of their campus leaders as a CDO, even though the role he or she plays may be inconsistent with the grounding logic and best practices consistent with a designated "chief" role that provides campus-wide leadership at the executive level in a particular area of administrative responsibility.

Absent a consensus definition of the CDO role, many institutions and officers themselves have begun referring to their highest-ranking diversity administrator as their CDO, regardless of seniority and responsibilities. Within this context, a program coordinator for multicultural student development, with little to no budget and staff, and buried deep in the student affairs chain of command, could be identified as the CDO. At other institutions, the chief diversity role might be assumed by a vice president who reports directly to the president, has 20 departments under his or her supervision, and controls an eight-figure budget.

Which of these two, the program coordinator or the vice president, can reasonably be called a *chief diversity officer*? From one perspective, both diversity professionals are clearly acting as their institution's CDO, because the CDO role can designate an institution's highest-ranking diversity administrator, regardless of seniority (Table 1.1). And yet the wide disparity in resources and responsibilities associated with this general definition of the CDO position can create confusion within and across institutions. The at times random designation or adoption of the CDO title is inconsistent with the convention generally associated with other "chief" roles that imply a position operating campus-wide at the highest levels of institutional life. This inconsistency reflects the ongoing inability of academic institutions to reframe diversity as an area of strategic importance, as well as the absence of a robust theory to describe the CDO role in a way that is grounded in the experiences and best practices of institutions that have developed effective CDO roles within their organizations (Table 1.1).

A Grounded Definition

The application of the CDO nomenclature in such a haphazard way limits the role's potential for leading change. First, it creates the false expectation that little strategy, much less change management science, rests at the core of the CDO position. As a result, the perception emerges that anyone with an interest in diversity can perform the job, regardless of knowledge, skills, or abilities. Second, and perhaps even more damaging is how this lack of clarity implies that the CDO role can be filled at any level of rank and administrative seniority. To fill this gap in the higher education administrative lexicon, and to ground our discussion, we define the CDO role in the following manner:

> The CDO is a boundary-spanning senior administrative role that prioritizes diversity-themed organizational change as a shared priority at the highest levels of leadership and governance. Reporting to the president,

TABLE 1.1
General Definition of the CDO Role Versus Grounded Definition of the CDO

General Definition of CDO	*Grounded Definition of CDO*
The highest-ranking diversity administrator regardless of seniority and positional mission.	The CDO is a boundary-spanning senior administrative role that prioritizes diversity-themed organizational change as a shared priority at the highest levels of leadership and governance. Reporting to the president, provost, or both, the CDO is an institution's highest-ranking diversity administrator. The CDO is an integrative role that coordinates, leads, enhances, and in some instances supervises formal diversity capabilities of the institution in an effort to create an environment that is inclusive and excellent for all. Within this context, diversity is not merely a demographic goal, but a strategic priority that is fundamental to creating a dynamic educational and work environment that fulfills the teaching, learning, research, and service mission of postsecondary institutions.

> provost, or both, the CDO is an institution's highest-ranking diversity administrator. The CDO is an integrative role that coordinates, leads, enhances, and in some instances supervises formal diversity capabilities of the institution in an effort to create an environment that is inclusive and excellent for all. Within this context, diversity is not merely a demographic goal, but a strategic priority that is fundamental to creating a dynamic educational and work environment that fulfills the teaching, learning, research, and service mission of postsecondary institutions.

Although no two roles are exactly alike, institutions need to appreciate the fundamental aspects of the CDO role that should be in place regardless of institutional size, selectivity, control, mission, or geographic location. This lack of clarity has led some institutions to develop high-profile positions that have little ability to move their diversity agenda. It has also resulted in some institutions hiring officers who are woefully unprepared for the complexity, challenge, and resistance that they may face when attempting to perform their responsibilities. Finally, it has resulted in officers using the title to describe their roles in ways that, although accurate in the general sense, are disconnected from the broader meaning that should be associated with the CDO role as a senior executive diversity leader of their institution.

Strategic Drivers of the Emerging CDO Role

Like all organizations, colleges and universities adapt to changing conditions. Many roles in our institutions did not exist as few as 10 years ago. Indeed, at one point in the history of higher education, the role of provost had yet to emerge as the president served as the "chief academic officer" of most institutions (Martin, Samels, & Associates, 1997). Yet as colleges and universities became more complex, the role of the modern-day provost became more common, and we have now reached a point where most institutions have someone who serves in a full-time chief academic officer role (Martin et al., 1997). Similarly, the role of the modern academic dean (e.g., Dean of the School of Nursing, Dean of Pharmacy, etc.), the vice president for student affairs, general counsel, and other roles evolved to meet the needs of a changing higher education administrative landscape, similar to the process that is happening with CDOs.

Changing demographics, turbulent political and legal contexts, persistent societal inequities, and other factors have created an increasingly complex diversity environment. For colleges and universities to face these dynamics effectively, new practices are essential. Developing a CDO role can help an institution meet its diversity imperatives and provide more proactive leadership in the context of diversity offices, units, committees, and plans. The emergence of the CDO role in response to a changing world is consistent with the guiding principles of contingency theory, which argues that the most successful organizations develop capacity allowing them to respond to different contingencies in their strategic environment by aligning their internal structures with the challenges and realities of their strategic landscape (Lawrence & Lorsch, 1967).

An important feature of contingency theory is that it does not prescribe any one best way to configure an organization, emphasizing instead the various possibilities that emerge when design is approached holistically and in response to a specific context. Hence, the optimal course of action depends on a combination of internal and external factors that must align with the big-picture strategy of the institution. Thus, the CDO role should be situated in a way that complements other roles, divisions, policies, and committees within the campus infrastructure. As a result, design decisions must take place through an iterative process that hinges on the strategic diversity goals of the institution, internal political dynamics, the external environment, preexisting campus diversity capabilities, and a host of other factors.

Conflicts Driving the CDO's Emergence

Although many institutions are moving toward the CDO role for strategic reasons, historically this has not always been the case. Indeed, one of the most prevalent drivers of the rise of the CDO position remains diversity-related conflict, what is referred to in the companion volume to this book, *Strategic Diversity Leadership,* as "cheetah moments." The very idea of creating diversity-themed capacity emerged in response to the civil rights movement and the growing populations of African American students in higher education. These early precursors to the modern CDO role carried titles like Vice President for Black Student Affairs and Special Assistant to the President for Minority Issues and Concerns. These positions dealt mainly with matters of racial equity. Peterson and associates (1978) note:

> New academic and supportive programs for blacks usually meant hiring black administrators to oversee their programs directly. Occasionally new positions concerned with a broad range of minority affairs activities might be created as umbrella offices which did not directly operate any minority academic programs but instead coordinated the non-academic programs for minorities. A third approach was to create new second and third echelon assistants to positions not designated to minority persons or explicitly responsible for minority programs but filled by black staff members. This practice was most common in admissions and financial aid, although it occurred with some regularity in some other areas such as student affairs and at the assistant or associate dean levels in academic affairs. A fourth pattern was to promote the director of a minority program to a position with a more general title . . . but still have them retain minority program responsibility. (p. 215)

A changing legal context and campus unrest drove these early institutional responses, just as they do in some cases today. For example, in the companion volume to this book we examine the controversial statements made by then Harvard University President Lawrence H. Summers. This cheetah moment led to the development of a diversity planning committee, which identified the need for a senior diversity administrator as an important building block for advancing faculty diversity initiatives on campus. In less than a year, this recommendation led to the appointment of a senior faculty member to serve as the inaugural Senior Vice Provost for Faculty Development and Diversity.

Similarly, at the University of Virginia, racial incidents in 2005 led then President John T. Casteen to appoint a commission on pluralism. A major recommendation of the commission's report was to hire a senior diversity officer early in the campus implementation process. After a national search, it hired an inaugural Vice President for Administration and Chief Officer for Diversity and Equity. In recent years, both Harvard and the University of Virginia have continued to evolve these roles, having now replaced their inaugural leadership with new officers with evolved titles and role functions. For example, Harvard University created an additional position in combination with the senior vice provost for faculty development and diversity that carries the title of Chief Diversity Officer and Special Assistant to the President.

Leadership Transition and Role Evolution Drivers of the CDO's Emergence

It is also common to see new CDOs emerge at institutions with the appointment of new senior leadership. This was the case at Miami University, University of Kentucky, Columbia University, and Ohio University, in the wake of hiring a new president or provost. After his hire at Ohio University, President Roderick McDavis reframed the institution's entire diversity infrastructure, eliminating a position of "special assistant" for diversity to develop a new Vice Provost for Equity and Diversity. When asked about his rationale, the president responded, "In order for us to achieve our commitment to diversity, we must be strategic and create key efficiencies to improve our campus climate. We need a centralized function in the presence of individuals who wake up each day empowered to identify ways to improve diversity and equity" (Athens News Staff, 2007).

Still others intentionally redesigned dedicated campus diversity officer roles to create a more highly ranked and potentially influential position out of a prior existing affirmative action officer, or other diversity leadership role. In 2011, for example, Chancellor Mary Anne Fox at University of California–San Diego (UCSD) created a full-time Vice Chancellor for Equity, Diversity, and Inclusion role out of a lower-ranking diversity leadership role that was occupied by a faculty member in a temporary, half-time appointment.

In a web article about the new position, UCSD described the development of the new position:

> Following campus and community consultation, we are pleased to announce plans to establish the position of Vice Chancellor for Equity, Diversity and Inclusion (EDI) and to conduct a national search for an experienced leader to guide our diversity initiatives. The full-time vice chancellor position will have direct responsibility for a range of diversity offices and activities for faculty, staff and students.
>
> The shift to a full-time diversity leader comes as Dr. Sandra Daley, who has served as Associate Chancellor and Chief Diversity Officer (CDO) in addition to her half-time position as Professor in the School of Medicine, concludes a three-year term as CDO on June 30, 2011.
>
> Reporting to the Executive Vice Chancellor–Academic Affairs and with an indirect reporting relationship to the Chancellor, the VC EDI will be supported by an Advisory Council representing campus constituencies and will be responsible for building on existing diversity plans to develop and implement a campus-wide strategy on equity, diversity and inclusion. The strategic plan will inform the final organizational structure for the office of the VC EDI, will propose metrics to gauge progress, and will identify potential additional areas of responsibility.
>
> The VC EDI will be a member of the Chancellor's Cabinet, continuing the practice of the Chief Diversity Officer as an integral advisor to the campus leadership. During the transition, Dr. Daley will serve as an advisor to the Executive Vice Chancellor–Academic Affairs.[2]

Diversity crises, strategic responses to a changing world, leadership transitions, and positional reframing are just some of the ways that the CDO role has emerged in the academy. Although the processes used to design the role vary, the stated intention in the beginning is always the same, namely to create a new CDO role that can establish a more formal approach to achieving diversity-related goals and objectives. This approach is often absent without having a senior administrative role that provides collegial leadership to this area of the institution's interests.

What Is Organizational Design?

In our work, we have seen the CDO role evolve through intentional organizational design and informal role evolution. The first process is one of deliberate formulation by senior administrators, consultants, planning committees, executive recruitment companies, and others to create an executive strategic diversity leadership role. The second process takes place when an existing institutional role evolves new patterns of interaction, language, and even definitions, often in response to shifts that may be happening elsewhere that senior leaders begin to import and model at their own institutions. Both approaches can be viable if they focus on developing a meaningful leadership role that is consistent with the theoretical and practical design concepts that we present in this chapter and in those that follow. Unfortunately, it is too often the case that many roles are poorly designed and inadequately positioned to be successful.

Indeed, since 2000 we have seen institutions shift the role multiple times in an effort to develop a position consistent with their strategic diversity leadership goals. Although the emergence of many roles reflects intentional efforts to respond to social, educational, and demographic changes that have elevated diversity's importance in the new economy, others emerged from the more classic root of political upheaval, diversity crisis moments, and transitions in leadership. Whether created proactively, or reactively, the stated goal is generally the same, namely to create a new position to help galvanize new possibilities on campus.

The process of developing a CDO position involves organizational design. Although for many administrators "organizational design" is largely synonymous with "organizational structure," in fact organizational design is a more robust concept that includes not just questions of vertical structure, but lateral relationships, human resources capabilities, and other dimensions (Galbraith, Downey, & Kates, 2002). We define *organizational design* as the creation of roles, processes, lateral structures, and formal reporting relationships within an organization. It is the process used to match the *form* of the organization as closely as possible to the *goals* of the organization (Galbraith, 2002; Lawrence & Lorsch, 1967; Mintzberg, 1979).

When design is limited to the vertical dimension, the process risks ignoring issues of strategy, human resources dynamics, enterprise-wide processes, and other key building blocks that should be included in the discussion to achieve optimal effectiveness (Galbraith et al., 2002). As a result, we hope that institutions endeavor to do more than simply add a new executive role to their already overburdened budgets. Rather, they should develop a new role that is fundamentally connected up, down, and across the institution.

Throughout this book we use the term *organizational design* to suggest that the CDO role must be developed in ways that are intentional, multifaceted, and interconnected. The focus should be on creating a role that is more than a job or position, because it rests at the center of a network of previously disparate capabilities, helping to bring about what Prahalad and Hamel (1994) refer to as *core competencies.* An institution's core competencies reflect its ability to integrate various strategies, policies, structures, people, and knowledge into a cohesive and focused approach to achieving its key goals. These competencies can only be achieved by blending expertise in new and unique ways that achieve more effective outcomes than when they operate in isolation. In this way, competence is activated and expanded as discrete capabilities are brought together and put into alignment with one another. For example, the role of the CDO must align with the work of the multicultural center, which must in turn reflect the central vision of a diversity plan. All of these disparate pieces must connect with one another if they are to define a core diversity competence.

Specialization

The evolution of new administrative roles can be further explained through the organizational design concept of specialization (Lawrence & Lorsch, 1967). The idea behind specialization is that work can be performed better if organizational tasks are subdivided into individual jobs or groups of jobs that form a department or division. Colleges and universities are full of specialized structures that organize employees around specific areas of expertise. For this reason, institutions of higher education are organized into schools and colleges, including business administration, education, medicine, liberal arts and sciences, engineering, and the like. These differentiated structures allow for trained specialists within the faculty or administration to offer a cohesive and specialized curriculum. For example, within an educational leadership department, some faculty members focus on K–12 administration and governance, whereas others focus on higher education administration; some focus on educational policy, and others focus on research design and evaluation of educational organizations. Each of these broad areas of emphasis defines the specialized areas of expertise that exist within a department. Taken collectively, they define an academic degree area that produces research and provides degrees in educational leadership.

Similar ideas rest at the core of having a diversity leadership role, whether that role is the director of the LGBT resource center, the chair of the department of women's studies, or vice president and CDO for an entire institution. Rather than have this work performed by a generalist, the goal is to match an area of work to an individual or a group of individuals who have a specific set of knowledge, skills, and abilities in this functional area. We thereby create a standardized ability to achieve the goals associated with each of these units in a more efficient and uniform way than if the dedicated leadership role did not exist.

In the example of the CDO, this means that he or she plays a specialized role in a domain of work responsibility that may include faculty diversification, multicultural marketing and external relations, student academic achievement, community engagement, intergroup relations, diversity-themed fund-raising, and a host of other areas defined by that institution as strategic diversity leadership work. The challenge with the role of the CDO is that it is by definition an integrative leadership role, as the boundaries of the officer's work will inevitably cross into the boundaries of other areas, including student affairs, human resources development, alumni relations, enrollment management, and academic affairs (Figure 1.1).

Specialization is central to understanding formal bureaucratic structures and the role of CDOs in the academy. The development of the specialized role of CDO should result in an expert ability to engage issues of diversity using evidence-based practices in a more coordinated manner. In the case of CDO departments and divisions, this type of specialized infrastructure facilitates the sharing of valuable expertise between leaders and subordinates. CDOs should have in-depth knowledge about diversity that allows them to supervise subordinate diversity infrastructures and roles with a greater degree of acumen than other leaders who may come from a functional area that overlaps with the role of the CDO.

Organizational Spans

Another organizational concept that complements this discussion is the notion of organizational spans (Simons, 2005). Most obviously, a span is the distance between two limits or points. Using the analogy of a bridge, Robert Simons notes that leaders have several tools to shape what he refers to as the "span of attention" (p. 25), or what people pay attention to, collect data on, lead, collaborate, and ultimately respond to through their actions. Table 1.2 provides an overview of the key spans in organizational theory.

Span of Attention

A position's span of attention can be either narrow or broad. If the core of a job is static, constrained, and limited in creative expression (Simons, 2005),

FIGURE 1.1
The Boundaries of the CDO's Role in the Context of Other Leadership Roles in Academia

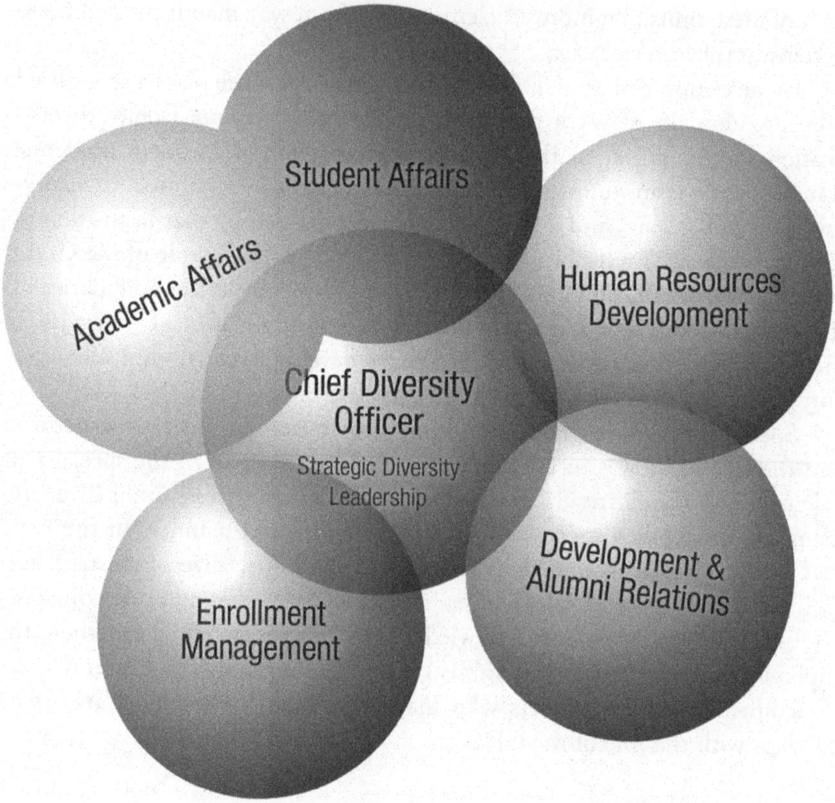

we can define the span as narrow. By comparison, the CDO generally has a broad span of attention, as he or she collects data from multiple sources; interacts with numerous constituencies; makes decisions across complex scenarios; and creates effect by mobilizing people across multiple contexts, whether administrative, academic, or cultural.

Three key spans constitute the planks or support systems of a CDO's span of attention: (a) the strategic span, (b) the span of control, and (c) the span of support (Figure 1.2). Leaders should adjust each of these spans as they respond to critical dynamics that must be aligned when creating a well-designed CDO position on campus. A position's *span of attention* is defined

TABLE 1.2
Four Types of Organizational Spans

Span of Attention		*Definition*
The *span of attention* is defined by what people pay attention and relate to, and ultimately respond to through their actions. A position's strategic span, span of control, and span of support operationalize its span of attention.	Strategic Span	The *strategic span* is defined as the breadth of diversity issues that are part of the CDO's portfolio. In other words, how broad is the CDO's purview on matters of diversity? Does he or she have an expansive or limited set of responsibilities?
	Span of Control	The *span of control* is defined as the range of resources over which a person has formal authority to direct. This span is consistent with the concept of vertical structure, and responds to the central question, "What resources do I control to perform my job duties?"
	Span of Support	The *span of support* is defined as the resources or individuals whose cooperation is vital to the CDO's ability to move the institution's diversity agenda forward. The shared nature of diversity work, as well as the integrative roots of the CDO role, means that CDOs need a broad span of support.

FIGURE 1.2
The Span of Attention Support Model: Strategic Span, Span of Control, and Span of Support

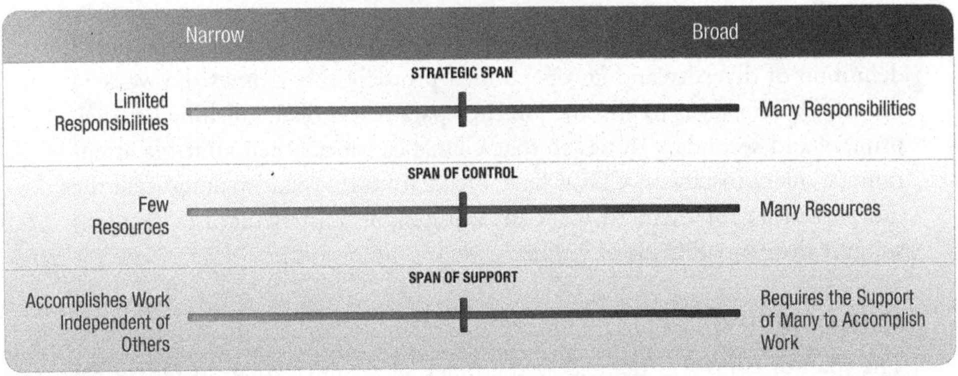

Adapted from Simons, 2005.

as the domain of activities that establish a particular role's strategic mission and resource base, as well as the key relationships required in performing the duties of the job. Spans provide labels to describe the internal characteristics of an organization and are key for designing and analyzing CDO roles and other infrastructures.

Strategic Span

The strategic span defines the breadth of diversity issues that are part of the CDO's portfolio. In other words, how broad is his or her purview on matters of diversity? Does he or she have an expansive or limited set of responsibilities? Do these responsibilities include all the dimensions that are part of an institution's definition of diversity? Does the definition include a focus on race and ethnicity, gender, sexuality, disability, national origin status, and so on? Does it include a focus on faculty? Students? Staff? Are the responsibilities focused on issues of curriculum and faculty development? Campus climate? Diversity education?

Because there are so many ways for institutions to define diversity, CDOs can possess either a narrow or broad strategic span. For example, the vice provost for multicultural and international affairs at a large research university we studied had a broad strategic span; his division played a key role leading the institution's domestic and international diversity issues. By contrast, we also located a vice presidential role tasked with diversity affairs that had a narrower span focused largely on issues pertaining to African American students, faculty, and staff, with a secondary focus on issues of diversity.

It is for this reason that institutions should create a clear institutional definition of diversity and an operational protocol that defines the work of the CDO. The key is to give the job clear parameters distinguishing between primary and secondary duties so that CDOs can focus their strategic attention. In many instances, CDOs have broad strategic spans making it all the more essential for them to work in well-designed infrastructures that can support their broad fields of vision.

Span of Control

The span of control is defined as the range of resources that an individual has formal authority to direct. This span is consistent with the concept of vertical structure, and responds to the central question, "What resources do I control to perform my job duties?" This span encompasses a position's formal authority and includes, among other variables, budget responsibility and formal line authority to create policy and hire, fire, and supervise the actions of others. A well-defined span of control is the most powerful way to ensure that strategic goals are aligned with policies and programs. The span of control defines the legitimate capacity that an officer has to direct the efforts of subordinates.

Although many CDOs enjoy a high rank, some simultaneously possess narrow spans of control because of limited budgets and staff. They therefore lack the direct ability to provide formal leadership to their institution's diversity agenda. A wide strategic span necessitates that the span of control also be broader, if the officer is to be successful. Otherwise, when conflicts emerge, the role's effectiveness will be limited because it will become evident that the position is more symbolic than material in its ability to influence the campus diversity agenda.

Span of Support

The span of support is defined as the unit resources, staff, and volunteer support whose cooperation is vital to the CDO's ability to move an institution's diversity agenda forward. Although some units may fall directly within the CDO's span of control, allowing him or her to supervise these areas, the bulk of a CDO's work requires a broad span of support to accomplish his or her responsibilities. For example, if a CDO is to play a critical role in terms of building off-campus community relationships, there are several potential spans of support he or she should consider, including the office of external relations, corporate strategic partnerships, and perhaps the institution's community service learning program. Depending on how the CDO role is defined, the span of influence might be broad enough to include students, faculty, community members, academic deans, student organizations, corporate stakeholders, alumni, and others. In another context, the span of influence might be narrow. The span of support encompasses the different groups that the CDO's work will influence, and is guided, in part, by an institution's overall strategic span.

The shared governance culture of most colleges and universities makes it difficult for even the most powerful presidents and provosts to lead without broad support for their initiatives. In the case of CDOs, this reality is even more prevalent. As we were told by a vice provost for diversity at a midsized institution in the Northeast:

> Relationships are everything. They are essential. The first item I try to accomplish is to get people to understand that I am here to help them. I

> try to let them know what I am about and that we are on the same page. Only then do they appreciate that I can help them move [their efforts] forward. For example, I can put them in touch with faculty diversity networks that can help them find the right talent, something they may not be able to do on their own. Once you have the relationship in place, you can actually do your job. You are solid with a lot of people and they want to support you even more.

CDOs cannot be effective if they work in isolated silos at the fringe of the institution. To be successful, the CDO role has to be integrated into the critical areas of the institution, at the heart of relationships, systems, and processes that define the diversity structures of the institution.

Only by working closely and collegially with faculty on a range of efforts—analyzing and even revising how potential positions are described, how searches are executed, and how talent is evaluated and nurtured—can CDOs help promote faculty diversification. In this case, integration of knowledge, most promising practices, and a shared understanding of how to move forward in a difficult direction are essential. Committees, task forces, and leadership councils are a critical part of integration infrastructure, particularly in higher education. Because so many colleges and universities have numerous committees and shared governance groups on campus, placing the CDO in the right groups can make all the difference in terms of helping the institution's strategic diversity conversation. For example, asking the CDO to chair an internal grants competition on innovation and strategic priorities may, in a very natural and organic way, elevate issues of diversity into this conversation in fresh and unexpected ways. As institutional leaders think about designing a CDO role, integrating the position into a myriad of institutional contexts is vital to success.

A Myriad of Different Spans of Attention

Our examination of CDO positions at a number of institutions revealed that despite similar titles, many officers had quite different spans of attention, which explains some of the discrepancies that we discussed earlier among officers. Some were responsible for affirmative action policies whereas others focused purely on issues pertaining to faculty diversification. Others had a mandate around community engagement and enjoyed significant division help to bring their visions to fruition. Some were focused more narrowly on faculty diversity and academic excellence, and still others touched all of these areas. In each of these models, the CDO required spans of influence and support allowing them to effectively advance the issues within their strategic span.

Comprehensively, the focus and resources that differentiate CDO roles vary from institution to institution. This point was made in a working document that we obtained from a midsized institution in the Northeast that had engaged in an extensive review of other institutions to develop a new executive-level CDO role. The report's author, a tenured faculty member in organizational psychology, observed the following:

> Benchmarking cabinet level diversity roles at a series of our competitor institutions and at institutions that were perceived as having a particularly effective model was incredibly challenging. A variety of models exist and even models that seem similar on the surface are called different things by different institutions. Absent a clear theme across the various institutions that we reviewed, we will have to synthesize our findings and develop a unique model for our institution.

This report concluded that CDO roles were established differently and that the field of strategic diversity leadership would benefit from a more integrated framework. This was a consistent theme not only among CDOs, but also senior administrative leaders, executive search firms, and diversity champions.

Redesigning Diversity Infrastructures

Between 2000 and 2010, we found no fewer than 60 of the nation's leading institutions engaged in efforts to reframe their senior diversity administrative role in some way. As we note in Table 1.3, these institutions included some of the most highly regarded colleges and universities in the United States, and represented a wide range of configurations, including public, private, large, small, highly selective, and open enrollment. Some used very intensive CDO processes to reframe their efforts, and others used less intentional, even haphazard processes.

Regardless of the intentionality and intensity of the process, we found several common questions at the core of the organizational design process. Among the most common were the following: At what level should we rank the CDO? Whom will the CDO supervise? How large should the office's budget be? Should we restructure current diversity offices like women's studies, multicultural affairs, or disability services? Should CDOs have tenure and

TABLE 1.3
Partial List of Institutions Developing or Reframing Their Senior Diversity Administrative Roles (2000–2010)

Babson College	Tarrant County College
Berkeley College of Music	Temple University
Boston College	Texas A&M University
Brown University	Texas Tech University
Bucknell University	Tiffin University
Clemson University	University of Arkansas
Colgate University	University of California–Berkeley
College of Charleston	University of California–Los Angeles
Columbia University	University of California–San Diego
Connecticut College	University of California–San Francisco
Cornell University	University of Denver
Duke University School of Medicine	University of Georgia
Eastern Carolina University	University of Iowa
Emory University	University of Kentucky
George Washington University	University of Massachusetts
Grand Valley State University	University of Minnesota
Harvard University	University of Missouri–Columbia
Indiana University–Purdue University Indianapolis	University of Missouri–Kansas City
Lafayette College	University of Nevada, Las Vegas
Loyola University	University of Oregon
Marquette University	University of the Pacific
Miami University	University of South Dakota
Michigan State University	The University of Texas at Austin
Middlebury College	University of Virginia
Naropa University	University of West Florida
North Carolina State University	University of Wisconsin–Madison
Ohio State University	University of Wisconsin–Stout
Ohio University	University of Wisconsin System
Oklahoma State University	Virginia Tech University
Purdue University	Wesleyan University
Rensselaer Polytechnic Institute	Wright State University
Rochester Institute of Technology	Xavier University
Syracuse University	Yale University

serve on the faculty? Should they have a legal or academic terminal degree? What should be their core responsibilities? On what committees should they serve? Who has to support their work for them to be successful? What data will they need to collect to have the type of information necessary to build institutional strategies? These questions and others define an officer's span of attention; they are at the heart of the design process and can help shape some of the organizational design processes that campus leaders need to put in place as they establish their CDO role.

The CDO Discovery Process

Many institutions begin their design efforts with some form of discovery process that they use to understand the field of strategic diversity leadership and the role of the CDO. Organizational discovery is often used in organizational development literature to describe the process of gathering information about a poorly understood phenomenon (Rasiel, 1999). In the CDO development process, it is vital to employ a range of tools, techniques, and sources to gather as much data as possible.

We use the term *discovery* to suggest the broad fact-finding mission that institutions have launched and sustained, sometimes in collaboration with national policy organizations like the American Council on Education, as well as researchers and scholars with diversity expertise. The most intense efforts combined a number of techniques, including institutional benchmarking. No matter who led the process or how it began, the goal was the same: to gather as much information as possible on the CDO's capability and present a context for informed decision making. Because the diversity management literature is sparse, particularly as it relates to building new leadership roles and higher education, the majority of institutional discovery efforts have centered on collecting data from individuals and institutions of relevance.[3]

As we identified the range of activities that designers put in place, we noticed that some were more frequently applied than others (Table 1.4). For example, many performed literature reviews, contacted national higher education associations, and talked with sitting CDOs at peer institutions. These important first steps helped administrators get up to speed on what others were doing and collect best practices, even if anecdotally. Less common techniques included hiring external recruiters to help design the role and find potential applicants, assigning point leadership to help guide the design process, developing a campus-wide CDO planning team to provide collaborative thinking about what the role should entail, sending brief surveys to other institutions to gather information, and attending higher education diversity conferences.

Only a few institutions put in place some of the most aggressive and labor-intensive design processes. These techniques included writing a CDO

TABLE 1.4
Common Discovery Process Techniques

Discovery Technique	*Description*	*Prevalence*
Perform literature and Internet searches	Institutions engaged in a number of literature and Internet searches. These searches helped leaders develop a list of institutions to examine as part of their benchmarking and interview process.	High
Contact national higher education policy organizations	Organizations such as the ACE, the AAC&U, the NADOHE, and others were contacted regarding best practices for establishing diversity officer roles and capabilities.	High
Interview established chief diversity officers	Sitting officers were interviewed to learn more about their spans of focus and control. Little attention was given to their spans of influence and support, as the focus was generally on who reported to whom and the scope of duties they performed.	High
Hire an external higher education consultant	Institutions hired external higher education executive recruitment consultants to guide the articulation of job descriptions and to facilitate national searches.	Moderate
Assign point leadership for the design effort	Often, the president or provost would appoint one individual to serve as the point person for the design effort. At times, he or she would also lead campus-wide design committees; in other instances, the design process took place without the benefit of a committee structure.	Moderate
Develop a campus-wide CDO planning committee	Institutions developed CDO planning committees. This type of group was usually the outgrowth of campus-wide diversity committees or task forces focused on broader institutional diversity efforts.	Moderate
Attend national diversity conference and meetings	Interested parties attended diversity conferences and meetings such as the annual NCORE and the AAC&U Diversity and Learning Conference.	Moderate
Launch electronic outreach strategies	Institutions deployed electronic information-gathering strategies by sending brief surveys to diversity listservs and e-mailing groups across organizational sectors.	Moderate
Interview diversity scholars and thought leaders	Diversity scholars and thought leaders with relevant research agendas were contacted to obtain insights into developing the CDO role.	Moderate
Engage in peer institutional benchmarking	Institutions examined the diversity infrastructures of peer institutions of similar size, complexity, control, and selectivity.	Moderate
Write a CDO concept paper	Institutions developed concept papers summarizing major findings and providing context for institutional decision-making and CDO organizational designs.	Low

TABLE 1.4 (Continued)

Discovery Technique	*Description*	*Prevalence*
Perform a campus-wide diversity audit	Institutions engaged in internal examinations of their institutional capabilities and then applied this information to develop the vertical and lateral infrastructures of the CDO role.	Low
Engage in campus-wide diversity discussions regarding CDO design effort	Interested parties engaged in internal conversations with key faculty, staff, student, and administrator constituencies to obtain feedback and participation in the CDO design effort.	Low
Hire an external diversity organizational design expert	Institutions hired experts with organizational design expertise to guide the discovery and design process.	Low

AAC&U, Association of American Colleges and Universities; *ACE,* American Council on Education; *NADOHE,* National Association of Diversity Officers in Higher Education; *NCORE,* National Conference on Race and Ethnicity in American Higher Education.

position paper grounded in their discovery process and the literature, conducting a campus-wide diversity capabilities audit, and hiring an external diversity expert to assist with the process of organizational design.

Assigning Point Leadership to Guide the Design Process

At a number of institutions, senior leaders appointed individuals to gather information from a number of different sources. The individuals were generally members of senior administrative staff, representatives from the human resources department, senior faculty members, and key members of diversity planning committees. Institutions with a clearly defined lead designer often deployed a number of discovery techniques in their efforts to develop perspectives on the key elements of an effective design process. As he reflected on his experience participating in the design process for reframing a CDO position, an administrator at a large research university in the Northeast offered this general reaction:

> It was like finding a needle in a haystack. There was no place to go for information. We had to work the phones and pull something together. When we built this office ten years ago, we had no idea what the person in this job should be doing, much less what type of staff was needed or what units might be included in his or her administrative portfolio. We called places that we respected and talked to professionals who were doing the work, and slowly our model began to emerge. Ten years ago there was

> even less literature in place and it was even more difficult to find your colleagues across the country. .

In addition to a firm grasp on diversity issues and capabilities on campus, the most qualified designers have experience working across organizational lines. Moreover, lead designers are personally committed to the process. Their engagement reflects their desire to get things right and help the campus develop a role that succeeds over the long haul. Their efforts ideally will result in a concept paper that articulates a range of options while simultaneously recommending the critical steps necessary to implement an effective CDO role.

Executive Search Companies

Executive search companies have played an increasingly prominent role in helping institutions hire CDOs. These executive search companies can reduce the amount of time required to complete the early steps of the screening process. They can both sort through outside applications and access their own databases of potential CDO candidates. It is common for the companies we researched to conduct background checks, hold preliminary interviews, and follow up on references. Although they are often brought into the search and screen process early on, our research suggests that they ultimately provide only limited guidance regarding the design of the CDO position. Indeed, one administrator who had recently been involved with a CDO search featuring a recruitment company found its overall effectiveness questionable:

> They cost a lot of money, and at the end of the day, I wonder what we really got out of the process. They wrote a good position description, but in conversations with others who have used them, I learned that they seem to recycle the same list of candidates and use the same boilerplate job descriptions. I think they have a benefit, but I am not certain if we got as much out of the process as we could have.

In their defense, we found that a number of search companies we contacted discussed the challenges they faced in convincing institutional leaders not only to hire someone for the role, but also to fully commit to designing an effective CDO role. Executive search companies often feel that they are in an untenable position, recruiting candidates without having a clear understanding of the responsibilities of the position and the officer's direct span of control. These companies stressed a need for top leadership to make decisions on responsibilities and budgets, and the relationship between the CDO and academic deans and governance groups, *before* conducting the candidate search.

When asked why some institutions avoid engaging in a substantive design process prior to publicizing the new role, senior leaders invariably responded that they wanted to hire the new officer—in the words of one search committee chair—"to have him or her help us to figure out what we should do." This ambiguity in the organizational design process presents a great challenge for executive recruiters and search committees that then must go out and find experienced talent to take a position when responsibilities are still in the process of being formulated. As one executive recruiter told us, "At times I felt like I was in a no-win situation, trying to recruit really good candidates but not being able to clarify what the job role was, other than collaborating with people to move diversity efforts forward. The best candidates are wary and want a more substantial description of their responsibilities and the resources they will control." As this comment suggests, a lack of job role clarity may hinder the institution's ability to secure the best talent. However, as Box 1.1 illustrates, with the right candidate and circumstances, including a new CDO hire in an institution's nascent CDO design process can prove rewarding.

BOX 1.1

Involving New Chief Diversity Officers in the Design Effort at Indiana University–Bloomington

The decision to involve a new CDO in new or renewed organizational design efforts can prove beneficial in certain circumstances, especially when the new officer possesses the knowledge, skills, and abilities required to lead the process.

In 1998, Indiana University–Bloomington Chancellor Kenneth Gros-Louis hired Dr. Charlie Nelms, a former chancellor at two previous institutions, to serve as Special Assistant to the Chancellor. As part of his duties, Dr. Nelms was asked to develop an institutional infrastructure that would help the university move its diversity and equity agenda forward.

Dr. Nelms assembled a diverse team of higher education professionals and scholars from across the country to serve as an institutional review team. The review team examined the diversity capabilities at a number of comparable institutions from across the country. The team wrote a report entitled "20–20: A Vision for Achieving

(continues)

(continued)

Equity and Excellence at IU–Bloomington." This report discussed the history of inclusion and exclusion at Indiana University–Bloomington, described five existing higher education organizational diversity models, and presented a number of recommendations based on analysis of the literature and the landscape of higher education capabilities.

The report then articulated the need to implement a model that would synthesize a number of diversity and nondiversity offices under one administrative portfolio and tighten their potential for collaboration. The report called for the appointment of senior diversity leadership that would work across organizational lines and the various dimensions of diversity to create a more powerful campus-wide strategic diversity effort. The chancellor accepted the report, and Dr. Nelms was appointed as the institution's inaugural Vice Chancellor for Academic Support and Diversity. Over his nearly 10-year tenure, Dr. Nelms's title and role continued to evolve.

A key point to recognize is that Dr. Nelms, a twotime chancellor, had the personal leadership ability to negotiate the terms of this design process and require the full implementation of the recommendations as a condition of accepting the position. Even if they have the knowledge and expertise to lead the redesign process, many newly appointed CDOs are not granted the requisite political authority to move forward on implementation. It is vital that if they are to be brought into the process early they be given the resources to follow through on the recommendations they formulate. Doing less is a recipe for disaster because it immediately belies an institution's lack of confidence in its new CDO. If the goal is to design the best possible CDO role, senior leaders must be willing to imbue the position with actual authority, not out of political expediency, but because doing so leads to effective outcomes.

Source: Personal interview with Dr. Charlie Nelms, June 5, 2007.

Benchmarking

Institutional benchmarking affords design teams with a means of outlining the diversity capabilities and infrastructures of both peer institutions and institutions they aspire to emulate. Some data collection strategies include phone interviews with current diversity officers, simple surveys, Internet searches, and requests for information from various higher education diversity listservs.

Although some comparable institutions might mirror the home institution in terms of size, structure, and mission, institutions outside these parameters may provide the best context for developing state-of-the-art diversity offices. For example, a small liberal arts institution may learn more from a large research institution with a long-standing CDO role than it might from a peer and vice versa. Our research found a number of shared beliefs, strategies, characteristics, and best practices among CDOs, regardless of institutional type, size, and mission. Indeed, the presence of multiple types of comparative contexts may help institutions avoid flawed organizational designs and assist them in developing new capabilities that can be adapted easily from one institutional type to another.

Internal Diversity Capabilities Audits

As we discussed earlier in this chapter, the CDO requires a broad span of support to accomplish his or her work. Nevertheless, we learned that this issue is often ignored in the design process. Very few institutions perform campus-wide audits of the diversity committees, student organizations, offices, units, initiatives, and personnel engaged in various diversity, equity, and inclusion efforts. As a result, there has been too little consideration of how the CDO role interfaces with other diversity capabilities and stakeholders on campus.

A lack of understanding of the institutional diversity context can be particularly problematic at large institutions. These institutions may have hundreds of programs to expand the pipeline for diverse groups; support diverse constituencies; pursue diverse areas of scholarship; expand global relationships; create inclusive campus environments; and prepare students for a diverse, interconnected global economy. Yet very few of the institutions that we reviewed engaged in serious efforts to understand the diversity capabilities that already exist on their campuses. In those instances where diversity capability audits were performed, leaders often defined diversity narrowly, focusing exclusively on race and ethnicity, or how diversity affected students. Many of these audits did little more than provide a list or catalogue of efforts.

Only rarely did we encounter an institution that was intentional about how the various campus diversity elements might best fit together to provide a platform for the CDO to lead in a more proactive and dynamic way. Consequently, many CDOs often emerged on campus without a clearly defined understanding of how their role was charged to lead, organize, or facilitate the activities of other diversity units on campus. This organizational dissonance is most common in areas where leadership responsibilities overlap.

A Lack of Deep Engagement With the Campus Community

The process of role design is important because it provides a window into the level of commitment that campus leaders hold toward what are often lofty diversity goals. Despite the collegial dynamics of the academy, few institutions actually involve the campus community in the process of designing the CDO role.

The lack of a broad conversation about the CDO role is a recipe for failure. By not engaging campus community members in town-hall-style meetings and allowing them to participate in the process, institutional leaders miss an important opportunity to help new CDOs evolve their work. A new CDO at a midsized public institution in the South offered the following:

> I felt like I was thrown to the wolves on all sides. People had no idea what I was supposed to do. There were so many offices and I had no idea what I should be doing with them. A number of my peers did not know what to make of me either, which created a number of problems in terms of simply being a good colleague. It was one issue after another that first year, but I survived.

Absent a broad conversation with faculty, staff, and student stakeholders, flawed assumptions will cloud the CDO role. The CDO is a new role in higher education and many people have a limited understanding of how the role can ultimately provide leadership on campus. Perhaps the most common misguided notion of the CDO role is that as the "diversity messiah," he or she is the only person responsible for institutional diversity. In other words, the CDO division "ghettoizes" the campus diversity effort as the sole responsibility of one person. To succeed, the CDO role must be collaborative. The more work that campus leaders can do to understand current campus capabilities prior to hiring the officer, the more that the CDO can become a valuable member of the institution's senior leadership community.

Incomplete Role Design

Our research has uncovered many examples of institutions that give too little attention to the CDO job description. In Table 1.5 we examine the role description of a highly regarded private research university in the South. In this situation, the institution retained one of the nation's leading executive recruitment companies. The job description does an adequate job illustrating

TABLE 1.5
Flawed Span of Control at a Research University in the South

Strategic Span	*Span of Control*	*Span of Support*
Position Overview In keeping with its vision statement of being committed to an inquiry-driven, ethically engaged, and inclusive community, the university is seeking courageous leadership in the newly established position of Senior Vice Provost for Diversity and Community Development (SVP). This important leadership position will build on the university's heritage of fostering openness and diversity, lead efforts toward developing both internal and external community relations, and guide its future transformation into a recognized leader of community engagement and participation. In short, the SVP will lead the university in "the practice of community." At the core of this newly established position will be responsibility for envisioning and enabling an environment where community, diversity, and engagement are fostered. The SVP will model leadership by creating partnerships and establishing expectations that will differentiate the university from other universities and benefit the institution, the local community, and the world. Key Responsibilities • In line with the university's strategic plan, this leader will serve as the point person for the university's effort to create an academic environment that enriches the intellectual work and social experience of faculty, students, staff, and others. • The SVP will lead the discussion of community and diversity and develop a vocabulary around diversity and community that challenges assumptions, enlightens participants, and creates understanding among individuals, groups, and academic partners. • The SVP will champion and model personal engagement in developing and living as a community, and will promote the positive role of diversity and community in higher education. • Communication is a key competency of this position. The SVP will drive the conversation by challenging the current understandings of diversity and community, both on campus and elsewhere. The SVP will champion open dialogue and will model effective communication techniques that engage a variety of constituents.	Reports To *Provost and Executive Vice President for Academic Affairs* **No mention of budget, staff, or direct reporting units. More than 100 diversity offices, units, and initiatives exist on campus at this institution.**	The Senior Vice Provost for Diversity and Community Development will be a member of the provost's senior leadership staff. He or she also will work closely with the President's Commissions on the Status of Women, Race and Ethnicity, and Lesbian, Gay, Bisexual and Transgender Concerns. The SVP will work closely with these commissions to stimulate dialogue, address issues, and create solutions. Key Relationships President President's Cabinet Office of the General Counsel Council of Deans Human Resources Office of EOP Administrative Council Employee Council Faculty Senate University Senate University Healthcare Health Sciences Art Museum University Library Division of Campus Life Director of Sustainability Staff and Faculty

TABLE 1.5 (Continued)

Strategic Span	*Span of Control*	*Span of Support*
• The SVP must create and manage measurement systems that will serve as meaningful benchmarks. Diversity metrics such as public and personal perspectives of integrity, honesty, and respect will be refined so as to become a means to measure success and outstanding challenges. As a result, the community will identify common diversity and community goals. Such metrics will assess how well the university balances its success in the recruitment and retention of diverse applicants, sustains its ranking in national measurements, and improves its standings among other leading institutions. • The SVP will provide leadership in the organization and development of a structural framework for diversity and community efforts throughout the university. Such a framework will be the basis and infrastructure for efforts and programs undertaken by each school, the college, and its business operations unit. • The SVP will provide guidance, coordination, and support as entities develop their own specific plans, with a goal to include aspects of diversity and community in plans for programs, curricula, services, and functions throughout the campus. • The SVP will play a key role in integrating and connecting efforts around diversity and community, serve as an interface for innovative design, and provide a stimulus for creative relationships that foster exchange of ideas and resources.		

the scope of the role, the span of support that the role will enjoy, and a detailed overview of the institution. However, the job description is woefully inadequate in specifying the span of control the new CDO will have to accomplish his or her work. There is no mention of budget, staff, or units that the position might leverage to achieve results. Furthermore, there is no discussion of areas that the new CDO might supervise or lead as part of a dual reporting structure. Each of these design possibilities is critical for establishing this new position with the potential to fulfill its strategic span.

A Poorly Aligned Span of Attention

A lack of attention to the material needs of the position, or its span of control, is all too common in most newly crafted CDO roles. The job description typically places tremendous emphasis on the institution's national reputation, research infrastructure, faculty excellence, and presidential leadership. What is often ignored is any concrete discussion of the dedicated staff, budget, and resource capacity that the CDO can access to meet the institution's human, financial, symbolic, and technical goals. This lack of specificity demonstrates the inadequate attention that often typifies the design of the CDO role. Figure 1.3 shows how, in many cases, the CDO's strategic span, span of control, and span of support are misaligned.

In our national survey of academic diversity leaders, 55 percent of CDOs and 67 percent of non-CDOs felt that their role was not structured optimally. This point was reinforced by one officer we spoke with early in her tenure at a liberal arts college in the South, who noted,

> They brought me in and expected a miracle, but they have not given me what I need to perform even the most basic magic tricks—let alone make a rabbit disappear. I have none of the resources that I need to get the job done. And as a result, I think that their entire commitment to diversity is little more than lip service.

It was common for us to interact with officers who complained that their span of attention was characterized by a broad span of responsibilities (strategic span) requiring a number of individuals to support their efforts (span of support), but possessing little human and financial resources (span of control) to move their work forward. One officer commented on this reality, specifically noting how many of the institutions she had worked for

FIGURE 1.3
Misaligned Span of Attention

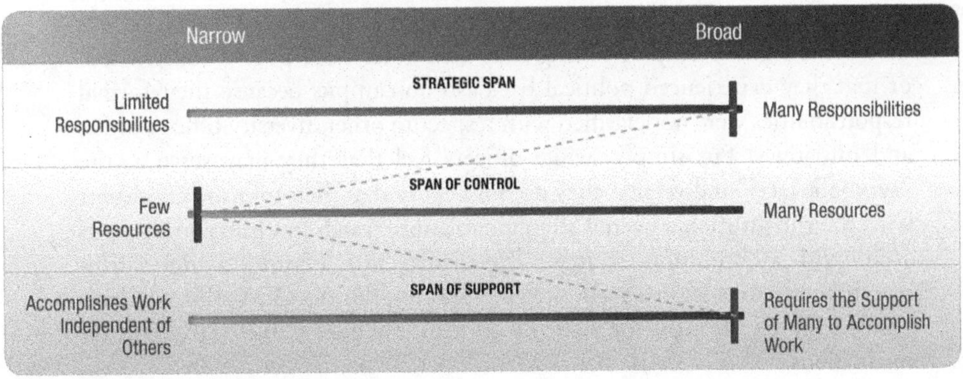

Adapted from Simons, 2005.

resisted moving any preexisting offices or units into her portfolio or providing her with an adequate budget:

> I have worked at four institutions and what I have concluded is that budgetary and institutional limits present the biggest challenge if you really are going to move the diversity effort forward. Your work is necessarily marginalized when your new chief diversity officer has no resources. It is striking that you never hear that same argument about budgets and resources in other areas of responsibility: just diversity! I have faced this at a number of institutions and it finally burns you out. I mean it just gets to a point where you are limited in how far you can take your program.

As these comments suggest, the implications of having a poorly aligned span of attention are multifaceted. First, it can lead to a high-profile role that lacks a strong foundation for success. It may also lead to low morale in the CDO, forcing him or her to feel as if it would be best to look for opportunities elsewhere rather than develop new programs and policies at his or her current institution. The most capable potential candidates are often uninterested in positions where they have little hope of succeeding. By comparison, a position that provides a clear understanding of the multiple dimensions of a role's span of attention is much more attractive and suggests that senior leaders have thought carefully about how the role can succeed on campus. Table 1.6 provides a well-developed span of attention overview associated with the announcement of the aforementioned new vice chancellor for equity, diversity, and inclusion position at UCSD.

Problems With the CDO Role Design

As we noted earlier, CDOs often identify their formal span of control as a key challenge to their effectiveness. Our research uncovered many CDOs who tell a similar story of feeling that their roles were poorly constructed, or that they experienced political backlash on campus because their formal responsibilities were not clarified with respect to other diversity offices, units, and initiatives. Put simply, while officers feel that they may serve as the "symbolic face" of diversity, they do not believe that their roles are consistent with their institution's overall strategic mission, much less position them to accomplish an ambitious strategic diversity agenda. Figure 1.4 summarizes recommendations we received after segmenting the 110 CDOs in our database about the vertical, or span of control, challenges they face at their institutions.[4]

TABLE 1.6

A Span of Attention Overview for the New Vice Chancellor for Equity, Diversity, and Inclusion at the University of California–San Diego

Strategic Span	*Span of Control*	*Span of Support*
Position Overview The proposal for the creation of the Office of the Vice Chancellor for Equity, Diversity and Inclusion (VC EDI) follows the "portfolio model" in which the VC EDI has direct responsibility for a range of diversity, equity, and inclusion initiatives and the offices and the individuals responsible for the initiative. Key Responsibilities • A key task of the new VC EDI will be to develop an appropriate organizational framework by collaborating and strengthening existing partnerships with diversity and outreach functions across campus that affect all members of the campus community. • The strategic plan will inform the final core administrative responsibilities, propose metrics to gauge progress, and identify potential additional areas of responsibility, reporting directly to the office of the VC EDI.	Direct Reporting Relationship The VC EDI will report directly to the Executive Vice Chancellor for Academic Affairs, and indirectly to the Chancellor. This reporting relationship is the most financially viable and cost-effective organizational structure. VC EDI Direct Reports • Associate Vice Chancellor for Faculty Equity • Assistant (Vice) Chancellor for Diversity • Full-time administrative assistant • Full-time administrative specialists for Campus Community Centers • Three Campus Community Center Directors • Eight additional professional staff in three Campus Community Centers Divisional Units • Cross-Cultural Center • Lesbian Gay Bisexual Transgender Resource Center • Women's Center Indirect Reports (Matrix) • Staff Diversity Liaison • Undergraduate Student Diversity Liaison • Graduate Student Diversity Liaison • Office of Academic Diversity and Equal Opportunity No mention of budget	Key Relationships The VC EDI will serve as a member of the Chancellor's executive cabinet and an *ex-officio* member of the Campus Climate Council and the Diversity Council. Advisory Support The VC EDI will establish an Advisory Council representing campus constituencies. With the Board's advice, the VC EDI will develop and implement a campus-wide strategic plan on equity, diversity, and inclusion. Advisory Groups • Faculty Equity Advisors • Graduate Diversity Coordinators • Staff Associations (11 staff associations) • Committee on Gender Identity and Sexual Orientation Issues • Committee on the Status of Women • Campus Council on Climate, Culture and Inclusion • Diversity Council

Source: Retrieved June 11, 2011, from http://chancellor.ucsd.edu/archive/2011_0504vc-edi.htmlon.

FIGURE 1.4
Recommendations of 110 Chief Diversity Officers on Best Practices for Improving Their Span of Control

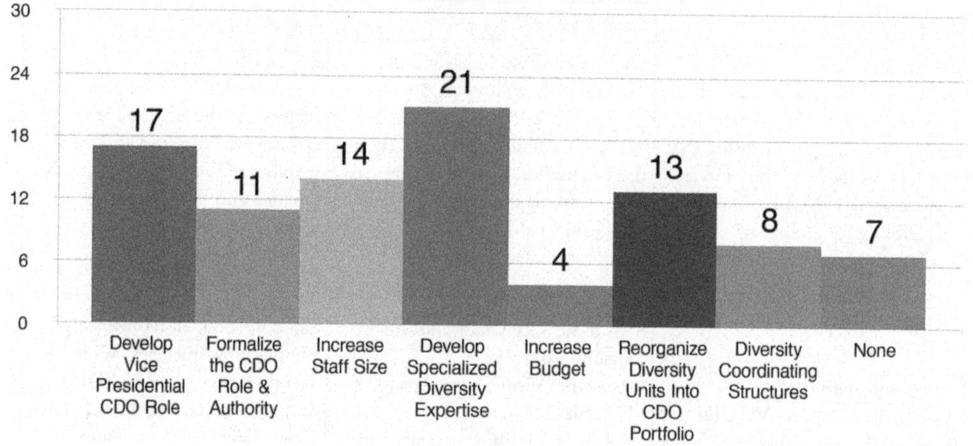

In 2007 we conducted a national survey that probed the question of vertical structure, asking CDOs to provide recommendations on ways to improve their roles. Like leaders in other positions, most officers felt that there are problems within most contemporary infrastructures. Of the 110 CDO respondents, only 7 felt that their infrastructures did not need improving. Others offered seven broad categories for improvement: (a) develop the CDO role at the vice presidential level; (b) formalize the CDO's role and authority on campus; (c) increase staff size; (d) develop specialized diversity expertise in specific areas of strategic diversity prioritization; (e) increase budget; (f) reorganize diversity units, placing them under the CDO's direct span of control; and (g) develop new campus-wide diversity coordinating structures.

CDO Role Misalignment

One of the common challenges that many CDOs discussed was the dilemma of having their job defined at a high level of rank and then being pressured into performing duties that were inconsistent with these broader expectations. For example, although it may be critical for a CDO to lead the design of a diversity-training program, it is questionable whether the individual should then bear sole responsibility for implementing five to seven trainings per week. One CDO offered that he felt more like a "diversity trainer" than a CDO, and that no other senior leaders had such operational duties associated with their positions. As he explained, "It would be like the Chief Information Officer conducting five to ten technology workshops a week, when they are supposed to be working on bigger issues like infusing technology into our classrooms."

This criticism is not meant to convey that diversity trainings are unimportant. To the contrary, diversity training, intergroup relations, intergroup dialogue, and diversity-themed leadership development workshops are critical to moving a campus's diversity agenda forward. The problem is when we title, rank, and create a more strategic set of expectations for the CDO and then expect him or her to lead in such an operational fashion, engaging in the larger priorities of the institution quickly becomes impossible. By spending all of their time in training, CDOs can find themselves distracted from their other primary responsibilities, which include improving strategy, creating innovations, representing the institution's diversity interests with key constituents, and amplifying current diversity capabilities. This inconsistency is a structural design challenge and one of the main reasons that institutions need to think seriously about how they design the basic role and expectations of the CDO early on.

A Need for More Specialized Capacity

The most frequent recommendation of CDOs was the need for specialized capacity to help them tackle strategic priorities more directly. One vice provost at a midsized institution on the West Coast noted that institutional leaders "just need some help to focus on the issues. If I had more staff who could work with students directly, or work with curriculum, I could get so much more done. As it stands now, I just cannot hit all of the areas that I need to cover." This comment is a good illustration of the challenge of capacity, specialization, and reorganization that typifies the reality for many CDOs.

As we noted previously, specialized capacity is a vital concept in organizational design. When there is an area of responsibility that is critically important, it becomes natural for the organization to hire specialists who are experts in the area. Ideally, the development of the CDO role marks a step toward creating specialized capacity to engage in strategic diversity leadership work. An additional step in this process is to create specialized capacity that will further enhance the officer's capacity to focus on specific aspects of the strategic diversity agenda, rather than leaving these tasks to be done by others or not at all.

At the heart of the idea of specialized diversity capacity is a belief that strategic diversity leadership is a knowledge-intensive field that requires expertise and dedicated staff to accomplish. CDOs also expressed a need for enhanced staff capacity, noting that staff resources are vital to achieving the following outcomes: (a) increasing the diversity of the faculty; (b) improving intergroup relations and campus climate; (c) conducting research and assessment into the educational benefits of diversity, campus climate, and program effect; (d) engaging student retention and graduation issues; (e) conducting diversity training and leadership development activities with faculty and senior leaders; and (f) working on diversity curriculum integration projects.

The presence of specialized capacity in any of these areas creates a potential advantage for the institution that develops capabilities in a particular area. In many ways, specialized diversity roles are the next logical step in developing focused capacity to tackle difficult diversity challenge areas. Although the idea may seem foreign to some, developing specialized diversity capacity that supports the leadership and vision of the CDO is no different from having dedicated assistant coaches who focus on offense, defense, and conditioning for a sports team.

Instead of splitting time between several different roles, strategic diversity specialists should hone their work in a particular area of responsibility, like conducting diversity trainings or assisting faculty search committees. The more that specialized capabilities are built into a particular area of priority, the better the diversity office will become at delivering the CDO's strategic diversity platform, and ultimately the institution's big-picture strategic diversity agenda. For example, although it may seem at first unfamiliar to ask someone from the CDO staff to advise a faculty search committee on best diversity practices, over time the process will become more routine.

Campus Politics and the Design Process

Too often the campus design process focuses on campus politics and symbolic messages rather than creating the best diversity infrastructure possible. In our research and experience, we found that over the life course of the CDO role, the political context will inevitably shift as new circumstances emerge, such as the arrival of new leadership. Although institutional politics is part of any organization, it should not be allowed to control design decisions. Frequently, new and encouraging possibilities are limited or ignored because they violate long-standing structures that may not be serving the institution's best diversity interests.

As we highlight in the companion volume to this book, senior leadership, the definition of *diversity*, the presence of dedicated diversity infrastructure, financial resources, and other variables represent an institution's Diversity DNA. Every time an institution's Diversity DNA shifts, a new set of powerful dynamics emerges. Yet just beneath the formal discussions of strategies, job roles, policies, and processes circulate a number of informal dynamics that define how changes actually take place on campus. This is the murky domain of institutional culture and politics that in many instances determines the distribution of power on campus and how CDO design decisions are made, for better or worse.

Although strategy and structural alignment are key to advancing a cohesive campus diversity agenda, many people seek to use organizational redesign efforts as a means to advance their administrative territory (Pfeffer, 1992). In these instances, interpersonal relationships with key decision makers and strategic coalitions often trump best practices and other rational arguments for change. We encountered this dynamic often in our consulting work helping campus leaders redesign and optimize their CDO infrastructure. In many instances, campus leaders would resist suggestions for achieving strategic and structural alignment for political and symbolic reasons.

Among the arguments put forth to resist diversity offices, perhaps the most nefarious is the claim that such work ends up "ghettoizing" diversity units. The real needs for diversity policies and the expertise to implement them should drive the institution's big-picture diversity agenda, not political posturing. And the only way to achieve successful outcomes is by aligning strategy, structure, and leadership. To get to this place, senior leaders have to recognize that the work of the CDO must be viewed through a formal structural lens. Hence, we emphasize that institutions embrace a multidimensional strategic diversity leadership tool kit upon which to engage and lead around issues of diversity. In the next chapter, we explore the varying and multidimensional leadership tools that an effective CDO can expect to draw on.

Another concern expressed is that by removing diversity offices from the student affairs division, student affairs professionals will be unable to serve diverse students. One of the great diversity challenges in higher education is that the work of diversity falls on the backs of one office or a relatively small number of organizations, allowing prominent campus-wide offices—including Greek life, career planning, study abroad, and student governance—to ignore the needs of diverse students who often feel marginalized by majority culture. The key is not to create separate but unequal diversity offices that service minority, LGBT, disabled, and women students, but to build strong diversity programs into both diversity and general campus units, such that they are able to work together and creatively leverage the strength and efforts of both communities.

We consulted with a small liberal arts college on the West Coast where the extent of its design effort hinged on the provost and members of her staff, who sat around a table shuffling 20 index cards with different names and placing them into various structural configurations. A faculty member who served on this committee told us:

> The conversation would always focus on relationships and campus politics, not what was best for diversity or the institution. The provost would say, "Well, if we do it this way, Susan would now report to Bob, and you know they have not gotten along that well in recent years. And if we move this role out of a direct reporting relationship to the president and place it with the chief diversity officer, they will view this move as a demotion and that we now do not value the contributions of their area." We never addressed the serious issues, including what we were trying to accomplish by creating a new position. It was frustrating because we did not know the major issues or how to get the process right.

As this passage illustrates, personal politics can often guide decisions around organizational design, rather than efforts to find the best structural solution. Too often, vice presidents for student affairs, deans of students, academic deans, and leaders of undergraduate education areas are asleep at the wheel on issues of diversity, unless the conversation moves toward a particular member's span of control. At this point, senior leaders move quickly and decisively—to protect their interests over the effort to implement best diversity practices.

Organizational realignment should always be approached with caution. As Kates and Galbraith (2007) note, strategy-structure-alignment is a classic principle of organizational design that is used to justify the creation of various roles, including the vice provost for enrollment management divisions, vice president for research divisions, and vice president for student affairs. If a new high-ranking CDO role is created to provide strategic leadership on campus across diversity issues, then why not vertically align the campus diversity function as well? If the diversity plan has not performed well, why not turn to this powerful lever of change as part of the campus diversity strategy? With so many powerful organizational realignment options, both vertically and laterally, the resistance of some senior leaders to even trying suggests a number of discouraging possibilities. They either do not value diversity, do not understand its clear connection to improved educational outcomes, or do not care about promoting it because diversity seems unrelated to their sphere of control. But designing a CDO role that is merely symbolic is worse than doing nothing at all.

Summary

Because the CDO role has emerged with little administrative and conceptual guidance, some are confused regarding the definition of the CDO role and use this designation in ways that are inconsistent with the spirit of a senior, high-ranking role engaged in strategic leadership work. In this chapter we defined the CDO role in higher education, demarcating a *general* and *grounded* definition of this senior leadership position in the academy. Although a diversity program coordinator in student affairs may serve as a "chief diversity officer" from a general perspective, we argue that institutions should recognize and respect the authority and responsibilities actually embedded in the traditional definition of a "chief" officer role. It is for this reason that we strongly recommend that institutional leaders define the CDO role using the grounded definition presented here, and situate the position at the highest levels of institutional life. With clearly defined and appropriate levels of support and control, the CDO can serve as an ideal catalyst of institutional change around issues of diversity and inclusion.

As we discussed, role design is a matter of formally defining an area of performance that we call "strategic diversity leadership work" and making this body of work the CDO's primary responsibility. The CDO role is predicated on the need to have specialized leadership that focuses on diversity issues as a matter of first institutional priority. Although many people should be engaged in issues of diversity, the CDO role is unique in that the person filling this institutional position will engage issues of diversity as a functional area of responsibility, focusing the issues, challenges, and capacities of diversity that exist across campus. Although many play a role in moving the institution's diversity priorities, even if they are able to make the work primary, they still may not have a sophisticated enough understanding of the literature, theories, and best practices that one must know to meaningfully move the agenda in innovative and effective ways.

In some respects, leading diversity work is like teaching kindergarten. Although every person has some experience with young people, this does not mean that anyone can cultivate a high-caliber learning environment for children. The same is true with diversity; simply because one has some experience with diversity, or is oneself a member of a minority group, does not mean that one knows how to create diversity education platforms, lead campus climate surveys, or develop a campus-wide diversity accountability process. The best CDOs lend expertise in an effort to help their colleagues and other members of the campus community become leaders in a collaborative change effort, rather than shouldering all the work directly. Indeed, diversity efforts only succeed if they are done collectively and collaboratively.

Too often, the CDO role is limited in its effectiveness because of a misaligned span of attention, in which the CDO has a broad mandate, but has few staff, material, and budget for human resources to move the diversity agenda forward. The bottom line for a successful organizational design process is grounded in being intentional, evidence based, and centered in the unique realities of the institution. To avoid the detrimental effect of personal and institutional politics, CDO design decisions should be made from a purely strategy-structural perspective. In the coming chapters we explore this challenge further, and provide several helpful frameworks for aligning strategy and structure. Indeed, we explore in detail the best practices associated with building the most effective—and potentially most contested—vertical design infrastructure.

Notes

1. 2005–6 University of Minnesota, March 2, 2006, University Senate Minutes: 3, Faculty Senate Minutes No. 3, Student Senate Minutes No. 4. Downloaded February 6, 2012, from www1.umn.edu/usenate/usen/060302sen.html.

2. Office of the Chancellor, Office of the Executive Vice Chancellor–Academic Affairs, May 4, 2011. Downloaded May 20, 2011, from http://chancellor.ucsd.edu/archive/letter 2011_0504.html.

3. For an in-depth discussion of the diversity management perspective, see the work of Roosevelt Thomas (1991), David Thomas (2004), and Taylor Cox (1991, 2001). Although their work has timely importance for leading diversity efforts in higher education, they do not focus on the direct needs of higher education diversity leadership. Authors who have made contributions to this conversation include Daryl Smith (2009), Jerlando Jackson (2006), Adrianna Kezar (2009), Marv Peterson and colleagues (1978), and others.

4. Figure 1.4 reflects responses to an open-ended question where we asked chief diversity officers to indicate any changes that they might make to the vertical structure of their organization. Among the 110 respondents, only 95 offered responses. Fifteen respondents did not complete this question and are not reflected in the figure.

2

RUNNING THE TRIANGLE OFFENSE

The Integrative Leadership Role of the Chief Diversity Officer

> In making this appointment of a vice provost for institutional diversity, Columbia reaffirms its commitment to promoting intellectual excellence, recognizing that this goal can be realized only if the university, in all of its aspects, reflects the diversity of American society and of the complex world in which we live.
>
> —Lee C. Bollinger, president, Columbia University (downloaded May 11, 2009, from www.columbia.edu/cu/news/04/09/jeanHoward.html)

Legendary basketball coach Phil Jackson is the winner of 11 National Basketball Association titles and mentored both Michael Jordan and Kobe Bryant during his time coaching the Chicago Bulls and Los Angeles Lakers. Coach Jackson has often said that these singular talents would never have become champions if they had failed to tap the roles and skills of their teammates. For all their superlative abilities, Jordan and Bryant benefited from their teammates—key performers who understood their roles and helped deliver the overall team strategy.

Coach Jackson is also famous for utilizing a particular offensive system known as the "triangle offense." A key premise of the triangle offense is to position three players on the floor in the shape of a triangle and direct the other two players to weave between and among them, creating the open space needed for an open shot. In this offense, players react to each other's movements, moving fluidly and efficiently with each player coordinating his or her part within the greater whole.

Basketball is a game of constant movement. Regardless of position—whether guard, forward, or center—each player is capable of dribbling, passing, and shooting from any space on the floor. Although certain positions favor dribbling and passing over shooting or rebounding, each player must contribute some element of all these skills, while harmonizing his or her movements with the rest of the team. And as in basketball, building sustainable diversity capacity requires the integration of often-disparate offices, coordinating policies, committees, and skills into a collective effort that reflects the contributions of the entire campus community.

The Chief Diversity Officer as Facilitator of the Campus Diversity Strategy

A key aspect of coach Jackson's championship philosophy is having someone who serves as an "organizer" or "facilitator" of the offense and the defense. This person, although not the only player who handles the ball, is charged with implementing the coach's vision and ensuring that the team is on the same page. On the teams coached by Phil Jackson, this player is also entrusted with taking big shots in critical moments, providing key leadership as time runs down, either by shooting or by advancing a deft pass to an open teammate.

Like Jackson's "facilitator," the chief diversity officer (CDO) plays a key coordinating role, helping the campus community define its strategic priorities. And in this analogy, the president or chief academic officer acts as the coach or manager of the CDO. He or she authorizes the overall strategic direction of the team, ensures that the team has an adequate budget to acquire and keep talent, and sets the overall strategy. The CDO is key to engaging the campus community and helping colleagues, peers, subordinates, and others to get involved, distributing opportunities as a basketball player does passes, and generally moving the diversity game forward in collaboration with a shared governance process that includes faculty, staff, and students. However, also like Jackson's "facilitator," during critical moments, the CDO provides key leadership, coordinating with a diverse set of stakeholders to implement a strategic vision that may include a range of campus diversity plans and efforts.

In this chapter, we define the *organizational DNA* of the CDO as a strategic facilitator and integrative specialist, outlining the foundational building blocks on which the role must be developed. Establishing a robust

CDO role is a potentially powerful step toward activating an institution's commitment to diversity, but only if the role is designed well and is empowered to be successful. We therefore begin by addressing the CDO's complex mandate, uncovering some of the myths and misperceptions that surround the role. Next we outline the major dimensions that give it shape. We conclude with a brief discussion of the myriad ways that CDOs affect their institutions and help them to build sustainable diversity capacity.

The Complex Mandate of the Chief Diversity Officer

Perhaps more than any other campus administrator, the CDO role is a lightning rod for criticism. Of course, some people simply fundamentally oppose efforts to increase access, equity, and inclusion for diverse students. But even people committed to diversity can object to the presence of these officers on the grounds that the CDO is often the symbolic "face" of diversity, and thus ends up being the go-to person, no matter what the diversity issue. Some critics are worried that having a central position means that the community has an easy means of avoiding a priority that should be everyone's responsibility.

Some diversity supporters who are critical of the CDO model believe that hiring a CDO removes the responsibility for diversity and inclusion from other senior leaders and members of the campus community. They argue that the presence of a CDO puts the full burden of diversity challenges on the shoulders of one person, potentially setting this individual up as a "diversity messiah" who is solely responsible for advancing the strategic diversity agenda. Others worry that the CDO is little more than a symbolic figurehead who possesses no real administrative authority or capacity to create change. They argue, quite rightly, that diversity must be everyone's responsibility and that no one person can or should provide leadership in an area that is already so hard to define.

Still other critics argue that CDOs threaten institutional quality by pushing a narrowly defined political agenda that has little to do with academic excellence, much less with meeting the needs of a changing world. Consistent with the "reverse discrimination perspective" discussed in the companion volume to this book, these individuals often focus their critique not only on CDOs, but on any level of institutional support for diversity efforts, arguing that they discriminate against White students. They argue that CDOs are pushing an agenda of "political correctness" that erodes quality, essentially working to admit students, or hire staff and faculty, who are not well qualified or meet the institution's standard of excellence. Finally, there are critics who believe that the CDO role, whatever its merits, constitutes a drain on financial and staff resources that could be better spent elsewhere. For these individuals, diversity is a low priority and they wonder why the institution has created a position dedicated to diversity efforts in the first place.

Among all these criticisms, perhaps the most widespread is the notion that implementing a CDO position precludes others from owning the diversity change process, which brings us back to the myth of "ghettoizing diversity" by investing diversity efforts in a single person or office. Although this attitude is inconsistent with what we know about the role and its potential influence on all areas of academic life, this notion will persist as long as there is a lack of clarity about the organizational best practices that must inform the work of a high-performing CDO.

Just as the chief academic officer should not be held singularly responsible for teaching and learning, the CDO is not singularly responsible for diversity. As noted in the companion volume to this book, implementing affirmative action and equity, learning and diversity, and multicultural diversity model goals is a collective process. CDOs do not hire faculty, admit students, or independently establish curriculum and campus policy. They necessarily operate within a set of institutional and social boundaries, and thus rely heavily on collaborating and building bridges to achieve their outcomes. In visits to institutions across the United States, we noted that these flawed beliefs often stem from an incomplete or misguided understanding of the context, mission, and role of the CDO. Rather than focus on the substance of what these officers do on a day-to-day basis, critics often made assumptions that reflect their own personal ideas about diversity, equity, and inclusion. Part of a CDO's work, therefore, needs to include conscious, intentional efforts to educate his or her colleagues about the day-to-day business of the CDO as an integrative, partnering force, whose work is centered on building synergies and engaging diversity as a matter of improving both academic and social outcomes on campus. If there was one common thread in our research with dozens of officers around the country, it was their strong conviction that it takes an entire campus community to create traction on diversity efforts, just as it takes an entire campus community to create a productive learning environment for students. Box 2.1 provides a description of the activities involved in a typical day in the life of a CDO.

BOX 2.1
A Typical Day in the Life of a Chief Diversity Officer

The work of a CDO requires a host of different capacities and skill sets.

The typical day begins early, perhaps with a morning meeting with the president's cabinet, briefing members not merely on programs and initiatives, but the management of any crisis incidents. A meeting with faculty pursuing a diversity-related grant opportunity, or an associate dean who is requesting financial support for conducting a study of the campus climate in his or her school or college, might follow the presidential briefing. From here, the officer might meet with a student interested in interviewing him or her for a class project on diversity in higher education, and then head to lunch with a campus dean, where the goal is expanding or deepening the network of strategic allies and partners who can be called on to engage issues of diversity.

As the administrator with point leadership for the university's diversity efforts, the CDO may be responsible for supervising programs in his or her area, but also supporting the diversity-themed and public relations efforts that advance the institution's overall mission. As such, the CDO's range of interactions extends off campus as well. In a typical day this might involve a meeting with the president of the NAACP to discuss how they can partner with the university to secure more tutors for a community-based after-school program. It may also involve meeting with high-capacity donors interested in supporting campus diversity efforts.

Because the CDO cannot be at all places at all times, a normal day will also involve members of his or her senior staff participating in meetings on the CDO's behalf, facilitating a meeting with a local company interested in recruiting more diverse candidates, meeting with student life regarding a sensitive campus climate issue in the residence hall, and connecting with students who may have requested time with the CDO, but who have been unable to get an appointment for several weeks.

The CDO's public-speaking skills are in constant demand. In the late afternoon, the officer may visit a class to give a talk about the influence of changing demographics in a global knowledge economy, before hustling to a dinner hosted by the dean of the Law School, where he or she is expected to give remarks on behalf of the provost, discussing not only the campus's diversity agenda, but the big-picture priorities of the institution moving forward.

Thus, the typical CDO workday generally runs late, because strategic and collegial partnerships are formed not only during office hours, but also at the academic, athletic, and cultural events that are the social lifeblood of an academic institution. Unlike some roles in the academy, the CDO must be capable of moving in and out of different spaces with a high level of aptitude, and across a range of administrative, academic, corporate, community, and fund-raising spaces.

(continues)

(continued)

On most college campuses, only the president, provost, academic deans, and a small number of other administrative roles have the leadership dexterity that is required to serve as a top-tier CDO. This breadth of potential activities is one of the reasons that the CDO role must be designed in ways that align the officer's span of attention with the types of leadership capacity that will deliver the diversity and strategic priorities at the heart of the institution's mission.

Diversity as a Functional Area of Specialized Leadership Attention

Within organizations, the assignment of responsibilities constitutes an important mechanism for promoting coordination and leadership in a given area (Galbraith, Downey, & Kates, 2002). By creating a CDO role, institutional leaders affirm that diversity is an area that requires dedicated and specialized leadership. It is a move indicating that the institution is formalizing its campus diversity capabilities by creating an administrative role that prioritizes, engages, and elevates the diversity discussion for the entire institutional community.

Diversity as a Matter of First Role Priority

The role and duties of a CDO are complex and hard to predict. By investing in the CDO role, institutions are asserting that they need dedicated expertise on diversity-related matters and an ability to integrate this expertise throughout the campus environment. The decision to define diversity as an area of work is similar to any other area of functional leadership, such as student affairs, legal affairs, and financial aid. A CDO serving a liberal arts college in the Northeast told us the following:

> When creating a CDO role, the institution is saying that there is an area of work responsibility on campus that we define as diversity work, and we want to establish a high-level person to help people embrace more broadly what that work means, whether it is educating the community, setting policy, or leading different initiatives and programs. The key is to make sure that diversity is not just out there floating in the wind. We need a senior person and a team working to reach certain goals every day, and helping others to meet those goals as well.

Greater Intentionality and Focus on Issues of Diversity

The development of the CDO role implies a great degree of intentionality and focus. Moreover, it implies that the institution's diversity interests must be addressed collectively and in a way that more tightly binds an often loosely connected campus diversity infrastructure. When diversity is defined as a functional area of leadership attention, CDOs can serve as a guiding voice in the campus's effort to conceptualize, define, assess, nurture, and cultivate diversity as a social, academic, and institutional priority. Although specific duties may include maintaining traditional priorities like affirmative action and equal opportunity, a CDO's mission is to provide leadership for diversity matters broadly defined. The only exception is when the role is further specialized to have a singular focus on a particular area like diversity faculty recruitment, student diversity and retention, or some other demarcation of the role's formal span of attention.

Assigning Accountability for Diversity

Similar to other sectors, higher education organizational charts typically show senior academic leaders at the apex of formal authority. When viewed in simple terms, each individual at the top of the pyramid is responsible for accomplishing an institution's goals or objectives. The domain of the CDOs is to advance institutional diversity goals and objectives, however they are specifically defined.

At the same time, diversity leadership is an area in which it is actually detrimental for one person to have absolute and final authority for accomplishing an institution's wide-ranging diversity goals. As mentioned earlier, diversity only works when it becomes a cultural value shared by the broader community. In addition, academic institutions are by nature typified by governing structures characterized by democratic principles and shared authority. Finally, the institutional culture of academia is deeply resistant to change (Birnbaum, 1988; Chaffee, 1985; Ellström, 1983; Rowley & Sherman, 2001). Hiring an ethnically and racially diverse faculty, creating general education diversity distribution requirements, and holding deans and vice presidents accountable for implementing campus diversity plans require a group effort and the involved participation and leadership of the president, provost, search committees, deans, CDOs, and faculty senate, to name only a few.

In many ways, the process of differentiating responsibilities and assigning accountability for achieving a particular organizational goal is foundational to the organizational design process (Simons, 2005). For example, in the case of undergraduate admissions, clear lines of accountability are fairly easy to delineate and enforce. First, the domain of organizational activity, such as admissions decisions, is narrowly defined. A specific department within the institution can be held accountable for visiting high schools, distributing marketing materials, collecting and processing applications, and making admissions decisions based on clear criteria. Second, a clear set of indicators exists to determine success or failure in the admissions process. Third, the process is clear and occurs annually, allowing for a rigorous evaluation of success or failure every year. Fourth, the enrollment of a cohort of full-time-equivalent students has immediate implications for the financial solvency of the institution. Consequently, the ability of the institution to operate and function may be affected by the quality and quantity of the applicant pool.

The same narrow dynamics do not exist when developing role responsibility for pursuing most institutional diversity goals. The boundaries for diversity are less clear than the boundaries of enrollment management. Although institutional leaders can develop indicators to track diversity progress and measure goal attainment, those objectives can be achieved only through the collective efforts of many within the institutional community. To stay with the question of undergraduate admissions, although the CDO may play a role in helping to drive the diversity of the undergraduate or graduate student body, the primary responsibility for enrollment rests with the admissions office. Unless the admissions office reports to the CDO, as it does at a limited number of institutions, the CDO is able to influence this goal only through a number of complementary strategies. He or she may engage in pipeline development activities, collaborate on the development of admissions criteria and review processes, establish strategic partnerships with diverse school systems, host various strategic yield events, involve current students in the recruitment process, and build new diversity recruitment programs. But, at the end of the day, CDOs cannot run separate admissions processes for ethnic and racially diverse students—nor should they. Even if the CDO can influence the process in a multitude of ways, admitting a diverse class rests with the admissions office.

The same is true regarding the goal of enhancing the campus climate. Many institutions have an established goal of improving the campus climate for the benefit of diverse constituencies. CDOs and their teams can play a critical role in helping to develop strategy, gathering data to drive organizational learning and new initiatives, and ensuring that campus climate issues remain a part of the big-picture institutional discussion. Nevertheless, the CDO cannot be held solely responsible for improving the institutional climate, retention, or faculty diversity. It is beyond any one person's ability to implement this goal, although many should play a role. It is for this reason that CDOs should never be labeled as the "person responsible for diversity." To the contrary, if meaningful change is to happen on campus, the entire institutional community needs to be involved.

As an area of functional responsibility, diversity flows into every aspect of the institution. Therefore, diversity cannot be singularly defined as the sole responsibility of student affairs, human resources, or even the CDO. To do so would result in a diversity infrastructure that is doomed to failure. Hence, to achieve meaningful organizational change, diversity efforts must be spread across many offices, units, and stakeholders. Accountability for accomplishing institutional diversity goals must be shared. The political and technical complexity of implementing diversity requires participation in decision making and accountability across a number of arenas, including academic, administrative, and student affairs. Rather than having full authority to accomplish the most critical diversity projects on their own, CDOs work collaboratively by using their expertise, political capital, resources, and influence to build new institutional diversity capabilities. As a result, the success of the CDO is largely determined by the clarity of how the position is defined and nested within the institution's broader organizational dynamics.

Leading Through Status and Influence

CDOs generally have little formal authority to hold accountable individuals who do not report directly to them. As a result, a CDO's source of power is often grounded in persuasion, symbols, and his or her ability to bring human and financial resources to the conversation. Similar to the position of chief information officer or chief technology officer, the CDO serves as an integrative force. CDOs may supervise staff and have line authority over different units that support the larger diversity agenda of the institution. Nevertheless, they accomplish their long-term goals by coordinating and amplifying the efforts of administrative, faculty, student, and staff members across all levels of the campus community. The challenge for CDOs is to provide enterprise-wide leadership in an environment where their formal roles often lack the authority and resources usually required to accomplish an institution's most ambitious diversity goals.

The Importance of Title and Rank

Title and rank are important to the success of CDOs, particularly if they are situated at the vice or associate vice president, provost, or chancellor level, or placed in a senior leadership cabinet of the campus chief executive or chief academic officer. Situating the CDO at this level sends a powerful message to the entire campus community regarding the importance of the CDO and diversity on campus. A diversity committee at a large research university in the Southwest offered the following in a position paper discussing the need to develop a new CDO role:

> The senior-level administrator responsible for directing the University's diversity efforts should have a title of Vice President and report directly to the President. . . . Universally, both experts in the field and University constituents have conveyed that the person in this role must have both perceived and actual authority to effect positive change. Because the President sets the tone, standards, and expectations for the University's commitment to its diversity initiatives, there should be a seamless connection between the President and the individual who directs the University's diversity plan. This person should have the authority to speak on behalf of the President regarding diversity issues, and to hold individuals accountable for their actions. It is vital that the position also have authority for directing diversity efforts at the institutional level, and not just among students and staff. This individual will be expected to work across all levels of the organization to move the university's diversity priorities forward.

Because the president sets the tone, standards, and expectations for the university's holistic commitment to a major initiative such as diversity, there must be a seamless connection between the president and the individual who directs the university's diversity plan. If the person in this role does not have both the perceived and actual authority to effectuate change, to speak authoritatively on behalf of the president regarding diversity and related issues, and to create accountability systems that will hold individuals accountable for their actions or inactions, the institution will have rendered the position an empty, symbolic role and limited its campus diversity plan.

Using the Bully Pulpit

When a highly ranked CDO has a "bully pulpit," he or she is able to bring diversity issues to the fore. CDOs can leverage their position and its visibility to broker high-level meetings, raise attention about promising campus initiatives, and bring different voices to the table in ways that may not happen otherwise. This ability is anchored in the position's location at the presidential or provost level of formal administrative rank and, at its best, grants the

CDO the reflective voice of the institution's chief executive or chief academic officer.

Participation in the executive cabinet of the institution ensures that the position has visibility, access, and symbolic effect. When located at a high level of rank, CDOs can infuse diversity into often highly politicized discussions about budget allocations, new initiatives, and future priorities of the institution. Although many voices should champion and engage issues of diversity in these meetings, having a CDO in the president's cabinet ensures a level of expertise and perspective that can help guide the discussion in significant ways that may not exist even at the provost level, a point that drives many to believe that the CDO should be ranked at the vice president level.

Orchestrating New Institutional Behavior

CDOs must be able to orchestrate new administrative possibilities, which is one of the main reasons that it is important for these officers to have the financial resources that allow them to advance the institution's diversity goals. When under the control of a seasoned CDO, these resources can create incentives to spur new interactions, seed innovation, and bring an often-disconnected campus community into a common conversation of shared purpose and change. One of the most experienced officers in our study, a CDO at a large research university in the Midwest, noted:

> I have always been in a position where I had resources to work with. If you do not have resources, you are just blowing steam. You need resources in order to provide direct services and to leverage behavior. You need to be able to leverage behavior from academic, faculty, student and administrative units. With proper budget support, you can do collaborative programming. Having resources can allow you to lead with a light touch and in a spirit of helping people to see the world differently. If you're just asking them to do something, with no material support, it can be nearly impossible.

Because CDOs must shape behavior in new ways, it is essential that they have a sufficient amount of discretionary resources to creatively partner and build new initiatives with colleagues across campus. If the CDO controls no incentives to inspire campus leaders to try harder, work differently, or develop new initiatives, it will be extremely difficult to accomplish diversity-themed change. The ability to experiment and seed new ideas is key to organizational innovation, and is foundational to the leadership DNA of an effective

CDO, a point we return to in our comparison of higher education and corporate CDOs at the end of this book (Dyer, Gregersen, & Christensen, 2011).

An Integrative Leadership Role

Despite the importance of rank to the success of the CDO, this is not a top-down autocratic role, and Figure 2.1 presents a diagram of a flawed perception of the CDO role. By contrast, Figure 2.2 provides a more accurate reflection of the CDO role as nested within an elaborate social network of internal and external campus stakeholders. Anyone who envisions the officer as John Wayne leading a cavalry charge is missing the importance this role places on building consensus and establishing strategic partnerships.

Even when leading a large and well-resourced CDO division, the CDO rarely has the ability to overcome alone the most challenging diversity tasks. He or she needs the help and partnership of others. For example, our research identified no CDO with the authority to hire faculty members without support of the academic department or dean, even when the CDO had the resources to provide a portion or all of the salary necessary to fund the position. Nevertheless, some officers can persuade department chairs to pool

FIGURE 2.1
Flawed Model of the Chief Diversity Officer as a Top-Down Vertical Role

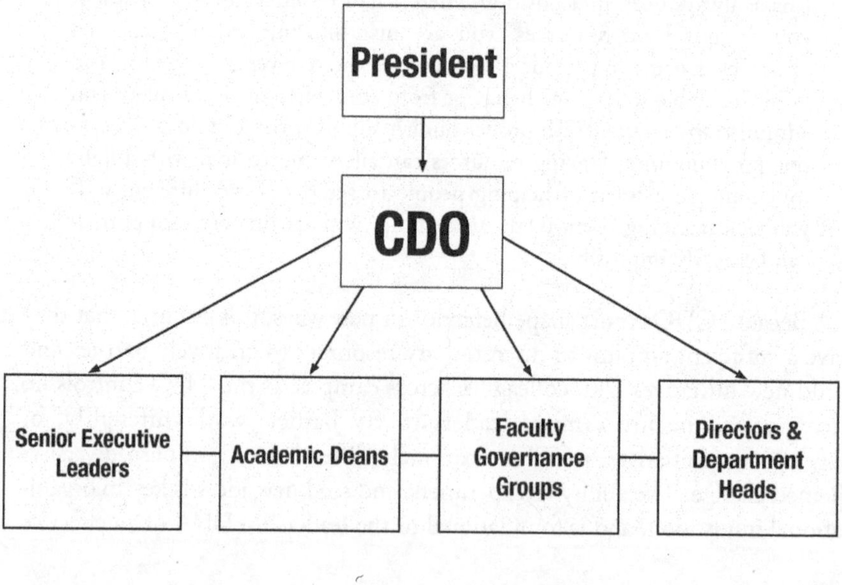

FIGURE 2.2
The Chief Diversity Officer as Part of an Effective, Horizontal Organizational Network

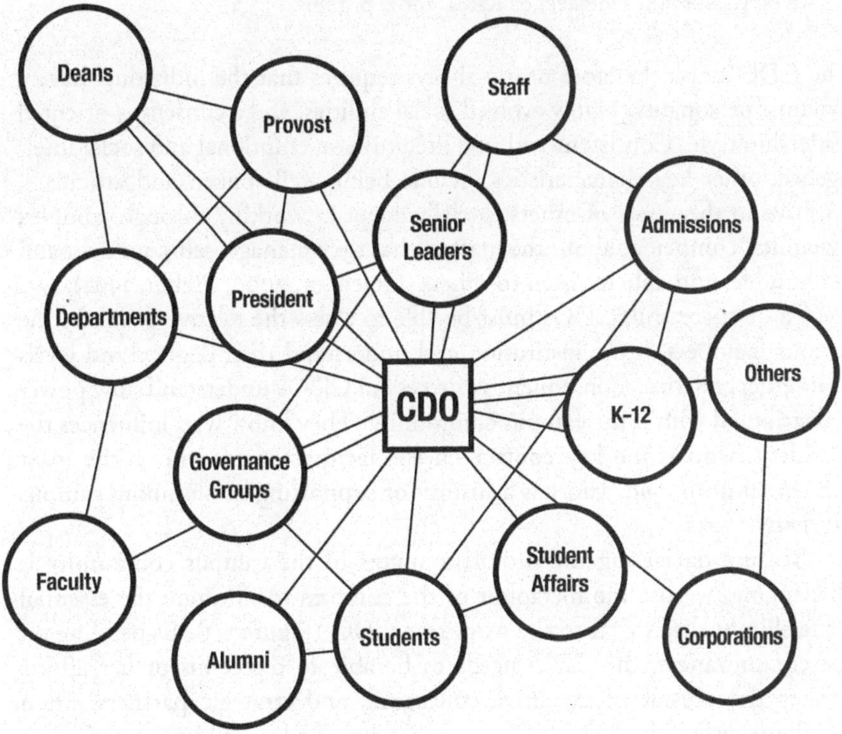

resources and hire a potentially high-caliber diversity candidate by offering these resources as an initial incentive and helping to find talented diversity candidates for the applicant pool.

Although some officers may have several units under their direct authority and control large resources, none enjoy sole responsibility for all academic hiring, curriculum development, and the myriad of other areas related to an institution's diversity agenda. Because most people naturally view the world from a perspective of self-interest, the role of the CDO is difficult. According to Jay Galbraith:

> Integrative roles, irrespective of type, rely heavily on the holder's interpersonal skills to build credibility. People in integrative roles usually do not command resources or have the authority that comes from overseeing a

> particular department or area. A person must be able to convince and motivate others to work across business lines, be solution-driven even when it's not their problem, and be willing to see things from multiple perspectives. (Galbraith, Downey, & Kates, 2002, p. 168)

The CDO's task therefore nearly always requires that the individual have a dynamic personality, highly evolved social abilities, and a consensus-oriented leadership style. Consistent with the literature on emotional and social intelligence, other key characteristics include being well spoken and articulate, sensitive to the needs of others, socially adept at working through complex dynamics, competent about the matters that they manage, self-confident and yet humble, and able to listen to others (Goleman, 2006; Pfeffer, 1992).

To be successful, CDOs must be able to assess the relative power of the various members of the institution and understand their degrees and levels of interdependence. Consequently, successful CDOs understand how power is distributed within the campus community. They know who influences the president, who is the key contact on the faculty senate, who is the most influential dean, and who has a history of supporting or shunning campus diversity efforts.

Because navigating the turbulent waters of the campus community is challenging, we use the metaphor of the compass to illustrate the essential leadership qualities vital to the work of a CDO (Figure 2.3). Depending on the circumstances, the CDO needs to be able to direct his or her efforts toward the president, executive colleagues, and strategic partners, often simultaneously. The key is to know what style of leadership is required to achieve collaboration and overcome obstacles. As we explore in Chapter 5 of the companion volume, *Strategic Diversity Leadership,* at different times an officer's leadership style is structural, collegial, political, and symbolic. Yet at the core he or she must always be actively engaged in an organizational learning process that seeks to leverage information, data, history, and relationships to move the institutional diversity agenda in dynamic and nuanced ways.

Successful CDOs are part of a broad information network that allows them to act in ways both subtle and decisive. For example, the CDO at a public research university in the Midwest told us how he regularly receives updates from various diversity champions across campus, allowing him to immediately use that information in his interactions with senior campus leaders. As Pfeffer (1992) notes, "One's access to social knowledge depends on one's position in the network of communication and social interaction.

FIGURE 2.3
Navigating a Course of Change Using Strategic Diversity Leadership

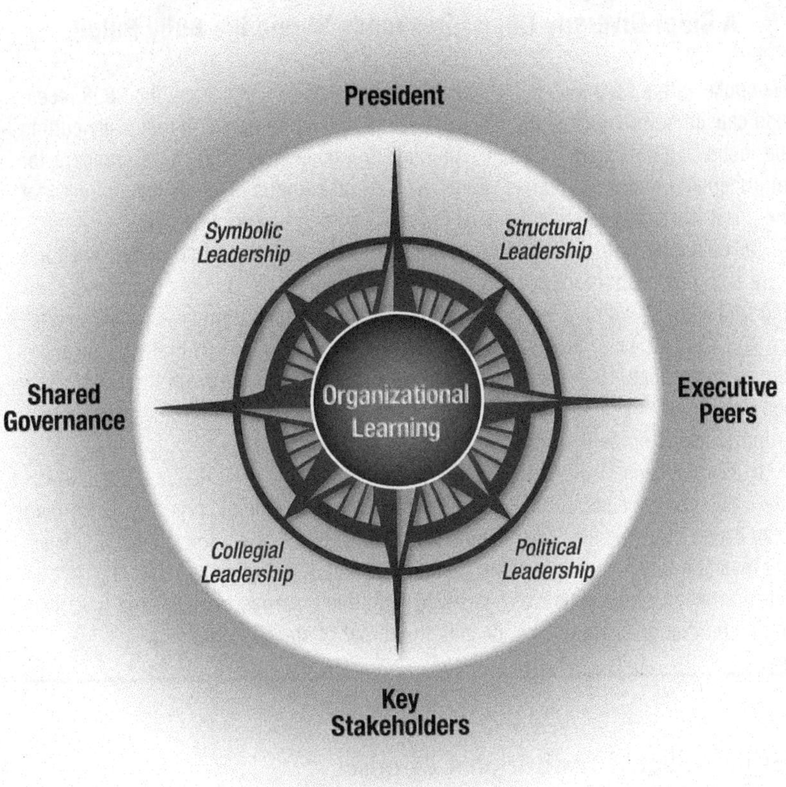

People who are well placed in the communication network also tend to be the central players in terms of power and influence" (p. 111). The best CDOs participate in a number of networks and actively cultivate friendships and contacts with influential stakeholders in an effort to build a broad base for their leadership. Box 2.2 illustrates how important communication was to one CDO at a large public university in the Midwest as he responded to proposed budget cuts.

BOX 2.2

Budget Cuts at a Large State University: A Chief Diversity Officer Responds Within the Bully Pulpit

We spoke with a CDO who noted how a budget crisis brought on by the 2008 recession caused several deans and divisional leaders to contemplate dramatically cutting the institution's diversity capacity. Although the ostensible goal was to prepare for an impending statewide budget reduction, several campus diversity leaders felt that the crisis was being used as political cover for cutting diversity capacity.

By obtaining information from multiple sources reporting that diversity efforts were being disproportionately targeted, the officer was able to act accordingly, setting up meetings with individual colleagues, creating a formal presentation, and writing directly to deans and divisional leaders entreating them to preserve diversity efforts on campus. He based his argument on the fact that although the entire campus community must share in the sacrifice, taken collectively, these cuts would disproportionately erode the institution's diversity capacity.

In every speech, presentation, letter, and interview, the CDO also noted that diversity was among the institution's top five academic and strategic priorities, according to an earlier strategic plan. His statements raised the question: How could the university maintain that campus diversity capacity was a top priority while inflicting greater cuts to it than other initiatives? Working with allies across campus, the CDO was able to protect diversity efforts, despite the threat of steep budget cuts.

Creating a Shared Institutional Mindset

Another way that CDOs exercise integrative leadership is in their efforts to create a shared understanding on issues of diversity. Here it is not about having the right answers, but asking the right questions. In this way, the CDO can use his or her role to encourage new ways of framing the diversity discussion, and finding innovative solutions to an institution's diversity challenges. For example, by introducing the idea of the "educational benefits of diversity" into the development of a new strategic plan, rather than solely a moral imperative, the CDO can connect diversity efforts to an institution's core academic mission. As one officer at a highly selective faith-based institution in the Midwest told us:

> Before coming on board, I was shocked at the institution's diversity language. It was really out of date. One of the first actions I took was to become very

intentional about getting the right language into the conversation and moving the discussion in a direction consistent with the twenty-first century. That meant talking about an educational and business case for diversity, and really pushing us to define our work in a more contemporary way.

This subtle reframing may not happen if the CDO is not part of these conversations. Yet the implication is potentially far reaching as this new plan may guide how resources are allocated, what issues are given greater strategic priority, and how the institution frames its diversity conversations for years to come. In their role as an integrative leader, CDOs can help influence the perspective of campus stakeholders, thereby building a more comprehensive campus diversity agenda.

Building Strategic Partnerships

Organizations are necessarily made up of boundaries, from vertical boundaries that separate people by rank, to horizontal boundaries that determine different functions and disciplines. There are also internal and external boundaries, which help distinguish the organization from its stakeholders and policy environment (Ashkenas, Ulrich, Jick, & Kerr, 2002). As Figure 2.4 illustrates, because of their unique history and multidimensional mission, colleges and universities are often characterized by disconnected silos—various entities pursuing their own independently crafted agendas.

As an area of functional leadership and responsibility, diversity cuts across these silos in myriad ways, and includes infusing diversity into the curriculum; enhancing the demographic diversity of students, faculty, and staff; and developing campus-wide diversity policies and programs. As such,

FIGURE 2.4
Administrative Silos in Higher Education

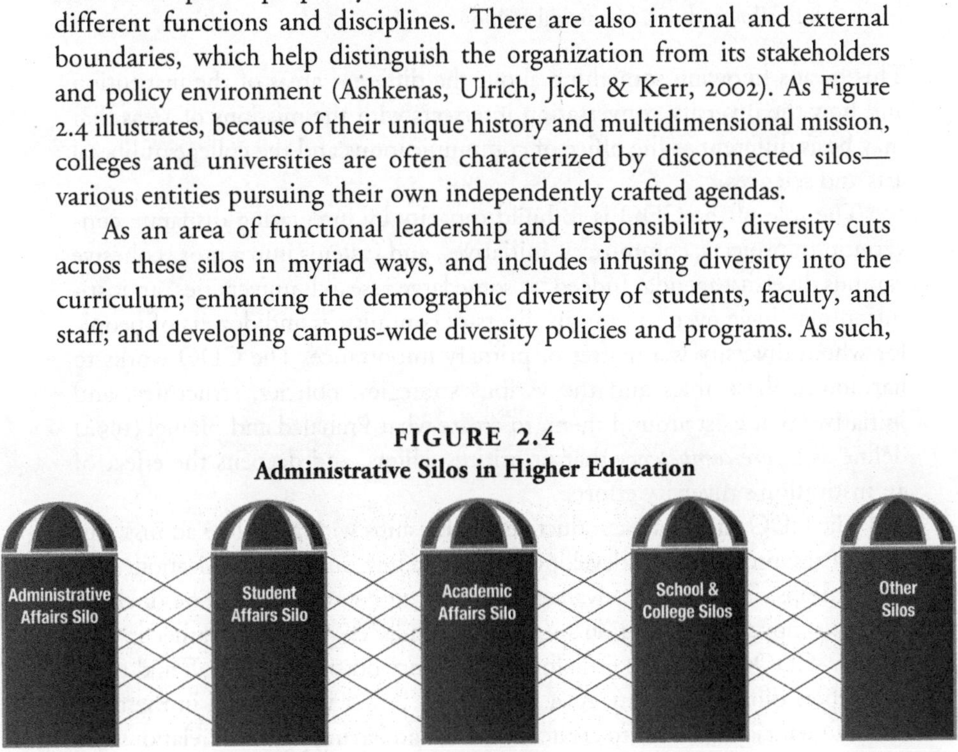

diversity does not fit into a traditional administrative box. Unlike very narrowly defined campus roles, the CDO's span of attention is broad, intersecting with nearly every facet of the institution.

Similar to other integrative roles, diversity is a functional area nested in the work of many people across campus, just as technology is nested in the work of any member of the campus community who logs into the campus network or has an institutional e-mail account. At their best, CDOs connect the diversity conversation across the white space of an institution by linking the various silos presented in Figure 2.4. In the words of a national leader on diversity who is currently serving as special assistant to the president and vice chancellor for diversity at a large university on the West Coast:

> When you have an issue like diversity that affects people across the entire university, one of the challenges that you encounter is that the organizational structure is not set up to allow diversity efforts to cross-fertilize easily. The key is to be intentional and think through the challenges in terms of organizational management and organizational change. Even though we all talk about the importance of diversity in our community, we tend to work in silos and in a hierarchal fashion.

This means knowing something about the different areas of the institution and how the diversity conversation intersects with the missions of areas that may be as different as the office of communications and the college of liberal arts and sciences.

The role of the CDO is to build capacity by integrating disparate conversations, projects, committees, initiatives, and systems into a more cohesive campus diversity agenda. Indeed, at some large research universities, an institution may have over 30 campus diversity committees and dozens of people for whom diversity is a matter of primary importance. The CDO works to harmonize these roles and the various strategies, policies, structures, and initiatives that exist around them, to create what Prahalad and Hamel (1994) define as a *core competency* that prioritizes, aligns, and deepens the effect of an institution's diversity efforts.

The CDO must have productive relationships with areas like admissions, human resources, faculty development, marketing and communication, academic deans, institutional advancement, and numerous others, if he or she is going to move the institution's diversity agenda. As we noted earlier in this chapter, CDOs often have little formal authority outside of the staff and units that report directly to them. As a result, their power is grounded in the presence of financial resources to create alliances, and having powerful relationships with their colleagues, possessing knowledge of both diversity and higher education, possessing an ability to work with the support of the president and the provost, and cultivating relationships throughout the institution.

In our survey of CDOs, 98 percent of participants reported using "informal networks and campus contacts" to advance their institution's diversity efforts. Similarly, 96 percent placed a premium on "building strategic campus partnerships and alliances" to implement campus diversity work. One CDO at a midsized institution in the Midwest described her strategy for building these informal networks:

> I attend a number of events to ensure that I get to know my president and his family, and my VP and Dean colleagues and their families, in a social as well as professional environment. This makes it much easier for me to talk with them as equals on issues of importance, to gain their support—and avoid their objections. I have one-on-one lunches with them to chat and discuss business issues in a collegial context. I invite them to community and professional organization activities that I am involved with so that important individuals in constituent communities can get to know them and be impressed with the great relationships we have, including parents of current and potentially future students.

The challenge of building relationships can be difficult as colleges and universities are hyperpolitical environments, and diversity can often be one of the most contested areas. For example, when the CDO enters into different areas of administrative purview, it forces the renegotiation of boundaries and identities because the CDO now occupies an institutional space (whether of human resources, academic departments, student affairs, institutional planning, etc.) that others view as their territory. When the CDO crosses into this territory, some will view his or her arrival as a threat, whereas others will embrace it as an opportunity to build collaborative solutions to the institution's diversity challenges. Box 2.3 explores the challenges of this integrative role with respect to admissions.

BOX 2.3
The Challenge of Chief Diversity Officers Working Across Administrative Boundaries

Integrative roles are difficult to implement because they can generate confusion, and in some cases conflicts, when people are engaged in a particular area. One of the

(continues)

(continued)

most challenging settings in academia can be found when a CDO is involved in diversity admissions policies.

For example, let us imagine a scenario in which the parent of a minority student asks the CDO to accept an application after the stated deadlines have passed and the admissions office has refused to review the application. The parent explains that the application was delayed because of a death in the family and that they are not looking for any special admissions provision, only that their child's application be considered. It turns out the student has a score of 20 on the ACT, a nearly perfect GPA from a well-regarded school, and is highly involved in several service-related and leadership activities.

How is the CDO to respond? If the CDO does nothing, he or she may potentially alienate the parents and lead them to conclude that the institution is not sincere in its espoused commitments to diversity. If the CDO acts on the student's behalf and strongly encourages the admissions office to review the application, he or she may be viewed as trying to "bend the rules" for a student of color. The situation is delicate and suggests the highly political nature of the CDO and the difficulty of integrative roles that span so many areas of institutional responsibility.

In a best-case scenario, the CDO will have built a strong personal relationship with the admissions office and can appeal to them on a personal level, explaining the situation and hopefully arriving at an agreeable outcome that maintains integrity in the process while serving the interests of diversity. After all, the CDO does not supervise admissions and cannot require the office to do anything. The officer can request that the office of admissions consider the student's application, but should be careful not to set unreasonable expectations of the family or applicant.

Most importantly, the CDO should have been working all along to establish a set of guidelines, however informal, to deal with these kinds of situations. The decision should not come down to the judgment of the two leaders in question, the director of admissions and the CDO. Because diversity success often requires doing things proactively, it necessitates leading through the back channels of traditional institutional policy, relying on both process and discretion to arrive at the desired outcome.

Building External Relationships and Partnerships

Beyond their internal concerns, CDOs also focus on building external relationships to help attract new energy, resources, and attention to their change initiatives. To this end, 93 percent of the officers we surveyed stressed the importance of building off-campus relationships to bring attention to and strengthen campus diversity efforts.

One particularly compelling program we encountered was a targeted alumnae event designed to link current undergraduate students and the development office with prominent minority alumnae. The president began the event by presenting the institutional vision of diversity. The office of the CDO summarized its campus diversity initiatives and paired current undergraduate students with minority alumnae mentors in their areas of study. Meanwhile, the development office proposed several diversity-centered projects to encourage alumnae contributions. This type of collaborative effort proved rewarding as diversity advocates built alliances that allowed other members of the campus community to develop initiatives that would not have existed without CDO involvement.

At other institutions, CDOs have played a key role in strategic fund-raising for campus diversity efforts. These efforts have included participating in high-profile fund-raising events with the president, provost, deans, and others, and partnering with the primary fund-raising office of the institution to pursue grants; major gifts; and strategic relationships with corporations, nonprofit organizations, wealthy donors, alumni, and foundations. In times of economic challenge, the CDO may be critical in spanning the divide that often exists when minority and other diverse students graduate and, over time, become disconnected from the institution.

Consultative Focus

Collaboration is often achieved through consultative relationships. As the campus's leading diversity expert, CDOs often consult with stakeholders to help build diversity capacity in offices, grants, projects, and initiatives. To this end, 93 percent of our survey respondents identified themselves as "internal consultants" on issues of diversity. Many of these officers were coauthoring grants, writing letters of support, and building relationships with community colleges and historically minority-serving institutions to strengthen the grant-writing efforts of faculty members. In each of these cases, the CDO was able to add value and strengthen the diversity components of these initiatives, thus enhancing their potential for success.

CDOs also mentioned their role in helping their colleagues develop new strategies to diversify services that may not previously have reached diverse constituencies. For example, one CDO assisted the honors program to increase the number of its African American and Latino students. The CDO and the honors program explored possible reasons why these students were not applying to the program and then collaborated to design strategies to encourage more to apply to the program.

Furthermore, the CDO involved the honors programs in several ongoing campus conferences and symposia, and then provided a roster of students who were qualified to enter the honors program. The two areas jointly hosted an information event that exposed ethnically and racially diverse students to other mentoring and leadership development initiatives like study abroad, service learning, and the leadership development program in the career planning office. Over time this targeted event raised the number of African American and Latino honors students in the honors program and other campus opportunities. The CDO was instrumental in identifying the target audience, helping other campus units understand ways to resonate with this audience, and using their status on campus to get a number of different constituencies involved in the effort.

This example shows the importance of building alliances with members of both internal and external communities. These alliances enable CDOs to amplify their efforts and create a sense of collective responsibility for campus diversity priorities. Although accountability structures were also required, meeting this commitment was only possible thanks to these interpersonal, consultative, and strategic partnerships.

The CDO leads campus-wide diversity planning committees, works to create diversity experiences both within and outside of the classroom, and at times leads a broad portfolio of units. In addition, he or she should serve as an advocate for diverse groups of students, faculty, and staff, including constituencies on the basis of race, gender, ethnicity, sexual orientation, domestic status, religion, disability status, and national origins, among others. Traditionally, diversity leaders have focused their efforts more narrowly, addressing the needs of particular student populations; implementing a narrowly defined set of initiatives; or enforcing campus-wide equal employment opportunity laws, regulations, and statutes.

Finally, the CDO integrates and amplifies the efforts of others across campus. This may include supervising or working closely with campus diversity units and initiatives, including cultural centers, ethnic studies, affirmative action, multicultural affairs, international affairs, study abroad, and grant-funded projects. He or she can also serve as a strategic resource for the admissions office, human resources departments, teaching and learning centers, academic schools and colleges, and the alumni office. Although the president holds final authority for ensuring that diversity is a top priority, the CDO is often the central leader who cultivates a campus-wide conversation, articulates a collective vision, and serves as a primary catalyst in developing the strategy to bring this vision to life.

Change Management Specialists

Because of the importance they place on strategies designed to move the culture of their institutions forward, CDOs can best be defined as "change management specialists." At least on the surface, no CDO is hired to maintain the status quo, even though some institutions only extend superficial support to their officers. Nevertheless, change is a fundamental aspect of the CDO role, whether leading campus-wide diversity planning and implementation efforts; seeding new diversity initiatives that involve others in change projects; developing diversity training and educational strategies for administrators, faculty, staff, and students; developing high-profile campus diversity events; or creating new systems to ensure that faculty and staff search committees cast a broad hiring net.

At institutions across the country, CDOs are building diversity capacity in a number of innovative ways. The CDO's task is to help the institution become more active on diversity efforts, whether the goal is defined in terms of increasing access and equity, building international relationships, or improving the learning environment. Although diversity broadly defined serves as the overall domain area, each of the following initiatives has the power to create both institutional and cultural change:

- **Elevating visibility and credibility of the campus diversity function:** Having a point person at the upper tier of an institution's leadership helps elevate the visibility of the CDO and other diversity-related offices, enhancing the credibility of the institution's commitment to infusing diversity into all aspects of campus life.
- **Leading strategic diversity planning efforts:** In our research, many officers mentioned the need to develop and refine strategic diversity plans. Furthermore, they advocated that diversity goals should be incorporated as a formal aspect of the overall institutional strategic planning process.
- **Building new institutional diversity infrastructure:** Launching a diversity council is just one example of productive infrastructure. These councils can be responsible for a variety of functions, such as conducting climate surveys and audits, supporting the development of major cultural programming events for the campus community, and planning seminars and forums centered on diversity issues.
- **Enhancing demographic diversity, equity, and success:** CDOs often work toward increasing the number of underrepresented faculty, staff,

and students on campus through enhanced recruitment strategies. These efforts include developing strategies and initiatives that seek to raise the retention and graduation rates of underrepresented students so as to achieve parity with majority students, as well as create targeted faculty diversification efforts like those discussed in Chapter 7 of this book.

- **Informing the search process:** CDOs interface with various phases of the search process for faculty and administrative hires, helping to develop and review job descriptions; debriefing search personnel on matters of institutional diversity; encouraging new people to participate in searches; reviewing the pool of candidates; and providing strategic resources to assist with competitive offers, dual-career challenges, and other issues.
- **Cultivating diversity awareness and appreciation:** This process entails launching campus-wide diversity-training and briefing sessions. These sessions increase diversity awareness and cultural competence across the campus and among administrators, faculty, staff, and students. Developing community outreach and diversity programs that effectively bridge the gap between campus and the community is also a key component of the CDO's role.
- **Interfacing with institutional accountability systems:** Many officers report interfacing with the institution's formal accountability systems as they relate to diversity. They engage in activities like evaluating cultural competence in all performance reviews of administrators and staff in their purview, advocating for the inclusion of diversity content and achievements in the merit performance review process for the entire institution, outlining diversity actions and achievements in annual reports, and giving presentations to institutional leadership and governing boards.

CDOs also mentioned creatively leveraging the knowledge and insights of experts and scholars in areas ranging from strategic planning and change management to scholarship examining the educational implications of diverse experiences on both classrooms and the campus climate. CDOs often talked of the need to engage external consultants who are able to provide trusted counsel because it draws on sources outside and independent of the institution. One high-ranking and nationally influential CDO working at a midsized public institution in the Southeast had this to say:

> Even though I am widely respected on these issues, it is important to bring other voices to the conversation. No one can be a prophet at home, and external expertise can help move the discussion of some difficult issue in an innovative and compelling way. I understand that some may view bringing in an external expert as frustrating, because often what the expert offers varies little from what the CDO has been saying for years, to no effect. However, bringing in these expert voices can help validate a CDO's perspective, coaching, and ideas. Ultimately, these consultants can help build the type of political capital and energy necessary to move the agenda forward.

Thus, it is vital that diversity leaders engage the expertise of external voices to help drive the change conversation. This might involve both hiring leading consultants in the diversity leadership field and sending campus leaders to participate in conferences and leadership trainings elsewhere. In both scenarios, the goal is to inject new energy into the diversity conversation, prompting movement that might not occur otherwise.

When using these techniques, we recommend that campuses only work with credible individuals and institutions. In the academy, this means accessing leading intellectuals and scholars who not only possess the requisite academic credentials, but a proven track record of success. They should be associated with leading higher education policy organizations and groups, or perhaps come from respected institutional peers.

The Multivariate Role of the CDO

Up to this point we have emphasized the formal definitions of the CDO role and his or her core focus on leading change, creating integrative energy and conversations, and spanning campus silos in an effort to advance the institutional diversity agenda. Nearly always, the CDO position launches with a job description; a statement of formal role responsibility; and perhaps some articulation of formal lines of authority, control, and relationships that set the position's span of control. And yet, the CDO role is generally much more complex than what appears in the formal job description.

Table 2.1 analyzes the features of the CDO role from a multivariate perspective, including the formal, negotiated, and manifest and latent core functions of the position. The formal role comprises official duties and areas

TABLE 2.1
Potential Formal, Negotiated, and Manifest/Latent Core Functions of the Chief Diversity Officer Role

Formal Role Duties	*Negotiated Role Duties*	*Core Functions*
Provides point leadership in setting the big-picture vision for diversity.	Supervises diversity units, offices, staff, and initiatives.	Catalyzes diversity-themed change.
Coordinates and aligns the activities of campus diversity committees, units, and initiatives.	Authorizes campus diversity budgets.	Serves as the institution's conscience on matters of diversity, equity, and inclusion.
Leads the campus-wide diversity planning and implementation process.	Leads campus fund-raising activities associated with issues of diversity.	Educates the president regarding diverse constituencies that he or she is not well equipped to engage.
Advises the president and other leaders on diversity matters.	Hosts diverse constituent alumni events.	Acts as cultural ambassador to diverse constituents around their issues, priorities, and actions.
Represents the institution on diversity matters before the media, internal and external constituencies, and key stakeholders.	Manages the campus's strategic faculty diversity hiring resources and programs.	Makes the institution look strong on issues of diversity.
Develops regular diversity progress reports and updates for relevant internal and external stakeholders.	Develops strategic partnerships with companies and nonprofit, K–12, and government organizations.	Gives hope to the campus community on issues of diversity.
Assesses campus-wide diversity programs, policies, and activities.	Conducts diversity trainings, search committee workshops, and other diversity education initiatives.	Protects the institution during diversity crises and periods of political and social unrest, often serving as a "diversity fixer."
Infuses best practices into campus diversity initiatives and programs.	Advises diverse student organizations, affinity groups, and individuals.	Evolves the campus community's thinking on issues of diversity, including not only issues of access and equity, but diversity-themed teaching, learning, and scholarship.
Develops new diversity initiatives, policies, and processes to drive organizational change.	Leads and partners on campus research efforts centered on issues of campus climate and diversity among students, faculty, and staff.	Mitigates risk around issues of diversity.
Oversees diversity discretionary resources to seed new initiatives and promote change.	Participates as a formal member of tenure and promotion decisions.	Provides a visible leadership presence at campus diversity events and programs.
Chairs the campus diversity planning committee.	Assists deans and divisional leaders in retaining diverse faculty and administrative professionals.	Provides a visible presence in diverse local communities on behalf of the institution.
Creates accountability and incentive strategies to drive organizational change.	Sits on external campus diversity advisory groups and community organizations.	Serves as a symbol of the institution's commitment to diversity.

of responsibility (Greenwald, 2008). Most people are aware of their formal responsibilities and those of their colleagues, at least at the time of their hiring, because their responsibilities find expression in their job descriptions. But negotiated roles are harder to pinpoint and include responsibilities and actions that can be added or subtracted at any time, depending on context (Greenwald, 2008). Finally, core functions represent the base or fundamental contributions that people make as a function of their role within an organization (Greenwald, 2008).

Formal and Negotiated Roles

Formal job requirements are easy to discern and include leading the campus diversity planning process, evaluating campus diversity offices and units, chairing campus diversity planning committees, advising the president and senior leadership, representing the university around matters of diversity, developing accountability and incentive strategies, supervising diversity discretionary resources, and others (see Table 2.1). These duties comprise officially assigned duties that are generally part of the portfolio of CDO responsibilities. Upon being hired, a new CDO initially sees only formal roles, both their own and those of their colleagues.

Negotiated role duties are the variable job roles that could potentially be added to or subtracted from the position's formal responsibilities. Whereas formal job roles are generally associated with the CDO role, negotiated roles are highly contextual and dependent on how the role is operationalized at a particular institution over time. Many negotiated roles have to do with the span of control and strategic foci as the CDO position can be enriched by infusing supervision of campus diversity units, personnel, and budgets; adding responsibilities to develop diverse strategic partnerships; engaging diverse alumni; and diversity fund-raising, to name a few that we highlight in Table 2.1.

In addition to the formal assigning of duties, some aspects of the negotiated role happen at the CDO's discretion as he or she becomes acclimated on campus and the role evolves to meet the demands of the environment. Indeed, it is common for the CDO to discard or assume new roles once he or she arrives on campus. Because many CDO roles are relatively new, it is typical for institutional leaders to reformulate over time the list of roles, granting them the gravitas and weight commensurate with their responsibilities on campus. Box 2.4 explores these formal and negotiated roles.

BOX 2.4
The Formal and Negotiated Roles of a CDO

The authors visited one large research institution where a newly appointed CDO talked about the importance of defining her job duties in a way that would allow her to focus on the big-picture strategic issues that had historically gone unaddressed by her predecessors. In this particular instance, the CDO noted that her predecessor had conducted diversity-training workshops with faculty search committees as one of his top job role responsibilities, despite serving in an institution with over 40,000 students and nearly 3,000 faculty and staff.

Thus, even though he was ranked at the highest levels of institutional life, her predecessor would regularly conduct 90-minute training workshops for as many as 50 search committees a year, which swallowed a tremendous amount of the CDO's capacity. Although the search process unquestionably provides a key opportunity for diversifying the faculty and administration, the former officer did not distinguish between the level and types of search committees. As a result, he often had little effect on increasing the proportion of ethnically and racially diverse faculty.

Although the new CDO agreed that every search committee should receive a well-designed training experience, she felt that her time would be better spent working on big-picture strategic issues, including efforts to author a new multidimensional faculty diversity strategy that would itself provide guidance on faculty search procedures. She also felt that it was important to conduct research that investigated the disparity in diversity capacities across campus, and then educated senior leaders and campus governance about how to redress these imbalances. Indeed, she was hired and titled at a certain level to move the institution's agenda strategically. If she spent her time instead doing what a diversity or human resources trainer could do, how could she serve the long-term diversity interests of the institution? How could she develop research, strategy, and networking opportunities if she had to maintain her predecessor's training schedule? Her solution was to empower others who could conduct the workshops, allowing her to focus her own energies on the considerable responsibilities of her position. The final result was that diversity trainers and consultants trained junior search committees and the CDO reserved her training time for the most senior administrative searches and positions on campus.

Although the diversity-training duties noted in Box 2.4 represent a set of negotiated responsibilities that may be inconsistent with the role of a high-ranking CDO, negotiated roles are not always negative. Indeed, negotiated roles are a potentially powerful way to position the CDO to influence the institution. In fact, the negotiated role is one of the places where one can see the skills of the savviest and most experienced CDOs come to the fore. Take, for example, those CDOs who supervise a hybrid portfolio of nondiversity-focused areas, such as institutional research, admissions, community engagement, financial aid, or even the honors program. As we discuss in subsequent chapters, the presence of a portfolio of diversity and general campus units in many ways symbolizes a deep commitment to ensuring that diversity is integrated into the fabric of key campus departments.

As a general rule, the supervision of nondiversity-related units is not a core aspect of the CDO role in the same way as guiding the institutional diversity planning process. Given the right circumstances, however, these duties can be included in the portfolio of the CDO during the organizational design process at the time of a new role's creation, or at some point in its evolution over time. This particular negotiated role is rare as it requires an institution consciously to move nondiversity-themed areas into the CDO portfolio, a decision that requires staunch support from senior leadership, a clear set of institutional goals that support the move, and capable leadership able to lead in a diversity and nondiversity-related area without sacrificing the mission of either.

Core Functions of the CDO Role

Core functions capture the base contributions that people make as a result of their role within the organization (Greenwald, 2008). A role's function constitutes how the position helps the institution to operate and meet its objectives. Although formal job roles are relatively easy to identify, core functions are often difficult to discern. According to Howard Greenwald (2008):

> Formal and negotiated roles are recognizable as concrete, observable actions by their incumbents. Core functions must be inferred indirectly by watching people carry out their roles over time. Different types of functions may be associated with a given role. Manifest functions are those that are visible, explicitly recognized, and official. Alternatively, many roles have latent functions. These are often invisible, ignored, or purposely kept secret. But latent functions are often more important than manifest ones. (p. 77)

Latent duties generally reveal themselves over time, rarely appearing in any formal job description, brochure, or website. They are often implied and in many instances unstated. The CDO is the symbolic face of diversity, playing a key role by providing a presence both on and off campus at different events. Although this symbolic responsibility should not be the only role that the CDO plays, similar to the symbolic role of the president, the CDO adds value simply through his or her physical presence. This latent role can be incredibly time-consuming, and must be balanced with other responsibilities and priorities.

Other latent responsibilities often include the CDO serving as the "conscience of diversity," giving voice to issues when no one else will, even though his or her formal job description implies a responsibility for involving many stakeholders with campus diversity efforts. This is a heavy burden for any CDO to carry, but it is not uncommon for the CDO to occupy this role. In these scenarios, the CDO is often an institution's conscience on matters of diversity, equity, and inclusion, a point that is never publically presented in a statement of job duties and responsibilities, but a characteristic that is latent in the role at many institutions. Because the CDO risks eroding his or her political capital if he or she is the only person to raise these issues, it is essential that the president and other senior leaders lead and contribute, thereby lessening the need for the CDO to play this latent role.

In a related fashion, the latent duties of the CDO may include educating the president regarding the concerns of diverse constituents whom he or she is not prepared to engage, serving as a cultural ambassador to diverse communities, and protecting the institution during times of political unrest and social upheaval (see Table 2.1). Officers in our study were clear that they often felt pressured to fulfill these latent roles and others. Although the formal duties associated with the CDO role are generally written in ways that focus on matters of strategy and policy, they do not capture the full complexity of diversity dynamics that CDOs will encounter around issues of race, gender, sexuality, and more. According to one experienced vice president for diversity at a large research university in the South:

> I cannot tell you how many times that I have felt pressure from the president to talk with minority students, just because I am the CDO and a minority woman myself. It was almost like these were not students, or that they would attack him or something. It is in these moments, where the cultural limitations of our leaders is a problem, and you [as CDO] have to determine how far you will go to buffer him from difficult conversations, protect the university, and put yourself into uncomfortable situations. It is never in the job description, but it is in the job, and you have to balance these unwritten pieces.

In moments like the one noted here, the CDO may face pressure to serve in the latent role of "diversity fixer," working to help the institution navigate a difficult diversity moment without it boiling over into something even more unpleasant. As we talk about this potential latent role of "fixer," it is critical that we point out the potential role conflict that may emerge when a president or provost exerts influence over the CDO to intervene in a situation and make it "go away." One officer at a small liberal arts institution had this to say:

> Sometimes they want you to do the "master's bidding" but you have to balance that request against the very real need to maintain your integrity as a credible member of the community and a champion of diversity. I always work to protect and ensure the best interests of the college; at times, however, what is best for the institution is to feel a bit of the pain and embarrassment that diversity unrest can bring. In my twenty-year career, I find that sometimes this is just what the institution needs to take a step forward.

This type of job role conflict is common and requires senior leaders to think about situations and challenges holistically. Although CDOs play a critical role in navigating difficult diversity politics, they should always be ready to share their true perspectives and help ensure the integrity of their position. The president or provost is rightfully the face of the institution in these moments, but it is often the CDO who is quietly working behind the scenes in an effort to bridge the divide and bring resolution to what our companion volume calls "cheetah moments." In the twenty-first century, these incidents can include campus demonstrations, negative media attention, and sudden shifts in legal and legislative policy. During diversity crisis moments, the CDO is often the primary communicator with disgruntled communities of color and other diverse groups threatening to mobilize political energy and media attention. This latent dimension of the CDO role may not be understood or even valued until one of these moments occurs.

Presidents and others may never understand why the CDO may spend an inordinate amount of time with community organizations. These relationships are necessary to ensure that the CDO has a personal network of community members, tenured faculty, key alumni, political allies, and student leaders who personally trust the judgment of the CDO. In short, when a crisis incident emerges, the CDO must know whom to call.

Summary

The CDO role offers no magic bullet that will lead to dramatic diversity change overnight. Nevertheless, the CDO can prove a pivotal part in building infrastructure and capacity. The ideas explored here constitute just some of the ways to accomplish one's diversity objectives. By themselves, these strategies will not narrow achievement gaps, enhance the campus climate, or lead to more diverse student bodies. Nevertheless, we believe that the work of CDOs represents a foundation on which to build improved diversity outcomes.

Over the past several years, the diversity discussion has widened from one focused initially on the access of African Americans in higher education, to a discussion of the rights and opportunities of individuals on the basis of race, gender, ethnicity, sexual orientation, age, disability status, national origin, and a host of other factors. This shift only underscores the powerful need for executive leadership that spans the academic, administrative, and student affairs silos. There are a number of ways to supplement the work of a CDO. They include creating campus diversity coordinating committees, encouraging or requiring faculty and staff to become involved in campus diversity initiatives, and promoting lower-ranking diversity leadership roles, to name only a few. Institutions should view CDO positions as part of a broader set of institutional diversity capacities that must be built up, down, and across the institution.

CDOs must be malleable, innovative, and committed to working in areas outside of their core area of expertise. Diversity does not fit into a traditional administrative box; hence, the duties of a CDO span the boundaries of their institution, and success is often a function of how well he or she can work with and through other people. Furthermore, CDO success is often a function of how well the CDO can coordinate the structures, policies, and capacities of the institution. Given this complexity, these senior administrators must be relational leaders who can inspire and supervise the people and units that report directly to them, while engaging the people and units who do not, moving collaboratively toward the institution's overarching diversity goals.

In the next chapter, we discuss some of the key frameworks, questions, and action steps required to develop the CDO role on campus. More specifically, we present the Chief Diversity Officer Development Framework and explicate the various dimensions of this framework and the key ideas necessary to developing the CDO role on campus, while more broadly building a powerful and effective campus diversity infrastructure.

3

THE CHIEF DIVERSITY OFFICER DEVELOPMENT FRAMEWORK

A Tool to Aid Design

> The key organizational task is not to design the most elegant structure, but to capture individual capabilities and motivate the entire organization to respond cooperatively to a complicated and dynamic environment.
>
> —Bartlett and Ghoshal (1990, p. 140)

In our research and travels we have encountered a dizzying array of diversity infrastructures that have emerged from a myriad of different processes. Some are more effective than others. We have consulted on cultural and multicultural centers that are located in student affairs but that enjoy little or no relationship with the chief diversity officer (CDO), and CDOs who hold a vice provost–level title but do not supervise even one dedicated staff member. When developing the CDO role, campus leaders must navigate several organizational challenges if they hope to create an effective and integrated infrastructure that will build both symbolic and material capacity.

As we have stated, for a variety of reasons the CDO role has often been disconnected from the broader campus diversity infrastructure. As an alternative, we propose a model of strategic diversity leadership that seeks to frame diversity efforts in a more coordinated, intentional, and systematic way, despite the complex dynamics and diffuse, lateral governing structures that characterize academic institutions. Indeed, we believe our collective inability to operate in this way helps explain why campus diversity efforts so often do not achieve their objectives, even when the institution holds diversity as one of its core values.

The decision to create a CDO position indicates that the institution seeks a more formal approach to coordinating and galvanizing its diversity possibilities by making diversity leadership more formal, prominent, and systematic. Without sound organizational design and staunch commitment from senior leaders, many CDOs end up simply grafted onto the existing structure of their institutions like an added and redundant appendage to a body. It becomes highly debatable how much this new appendage will enhance the institutional body's ability to accomplish all its complex functions.

This chapter seeks to take a formal structural approach to elaborating the CDO role, and by extension the campus diversity infrastructure. Our approach is defined by an integrated and multidimensional system of variables that we call the *Chief Diversity Officer Development Framework* (CDODF). More than a how-to guide, the CDODF emerges out of the formal structural Strategic Diversity Leadership Model articulated in the companion volume to this book. Together, these systems offer an organizational theory for designing the CDO role. In our experience, organizational design science has too often been ignored when it comes to building dedicated diversity capacity, whether in academia or other spheres of organizational life.

The chapter begins with a general overview of the CDODF before moving into a specific discussion of each of its dimensions. We address, in succession, the related concepts of the (a) strategic diversity platform, (b) formal vertical structure, (c) lateral diversity capabilities, and (d) change management systems. We conclude with the model's fifth dimension, an explication of the knowledge, skills, and abilities that CDOs must possess, as well as key principles for applying the CDODF tool at an institution. Each dimension is addressed from the vantage point of designing an effective CDO role, and we return to earlier themes as a way of contextualizing the CDO role as an integrative expression of an institution's approach to strategic diversity leadership capacity. We also foreshadow a number of vertical dimension themes that are explored in Chapter 4.

The Chief Diversity Officer Development Framework

The CDODF grew out of our analysis of the qualitative data we collected through our research and consulting work, site visits to institutions in different phases of the design process, and experiences working in different CDO structures. The framework's foundation rests on Jay Galbraith's five star model of integrated organizational design (Galbraith, 2002), which provides a powerful conceptual model, which we illustrate in Figure 3.1.

FIGURE 3.1
The Chief Diversity Officer Development Framework

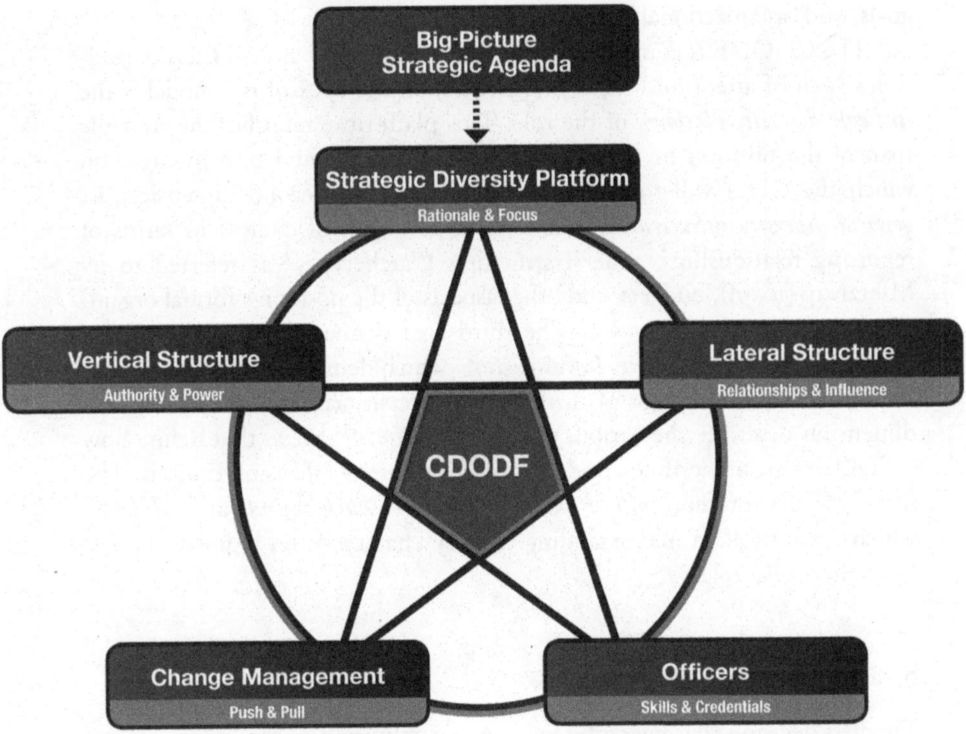

The CDODF can help senior leaders, researchers, diversity professionals, consultants, executive search companies, and others think through the various design elements that must be considered when developing the CDO role. The framework is also useful for researchers interested in examining these roles for both scholarly and programmatic purposes. In many ways, the issues addressed by each element of the design play a determining role in the CDO's potential for success with regard to providing strategic diversity leadership in an institutional setting.

The CDODF is guided by the big-picture strategic agenda of the institution and has been conceptualized to be consistent with the design principle stating that strategy should guide organizational design (Galbraith, 2002). That is, the design of the CDO role should flow from the institution's diversity definition and rationale, the diversity strategic plan, the overall strategic plan, and the fiscal reality of the institution. The design of the CDO role must take its cue from this overall framework if it is to align with the vision, goals, and organizational capacity of the institution.

The CDODF is composed of five basic elements that establish the position's span of attention (Table 3.1). Situated at the apex of the model is the *strategic diversity platform* of the role. This platform establishes the strategic span of the position in terms of the mission, scope, and priority areas on which the CDO will focus his or her efforts. The second dimension, or *vertical diversity infrastructure,* determines the span of control in terms of reporting relationships, general structures ("archetypes" as referred to by Mintzberg [1979]), budgets, and other aspects of the position's formal organizational authority and power. The third area defines the CDO's span of influence, or *lateral diversity infrastructure,* which defines the numerous ways the CDO is an integrator of institutional diversity capabilities. The fourth dimension describes the various *change management systems* that define how a CDO drives, orchestrates, and encourages diversity efforts on campus. The fifth category presents *officer skills, knowledge, background,* and *abilities,* which are critical to understanding the key characteristics required to perform the CDO role.

Strategic Diversity Platform

The first decision that has to be made is the definition of the organizational reality of the CDO within the specific context of his or her institution. This definition should be shaped by the grounded definition of the CDO that we provided in the previous chapter and the various negotiated roles that should be embedded into the position. Articulating a clear strategic diversity platform is essential to this process as it determines the CDO's strategic span and is the first dimension of the CDODF. Moreover, the strategic diversity platform defines the specific areas in which the CDO will provide integrative leadership regarding campus diversity issues, as well as a ranking of the primary and secondary priorities of the role. The definition of an officer's strategic diversity platform should shape decisionmaking in terms of defining vertical and lateral structures, the skills and backgrounds of staff hired to work with the CDO, and the change management principles that are put in place to advance the institution's diversity agenda.

By definition a CDO's rank should be set at the highest levels; nevertheless, the officer's specific job duties should be determined in accordance with

TABLE 3.1
Chief Diversity Officer Development Framework

Dimension	*Definition*	*Span*	*Key Elements*	*Central Questions*
Strategic Diversity Platform	The strategic diversity platform defines the specific areas of the CDO's involvement, including primary, secondary, and tertiary priorities. The strategic diversity platform provides the conceptual framework that determines the parameters of the CDO's work. Depending on how an organization wants to design its CDO capabilities, these include the organizational-conceptual level, diverse membership level, stakeholder membership level, and strategy-tactical level.	Strategic Span	Mission of the office Constituencies Strategic priorities Secondary priorities Tertiary priorities	How is diversity defined institutionally? What is the overarching mission of the CDO in terms of advancing the institutional definition of diversity? What are the primary, secondary, and tertiary diversity priorities that the CDO will pursue? Will the CDO serve as the affirmative action officer for the institution? Will the CDO serve as the Americans with Disability Act coordinator for the institution? Will the CDO center his or her efforts on faculty, staff, student, or community concerns? Will the CDO serve in a hybrid or dedicated diversity leadership role on campus?
Vertical Diversity Infrastructure	This dimension defines the formal authority, or span of control, of the CDO in terms of direct reporting relationships, archetypes of vertical structure, line authority, and budgets. Three primary archetypes of vertical structure exist: (a) the collaborative officer model, (b) the unit model, and (c) the portfolio divisional model.	Span of Control	Formal authority Reporting relationships Vertical archetypes Formal budgets	What is the formal vertical authority of the CDO? Who is the CDO's direct supervisor? Is a matrix reporting relationship up, down, or across the institutional environment necessary? What is the CDO's level of rank? What is the formal title? What is the primary archetype of vertical structure? Which areas report to the CDO? What is the budget authority of the CDO? What is the role's formal ability to set institutional policy?

TABLE 3.1 (Continued)

Dimension	*Definition*	*Span*	*Key Elements*	*Central Questions*
Lateral Diversity Infrastructure	The lateral diversity infrastructure represents those diversity capabilities that exist across campus that define the institution's ability to deliver its diversity goals. It also further defines the CDO role as focused on integration, coordination, amplification, synergies, and the sparking of diversity innovations.	Span of Support Span of Influence	Campus leaders Diversity committees Diversity areas outside the CDO's span of control Diversity professionals across campus Diversity point people among nondiversity units Affinity groups Student organizations Other groups	What is the lateral diversity infrastructure of the institution? What coordinating diversity capabilities must be established to accomplish the goals of the strategic diversity platform? What coordinating structures must be put in place to complement the vertical structure? What types of lateral leadership skills are required for one to lead as a CDO? How will diversity efforts be coordinated and integrated across campus? What are the coordinating mechanisms that connect the white space that exists between the formal areas of the organizational chart? What key relationships must the CDO have to accomplish her or his work on campus? What affinity groups are in place and how do they interface with the CDO role?
Change Management Systems	This dimension focuses on the primary change management techniques employed by CDOs to implement campus diversity efforts.	Strategic Span Span of Support Span of Influence	Educational strategies Entrepreneurial strategies Accountability systems Communication strategies Political strategies	What tools does the CDO use to drive, influence, and encourage change? What is the role of senior leadership in supporting the CDO to ensure that he or she can accomplish goals? What is the primary change management technique required to lead diversity planning and implementation in higher education? What are the key aspects of a campus diversity plan? What are the key principles and issues for understanding how to implement a campus diversity plan?

TABLE 3.1 (Continued)

Dimension	*Definition*	*Span*	*Key Elements*	*Central Questions*
Officer Skills, Knowledge, Background, and Abilities	This dimension refers to the different types of knowledge, skills, and abilities required to lead as a CDO.	Span of Control	Background Knowledge Skills Abilities	What knowledge, skills, and abilities are necessary to provide optimal strategic diversity leadership to the CDO role? Should the CDO have tenure? Should the CDO have a law degree? What are the most important characteristics of the CDO?

the institution's strategic diversity agenda. Hence, the questions that drive this dimension of the framework include the following: What areas of institutional diversity are the CDO expected to address? For example, should the CDO have responsibility for affirmative action and equity issues or should the officer simply consult on these issues, leaving someone else to serve as the institution's affirmative action and equity officer? Should the CDO focus on study abroad and international diversity issues or only solely on domestic diversity issues? Should the officer be involved in community engagement activities, alumni relations, and fund-raising, or focus narrowly on campus diversity matters? Will the CDO focus on student issues, faculty issues, and staff issues? Will his or her efforts focus on one or more of the following: race, ethnicity, gender, LGBT status, age, disability status, national origins, or other dimensions of the diversity equation? In other words, what is the CDO's mission?

Mission and Institutional Diversity Responsibilities

The institutional definition of diversity and the institution's strategic diversity agenda should guide the mission, priorities, and responsibilities of the CDO. Determining the mission of the office and its primary responsibilities should be among the first issues addressed when developing, reframing, or optimizing an institution's CDO capabilities. As we outlined in Table 3.1, CDOs can engage in a range of different diversity-related responsibilities on campus, including recruitment and retention activities, human performance enhancement or training programs, campus climate improvement activities, external relations and development, curriculum and research initiatives, strategic communications, and building accountability and evaluation efforts to enhance the institution's diversity agenda, to name only a few.

We recommend that institutional leaders categorize these various duties as either primary, secondary, or tertiary responsibilities (Table 3.2). In those areas of primary responsibility, the CDO will serve as the process leader in the conceptualization and development of work in this area, maintaining ultimate authority for making strategic decisions and implementing the tactical activity that will follow. With respect to secondary responsibilities, another unit or individual should guide process, with the CDO serving as a strategic partner to develop shared priorities and strategies. Finally, tertiary areas of responsibility require the CDO to be aware of work going on in these areas, participating in an as-needed capacity but with no ongoing direct responsibility to advance the particular project or policy.

Although these classifications may seem somewhat formal in a setting where numerous higher education leaders assist with several different responsibilities on campus, they are absolutely essential to defining the CDO role. A CDO needs realistic parameters so as not to be overwhelmed by so many varied and time-consuming duties. As we noted previously, only the president, provost, and academic deans touch on as many areas of the university as a CDO. Even with a narrowly defined role, an effective CDO invariably ends up working on a broad range of issues throughout the campus community. If indeed this happens, the strategic diversity platform may require redesign, setting in motion a series of other design decisions that affect the position's span of control, influence, and responsibility.

Institutional designers should therefore ask themselves, "What human, financial, technical, and symbolic resources are necessary to empower the role's strategic diversity platform and deliver on our big-picture strategic diversity agenda? And how can we align the CDODF with our broader mission?" How this theme is tackled in the design process will help determine whether the institution conceives and delivers a well-balanced CDO position, or ends up with a position that is woefully misaligned with the intentions that led to its development in the first place.

Dedicated and Hybrid Chief Diversity Officer Roles

An important part of the CDO design process is determining if the CDO role should have a *dedicated* or *hybrid* mission as part of his or her strategic platform. As we outline in Table 3.3, both these roles share similarities and differences, as well as strengths and weaknesses, in terms of their strategic span of attention.

In the dedicated CDO role, the officer should possess a 100 percent focus on advancing diversity issues as his or her formal area of institutional

TABLE 3.2
Chief Diversity Officer Primary, Secondary, Tertiary Diversity Responsibilities Matrix

		Primary	*Secondary*	*Tertiary*
Definition		The CDO serves as the primary process leader in the conceptualization and development of work in this area and has ultimate authority for making strategic decisions and implementing the effort.	The CDO serves as a strategic partner in this area of responsibility, developing joint solutions with others to the particular project goals.	The CDO is aware of these areas of responsibility and participates as a contributor when called on.
Responsibilities	*Strategic Goals*			
Recruitment and retention of diverse faculty, staff, and students	Diversifying the faculty, staff, and student bodies of the institution and improving rates of promotion, tenure, and graduation			
Human performance enhancement: training and leadership development	Developing diversity leadership and training programs for students, faculty, and staff that prepare them for a diverse and global world			
Establishment of a supportive and inclusive campus climate	Developing programs and initiatives to improve the campus climate for all, with a particular focus on diverse groups			
Curriculum and research	Establishing courses, centers, think tanks, and research institutions to advance the intellectual diversity agenda of the institution			

TABLE 3.2 (Continued)

Responsibilities	*Strategic Goals*	*Primary*	*Secondary*	*Tertiary*
Strategic communication	Communicating the institution's diversity brand in print, digital, and face-to-face forums, and other outreach efforts			
External relations and fund-raising	Fostering positive community relationships with key diverse constituencies, including alumni, donors, local community members, corporate allies, minority-serving institutions, and others			
Assessment and evaluation	Assessing the diversity outcomes of campus-wide diversity offices, units, and initiatives, and assessing the efforts of senior leaders to advance the institution's diversity agenda			
Other	Additional areas of responsibility that may require the CDO's leadership and attention, including nondiversity-themed duties and responsibilities			

responsibility. We refer to this approach as the *dedicated diversity model.* Although the CDO will inevitably collaborate on broader campus priorities from a diversity perspective, general administrative duties are not fundamental to the position's mission and duties (although it is essential that the CDO understand the culture of the academy and higher education issues broadly).

TABLE 3.3
Dedicated CDO Role Versus the Hybrid CDO Role

Dimension	*Dedicated CDO Role*	*Hybrid CDO Role*
Title and Rank	Diversity-themed title Potential title: Vice Provost for Multicultural Affairs and Chief Diversity Officer (CDO)	Diversity-themed title and general administrative title Potential title: Vice President for Diversity, Dean of the College, and Chief Diversity Officer (CDO)
Supervisor	The CDO should report to the president or provost as articulated in the grounded CDO definition.	The CDO should report to the president or provost as articulated in the grounded CDO definition.
Strategic Span	The CDO's primary focus covers issues of diversity, equity, and inclusion defined through one of three potential strategic diversity leadership models elaborated in Figure I.2 and Table I.1 in the introduction. These models are the Affirmative Action and Equity Model; the Multicultural and Inclusion Diversity Model; and the Learning, Diversity, and Research Model.	The CDO focuses on issues of diversity, equity, and inclusion defined through one of three potential strategic diversity leadership models: the Affirmative Action and Equity Model; the Multicultural and Inclusion Diversity Model; and the Learning, Diversity, and Research Model. The CDO also focuses on any number of responsibilities that might include undergraduate education, general academic affairs, legal affairs, and student affairs, among others.
Span of Control	The CDO potentially leads one or more diversity-themed units across the various organizational diversity models, including a core team of diversity staff. Alternatively, the CDO may have a dedicated budget that he or she controls to advance issues of diversity broadly defined, in addition to leading diversity-themed committees and initiatives.	The CDO potentially leads one or more diversity-themed units across the various organizational diversity models, including a core team of diversity staff. Alternatively, the CDO may have a dedicated budget that he or she controls to advance issues of diversity broadly defined, in addition to leading diversity-themed committees and initiatives. The CDO may have a span of units that he or she supervises covering a range of responsibilities contingent on the position's hybrid quality. He or she could also lead a number of different committees and initiatives for the institution depending how the position is designed.
Span of Support	The CDO position requires a high level of support from senior leaders and other campus stakeholders to deliver integrative leadership to the strategic diversity agenda.	The CDO position requires a high level of support from senior leaders and other campus stakeholders to deliver integrative leadership to the strategic diversity agenda. Depending on any additional responsibilities and strategic span or control issues, the CDO may or may not require additional support.

TABLE 3.3 (Continued)

Dimension	*Dedicated CDO Role*	*Hybrid CDO Role*
Major Strengths	The CDO position allows for a dedicated focus on diversity challenges and opportunities as a matter of first priority, creating opportunities for potentially greater levels of alignment, optimization, and influence. There is the potential to hire someone with a high level of strategic diversity leadership expertise and an ability to add value across the various domains of the three organizational models of diversity. There is more focused potential to overcome major diversity challenges (e.g., graduation gaps, faculty diversification, etc.). Job role clarity creates an enhanced ability to establish new relationships and possibilities, and to advance the campus agenda more aggressively.	The CDO position allows for the structural linking of campus diversity efforts with other senior leadership functions, potentially creating a tighter conceptual and administrative tie between the campus's strategic diversity leadership role and other critical areas of institutional priority. There is the potential to leverage general campus resources more prominently to benefit diversity-themed areas of priority. There is greater direct potential to reimagine general campus priorities as diversity-themed priorities. The CDO role may require greater salary resources required to hire a hybrid leader to fill two senior leadership roles.
Major Challenges	There is the potential for the role to be marginal and not well integrated into the overall campus administrative infrastructure. There may be challenges finding a strategic diversity leader who has the skills to work creatively across the three main models of organizational diversity. There is the risk of a lack of institutional commitment to providing an adequate level of resource support to adequately activate the CDO mission.	There is the potential for a span of attention that is too broad for any one person to handle, causing limitations in the institution's ability to either prioritize diversity or deliver on additional institutional administrative areas of importance. There may be challenges finding a strategic diversity leader who has the skills to work creatively across the three main models of organizational diversity. There is the risk of a lack of institutional commitment to providing an adequate level of resource support to adequately activate the CDO mission; using the hybrid approach becomes merely a symbolic tool and does not spur genuine innovation. There may be difficulty identifying someone who is able to lead equally well in both areas of administrative mission. There may be limited ability to fully activate both sides of the administrative mission even if a suitable leader is found.

As a result, officers in these roles are able to dedicate their energies almost completely to the challenges and opportunities of diversity issues across the Affirmative Action and Equity; Multicultural and Inclusion Diversity; and Learning, Diversity, and Research models.

The Hybrid Model

By contrast, some officers may have a dual title and carry additional responsibilities in academic affairs, student development, or faculty development. We refer to this CDO approach as the *hybrid model.* This hybrid model offers a way not only of integrating two areas of responsibility, but increasing a CDO's stature on campus. According to one officer we interviewed, the presence of a title like "Vice Provost for Diversity and Academic Affairs," in combination with a portfolio of units and responsibilities in both areas, signals that the officer is "more than simply a resource on matters of diversity and suggests a fundamental connection between diversity and academic excellence." This point is made in an excerpt from a campus CDO-planning document at a large research university in the Southwest:

> There must be a clear sign from the chief executive officer that while diversity is the focal point of the new administrator's responsibilities, this person is qualified for a second role that includes a variety of functions directly connected to initiatives essential to the institution's mission. One senior leader who contributed to this report occupies the following hybrid role: Vice President for Student Development and Diversity and Vice Chancellor for the campus, and Professor of Higher Education Administration. In his role as Vice President, this individual has responsibility for the honors college, which is led by an academic dean and enrolls 2,600 students. He simultaneously works with chief academic officers across the university to design and implement a focused set of academic initiatives to enhance student retention. By bringing the honors college into the diversity portfolio, the message is clear that this officer is a valued administrator who has responsibility and expertise beyond diversity issues.

Designing a hybrid role should not be required, but there are cases for which a CDO is well suited to lead diversity and general administrative units like institutional research, the honors program, advising, student life, community engagement, outreach, and enrollment management. By comparison, the dedicated CDO role focuses energy directly on matters of diversity, leading diversity-themed units like multicultural affairs, cultural centers, affirmative action, intergroup dialogue efforts, and the like. A hybrid portfolio is also achieved by having a focus on both domestic and international diversity issues, particularly when it involves supervising core teaching, learning, and research units, such as area studies departments.

Configuring a hybrid position should only take place after carefully considering the goals, strategies, and relationships that will be assigned to the new role. In this instance, the CDODF can help determine how the new role will work from an organizational design perspective. For example, simply recasting the current vice president of student affairs as the institution's CDO may not provide the dedicated leadership required to spearhead new diversity initiatives. Moreover, it may compromise the campus student affairs agenda, because the CDO's primary duties should touch on issues of faculty and staff diversification, curriculum development, and teaching and learning. Indeed, in some instances a hybrid position presents clear disadvantages, especially if the portfolio grows at the expense of diversity work. The movement toward this model should occur only if both aspects of the job role can be fully activated and balanced.

Both large and small institutions have embraced the hybrid approach, and it has recently emerged as a compelling model among smaller liberal arts institutions. We spoke with members of the Liberal Arts Diversity Officers (LADO) consortium who were clear that the hybrid model is particularly well suited for their institutional context. These institutions generally boast a more intimate institutional culture and tend to have fewer campus-wide diversity capabilities as compared with large public research universities. LADO members also argued that the presence of both a diversity and more general themed area of academic responsibility allowed them to bring diversity into the conversation of institutional priorities more seamlessly. A vice president for diversity and dean of the college at a small liberal arts institution in the Southwest told us:

> By having responsibility for diversity and nondiversity areas, I am able to push the agenda in new directions because colleagues do not see me as an outsider to the general structure. I can do my job in student affairs and push the diversity agenda as well. The problem is when you have someone who really only knows the major aspects of the student affairs piece and are faking the diversity piece. Or they can only perform the student piece but do not have the credibility to get involved with issues like faculty diversity. Because I have also been a faculty member, I have the credibility to link the various worlds together.

The greatest strength of the hybrid approach is the potential for the officer to reframe general campus-wide resource and institutional priorities to more completely embrace diversity-related matters. Among these opportunities we can include leveraging general administrative budgets and offices to benefit issues of diversity, taking an aggressive stance toward ensuring that the staff of key areas of institutional responsibility are diversified, and using the more general campus leadership position to create visibility for the campus diversity agenda in new ways. Again, the challenge is to design a role in such a way that the person can fully operationalize both sides of his or her role. We spoke with one hybrid officer who noted, "They gave me both titles but they did not give me the budget or staff to do anything with the diversity aspect of the job." While designing a hybrid role is seductive, the position must be designed with a level of integrity to ensure that leadership is provided that will serve both aspects of the role.

Vertical Diversity Infrastructure

The vertical structure of the CDO must follow from the big-picture institutional agenda and more directly from its strategic diversity platform. To return to an earlier theme of contingency theory and formal structural leadership, strategy should drive structure. The key is first to look to the strategic diversity agenda and then align the formal chain of command, definition of rank, policy-making ability, financial resources, and span of control with the mission of the office. The decision to create a hybrid role must include the vertical diversity infrastructure of the CDO.

Chain of command is an old military idea that refers to the unbroken line of authority that extends from the supreme commander down to the unranked private. The institutional chain of command defines a role's span of control and determines the scope of its functional duties and identities within an institution's formal administrative hierarchy. The vertical structure of an institution defines the formal ways in which people and responsibilities are grouped together into a defined unit or area. It is one of the most contested dimensions of organizational design because it sets the CDO's parameters of power and authority, as well as how limited resources will be allocated and coordinated. Finally, the vertical structure defines which dimensions of the campus diversity infrastructure are under the direct operational control of the CDO as opposed to another senior leader.

Generally speaking, the chain of command within an academic institution is less stringent than in a corporate environment. In the academy, input can come from any combination of faculty, students, legislatures, governing boards, staff, parents, and alumni, and these interactions often cloud the chain of command. Simultaneously, colleges and universities possess several vertical dynamics that must be considered when developing the CDO capacity. Some of the most critical are institutional rank, financial resources and policy-making ability, archetypes of vertical structure, and matrices or dual reporting structures, all concepts that define the vertical capabilities of the CDO.

Position Title, Rank, and Supervision

A key first concept when designing the vertical dynamics of the CDO is determining the role's title, rank, and authority. These three aspects of vertical capability establish the basic context for the role's visibility, influence, and symbolic potential as a strategic diversity leader. Table 3.4 presents supervisor, rank, and role descriptions that our research uncovered. Given

TABLE 3.4
Potential Chief Diversity Officer Supervisor, Rank, and Role Descriptors

Supervisor	*Rank*	*Diversity Descriptors*	*Additional Descriptors*	*CDO Designation*
• President • Chancellor • Provost	• Vice Chancellor • Vice President • Vice Provost • Associate Vice Chancellor • Associate Vice President • Associate Vice Provost • Assistant Vice Chancellor • Assistant Vice President • Assistant Vice Provost • Dean • Executive Director • Special Assistant	• Academic Diversity • Affirmative Action • Campus Climate • Diversity • Diversity Initiatives • Equity • Faculty Diversity • Global • Inclusion • Inclusive Excellence • Intercultural Affairs • Intergroup Affairs • International Affairs • Global Initiatives • Globalization • Minority Affairs • Multicultural Affairs • Strategic Diversity Initiatives • Strategic Diversity Leadership	• Academic Affairs • Academic Excellence • Educational Achievement • Institutional Planning • Institutional Research • Human Resources • Strategic Planning • Student Affairs • Student Success • Undergraduate Affairs	• Chief Diversity Officer • Chief Officer for Diversity and Equity • Chief Officer for Inclusion and Diversity • Chief Officer for Diversity, Equity, and Inclusion

our grounded definition, the supervisor dimension is obvious and is located at the president or provost level, with either a single or dual reporting role. *Rank* refers to the formal positioning of the officer in the chain of command. The description can either contain exclusively diversity terminology or use another form of terminology that addresses some aspect of the institution's strategic interests. When a second type of descriptor is introduced into the CDO's formal span of attention, it may make sense for the role to possess a hybrid nature. Finally, the officer can have the formal designation of CDO, or another title option that symbolically and materially identifies this role as having the chief designation. In theory, a well-positioned role might report directly to the president; rank at the vice presidential level; have a formal title with the descriptors "diversity," "equity," and "institutional planning"; and possess the formal designation as the institution's CDO.

The CDO Designation and Formal Rank

Because the CDO role is so new to higher education, we do not recommend that institutions use the title of "chief diversity officer" as a stand-alone formal title. Although *CDO* describes the role that this position should play on campus, the use of this term absent a companion rank of *vice president, associate vice chancellor,* or *vice provost* lacks clarity and confuses the position's location in the institution's formal administrative hierarchy. Because the CDO role is generally misunderstood, it is essential that the role actually have a formal rank that allows for the campus community to calibrate the position's formal stature in the institutional environment. Unlike the CDO designation in the corporate sector, where the "chief" designation is common, higher education rarely uses the "chief" designation. Hence, it is important to give the role a formal rank, bestowing it with the political and institutional capital necessary to allow the officer to participate in different conversations and decision-making processes. As we noted earlier, a position's rank is as much symbolic and political as it is material. The higher the institution defines the CDO rank, the more prestige and symbolic capital the position will enjoy.

A CDO must be ranked in a way that is consistent with the role that the institution expects him or her to play delivering the institution's diversity goals. Whether the CDO is ranked at the vice provost, vice chancellor, or vice presidential level depends on the role's designers and the formal administrative context of the institution. These decisions must be made locally and then aligned with guidelines of how other senior administrators are commensurately ranked. Who wields parallel authority on campus in a different area? What rank will position the CDO in such a way that he or she can help lead the big-picture institutional agenda on issues that are fundamental to themes of diversity? What rank is consistent with the role that the CDO must play, whether leading others or working collaboratively through committees, task forces, and appointed roles?

When determining the supervisor for the CDO, one must address whether the position should be a part of the president's senior team, the provost's senior team, or both. Whatever is decided, we recommend that the position's formal rank be commensurate with the administrative culture of the institution. For example, if senior leaders at a large institution decide to place the CDO on both the president's and provost's senior leadership teams, they might consider granting the CDO a dual vice president and vice provost title. This dual title would illustrate that the position encompasses the president's and provost's strategic span of attention as it relates to diversity-themed chief executive duties, as well as diversity-themed chief academic officer duties.

Such an officer might serve as the point leader on the presidential leadership team charged to carry out diversity-themed initiatives that focus on fund-raising, external relations, legislative lobbying, and campus-wide decision making. As an extension of the provost, the CDO might be charged to cochair a faculty committee's review of the ethnic studies requirement; develop an academic achievement gap strategy to eliminate performance gaps between diverse groups; or develop a new faculty diversity strategy to increase the numbers of women in the science, technology, engineering, and math fields. Ultimately, the decision to title and rank the position must flow from the strategic diversity platform of the CDO and the institution's big-picture strategic agenda.

Although matrix relationships like the presidential–provost reporting structure can prove effective, they should be used with caution. We fundamentally believe in the unity-of-command principle and that each person should ultimately be accountable to one person, even if the individual aligns his or her work with others. When a person has more than one supervisor, as in these matrix reporting relationships, conflicts can develop in the command and communication structure.

Formal Resources and Policy-Making Ability

Rank and supervision are only two concepts that must be clarified when designing the CDO role. Perhaps even more fundamentally, design leaders must define the formal power and authority vested in the role. That is, what formal resources and policy-making capacity does the CDO have? What financial, staff, and unit resources are under his or her direct authority? And what new initiatives can he or she conceive and implement without supervision or assistance? Can the CDO host a campus diversity symposium? Authorize a campus climate study in a particularly problematic school or college? Author a campus-wide e-mail about a particular issue? Develop a new strategic relationship with a local nonprofit agency doing parallel work to expand access into higher education? Fund a new pilot initiative in the office of multicultural affairs?

Establishing the annual operating budget for the CDO is a critical decision that must be balanced against several institutional factors. They include the institution's overall budget, current strategic priorities, parameters of the strategic diversity agenda, and current diversity investments. Although this CDODF cannot account for all of these factors exhaustively, we suggest that institutional designers consult Table 3.5, which summarizes our analysis of 104 institutions, contrasting institutional size and CDO annual operational budgets, not including salaries and grant money.

We offer this table as a way to help institutional leaders determine how their budget allocation decisions compare with the budgets of institutions of similar size as defined by their undergraduate populations. The decision to create a $25,000 or $1 million budget must ultimately reflect the strategic diversity platform of the institution and the degree to which the institution desires to empower the CDO to have the material capacity to advance and encourage its strategic diversity agenda.

TABLE 3.5
Chief Diversity Officer Institutional Size and Budget Control

Undergraduate Size	*Description*	*Less than $50,000*	*$50,000–$150,000*	*$150,001–$500,000*	*$500,001–$1 million*	*Over $1 million*	*Total*
Small institution (*n* = 26)	Fewer than 5,000 students	61%	19%	4%	4%	12%	100%
Medium institution (*n* = 22)	5,000 to 10,000 students	41%	32%	14%	4%	9%	100%
Large institution (*n* = 24)	10,000 to 20,000 students	29%	17%	25%	17%	12%	100%
Very large institution (*n* = 32)	More than 20,000 students	9%	16%	25%	19%	31%	100%

N = 104 institutions.

When developing the CDO budget, we recommend that institutional leaders evaluate any current spending on diversity policies and programs to possibly subsume them into the CDO portfolio. Although this strategic reallocation is challenging, it represents the kind of integrated thinking needed to empower an institution's new CDO and to coordinate current investments with an emerging big-picture strategic diversity agenda. We return to this point in the next chapter, which specifically focuses on vertical structure in more depth.

Even beyond the campus diversity investments, institutional leaders may need to devise an enterprise-wide strategic reallocation from every budget to create a centralized diversity budget for the CDO. A 0.50 percent permanent adjustment of every budget across campus offers a novel and potentially powerful material and strategic approach to creating a strong diversity budget that can then be used to drive diversity efforts across the institution. Other options include dedicating new resources to the CDO and putting in place a number of dedicated processes to raise additional diversity funds for the CDO using a confluence of grant writing and development activities with private donors, corporations, foundations, and others. The most aggressive institutions will assign a dedicated development officer to assist with fund-raising activities, develop a targeted diversity capital campaign as part of their annual giving strategy, and even make diversity a major priority of any future fund-raising efforts.

Archetypes of Structure

As we worked to develop the CDODF, we looked to the pioneering work of Henry Mintzberg (1979). Mintzberg concluded that every class of organization has an underlying interpretive scheme that, once located, presents a relatively small number of general structural archetypes that define it in a fundamental way. According to Mintzberg, designs are built on archetypal templates that establish the general form of an organization, much like a skeleton provides internal structure of a body.

In the CDODF, we use the term *archetype* to describe a model's span of control, which includes the number of people who directly report to a particular position and the general pattern of vertical infrastructure that exists. The archetypal idea is critical to determining how institutional leaders establish a CDO's formal authority and financial and staff resources. Although collaboration is key, and a holistic design perspective is essential, it is the presence of human and financial resources that is fundamental to swaying opinion, securing new strategic partnerships, and launching initiatives across campus.

We identified four organizational archetypes in our research, the *Collaborative Officer Model,* the *Unit-Based Model,* the *Portfolio Divisional Model,* and the *Multi-Institutional Model.* The Collaborative Officer Model is characterized as having little or no formal vertical responsibility in terms of staff or the ability to supervise others. As a consequence, all of the officer's efforts are done either alone or with minimum staff, relying heavily on voluntary collaboration with others. The Unit-based and Portfolio Divisional models also emphasize collaboration and strategic partnerships, but these archetypes are typified by the presence of staff or offices and units that directly report to the CDO. By comparison, leaders operating in the Collaborative Officer Model may not even have administrative support. From a classic perspective of power and authority, the Unit-based and Portfolio Divisional models are better positioned to lead than the Collaborative Officer Model. The most vertically integrated CDO archetype is the Multi-Institutional Model, which operates across multiple campuses in a statewide system of higher education. (Box 3.1 provides an in-depth overview of the Multi-Institutional Model; the other three are addressed in depth in Chapter 4.)

Organizational archetypes are not clear-cut categories into which all roles fit neatly. Although some positions will fit seamlessly into one of these categories, others can take a hybrid approach, combining different archetypes. The point here is not to put CDOs into prefabricated boxes and then provide black-and-white "solutions" to their organizational challenges. In fact, our purpose is just the opposite, providing leaders with a tool for examining their own institutions so that they can devise an effective structure based on the goals defined in their strategic diversity agendas. Thus, the three archetypes presented here serve as potential models for designing the modern-day CDO role on campus. We focus on these three models in great detail in Chapter 4, which describes the three archetypes in depth along with other aspects of vertical structure.

Matrix Relationships

Another important aspect of vertical structure is matrix reporting relationships, or what Galbraith (2002) and others refer to as "dual reporting structures." As a way of creating connectivity up, down, and across the institution, matrix reporting relationships are often useful. For example, a CDO at the vice provost level may have a matrix reporting relationship that extends to the president on matters of affirmative action and equity, and to the provost on day-to-day issues relating to implementing the diversity strategic plan.

Matrix relationships introduce complexity that can be problematic, particularly if the dual reporting structure is deployed as a way to avoid difficult reorganization conversations. In these situations, the result is a matrix swirl in which no one is responsible and the organization flounders. For matrix relationships to work, individuals must have the ability to manage conflicts creatively, without constantly taking issues up the leadership chain in order to resolve differences. Thus, goals have to be set jointly and evaluations conducted by both sides in terms of organizational performance. Finally, individuals who report up to two supervisors have to be "matrix thinkers," able to navigate multiple worlds without getting bogged down, informing and aligning their supervisors with the big-picture goals of the institution. We return to this discussion of matrix relationships in Chapter 4.

BOX 3.1
Multi-Institutional Model of Chief Diversity Officer Structure

A fourth general archetype of structure is the *Multi-Institutional Model.* This archetype exists in public statewide systems of higher education, although it is not uncommon in large corporations or health centers that provide leadership to multiple companies or health organizations as part of their overall organizational infrastructure. The Multi-Institutional Model is characterized by a high-ranking CDO who generally reports to the president or chancellor and provides boundary-spanning diversity leadership to the various institutions that comprise a statewide system of colleges and universities. Some prominent examples include the Tennessee State System of Higher Education, the University of Minnesota, and the University of Wisconsin, to name a few that we have visited through the years.

Some of the key activities associated with this type of archetype are developing a shared campus diversity framework and executing collaborative initiatives designed to advance campus diversity efforts defined in myriad ways. Some of these efforts include campus climate studies using common survey instrumentation and methodologies, helping campus leaders to navigate shifts in the law and policy around issues of diversity and equity, and implementing regular accountability processes such as annual diversity reports, diversity-themed chancellor evaluations, and other initiatives designed to create transparency and greater intentionality in advancing campus diversity. It's also common for multi-institutional CDOs to host professional development meetings with campus diversity leaders, chancellors, and others in an

(continues)

effort to strengthen their strategic diversity leadership abilities. Officers in this model also talked about the important role that they play as a conduit to their regents or trustees, helping them through a combination of formal and informal activities designed to enhance campus diversity efforts. The most powerful multi-institutional CDOs control considerable budgets, allowing them to creatively provide resources to support campus diversity efforts through annual grant competitions, regular budget processes, and discretionary initiatives.

In some ways, the multi-institutional archetype is a meta-archetype, providing an overall structure that includes aspects of the Collaborative Officer, Unit-Based, or Portfolio Divisional models discussed previously. For example, a multi-institutional CDO may have little or no staff to support a broad mission, evidencing characteristics associated with the Collaborative Officer Model. In other examples, the CDO may lead a core team of diversity planners, researchers, support personnel, and policy analysts who assist with their efforts to provide integrative diversity leadership across campus—the Unit-Based Model. A third version of this archetype may involve the CDO leading a vertically integrated portfolio of units as part of a Portfolio Divisional Model, where they may supervise diversity research institutes, affirmative action offices, gender equity units, and other diversity- or nondiversity-related departments that have been formally organized into the CDO's direct span of control.

One of the complex archetypal structures might be a Multi-Institutional Portfolio Divisional Model, for which the CDO has both system-wide (multicampus) and institutional responsibility. To achieve the potential benefits of this type of archetype, several complexities must be addressed in the design. First, the CDO must have a sufficient core team that will allow for broad spanning connectivity across the flagship campus, as well as across the multiple institutions located statewide. Given the integrative nature of the CDO role, this will require the CDO and his or her team to develop innovative efforts to establish campus diversity liaison roles; schedule regular conferences, symposia, and meetings; leverage state-of-the-art communication techniques; and design common frameworks and timelines to ensure that each of the campuses is speaking the same language with one another. Second, because the demands on the CDO are so expansive, this model also requires that the division have a clear hierarchy of leadership that includes senior diversity leaders at the associate or assistant vice president level to limit the number of direct reporting relationships that the CDO will need to supervise on a day-to-day basis. Finally, it will be important for the CDO in this archetype to have a powerful ability to navigate not only his or her home institutional politics, but also the politics associated with the various institutions where the CDO will collaboratively lead around issues of diversity, equity, and inclusion

Multi-institutional leadership is more challenging and difficult than leading in a single institutional context. The mission, culture, priorities, resource base, diversity infrastructure, and history vary from one institution to another. These realities create

(continues)

(continued)
tremendous managerial complexity for CDOs and their teams who must balance institutional, diversity, and statewide concerns. Multi-institutional CDOs must have a tremendous appreciation of the different administrative and cultural dynamics associated with each institution and an ability to navigate the challenges and opportunities that they will encounter. Consequently, the CDO must have strong support from the system-wide president to ensure diversity efforts are not ignored when presented at the institutional level. But beyond this, the integrative collaborative process necessitates a need to shape policy and new initiatives in a way that respects the culture of each institution, while moving them toward common goals established at the enterprise-wide level. Institutional diversity efforts are both art and science; a common process, technique, or initiative may not fit for every campus environment. As a result, it will be important for the president to support campus leaders as they nuance new initiatives in such a way that they speak to the realities of the institution in which they will ultimately be nested.

Lateral Diversity Infrastructure

By definition, the CDO is an integrator whose formal job responsibility requires him or her to work collaboratively with a number of critical stakeholders. As a result, the span of relationships that CDOs routinely manage should be determined by the breadth and depth of their strategic span. This dimension of the framework articulates the lateral diversity infrastructure that CDOs use to accomplish tasks across the white spaces that exist between the formal boxes on the organizational chart (Galbraith, 2002). Figure 3.2 illustrates the coordinating structures, strategies, and relationships that CDOs interface with to complete their work.

As we alluded to in Chapters 1 and 2 and in our discussion of the "triangle offense," a CDO's success significantly depends on his or her ability to create, nurture, strengthen, and expand a network of partnerships with peers, students, faculty, academic leaders, external community members, and others. Professionals who work in integrator roles rise and fall by their ability to work across a myriad of relationships, each with its own set of unique expectations. An institution's lateral diversity capability is partially predicated on the CDO's ability to lead in this way. This aspect of the CDODF is closely connected to the model's fourth and fifth dimensions, which outline various types of change management systems and officers, as well as the leadership skills required to be effective in the CDO role.

FIGURE 3.2
Chief Diversity Officer Lateral Diversity Infrastructure

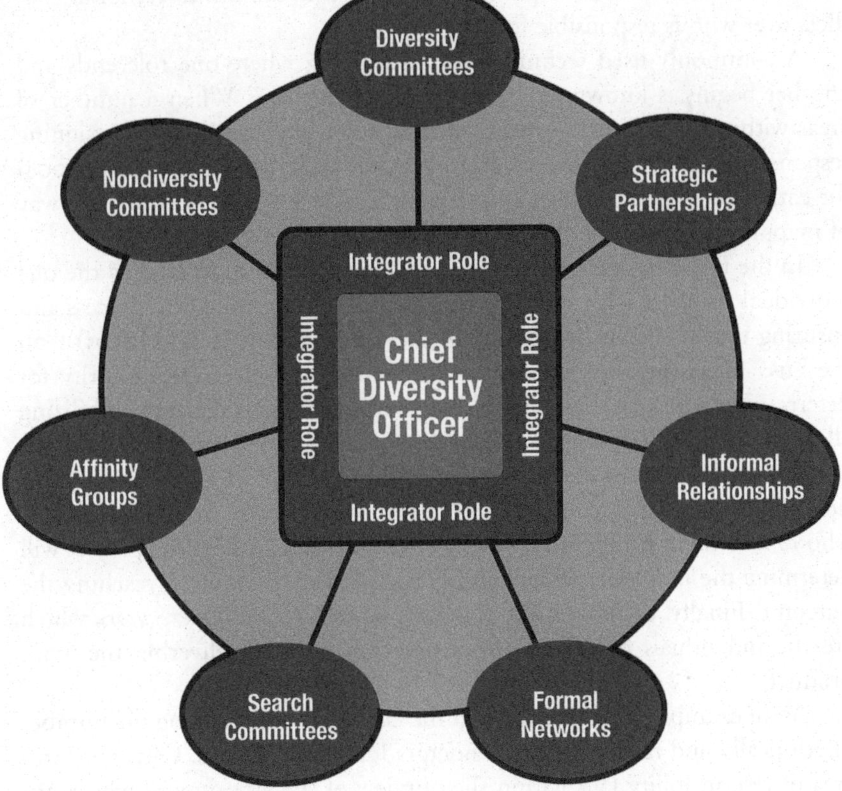

The lateral dimension of the CDODF specifically relates to fostering networks and strategic partnerships, leading diversity task forces and committees, supporting affinity organizations, creating communities of practice, participating in search committees and other nondiversity committees, and building strategic alliances both on and off campus.

Negotiating Boundaries in Areas of Overlapping Responsibility

A key step to promoting the CDO's long-term success is to identify and negotiate difficult boundary issues and political dynamics between the officer and other campus leaders. A critical component of this process is defining job-role responsibility for which leadership span of attention is shared by two or more positions. When both the CDO and his or her counterparts have a clear sense of role responsibility, both sides can avoid territorial conflicts over who is responsible for what.

A commonly used technique for identifying where one role ends and another begins is known as "responsibility charting." When a number of areas within the institution must work together interdependently, assigning responsibility is crucial. We recommend the PACE model (Modena, 2008) for early and ongoing design conversations. The PACE model offers a way of mapping job responsibilities when areas overlap (Modena, 2008).

In the PACE model, the *P* stands for *process leader* and refers to the one individual or office with ultimate responsibility for guiding the process and ensuring that the right people are, in the words of Jim Collins (2005), "on the bus." The objective is to grant one person or office sole authority for determining a project outcome so that they take ownership over mobilizing all human, financial, and technical resources required to ensure success. Meanwhile, *A* refers to the *approver* who ultimately decides what the institution will do in a particular situation. Next, there may be multiple *C* people who *contribute* in bringing the project to life, although here the project will determine the individual contributor's level of participation in reaching the outcome. Finally, the last aspect of the model refers to *E*, the *executors,* which are the individuals or offices responsible for actually delivering the work product.

As an example, we might look at the challenge of increasing the number of ethnically and racially diverse undergraduates on campus. Obviously this area of responsibility falls within the purview of the vice provost who manages enrollment and the office of admissions. At the same time, it may make sense for the CDO to play a role in developing or implementing the strategy. But what role should the CDO take? Should he or she develop the strategy? Should the CDO office pay for the effort? Should the CDO have an ability to veto a strategy that is inconsistent with his or her diversity expertise? These are the critical questions that come up not just when an institution is devising a new CDO role, but every time a diversity-related project raises issues of responsibility, leadership, accountability, and authority.

In this example, because he or she has direct responsibility for admissions, the vice president who manages enrollment might best serve in the process leader role. Next, because the goals of achieving a more diverse applicant pool will ultimately require a tactical shift in terms of branding, yield strategies, and a host of other areas, the ultimate approver in this example is the president or provost. As approver, the president will need to authorize an overall shift in philosophy, provide new resources to make the strategy happen, and perhaps engage the board of trustees and others in the process.

Contributors to the project might include the CDO, the vice president for communications, the president of the Black alumni association, and others. Particularly if the CDO has an extensive background in the areas of enrollment management and marketing, the CDO might serve as an important contributor in this effort, mobilizing diversity faculty, students, alumni, and parents. However, final execution of the diversity enrollment effort ultimately rests with the admissions office, as it changes its recruitment patterns, builds new relationships with high schools and guidance counselors, retrains staff members on new application criteria, and pursues any number of new tactics.

Budget Cut Scenarios and the Role of the CDO

The PACE model (Table 3.6) can be an incredibly helpful tool for aligning the formal responsibilities of the CDO. Indeed, recent budget challenges presented by the onset of the 2008 Great Recession provide a window for

TABLE 3.6
The PACE Model

Dimension	*Description*
Process	• Brings the organization to an aligned plan. • Facilitates the process and makes sure the decision gets made in a timely manner. • Is a single individual or unit.
Approver	• Ratifies the final decision. • Holds final decision-making authority. • Is a single individual.
Contributor	• Designated by *A* or *P* for advice and help. • Does not hold approval or veto power. • Not always required; never more than 2–10 individuals. • Evaluates proposal and provides input. • May be able to prevent a recommendation from being shared with approver. • May move into an executor role if necessary.
Executor	• Takes action to bring decision to life. • Needs to know rationale for a decision and outcomes. • Number is as needed to deliver the project or objective.

Source: Adapted from Modena, 2008.

understanding the important role of this framework in steering the efforts of the CDO. As institutions tighten their belts financially, diversity efforts are often among the first to be cut. Working within the PACE model, campus leaders can design a process for maintaining a viable diversity vision during economically challenging times and, most important for this discussion, outline the CDO's role as it relates to diversity (Table 3.7).

As we outline in Table 3.7, the CDO can play a number of different roles during budget cut negotiations, whether as a process leader, an approver, a contributor, or an executor. Clarifying these roles for the CDO is essential when the campus is faced with difficult budget decisions. For example, can the vice president for student affairs eliminate two full-time-equivalent positions in the Office of LGBT Affairs without having a conversation with a high-ranking CDO who has LGBT issues in his or her span of attention, but not span of control? Does the vice president for student affairs need to have a conversation with the CDO, notifying the CDO of his or her intentions? Should this decision, or other diversity-themed budget cuts, come before a group of faculty and academic leaders chaired by the CDO?

Although the CDO may enjoy a high rank and occupy a leading role on campus, if he or she is not empowered to engage on budget issues, then confusion, resentment, and a loss of faith in the office will result. For many, the budget is an area that the CDO should control entirely. Still others will view the CDO as, at the least, critical to the process. And there are some who will view budget decisions as the primary responsibility of the direct supervising unit, regardless of diversity's purported value on campus. The point that we want to emphasize is that clarity must exist in those areas where strategic spans overlap. When clarity does not exist about the relationship between multiple roles and their areas of shared responsibility, confusion results, morale is affected, and the campus diversity agenda is compromised. We recommend that campus leaders deploy the PACE model to help clarify the CDO's policy-making authority in areas in which his or her role inevitably overlaps with other leaders'. The more clarity that is developed early and throughout the life of the CDO role on campus, the more positive synergy and collaborative energy is possible. Problems inevitably emerge when these roles are not clarified, a point that we emphasize as we outline general parameters of the CDO's relationship to other campus leadership roles.

Critical Relationships and the Chief Diversity Officer

The CDO role represents a major structural change to the form of the organization by adding a new layer to the top leadership echelon. One of the

TABLE 3.7
PACE Model and the Role of the Chief Diversity Officer in Navigating Campus Budget Challenges

Dimension	*Description of PACE*	*CDO Leadership*	*Strengths/Weaknesses*
Process leader	The CDO guides the diversity budget-cutting process.	The CDO leads a shared governance committee that reviews the budget-cutting scenarios developed by schools, colleges, and divisional leaders, and weighs their implications for diversity before making recommendations to the president or provost.	Leverages shared governance. CDO is instrumental to process. Depends on president or provost, who may or may not have a commitment to diversity.
Approver	The CDO serves as the key decision maker in what gets cut, approving the plans of other senior leaders.	All schools, colleges, and divisional leaders must submit a report to the CDO, who will review the proposals and make a decision regarding diversity-related budget changes.	CDO is able to leverage formal authority consistent with role and rank on campus. CDO is empowered to act in the best interests of diversity. CDO is viewed as an adversary to other campus leaders.
Contributor	The CDO collaborates with other key decision makers in developing budget cut scenarios.	The CDO works with leaders in schools, colleges, and divisional areas regarding campus diversity cuts, helping to illustrate key themes, opportunity areas, and implications of different budget scenarios, often through direct one-on-one conversations with relevant deans and divisional leaders.	CDO is able to leverage the collegial dynamics of campus. CDO may clash with campus leaders who have no commitment to campus diversity issues. The campus diversity agenda may be co-opted by campus politics and other areas deemed more important than diversity.
Executor	The CDO defines the areas for budget cuts in those areas where they are the only formal supervising unit.	The CDO makes budget cut decisions in his or her unit alone, playing no role in campus-wide budget cut scenarios outside of his or her direct span of control.	CDO empowered only in areas in which he or she has span of control. CDO is not able to activate mission throughout campus. Diversity efforts are left to the decisions of individuals who may lack commitment and insight.

new officer's first challenges is to develop relationships with other key leaders across campus. The lateral relationships of every CDO will differ depending on the broader system of decisions governed by the CDO's strategic span. A narrow strategic span requires fewer interactions with the various offices and units listed here, whereas a broader strategic span requires more.

Table 3.8 outlines many of the critical relationships that the CDO should maintain, as well as some of the possibilities that may emerge. When designing the CDO role, these dynamics should be discussed to ensure the successful emergence of the CDO position. Positions that manage relationships that span from the highest institutional governing board, through the president, provost, faculty governance, alumni, and community, are rare. Indeed, only the president, provost, and the most influential academic deans maintain a similarly complex and diverse portfolio of relationships. Thus, the CDO must possess a wealth of leadership dexterity and relational skills, especially in regard to framing diversity issues, using the language of different audiences, and proactively working to lead change from a multivariate, strategic approach.

For this reason it is important for role designers to imagine lateral dynamics in connection with vertical capabilities. Because the CDO role is integrative by its very nature, relationship management and partnerships define the core of the officer's day-to-day work. Misalignment among the strategic, vertical, and lateral elements of the CDO role can lead to a number of problems.

The Pressure of Lateral Relationships

Although the integrative nature of the CDO role creates great potential for developing new possibilities institutionally, the crush of so many members of the campus community hoping to collaborate may render the CDO ineffective if he or she does not have the human and financial resources to meet these requests. This situation is particularly common among officers operating in the Collaborative Officer Model archetype. If their strategic span is too broad, officers run into a number of different challenges. One associate provost at a medium-sized institution in the South told us:

> I share a secretary with the other associate provost and so have to get out there and make it happen myself. From developing ideas, to setting my calendar, to running the meeting, even making my own photocopies, it is all on me. Now I am not one to think I am above anything, but it gets to a point where you start thinking, wow, how long is this sustainable? Am I really a senior officer, or just a fool trying to do it all?

TABLE 3.8
Strategic Relationship Between Senior Leadership and the Chief Diversity Officer

Senior Leadership	*Diversity Focus*	*CDO's Role*
Highest Governance Board	Trustees and regents provide broad stewardship of the institution's interests at the highest levels, often selecting the president or chancellor, providing opportunities to raise attention on issues of diversity, requiring the institution to provide strategic focus in this area, and hiring a chief executive officer who has a leadership philosophy that embraces the importance and merits of diversity.	The CDO provides members of the board with relevant information regarding the institution's diversity priorities, capabilities, challenges, successes, and needs. The CDO may also work collaboratively with a diversity-themed governance subcommittee or task force group.
Chief Executive Officer	Presidents and chancellors provide chief executive leadership to the institution's diversity agenda, creating a broad context for diversity planning and implementation as a matter of high institutional importance.	The CDO provides high-level strategic guidance regarding the president's understanding of the broad institutional diversity discussion, while supporting the implementation of the institution's strategic diversity agenda. The CDO should also serve as senior advisor during crisis moments. In the ideal scenario, the CDO acts as a trusted confidant capable of assisting senior leaders in various ways.
Chief Academic Officer	The chief academic officer, often the provost, sets the tempo for academic affairs by underscoring the connection between diversity and learning; promoting ethnic, gender, and international area studies; centralizing faculty diversity hiring funds; and infusing diversity into the curriculum.	The CDO advises and partners with the chief academic officer to help influence organizational change across campus, focusing specifically on the various academic and support areas of the institution. In particular, the CDO may be closely aligned with the office of the provost in terms of strategic diversity hiring and retention programs, reviewing difficult tenure and disciplinary issues, and aligning diversity efforts with new initiatives centered on issues of teaching and learning.
Chief Financial Officer	The CFO develops creative strategies to reallocate resources, lobby for new resources, or develop entrepreneurial strategies to bring new resources into the institution, including financial support for institutional diversity priorities.	The CDO advises the CFO on diversity priorities, helping in the creative assignment of financial resources to diversity areas of high priority. The CDO may also work with the CFO to audit campus spending relative to diversity, particularly if unique funding streams or accounts are specifically dedicated to fund diversity-related work.

TABLE 3.8 (Continued)

Senior Leadership	*Diversity Focus*	*CDO's Role*
Academic Deans	Academic deans can communicate the importance of diversity throughout every aspect of their schools or colleges by holding their department heads accountable for faculty diversity hiring and providing support for the strategic diversity agenda as it relates to their particular area of oversight.	The CDO supports academic deans as they advance their school's or college's diversity agenda, providing input on diversity-related issues within the specific context of that unit, school, or college. The CDO also helps monitor and communicate the diversity efforts and challenges within these units. The CDO may have a dual reporting relationship with diversity-related staff or committees in the various schools and colleges.
Chief Student Affairs Officer	The chief student affairs officer creates developmental opportunities that help students achieve intercultural competencies and leadership skills, and supports the cultural identities and experiences of diverse groups.	The CDO extends the capacity of the student affairs area by integrating diversity best practices into student development practices and helping to ensure that the activities of the student affairs area encompass diversity. In addition, the CDO may partner on several diversity-themed areas, particularly if the officer has supervising oversight for a number of student-centered diversity officer units. Finally, the CDO partners in managing campus climate issues that may arise, participating in bias incident reporting processes, weighing in on sensitive public safety issues, and developing proactive educational strategies that touch Greek life, student government, student media, and other areas where diversity crisis moments tend to arise.
Chief International Affairs Officer	The CIAO is engaged in activities ranging from building new partnerships around the world, establishing study abroad programs and other opportunities for undergraduate students, and engaging in international research and outreach.	The CDO collaborates with the CIAO on projects that illustrate the intersection of domestic and international diversity efforts in the academy. Efforts include hosting joint conferences, ensuring common support systems for domestic and international student communities, and engaging in joint scholarly efforts that combine multicultural studies and international area studies.

TABLE 3.8 (Continued)

Senior Leadership	*Diversity Focus*	*CDO's Role*
General Counsel	The general counsel ensures compliance with EEO and affirmative action rules and regulations, and supports the work of the Equity and Diversity Office.	The CDO partners with general counsel to ensure that the institution remains compliant with EEO and affirmative action rules and regulations, while encouraging all institutional leaders to be proactive in their diversity-related activities.
Chief Enrollment Management Officer	The chief enrollment management officer collaborates in establishing the institution's broad visions for diversity recruitment and financial aid, establishing culturally relevant pedagogies and techniques for recruiting and yielding diverse students.	The CDO ensures that the various enrollment areas employ diversity best practices in their outreach, recruitment, financial aid, new student programs, and related processes, including communicating directly with diverse parents and communities. The CDO plays a key role in the development of diversity-themed enrollment strategies, partnering in yield events, building new programs initiatives, negotiating transfer programs and articulation agreements with community colleges, and cultivating relationships with diverse communities.
Communications and External Relations	The chief communications staff person develops and distributes the institution's diversity brand to both internal and external stakeholders, including members of the broader community.	The CDO infuses multicultural competencies within the organization to create compelling messages that connect and resonate with diverse communities. This work includes multidimensional marketing efforts that target minorities, women, urban communities, members of the LGBT community, and others.
Faculty Senate	The faculty senate is the primary vehicle for elevating diversity issues within a powerful faculty governance setting and influencing the actions of high-profile faculty leaders.	The CDO reports to the faculty senate regarding institutional diversity priorities, seeking input on new academic diversity efforts and inviting its collaboration and support for moving diversity into the institution's academic core.
Student Leaders	Depending on the campus, student leaders can play a key role in directing their peers in support of diversity efforts, either informally, through student groups and organizations, or through student governance.	The CDO can help develop mentoring and leadership programs, support diverse student groups, and empower student leaders in partnership with student affairs and others.

TABLE 3.8 (Continued)

Senior Leadership	*Diversity Focus*	*CDO's Role*
Alumni Affairs	The alumni association is the primary conduit for maintaining a lifelong relationship with those who have attended the institution. These units can assist campus diversity efforts by creating diversity-themed alumni groups, like the LGBT Alumni Advisory, the Latino Alumni Association, and others.	The CDO can partner with the alumni association through targeted communications to diverse audiences, creating engagement experiences for diverse alumni to participate in homecoming, parents weekend, and alumni weekends. These relationships can prove instrumental for shaping diverse alumni perceptions of the institution, and cultivating new development possibilities and potential second- and third-generation applicants from diverse alumni.
Foundation/ Development	The institutional foundation or development office is responsible for raising new resources to drive diversity priorities and initiatives, including diversity efforts through a confluence of principal gifts, annual programs, grant writing, strategic partnerships, targeted events, and other efforts designed to generate new resources.	The CDO can partner with the foundation in several diversity-themed fund-raising activities that might result in operational or endowment funds to benefit issues of diversity. These might take the form of an annual giving program, setting the digital diversity fund-raising strategy, developing a diversity-themed campaign, requesting funds from corporate partners, and other efforts.

CFO, Chief financial officer; *CIAO,* chief international affairs officer; *EEO,* equal employment opportunity; *LGBT,* lesbian, gay, bisexual, transgender.

As we noted before, for better or worse, the CDO is often identified as the institution's face of diversity. Consequently, in addition to the more formal relationships mentioned here, CDOs are frequently sought out by individuals at all levels within the institution. The CDO can expect to be contacted by everyone, from an employee having an issue with his or her supervisor, to another wanting career coaching, to a student of color seeking mentorship opportunities, to an LGBT faculty member seeking to host a conference.

Because diversity efforts grew out of the social justice movement, the CDO can expect solicitations to join a wide variety of progressive callings and causes. Many within the community will have unreasonably high expectations that the CDO will be able to meet every request. As a result, role designers must take this into account as they create a role that requires a number of different relationships, but also requires a high level of operational discipline to activate.

CDOs will inevitably give presentations, mentor students, and meet with individuals and groups, but their work must center on big-picture priorities and delivering the institution's long-term diversity goals. This balance can be difficult to accomplish when members of the community may view the CDO as their personal counselor and desire to communicate directly with him or her about concerns both big and small. Although it is appropriate for the CDO to oversee the development of the campus diversity plan, tactical activities should be delivered by others, freeing the CDO to work on broad issues of institutional policy, strategic plans, cultivating new relationships, locating new revenue streams, and developing new campus diversity capabilities.

Managing External Relationships

CDOs may also play a prominent role in the external community. Some CDOs have an active presence in local minority communities, helping to mitigate the contentious relationship between community and institution. These "town and gown duties" can involve sitting on various boards; speaking at local events; fostering new partnerships in the K–12 school system; participating in citywide diversity efforts; and building new relationships with companies locally, regionally, and nationally.

In recent years we have noticed an increasing number of statewide councils and commissions that bring together diversity leaders from higher education, corporate, nonprofit, K–12, and public sectors.[1] Some of the most innovative partnerships include developing human resources strategies to assist with dual-career families seeking employment for trailing spouses, launching new diversity-themed magazines and publications, partnering on career fairs and professional development events, building broad-based corporate and community mentoring initiatives, and designing roundtable activities to allow for the sharing of expertise. Each of these activities might warrant the involvement of CDOs.

CDOs may also have their own external advisory boards that might include local leaders, diversity champions from the community, prominent alumni, and others. These boards can help guide the strategies of the officer and, even more importantly, provide a channel for officers to connect regularly with key stakeholders in different areas of importance. In our interviews, some CDOs spoke of their regular meetings with diversity-themed committees in addition to their boards of trustees and regents. These spaces allowed them to build relationships, create visibility for their work, and by turns directly and subtly advance their diversity agenda.

Diversity Committees, Commissions, and Task Forces

Another important component of any institution's lateral diversity infrastructure is its committees, commissions, task forces, and councils (Cox, 2001; Maltbia & Power, 2009). We recommend that campus leaders think of diversity committees as a critical element of the lateral diversity infrastructure, a point that is made in depth in Chapter 9 of *Strategic Diversity Leadership*, which focuses on the creation, design, and best practices associated with these critical cross-cutting structures. In our research and consulting engagements, we found that most CDOs work in close alignment with campus diversity committees serving as ex-officio chairs, funding their work and priorities, advising their efforts, and in some instances appointing their membership.

Diversity committees provide a means of integrating diversity efforts up, down, and across the institution. They bring together individuals with divergent skills, perspectives, and day-to-day roles, extending the collaborative dynamics of the institution's diversity agenda in meaningful ways. As with other dimensions of the CDODF, there is no single successful committee implementation process, only contingencies to be considered when designing the diversity capabilities of the institution. In our companion volume to this book, we explore diversity committees in detail, delving deeply into the contingencies that must be considered when developing these structures.

Diversity Affinity Groups

Terms for identity-themed diversity groups or organizations run the gamut from *affinity groups, forums,* and *networks.* We prefer to use the general term *affinity group* and define this dimension of the lateral diversity infrastructure as a group organized around common identities, challenges, and interests. These groups are generally made up of people who have been historically underrepresented within the organization and include, among others, racial and ethnic minorities, individuals with disabilities, gender groups, and members of the LGBT community. Affinity groups generally seek to:

- Advance the personal and professional development of their members.
- Expose members to increased leadership opportunities.

- Provide support and networking opportunities.
- Participate in community service.
- Engage in mentoring relationships with their members, as well as students.
- Assist the CDO and other diversity staff in achieving key organizational diversity initiatives, including recruitment, retention, promotion, and long-term success.

Colleges and universities have a long history of faculty, staff, and student affinity organizations and structures. With respect to the diversity movement, the oldest affinity groups grew out of the first minority affairs offices and ethnic studies programs. They were first used as a vehicle to advance the collective political concerns of African Americans and other historically underrepresented groups—referred to by some as *ALANA*: African American, Latino, Asian, and Native American groups. These affinity structures also exist centered around achieving the full participation of women in the academy.

In the current era, affinity groups remain a popular diversity tactic for many institutions. They are easy to set up and relatively inexpensive to run. For many organizations, the focus of affinity groups has evolved over time from their primary role—providing a forum for organization members who share common interests to meet and work together—to multifaceted efforts that influence a number of aspects of an institution's diversity structure. Although the benefit of these infrastructures has been largely unexamined in academic research, we view them as a critical component of the multicultural and inclusion capabilities of an institution.

These structures provide a forum for institutional community members to gather socially and professionally, sharing ideas outside of their particular academic or administrative units. Some institutions have a myriad of affinity groups that organize their own events and work to attract and retain a diverse community. Issues facing affinity groups today are more than simply social. For example, one issue of particular importance to LGBT affinity groups is extending employee benefits for partners in same-sex relationships. Table 3.9 describes the affinity infrastructure at a large research university in the Northwest.

Affinity groups offer one way to make diverse members of the community feel welcome and valued. They can play a key role helping new arrivals transition to campus life. For example, when a prospective minority faculty member moves to a town, members of the group often help that person get

TABLE 3.9
Affinity Group Infrastructure at a Large Research University in the Northwest

Affinity Group	*Mission Statement*	*Goals*
Asian and Pacific Islander American Faculty and Staff Association	Recognizing and honoring the rich ethnic, cultural, and social diversity of Asian and Pacific Islander American faculty and staff, the purpose of the APIAFSA is to create, engage, maintain, and sustain a visible and supportive APIA community.	• Increase education and dialogue on issues affecting Asian and Pacific Islander Americans. • Support leadership and career development and advancement among APIA faculty and staff. • Advocate for issues in higher education that affect APIA faculty and staff. • Assist in the recruitment, support, and retention of APIA faculty and staff. • Provide opportunities for professional and social networking. • Foster the exchange of diverse intellectual, social, cultural, and political perspectives. • Work in collaboration with other campus affinity groups and units to build a diverse, inclusive, and engaging intellectual and social environment for the entire campus community.
Black Faculty and Staff Association	The mission of the Black Faculty and Staff Association is to foster a greater sense of community and mutual support among the African American faculty and staff of the university through mentoring and networking in an effort to provide an organized support system that will enhance the cultural diversity within the university, as well as enhance and support the academic mission of the university.	• Create an enlightened environment where issues of inequity and injustice can be effectively identified, discussed, and addressed. • Support the recruitment, retention, academic excellence, and graduation rates of African American graduate and undergraduate students. • Promote the recruitment and retention, promotion and tenure, and professional development and career advancement of African American faculty and staff at the university. • Expand and strengthen the relationship and involvement of African American faculty and staff with the wider university community.
LGBT Faculty and Staff Association	The purpose of the LGBT Faculty and Staff Association is to foster and support a visible and vibrant LGBT community.	• Increase education and dialogue on issues affecting the LGBT community. • Honor the cultural diversity of LGBT faculty and staff. • Support leadership and career advancement among LGBT faculty and staff. • Advocate for issues in higher education that affect LGBT faculty and staff. • Assist in the recruitment and retention of LGBT faculty and staff. • Provide opportunities for social networking. • Foster the exchange of social, cultural, and political ideas.

TABLE 3.9 (Continued)

Affinity Group	*Mission Statement*	*Goals*
Latino/a Faculty and Staff Association	The LFSA is an advocacy, leadership development, and social networking group that addresses Latino issues in higher education, including the educational concerns and advancement of the Latino community.	• Highlight the scholarship produced about Latino communities; spotlight the contributions of Latino staff. • Assist in the recruitment, retention, and advancement of Latino faculty, staff, and students. • Create community and a support network that validates Latino people as a visible and viable part of the university's environment and leadership. • Enhance knowledge of educational contributions related to Latino communities. • Promote social and cultural activities that relate to Latino communities on and off campus.
Native Faculty and Staff Association	The Native Faculty and Staff Association seeks to focus on initiatives specifically related to the well-being of the university's Native faculty and staff community.	• Create and sustain a First Nations community that celebrates achievements, acknowledges milestones, represents concerns, and provides advocacy for community members. • Create an environment that attracts, welcomes, and retains First Nations faculty, staff, and students. • Acknowledge the service that Native faculty and staff provide to students formally and informally through mentorship and other student assistance. • Develop effective, ethical, innovative, respectful, and culturally appropriate research partnerships with tribal communities. • Improve the career pipeline for faculty and staff into the upper echelon of the university.

APIA, Asian and Pacific Islander American; *APIAFSA,* Asian and Pacific Islander American Faculty and Staff Association; *LFSA,* Latino/a Faculty and Staff Association; *LGBT,* lesbian, gay, bisexual, transgender.

adjusted to the community, finding everything from a suitable place to worship to a realtor. The goal is for the affinity structure to help new arrivals become productive members of the community.

Affinity groups also focus on the professional development of their constituents by holding workshops and seminars around institutional policies and programs. Senior members offer junior members tips from their experiences of having worked their way through the ranks. In particular, the social networks created in employee affinity groups can serve as a counterbalance to the "good ol' boy" network and help individuals to break through the glass ceiling of campus leadership, navigate tenure and promotion requirements, and generally understand how to negotiate the campus climate for diversity. With so few truly diverse campuses, a well-organized affinity structure can make it easier for community members to meet people in other departments, allowing for a greater sharing of resources and success stories.

These groups often provide training and workshops on issues of difference. We have encountered a gender affinity organization that sponsored a training series on gender issues on campus, an LGBT affinity organization that provided members to serve on a panel for new faculty, a Latino faculty and staff affinity organization that implemented a mentoring program for undergraduate students, and an African American affinity organization that established a scholarship program in the name of Martin Luther King, Jr.

Although it is a more common practice in the corporate community than in higher education, affinity organizations can play a key role in outreach and recruitment of new employees, from hosting booths at conferences to forging strategic partnerships with minority-serving institutions and networks. Some affinity groups even provide search committee training and awareness programs for members of the campus community.

Student organizations offer some of the most long-standing and consistent affinity organizations on campus, from minority-serving fraternities, sororities, and student unions, to diversity-themed pre-professional student organizations. Student affinity organizations assist students with becoming connected and engaged on campus, foster leadership skills and abilities, improve retention and graduation, and provide other positive benefits.

Alumni associations also make effective affinity networks. At Brown University, the Multicultural Alumni Committee (MAC) offers a vibrant alumni voice for diversity. This group strives to be a *conduit* for connecting diverse alumni with the Brown Alumni Association and serves as a touchstone for reconnecting graduates to diversity values. The group also engages alumni of color and LGBT alumni on diversity issues and activities. The MAC helps convene various diverse alumni affinity groups, including the Asian/Asian American Alumni Alliance, Transgender Bisexual Gay and Lesbian Alumni, the Latino Alumni Council, and the Black Alumni Council.

Alumni affinity groups have great potential for enriching the experience of current undergraduates through mentoring, internship opportunities, and professional development. These groups also can prove an invaluable asset in fund-raising and development activities, as many diverse graduates are more likely to give to specific diversity-themed scholarships and initiatives than general campus-wide programs. Affinity organizations can help to shape fund-raising efforts and cultivate relationships with diverse communities and constituents. Indeed, a prominent example of this is the Woman In Philanthropy Committee at the University of Wisconsin–Madison, a group that regularly contributes funds to drive issues of diversity and inclusion on campus, elevating gender equality as a strategic priority.

Table 3.10 outlines five key recommendations for affinity groups designed to strengthen their diversity efforts and support resources. One sign of an institution's commitment to these organizations is to allocate them financial resources. The dedication of real resources toward their work shows

TABLE 3.10
Recommendations for Successful Affinity Groups

Recommendation	*Description*
Assign the groups real-life institutional challenges.	To avoid having your affinity groups become a glorified book club, keep the members focused on real projects. Consider assigning the tasks of addressing problems faced by people from an under-represented group. A formal, well-articulated charter should provide measurable benefits to the broader organization, not just the particular group it seeks to serve.
Cultivate a diversity of seniority levels within each group.	If all the participants in your affinity groups are entry-level employees or in support roles, meetings will yield fewer valuable networking connections for career advancement. Therefore, encourage senior executives to get involved. Their insights into how the organization works and how to improve efficiency can be valuable for everyone involved.
Encourage different affinity groups to work together.	Affinity groups that work together can overcome the "silo effect," making their efforts more effective within the corporate culture. A company's affinity groups can accomplish more by pooling their resources, thereby demonstrating through their cooperative efforts the intrinsic benefits of diversity.
Make sure the affinity group respects all federal and state labor and antidiscrimination laws and regulations.	If you offer space and other resources to one group, make sure to offer similar resources to all other groups. Also, by law, an affinity group cannot exclude anyone from joining as long as he or she meets membership standards.
Provide resources to the affinity group, helping them to become a programming body.	The best modern groups are funded by senior leadership and are integrated into the diversity strategy and review processes. If you want to empower the group, give them a working budget that will allow them to develop programs, host social events, sponsor workshops, and proactively pursue their work. Without a budget, the institutional commitment to the work is less evident and the groups are less able to engage on diversity efforts.

Source: Retrieved from http://newdemographic.com/2009/02/24/how-employee-affinity-groups-can-help-you-recruit-and-retain-a-diverse-workforce

that an institution is willing to do more than talk about the value of affinity groups to the strategic diversity agenda.

Change Management Systems

The role of the CDO is to work collaboratively with stakeholders, both within and outside the campus environment, in an effort to drive the institution's big-picture strategic diversity agenda as well as the strategic diversity platform of its office. More than anyone else on campus, the CDO must be competent with respect to issues of strategic diversity leadership, diversity planning, and accountability techniques. He or she must possess an ability to analyze diversity challenges and move forward using organizational learning, structural, symbolic, collegial, and political leadership styles in the effort to drive change on campus. These techniques are explored at length throughout *Strategic Diversity Leadership* and are presented in Chapter 6 of this volume.

Our review of CDO efforts has led to the creation of a grounded understanding of the tactics that these leaders use to encourage institutional change. Table 3.11 has grouped these tactics under six broad headings: (a) engagement tactics, (b) entrepreneurial tactics, (c) accountability tactics, (d) symbolic tactics, (e) communication tactics, and (f) research tactics. Each is rooted in a particular organizational change tradition, and has been deployed by CDOs in their work as integrative diversity leaders.

These initiatives represent some of the key tactics that CDOs have leveraged to promote institutional change. The success of these strategies often hinges on the clarity of the CDO's strategic diversity platform and ability to leverage not only his or her formal vertical authority, but also the reflective voice of senior leaders and the institution's lateral diversity infrastructure.

Officer Knowledge, Skills, and Abilities

When institutional leaders decide to develop a CDO position, they must take care to find the right candidate. This task can be difficult when applicant pools yield hundreds of qualified applicants, including faculty members with a diversity research agenda, lawyers who are well-versed in affirmative action law, multicultural student development specialists, individuals from the corporate community, and others. In Chapter 2, we devoted extensive effort to defining the CDO role. All of the ideas mentioned there are critical in helping to find and empower an effective CDO. Yet these abilities must

TABLE 3.11
Institutional Change Tactics Applied by Chief Diversity Officers

Strategies	*Description*	*Examples*
Engagement Tactics	Tactics designed to educate, engage, and align students, faculty, staff, alumni, community members, external community members, and others in collaborative conversations, training, and leadership development around issues of diversity	• Diversity briefings with senior leaders • Diversity symposia; roundtables; conferences for students, faculty, and staff • Diversity training and leadership development programs for students, faculty, and staff • Intergroup relations programs • Search committee development activities • Assistance in the development of general education diversity distribution requirements
Entrepreneurial Tactics	Tactics either implemented directly by the CDO or designed to provide financial incentives to encourage involvement from the campus community, spurring innovation in campus diversity initiatives	• Faculty diversity challenge grants • Student diversity challenge grants • Seeding new faculty positions • Providing matching funds for new initiatives • Cultivating gifts from prominent alumni and community members • Writing private, corporate, and federal grants • Developing pilot initiatives and programs to seed new innovations and possibilities
Accountability Tactics	Tactics designed to align the systems and processes of the institution with institutional diversity goals	• Establishing search accountability mechanisms • Infusing diversity into performance assessments • Developing campus-wide diversity plans • Encouraging decentralized diversity plans • Establishing key diversity indicators • Infusing diversity into campus-wide strategic and academic plans
Symbolic Tactics	Tactics designed to leverage culture, myths, and political dynamics to achieve diversity goals and build support	• Encouraging regular supportive messages from senior leaders regarding diversity • Leveraging the reflective power of the president • Creating diversity awards and events that ritualize diversity within the culture • Participating in campus diversity and other events providing a visible presence of the institution's commitment to diversity
Communication Tactics	Tactics designed to communicate the institution's diversity values and capabilities	• Infusing diversity into mainstream campus publications and media vehicles • Developing diversity-targeted websites, brochures, and videos • Writing annual diversity progress reports
Research Tactics	Tactics designed to better define the current state of diversity on campus in terms of access and equity, student success, campus climate, and student learning and development	• Campus climate studies for students, faculty, and staff • Demographic studies • Salary equity analyses • Studies of the student experience with diversity • Retention and graduation studies • Longitudinal studies of the student experience with diversity

be fine-tuned within the context of the CDODF. This final dimension, which addresses the human capacity dimension of the CDODF, asks, "What are the knowledge, skills, and abilities that the CDO needs to succeed?"

The CDO position is notoriously difficult to fill because it requires a wide range of competencies. It was common for many of the searches that we examined to take between 6 and 12 months to complete. Indeed, even when a strong candidate emerged, the challenge of navigating such an arduous selection process, as well as the expectations of so many different constituencies, led to missed opportunities and disappointments.

When gearing up for a search, senior administrators face a number of difficult choices. Should the hire possess a doctorate or other terminal degree? Should he or she be placed in a tenure-track appointment? Does the officer need legal experience with federal and state compliance issues? And is belonging to a minority group a prerequisite for fulfilling the role? Table 3.12 provides a partial list of several key competencies of the ideal CDO candidate. Although the exact mixture of degrees, experiences, and qualifications is impossible to define, the most successful officers will demonstrate seven key attributes, regardless of academic and administrative background: (a) a technical mastery of diversity issues, (b) political acumen, (c) an ability to cultivate a common vision, (d) an in-depth perspective on organizational change, (e) sophisticated relational abilities, (f) an understanding of the culture of higher education, and (g) an orientation toward results.

Although these qualifications should drive the hiring process, the ultimate decision must also be informed by the institutional context and predicated on factors such as core job responsibilities; span of units and offices that the CDO will supervise; and the degree to which the officer intersects with issues such as tenure, promotion, faculty hiring, community engagement, and curriculum development. To say that a person is qualified simply because he or she is African American and a tenured member of the Art History Department, for example, is as inaccurate as putting an Irish American botanist in charge of the European Studies Department.

Another common mistake is to assume that only a tenured faculty member should serve as an institution's CDO. Our study of CDOs revealed that only 38 percent of survey respondents were tenured. Of all the CDOs we surveyed, only 44 percent possess the resources to assist in faculty hiring, and only 32 percent responded that they "play an integral part in the tenure and

TABLE 3.12
Chief Diversity Officer Competencies

CDO Competencies	*Description*
Technical Mastery of Diversity Issues	The CDO should have an excellent command of all aspects of diversity issues in higher education, including faculty recruitment and retention issues, identity development, access and equity, diversifying the curriculum, assessing the educational effect of diversity, measuring the campus climate, and the policy and legal dynamics of affirmative action and diversity in higher education. Furthermore, a CDO must be comfortable leveraging the social justice, educational benefits, and business case rationales for strengthening diversity efforts.
Political Acumen	The CDO must be particularly astute at navigating an institution's political landscape and able to respond effectively to politically charged or sensitive situations. He or she must possess an ability and willingness to find comprehensive solutions when crisis incidents arise, and know how to build consensus and buy-in by reconciling competing interests.
Ability to Cultivate a Common Vision	The CDO must be able to cultivate a common diversity vision on campus. He or she must be authentic with students, faculty, staff, and administrators, and be committed to working collaboratively with senior leaders to build positive policies and programs that result in strategic initiatives that holistically affect diversity.
In-Depth Perspective on Organizational Change	The CDO should possess an outstanding command of the elements and dynamics of organizational change, as well as extensive experience leading these kinds of efforts in the past. Change is rarely easy, and given the inherent difficulties embedded in what is often a politicized process, the CDO must have a commitment to navigate the change process through challenges and rough spaces. He or she must oversee the organizational change process from a holistic point of view by guiding the design, implementation, assessment, and evolution of key milestones over time.
Sophisticated Relational Abilities	The CDO must possess a high degree of emotional intelligence, charisma, and communication abilities. Given that much of the work will be accomplished through lateral coordination, a CDO must have the ability to cross numerous organizational boundaries fluidly and adapt language and styles to different audiences.
Understanding of the Culture of Higher Education	The CDO should possess an in-depth knowledge of the culture of the academy. Colleges and universities are different from other types of organizations, and to achieve success the CDO must understand the culture of shared governance; tenure and promotion; multiple and competing goals; decentralized campus politics; and the unique needs of students, faculty, staff, and executives with respect to diversity.
An Orientation Toward Results	Although not solely responsible for success, the CDO must be committed to encouraging and achieving significant results. Consequently, the officer must be able to demonstrate that diversity is integral to the institution's mission and fundamental to academic excellence in the twenty-first century.

promotion process." Our interviews supported these findings; only a few officers discussed their participation in reviewing tenure and promotion files as part of their portfolio of responsibilities. In those instances, the CDO was part of the provost's senior staff and read tenure and promotion files along with other senior members of the provost's leadership team. It was more common for CDOs to investigate into the tenure and promotion processes of diverse faculty members who had filed a grievance of some kind. In these instances, the CDO played an investigative role and made recommendations to the provost about the most appropriate course of action. Indeed, the lion's share of ways that CDOs became involved in the tenure and promotion process involved upstream planning, managing faculty diversification resources, and assisting both formally and informally with the search and retention process, the focus of Chapter 7.

Thus, although having a tenured faculty member provides some benefits, it should not be a requirement for the CDO role, especially if the officer is not going to hire faculty or participate in the tenure and promotion process. Every CDO should understand faculty culture and the principles of the academy, and tenure can be another component of relational capital that the CDO might use to build bridges, especially when working on academic issues. Nevertheless, its presence is not an automatic indicator that the CDO can lead change and build institutional diversity capacity, any more than it means that a particular candidate understands the culture of the institution. Our research uncovered that several search committees noted that *desiring* versus *requiring* tenure made a tremendous difference in the numbers of applicants they received. Indeed, limiting the search to tenured faculty sometimes undermined the search effort and meant that the position had to be redesigned to encourage a more robust applicant pool.

The overriding goals of providing leadership for diversity and guiding change must inform the selection process or institutions run the risk of hiring individuals who are woefully underprepared for the demands of such a complex, high-profile, and politically charged position.

Knowledge

Another key factor for CDOs is to have a broad span of knowledge that can be leveraged in different domains. The CDO should possess a detailed and sensitive understanding of diversity topics that span a number of different identity groups, ranging from race and ethnicity to sexuality, national origins, disability, and veteran status, among others. In a related fashion, he or she must have a working knowledge of key affirmative action and federal and state policies that intersect with his or her work.

We therefore recommend that officers have a depth of expertise in topics for which they will have a primary role, and at least a working knowledge of secondary and tertiary areas for which they might play a supporting or advising role. Thus, the CDO must be able to demonstrate the capacity to learn new information and assimilate it into the leadership toolbox quickly. The ability to learn and acquire new skills might be the most important quality of an effective CDO.

Finally, the CDO must demonstrate an in-depth understanding of the process for managing change and how this process might play itself out in different organizational contexts, whether at a small liberal arts college, a community college, or a large research university. The CDO should have an appreciation of the differences and similarities among different kinds of institutions and master several related topics, including diversity planning and implementation and techniques for overcoming cultural resistance. Although we would expect CDOs to be positive about their prospects to inspire change, they should always approach their work with a realistic understanding that change generally happens slowly in academic institutions, whatever their mission, scope, and size.

Skills

One of the most important skills an officer can have is the ability to communicate persuasively in both written and oral forms. Because the CDO is trying to lead change, he or she must be able to build evidence-based arguments and market these ideas to different constituencies. For this reason we recommend that the CDO build a team of people who have the ability to communicate effectively. We also recommend that the CDO bring someone on staff who can help manage communications for the campus community and other external constituents. The CDO has to tell the story of his or her work and how the campus community is progressing, and finding multiple and diverse messengers to carry the news offers an attractive way to demonstrate that multiple constituencies support his or her initiatives.

Although the majority of CDO units and divisions that we studied were full of individuals with a depth of content expertise on matters of diversity, the most effective were those units built around staffs with fluid and transferable skills. These skills included the ability to communicate effectively, think critically and solve problems, navigate complex tasks, work together in high-pressure situations, leverage technology, develop logistics, conduct and apply research, and produce clear deliverables for the campus community.

One senior diversity officer at a large research university in the Midwest was particularly savvy in his approach to finding and supervising the right talent. Not only did he have a highly competent full-time professional staff, but he creatively hired emeritus professors to lead research projects. He also hired a number of graduate students and undergraduates to lead high-profile projects. As he told us:

> You always need to have young people around who can do things. I like to have the desktop publishing and web programs in the office because young people can do many of the same things that a full-time professional can. You just have to find good students and make it clear what you need. In terms of graduate students, this is one of the best schools in the country. If you can get some of these brilliant graduate students working on staff, it is like hiring the best of the best to work for you.

The presence of a highly competent CDO core team is essential to an officer's ability to lead effectively. It's the presence of this staff that allows CDOs to fluidly consult with campus constituents around matters of diversity, develop new initiatives, maintain relationships with campus and external constituents, and innovate in ways that may be unforeseen at the time of their hire.

Abilities

The CDO must be able to leverage what he or she knows to deliver uncommon outcomes, despite what are often difficult working conditions. The organizational parallel that CDO designers might use when constructing the CDO role is that of top-tier management consulting firms like McKinsey & Company, Booze Allen Hamilton, or Accenture. These organizations leverage their human capital to flourish in a wide variety of areas, ranging from mergers and acquisitions to marketing, systems integration, and finance. When selecting talent, these high-performing companies often focus less on a particular area of expertise, and more on finding world-class talent.

At the nation's leading consulting companies, managers and partners provide overall direction, but at the base of the organizations are amazing professionals, often young people, who possess what one consulting firm refers to as "raw intellectual horsepower." The key qualities of this talent pool include a can-do approach to problem solving, a high capacity to learn and adapt, and the ability to work until desired outcomes are achieved. As a result, the CDO unit of the future may boast some people, particularly at the top of the organization, who know a great deal about diversity issues, whereas at the tactical level of creating and implementing solutions, highly capable generalists drive the process.

Guiding Principles for Applying the CDODF

We cannot stress enough how critical alignment is to the long-term success and viability of the CDO role. Each component of the organization, represented by a point on the star in Figure 3.1, should work to support the officer's strategic diversity platform. The more that the strategy, structure, lateral infrastructure, change management tactics, and skills of the officer reinforce the big-picture strategic agenda of the organization, the more effective the CDO will be in helping the institution achieve its goals.

Equally vital as a sound initial alignment is the ability to realign as circumstances change. The configuration of resources, the processes used, and the mental models that contribute to today's efforts must always be considered in light of the future. In a time of stability, organizations should work to promote efficiencies and maintain a focus on operational discipline in their approach. In a time of change, the inability to adapt can prove disastrous. Organizations must have alignment, but they also need the flexibility to respond to opportunities as priorities evolve and circumstances change, as when new legal rulings emerge or a new president is hired who has a different vision for campus diversity.

Lawrence and Lorsch (1967) were instrumental in developing the theory that strategy should guide structure. Contingency theory argues that design processes exist as part of an integrated whole and that each element of the design equation must complement other aspects of the design, as well as the organization's broader environmental strategic context. For example, if the strategic diversity platform has been established to focus primarily on faculty diversification, other aspects of the system should be designed to allow the CDO to accomplish this goal.

From a contingency theory perspective, therefore, *strategy must guide design decisions,* more than institutional politics, interpersonal relationships, or even past history (Birnbaum, 1988; Chandler, 1962; Galbraith, 2002). This is a difficult goal to achieve in college and universities, where a premium is placed on leading in ways that are political, symbolic, and historically entrenched, rather than focused on achieving optimal performance through the classic process of strategy-structure alignment (Alfred, 2006; Birnbaum, 1988).

To compensate, existing infrastructures in academic institutions should evolve to accommodate the presence of new or reframed executive leadership roles, whether of the CDO or anyone else. When a new CDO role is created, a series of ripples occurs, causing other individuals to adjust. Charging the CDO to work on a diversity communication strategy without aligning this new responsibility with the existing director of communications may result in conflicts, role confusion, turf warfare, and other problems. As a result, organizational design must be handled with a great degree of intentionality and focused on designing a campus role that will allow the institution to implement its strategic diversity agenda over time.

For example, faculty diversification efforts might require the CDO to dedicate a member of his or her staff to serve as a recruitment and outreach specialist to increase the number of individuals from historically underrepresented groups on the faculty. They might also require the CDO to control a fluid funding source that can be used at his or her discretion to increase the likelihood of hiring a historically underrepresented minority faculty member by joint funding the position. Another change management technique includes requiring search committee members to participate in a diversity hiring workshop to ensure that they understand how to cast a broad net in the recruitment process. This educational strategy might be supported by a complementary change strategy that allows the CDO, under the authority of the president or provost, to veto searches that do not fulfill a formulated plan to encourage a diverse applicant pool for each faculty opening.

Again, the beauty of the CDODF is that it is not static but dynamic, because each of the overarching five points will evolve over time. It is always easier to change an area of strategic focus than to change the institution's entire organizational configuration. When the strategic direction of the institution changes, the model's various supporting elements must also shift, or the resulting change will misdirect the CDO's ability to provide leadership. We suggest that leaders think of alignment as an ongoing process rather than a destination or end goal that is achieved as a onetime event.

Creating a Context for Success

Senior leaders must provide more than lip service in their support of CDOs. They need to establish a context that will allow the CDO to operate within a well-conceived span of attention (Box 3.2). This means ensuring that they have adequate staff within their span of control, such that they can work effectively with others. It also implies how important it is for individuals at all levels to make diversity a priority in their planning, decision making, and scope of activities. Finally, CDOs must have enough resources to provide incentives that will encourage others to become involved in their work.

BOX 3.2
Recommendations for Creating a Supportive Context for the Chief Diversity Officer

To assist the CDO getting off to a fast start, we recommend that the president take the following actions:

- Implement a multiphase organizational design process, leveraging the insights offered in this chapter and the next regarding theory, process, and critical frameworks for developing the role's strategic span, span of control, and span of support so that the role can succeed.
- Educate the organizational community throughout the design process to correct any mistaken assumptions that the new officer will operate as the "campus police" on diversity matters. It is the job of the president and other senior leaders to deliver a message that the institution's CDO is intended to improve organizational effectiveness, not to serve as a "diversity watchdog," even if affirmative action compliance might be a part of the role's strategic span. We recommend a dedicated website, press releases, a presidential editorial, and town-hall meetings throughout the process.
- Define the key relationships that the CDO will need to leverage for success and communicate directly with these individuals regarding your expectation that they will collaborate and support the CDO in his or her efforts to build institutional diversity capacity. This is particularly important in those areas in which the CDO's success may require the development of a matrix reporting relationship with particular individuals, offices, or units.
- Specifically articulate in writing how different administrative roles (e.g., student affairs vice president, vice president for human resources, diversity centers, etc.) that reside in the CDO's span of support may need to evolve to accommodate the new officer's presence.
- Allocate sufficient financial resources to develop new campus diversity initiatives. Without resources, the CDO is limited in his or her ability to lead and collaborate.
- Establish a transition team to assist the new officer with meeting key stakeholders, learning the institutional culture of inclusion and exclusion, and developing a better sense of institutional norms. One approach is to have the CDO search or design team continue standing for a semester or year.

(continued)

- Charge the CDO to draft a strategic framework for his or her office that describes how the position might evolve, major initiatives that he or she might undertake, and the resources he or she will need. This is an important part of the officer's first 100 days. Furthermore, this provides a document that both the CDO and senior leadership can use to establish key indicators and milestones for determining the success of the new CDO in building an enhanced diversity infrastructure across campus.

Although the CDODF provides key concepts necessary to develop a successful CDO role, it is not intended as a recipe. Instead, the framework should be used as a tool to provide rigor and discipline to the CDO design process. In many ways, achieving the right structure is less important than the journey of asking the right questions, exploring possibilities, and making decisions that are in the best interests of the institution. Whether the goal is to launch a new CDO position or reframe a long-standing affirmative action and equity role, the CDODF can help provide a clear and intentional process.

It is always easier to change a particular component of the model than to change an organization, just as it is easier to change a large ship's course before its journey is over. The more rapidly the institution can be realigned, the faster its leaders can execute new strategies and opportunities as they arise.

Note

1. For more information on a leading agency in this emerging trend, visit the National Diversity Council at www.nationaldiversitycouncil.org. Founded in 2008 by Dennis Kennedy and responding to the need to champion diversity and inclusion across the country, the National Diversity Council is a nonprofit 501(c)3 organization that now boasts councils in Texas, California, Florida, Michigan, Georgia, Ohio, and elsewhere.

4

MORE THAN SYMBOLIC LEADERSHIP

The Critical Role of Vertical Structure

> To be taken seriously, the chief diversity officer has to be at the table with the president and provost, and have some resources. If you are not at that level of the institution, it becomes difficult to effect change. Beyond that, your role has to be viewed in the same way as other vice presidents and senior officers. If they have budget, staff, and units, you should have budget, staff, and units. When I see other chief diversity officer colleagues who do not have these commitments in place, I do not criticize them, but I do question whether or not their institutions' commitment to diversity and the chief diversity officer is real, or symbolic.
>
> —Vice president and vice provost for diversity and equity at large research university in the Northwest

Although personal charisma, lateral relationships, and integrative thinking are key to leading in the chief diversity officer (CDO) role, success is also contingent on having suitable resources in a position's formal span of control. We believe that CDOs should have an ability not only to provide symbolic and collegial leadership, but also to provide formal leadership with regard to an institution's diversity capabilities. Whether at an institution of 1,500 or 50,000 students, vertical structure is foundational to establishing the CDO's ability to provide strategic diversity leadership.

Our research found that vertical design varied greatly from institution to institution, often with no clear relationship between the size of the institution and the structural configuration of the CDO role. One former CDO told us, "Institutions just do not know how to build the position at a level that is going to have an impact." The structure of the CDO role sends a powerful message about the role's importance on campus and illustrates the values of an institution. More than any other design dimension, it establishes a basic power configuration and determines how people and funds will be allocated and coordinated.

It is for this reason that we titled this chapter "More Than Symbolic Leadership: The Critical Role of Vertical Structure." Here we dive deeply into the most contested dimension of the CDO design process, its vertical structure. In this chapter, we address critical concepts like title and rank, dual reporting relationships, archetypes of vertical structure, dynamic diversity deployment, and the process of divisional reorganization. Although we introduced some of these concepts in the previous chapter, we developed this chapter as a way to explore each of these essential concepts for developing the vertical capabilities of the CDO role on campus.

Vertical Structure and Formal Power

When defining the material power and resources that exist in a particular role, we are often asked, "What is the best way to structure the CDO role?" Behind that fundamental question is a whole series of smaller motivating questions. Should the affirmative action officer report to the CDO or someone else? Should the CDO be the institution's affirmative action officer? Should the Office of Multicultural Affairs be in the CDO's portfolio? Should the CDO play a role on issues of race and gender? Disability rights? International issues? Should we move the LGBT center into their direct reporting portfolio? What about African American studies? Can a CDO supervise an academic department? As we discussed in previous chapters, numerous design solutions can be implemented to respond to these questions, each with its own implications for helping an institution achieve its goals.

As indicated by our discussion of the Chief Diversity Officer Development Framework (CDODF), vertical structure is simply one aspect among many that must be harmonized to ensure a strong campus diversity infrastructure and an effective CDO role. The CDO is not a magic elixir for resolving diversity. Rather, the CDO is one of several key mechanisms for strengthening current programs while bringing forth new possibilities designed to move the campus diversity agenda forward.

A broad array of vertical design solutions can work when aligned with other dimensions of the CDODF and the big-picture strategic agenda of the institution. Failure to align these dimensions makes it nearly impossible for the CDO to provide effective integrative leadership. CDOs go to work each day focused on contributing to their institution's strategic diversity agenda. Too frequently, the very structures that they operate in serve as barriers rather than enablers of their leadership.

How people are grouped within the organization and the way their roles are defined is essential to determining their formal power and authority. Galbraith, Downey, and Kates (2002) use the metaphor of the human body to describe organizational structure, arguing that it is akin to the skeletal system of the human body. Structure establishes the shape of the organization and frames all of its strategies, structures, processes, and reward systems. Organizational roles can be defined as the organs and muscles where work occurs. The *structure* of the organization refers to the way that people and work are grouped into defined units. Grouping creates a common focus by standardizing processes, making information accessible, and establishing a clear chain of authority. Over time it can allow for a more efficient use of organizational resources and provide employees with an identifiable home within the broader institutional community.

The development of a CDO position is a process of job role specialization. As we emphasized, the position's designers should create boundaries around an area of work they define as "strategic diversity leadership work." As the CDODF articulates, how an institution specifically defines this work in its strategic diversity platform should guide every aspect of CDO role design, including vertical structure.

Determinants of Structure

A number of factors determine what actually goes into the construction of a CDO role and vertical portfolio of responsibility. These include the institution's big-picture strategic diversity agenda, the values of key leaders in administrative and shared governance positions, the social context, and even the geographic and cultural setting of the institution.

Senior Leadership

The beliefs and values of senior leaders play a key role in the process of diversity planning, strategic diversity leadership, and accountability. In our experience, one of the quickest ways to derail the diversity progress of a CDO is to hire a new president or provost who is unfamiliar with or uncommitted to the goals, structures, and best practices associated with diversity-themed change and the role of CDOs. It is especially common for new senior administrators to seek to change the organizational structure as an easy way to assert their leadership without engaging in the process of shared governance. When the experience and values of these leaders depart from or subvert campus diversity efforts in general, and the CDO infrastructure in particular, disaster often ensues. In these instances, the CDO role and campus diversity efforts become stunted and conventional.

Our research uncovered several examples in which CDOs noted how their infrastructures were eroded and made more conventional by removing the honors program, institutional research, international affairs, ethnic studies units, and other more academically themed units from the CDO portfolio. In other instances, all of the vertical units were stripped from the CDO portfolio, or their budget was dramatically reduced, and in some instances the role of CDO was eliminated altogether. Often these changes occur when the CDO has resources and yet occupies a nontraditional position of power and influence that is defined in many ways by its vertical infrastructure. Moments of change or transition present the greatest risks to an innovative CDO's position to lead diversity-themed change. The damage inflicted often remains until new leadership arrives, or a significant crisis incident forces the institution to reexamine its practices and initiate a new conversation on its diversity efforts. Box 4.1 offers five recommendations to secure the position of the CDO during times of change and transition.

BOX 4.1
Recommendations for Strengthening the Chief Diversity Officer Infrastructure in Times of Transition

1. **Develop a high-profile and politically capable advisory board.**
   Develop a diversity advisory board of influential internal and external stakeholders who bring together a high level of visibility, credibility, and political capital. These individuals can speak to the work that is being done to advance the institution's strategic diversity agenda and the role of the CDO in providing integrative leadership to help advance campus diversity.

2. **Communicate relentlessly to both internal and external stakeholders.**
   Communicate through e-mails, diversity reports, updates, webinars, blogs, press releases, targeted articles, and other mediums about the progress and role of the CDO. The CDO should have a regularly updated online social media communications system and other capabilities to help drive his or her message across campus and in the broader community.

(continues)

(continued)

3. **Build relationships with shared governance leadership.**
Consistently build and leverage relationships with governing bodies, making them aware of campus diversity challenges and successes, and the role of the CDO. We recommend that the CDO meet with these groups at least once a semester to ensure that faculty, staff, and student leadership groups are aware of the officer's activities and initiatives.

4. **Highlight accomplishments locally and nationally.**
Look for ways to highlight the strategic diversity agenda, infrastructure, and successes in local and national media. This may involve highlighting diversity contributions and the role of CDO in national publications like *Diverse Issues in Higher Education, The Chronicle of Higher Education, Inside Higher Education, Change Magazine, About Campus, Strategic Planning for Higher Education,* and others. These efforts may also involve developing presentations and workshops at high-profile conferences and competing for diversity grants and awards.

5. **Be involved during moments of leadership transition.**
During moments of leadership transition, it is imperative that the CDO become even more proactive, elevating the campus diversity agenda and the role of the CDO in advancing that agenda. This means ensuring that diversity issues feature prominently among the priorities of the campus search committees charged with hiring a new president or provost. The more that new senior leaders embrace issues of diversity, the more emboldened the CDO can be in leading change across campus.

Diversity Goals, Institutional Values, and Structural Alignment

Another important design determinant is the institution's diversity goals. As the CDODF makes clear, the institution's big-picture strategic diversity agenda should guide design decisions. If the institution cares about the graduation and retention of historically diverse groups, or enhancing the educational benefits of diversity for all students, these values should be reflected in the institution's diversity infrastructure. These values are then expressed in reporting relationships, budgets, and formal decision-making authority. The late Dr. Frank Hale, Jr., vice provost emeritus of The Ohio State University, often warned about "commitment without currency being counterfeit." If an institution is not financially committed to building a well-resourced diversity infrastructure, its diversity efforts will amount to little more than lip service.

The question of values and commitment plays out every day in terms of vertical and lateral structures, what committees and task forces the CDO serves on, and who ultimately makes key decisions when a key issue falls under the responsibility of multiple leaders.

Sociopolitical Context and Geographic Dynamics

Historical, political, and social forces have always been critical to the development of diversity capabilities in the academy. The diversity efforts taking shape today depart in important ways from the first efforts founded during the civil rights movement (Patton, 2010; D. L. Stewart, 2011). Historically, these units focused primarily on the rights and interests of African American students, although a few did prioritize needs of Latino, Native American, and Asian American/Pacific Islander students. Today, most contemporary cultural centers embrace a broad conception of diversity, engaging in diversity, multiculturalism, and inclusion issues as they work to serve "ethnically and racially diverse" communities, as well as members of the LGBT community, women, disabled students, and veterans. When the first cultural centers and Black student affairs offices were created, few people thought about using a more inclusive definition of *diversity*, or recognized the clear connection between diversity and improved educational outcomes.

The geographic and cultural setting of an institution also helps shape its diversity infrastructures. On the West Coast, for example, strong and growing populations of Asian and Latino students have shaped diversity efforts in ways that differ from diversity efforts in the South, where dynamics have largely centered on relations among African Americans and Whites. Within urban areas the landscape is even more varied, with colleges and universities in cities like New York and Los Angeles experiencing incredible diversity, even among minority subgroups. For example, both Puerto Rican and Dominican communities have flourished in New York, although their interests and concerns are not necessarily the same. Moreover, the roots of these communities run deep; some institutions on the East Coast boast Puerto Rican cultural centers that date back over 50 years.

Reporting Structure and Rank

A reporting structure that connects the CDO to the president or provost sends a powerful message to the entire campus community and allows CDOs to raise issues of access and equity, and the educational implications of diversity, within the highest levels of institutional leadership. Without the presence of a CDO, these issues might not be treated in a manner consistent with the institution's strategic diversity plan. Among the 110 CDO respondents to our survey, 70 percent responded that they report to the president, whereas the other 30 percent reported a primary reporting relationship to the provost.

As we have already emphasized, rank is also vital to imbuing the CDO with the requisite authority to carry out his or her duties. Our national survey found that the largest number of respondents reported their primary institutional rank at the special assistant to the president level (36 percent). The second most reported rank was at the level of vice president, vice provost, or vice chancellor (33 percent). The third most reported rank was at the level of associate vice president, associate vice provost, or associate vice chancellor. Over 50 percent of CDOs at the vice president, vice provost, or vice chancellor level were in "new positions" created within five years of our original data collection reported in 2008 (See Figure 4.1; Williams & Wade-Golden, 2008). Indeed, only 17 percent of CDO roles at the "vice" level had existed for more than 10 years, reflecting that the trend of developing new roles at the senior level is fairly recent.

FIGURE 4.1
Percentage of Chief Diversity Officers at Different Levels of Institutional Rank (N = 110)

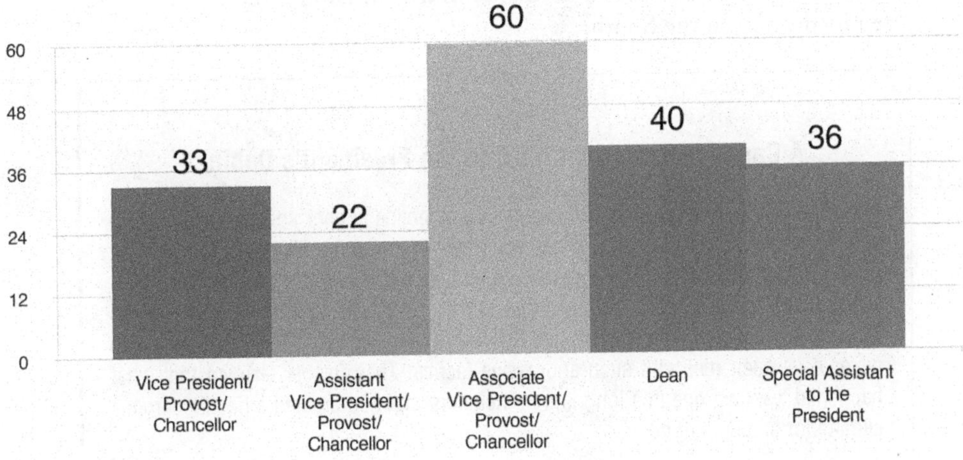

Implications of Rank

From a strategic diversity leadership perspective, title and rank are foundational for a CDO's ability to lead on campus. To accomplish this end, the CDO must have a presence on the senior-most leadership teams, and an opportunity to contribute regularly to diversity- and nondiversity-related matters, just as any other senior officer would. One officer at a midsized liberal arts institution in the Northeast had this to say about the importance of rank:

> In my current job I report directly to the president. In my previous CDO position, I had to go through the dean of the faculty, or chief academic officer. I should not have had to call the special assistant to the dean of the faculty and she, in turn, should not have had to call the dean, in order to put me in touch with the president's chief of staff, who would then coordinate with the administrative assistant for the president, just for me to be able to see the president for a regular status update or to advise him on a particularly sensitive matter. This arrangement put me, the CDO, in the position of a junior player instead of as the key consultative voice on diversity matters. You need to live near the top if you're going to be effective.

By situating the CDO position near the top of the administrative hierarchy, officers find it easier to collaborate with other senior officers; interface the institutional governance systems; and gain buy-in from faculty, staff, and student leadership committees. Finally, their seniority allows these officers to help keep diversity issues on the front burner of institutional decision-making and campus-wide conversations. Box 4.2 offers a case study of a CDO who was not included in the central command structure at a midsized institution in the South.

BOX 4.2
A Case for Having the CDO in the President's Cabinet

At a midsized institution in the South, university police pepper sprayed several African American students at a Black Greek letter organization dance in the student union. Responding to what they perceived as police brutality, the community mobilized, calling for an investigation and disciplinary measures against the participating officers. A coalition of students argued that a fraternity party of White students would never have been met with such aggressive tactics. They further claimed that what happened was just one in a long line of incidents that had created a hostile campus climate for students of color.

(continues)

The chief of police briefed the president on the situation and convinced the vice president of communications to keep the incident out of the university newspaper and online media services. The CDO, an assistant provost and experienced leader on campus, was not included in conversations about how to respond. In part, this was due to the fact that she was not part of the president's cabinet and had never been invited to discuss diversity issues with the president, much less participate in broader leadership decisions. Despite her considerable skills and experience, she was not included in efforts to defuse this explosive situation.

A broad spectrum of faculty, students, and staff had long been frustrated with the college's police force and felt that the president should be a stronger leader on diversity issues. They circulated a letter of no confidence and called for the firing of the chief of police and the officers involved in the incident. They also staged a major demonstration at the next board of trustees meeting and mobilized the Black Alumni Association, which had been preparing to assist with a major capital campaign. The students used social media, developing an Internet strategy that included a phone video of the incident and student commentary about the institution's lackluster response. In a matter of weeks the incident became a major public embarrassment for the university, even getting attention in the national press.

The CDO had been in only periphery conversations with the coalition guiding the emerging campaign against the institution. She felt confident that the situation could have been avoided if she had been made part of the conversation from the beginning and allowed to provide advice, work her campus and community network, and coordinate the conversation. Although not closely tied to the president, she had always found him to be fair, thoughtful, and supportive, even though he very rarely discussed diversity matters publically.

Whereas the president and the chief of police wanted to keep things quiet, the CDO knew that getting out in front of the issue was the best strategy. She knew that giving the students a voice, stressing the positive efforts that were taking place, and outlining the investigation process that was underway were critical to defusing the situation. She had considerable expertise in conflict resolution from her training in social justice education and years spent as a faculty member in social work. She also had good relationships with many campus community members and was more than willing to serve as an emissary, acknowledging the community's pain, while using the situation as a learning moment that could spark positive change on campus.

Had she been part of the president's leadership cabinet and emergency response team, she could have worked with senior leaders to defuse the powder keg before it exploded. As it evolved, the situation on campus continued to become more explosive, leading to a massive group of students protesting on campus, increasing conflict with institutional police, and a series of poor statements that served to further anger students and local community leaders regarding the campus's lack of sensitivity and support for issues of diversity. What began as a serious, if manageable,

(continues)

(continued)

situation, ultimately became a major setback for the institution and an erosion of the president's leadership capital and the institution's diversity brand as it began to move virally through the Internet.

Although having a seat in the president's or provost's cabinet will not automatically strengthen the campus diversity conversation, it does provide a space for the CDO to contribute in positive ways. For example, a CDO might start working with the institutional research office to determine the effect of tuition increases on the campus's most economically vulnerable populations. In a best-case scenario, the CDO is positioned not only to share information, but offer recommendations on balancing budgetary decisions with the value of maintaining economic diversity. But more importantly, the CDO is part of the team that can then partner in managing the tuition increases with media, parents, public officials, students, and community members. Depending on the issue, having the CDO involved at a high level can help to sway support around an issue and give confidence to communities that may feel as if they are particularly vulnerable. When a CDO is not reporting at the top levels of the institution, it makes it more difficult to have conversations that are critical to the institution's future. Box 4.3 lists several reasons for participating at the highest levels of rank.

BOX 4.3
Rationale for Participation at the Highest Levels of Institutional Rank

Participation at a high level of rank and in the institution's senior-most leadership teams allows the CDO to:

1. Regularly access key decision makers.
2. Influence the strategy development process about diversity-themed topics.
3. Provide insight into major institutional challenges, issues, and opportunities.
4. Focus on critical alignment issues regarding diversity and other institutional priorities.
5. Send a powerful symbolic message regarding the importance of diversity issues on campus.

(continues)

(continued)

6. Build relationships with key decision makers whose support is needed for diversity initiatives.
7. Share information in an informal and nonthreatening style.
8. Work collaboratively with top student, faculty, and staff governance committees in a formal capacity.
9. Provide voice to the issues of historically excluded and silenced communities to top leadership.
10. Ensure that diversity is an institutional priority.

It is worth noting that just because the CDO is a member of senior leadership does not necessarily mean that the CDO enjoys the confidence of other senior leaders. It simply means that he or she is in the group. Regardless of rank and title, presidents and other senior leaders have a responsibility to engage the CDO if he or she is to work effectively. For the president in particular, this means proactively inviting the CDO to contribute during meetings, encourage informal conversations outside of meetings, and assign the CDO to participate in valuable initiatives that may or may not directly involve diversity issues.

Achieving Structural Clarity Between Diversity Roles

As noted in Chapter 3, if the CDO designation is desired, leaders should pair this designation with a formal rank that clarifies the officer's position within the institution. Pairing the CDO designation with a traditional rank informs the campus community that this person's office has a special charge on diversity issues, even when there is another senior diversity officer who may be high ranking and may not report directly to the CDO.

The CDO designation implies that the holder is the most senior person with a titular-structural designation around issues of diversity. Some may gravitate to the CDO term without reading this book or any other guidance on diversity-themed organizational design; nevertheless, we recommend that the CDO title be used to signify a formal role of leadership that complements one's rank. It should not be a designation of convenience but should formally express a leadership role consistent with the grounded definition we offer.

In the absence of a formal "CDO" designation, a lack of clarity abounds. For example, take a situation in which there is a vice provost for affirmative action and equity and a newly created position of vice president for diversity, equity, and inclusion. In this scenario, the vice provost does not report to the vice president and the vice president does not hold the CDO designation. Do the two leaders work together or not? How do they align their efforts? Who is the campus CDO? Can one be the campus CDO and have no formal expressed relationship to the other? Is the new vice presidential role operationalized in such a way that the person has no charge to advance the affirmative action and equity agenda on campus? If this is the case, why is "equity" a part of the title? These are the questions that campus leaders must ponder when they consider whether to use the CDO designation to promote a vertically integrated divisional model, or leave the existing diversity infrastructure unchanged.

If the CDO designation was formally granted to the vice president, then the key design decision would involve defining how he or she should activate the "CDO" component of the vice presidential role as it relates to the vice provost. If we return to our discussion of the CDODF, this could result in several design options. One option is to put the two officers into a matrix reporting relationship, in which the vice provost for affirmative action reports to both the vice president for diversity, equity, and inclusion and the provost or the president. Another option is that the vice president may lead a council of the campus's senior-most diversity leaders and use that coordinating structure as a tool to align the perspectives and interests of the vice provost and other key leaders around campus-wide diversity priorities. Finally, a third option is that a new direct reporting relationship could emerge between the two roles, in which the vice president becomes the immediate supervisor for the vice provost. Regardless of the solution, campus leaders should resolve these design tensions early in their efforts to develop or reframe campus diversity capacities, whether they desire to create a CDO function or not.

In the absence of a formal "CDO" designation, there is the risk of confusion. Disputes over who will supervise what resources, who will lead what projects, who has the power to define the process for how work should be done, and who has leadership over particular issues are just some of the reasons that dissonance may emerge. Confusion is particularly common when dedicated diversity capabilities are not placed within a single officer's formal span of control and relational dynamics are not clarified regarding shared responsibilities, the process of alignment, and decision making.

Even in a best-case scenario, communication conflicts usually result in diversity efforts that are not mutually supporting or synchronized. In a worst-case scenario, the conflict leads to competition over limited resources and infighting between leaders. In these contexts, authentic conversations are supplanted by back-room deals, while decisionmaking becomes a constant battle to determine who has the power. Meanwhile, the formal needs and priorities of the institution are subsumed by the narrow interests of those who possess the raw political capital to move their agendas forward, rather than by those who support the institution's mission.

Matrix Leadership and the Role of the Chief Diversity Officer

As we suggested in Chapter 3, dual reporting structures are a critical facet of vertical structure, and have existed in organizational life since the 1970s (Kates & Galbraith, 2007). As we intimated in our previous example of role confusion and the CDO designation, matrices offer another approach to handling organizational complexity and role overlap between two or more units (Kates & Galbraith, 2007). Matrix leadership is among the most complex types of lateral organizations, as it requires a power balance between two or more leaders and clarity in defining who will oversee particular aspects of an area of shared responsibility. Matrix structures are often politically expedient, looking good on paper and creating what seems to be a straightforward solution, while avoiding the difficult decision of choosing between two leaders who share a stake in a particular area of the strategic diversity agenda.

At times reorganization may result in a matrix organization as a way of ensuring that decisions are made with a dual focus on multiple areas of responsibility (Kates & Galbraith, 2007). According to this theory, for the best outcomes to emerge, two or more leaders need to exercise authority over a particular staff member, unit, funding source, initiative, process, or even committee. Our research has uncovered dual reporting structures that involve the CDO sharing responsibility for some aspect of the institutional diversity agenda with either the chief student affairs officer, the provost, the vice president for human resources, the dean of the graduate school, the vice provost for undergraduate education, or leaders in faculty affairs, to name some of the most common.

The inspiration to develop a shared leadership structure should ideally emerge out of the nature of the work and not institutional politics. In a successful matrix, each leader has specific control over certain operational decisions, while collaborating on other decisions. Often these joint decisions focus on hiring personnel, establishing goals, and assessing the performance of the initiative or unit and the people who report to both leaders. Many institutions avoid matrix relationships because they often lead to conflict and organizational dissonance, which creates confusion in moving the institutional agenda forward.

Managing a Shared Faculty Diversification Fund

Many CDOs prioritize increasing the numbers of historically underrepresented minority and women faculty as a major priority. As a result, one of the most common dual reporting structures that we have uncovered involves the oversight of a centralized faculty diversity fund or initiative to assist with the recruitment and retention of diverse faculty. As we discuss in Chapter 7, several of these efforts are designed to provide the campus community with additional leadership tools to help drive their faculty diversity agenda forward. Examples include developing new recruitment efforts, issuing best-practice guides, conducting search committee awareness workshops, hosting faculty diversity conferences, and providing funds for opportunity hiring and supplemental compensation packages.

Although some CDOs have total oversight of these funds, it is common for the design and execution of the fund to be shared between the CDO and senior leaders in the human resources or faculty development office. Other alliances might exist between the CDO and a faculty diversity committee or the provost's office. Although some are critical of these alliances, our experience suggests that they can work if clarity and respect exist between both officers. Faculty diversification is one of the most difficult challenges facing the academy, and requires collaborative leadership if it is to succeed.

In the best faculty diversity collaborations, the CDO partners with a human resources or faculty development officer to develop the overall strategy that will allow the central administration to help campus deans, department heads, and search committees to diversify their applicant pools. The CDO may take a lead on one aspect of the fund's execution, while the partnering leader may take responsibility for another aspect. Although one office may fiscally host and manage the funds, expenditures at a certain level may require dual signatures to move forward. This procedure helps forge alignment between the two officers. In situations in which alignment cannot be achieved, the issue may be presented to a faculty diversity oversight committee that makes a recommendation to the president or provost regarding the way funds should be utilized.

Point Leadership to Campus Diversity Units on Campus

Another example of matrix leadership is when a diversity point person or committee exists in each school, college, or divisional area. For example, campus leaders decide to enhance diversity capacity in a given functional area of the institution, like the nursing school, school of education, or division of graduate studies, in a means similar to the CDO's efforts campus-wide. This is common in large research universities, where capacity often exists in many areas. It is also common to see these types of structures under a decentralized diversity planning process, where multiple schools and departments have their own campus diversity plans.

Our research has uncovered a large institution in the West that has established a matrix relationship between the CDO and several roles and units across campus that annually receive a centralized allotment of resources that are specifically allocated to drive diversity-themed efforts such as the recruitment, retention, and precollege development of historically underrepresented minorities and first-generation college students. Units that receive this funding are required to participate in regular meetings, provide accountability reports, and periodically participate in campus audits of their funding processes and protocols. We recommended to central administration that the CDO should host alignment meetings with the dean of each area before a new diversity officer role can be filled, to make sure that both hiring and funding decisions align with the institution's strategic diversity agenda and the imperatives of the dual reporting relationship.

Challenges of Dual Reporting Structures

What makes dual reporting structures difficult is that they create political turf battles. These battles often stem over confusion regarding priorities, decision-making authority, and the potentially conflicting visions of the CDO and other officers. Take a potential dual reporting structure between a CDO and the vice president for student affairs. In theory, the director of the intercultural affairs office would report directly to the chief student affairs office on day-to-day management issues, such as vacation and leave policies, student affairs divisional issues, and maintenance issues related to their facility. The director would then report to the CDO in terms of the unit's alignment with the campus's strategic diversity agenda, use of best-practice diversity techniques, and efforts to work collaboratively with other diversity-themed units across campus. The CDO and chief student affairs officer would need to coordinate on hiring and promotion decisions, annual reviews, adjustments to formal budget authority, and establishing unit priorities and initiatives.

Challenges result when there is only a ceremonial reporting line to the CDO in the dual reporting relationship. In instances in which the two supervisors are at odds, the subordinate director is forced to make uncomfortable loyalty choices. The success of dual reporting structures often depends on the level of intentionality that was put into defining what that structure should look like. Thus, it is vital that the two leaders sit down and jointly create and revise the subordinate's job role together. If a new position is being created, it means jointly appointing search committees as a combined effort and negotiating priorities as a senior leadership team.

Because accomplishing one's goals invariably depends at least partly on having institutional authority, we are far from convinced that matrix relationships are the direction to go, given their obvious challenges. We emphasize it here because it is critical to clarify the challenges of this particular organizational design, given that so many institutions often turn to it. Perhaps even more than authority and a dual reporting relationship, what is important is aligning the work of units across the white space of the organizational chart to move the campus diversity agenda in important and powerful ways. This means mapping the types of relationships that need to exist using the PACE framework discussed in the last chapter (Modena, 2008). This type of tool can help leaders to understand the type of support and leadership required to manage processes from start to finish.

Archetypes of Structure

The most direct way of addressing organizational confusion is through the vertical authority of the CDO role. By addressing the role's span of control, institutions can clarify the CDO position across an entire spectrum, from basic one-person offices to more complex multiunit configurations that may include over 20 direct reporting units and eight-figure budgets. Mintzberg (1979) argues that the process of designing organizations is simplified by determining the core organizational archetypes essential for designing an effective role.

As we discussed briefly in Chapter 2, our research identified four basic archetypes of the CDO structure: the *Collaborative Officer Model*, the *Unit-Based Model*, the *Portfolio Divisional Model*, and the *Multi-Institutional Model*. Each archetype presents a general template for how an institution might design the vertical capabilities of the CDO's role. In some instances, a particular unit may not fit easily into one category and will possess characteristics of two or more archetypes. Thus, it is possible to posit a blended administrative portfolio of responsibilities and priorities. This chapter highlights the key characteristics associated with the three campus-based archetypal models outlined in Table 4.1.

Our research (Figure 4.2) discovered that most CDOs, or 40 percent of respondents, operate within the Collaborative Officer Model. The second most common archetype is the Unit-Based Model, which characterized divisional infrastructures in 31 percent of cases. We found CDO roles following the Portfolio Divisional Model in 28 percent of cases. The particular CDO archetype provides important insights about the level of leadership and resources an individual CDO wields in advancing particular aspects of his or her strategic diversity agenda. However, regardless of archetype, the CDO is responsible for working with executive peers, partners, faculty leaders, and others to establish and implement overall diversity strategy. Nevertheless, a CDO's job is more straightforward if he or she has line responsibility for diversity units, and even nondiversity units. Line manager leadership is characterized by the CDO having responsibility for performance management, ensuring adequate training and development of staff, hiring, firing, setting goals, motivating staff, and generally leading through people in their direct span of control.

The Collaborative Officer Model

The Collaborative Officer Model is characterized by a single CDO and little else (see Figure 4.3). By definition, these officers operate in a "one-person" shop, having limited or no ability to hire, supervise, or evaluate the performance of subordinates who report directly to them (Galbraith, 2002). If they have any staff, it is often either one full-time appointment, a shared administrative assistant, or student assistants. As a result of human resources limitations, nearly all projects and initiatives are implemented through collaborative relationships and lateral coordination. In some instances the CDO may share administrative support with another colleague.

Because of these constraints, these officers have a limited ability to implement programs and initiatives independently. Notable exceptions occur when officers control sizeable budgets and are able to outsource services and support for initiatives implemented through their offices. Successful officers in this model rely on the reflective power of senior leadership,

TABLE 4.1
Archetypes of Chief Diversity Officer Vertical Structure

Archetype	*Key Characteristics*	*Strengths*	*Weaknesses*
Collaborative Officer Model	Limited human resources characterize this model as officers may only have administrative and student support in their immediate span of control. In the absence of a staff, a high-ranking title, personal leadership, and the ability to negotiate with limited financial resources are essential.	Maintains the current campus organizational structure. Is low cost. Is characterized by flexibility in changing and redefining the role. Establishes a dedicated role to advise on matters of diversity. Creates a symbolic expression of commitment.	Is more symbolic than material commitment to CDO role design. Renders the CDO as a thought leader—with little ability to activate new initiatives. Limits ability to collaborate with others. Does not create economies of scale. Creates unequal footing between the CDO and comparable senior administrative roles.
Unit-Based Model	This model requires the same type of leadership as the Collaborative Officer Model but is distinguished by the presence of a central CDO staff of administrative support professionals, programming and research professionals, and other diversity officers.	Is integrated moderately into the campus organizational structure. Establishes a dedicated role to advise on matters of diversity. Creates a symbolic expression of commitment. Enhances capacity to create new diversity deliverables in terms of initiatives, projects, and events. Enhances capacity to engage in collaborative relationships with others and seed new possibilities. Is a more structured and professional archetype for engaging diversity issues as a strategic priority.	Potential organizational conflict with diversity units not in the CDO portfolio. Potential organizational conflict with general campus-wide units not in the CDO portfolio. More cost-intensive model than the Collaborative Officer Model in terms of staff and hosting a dedicated unit on campus.

TABLE 4.1 (Continued)

Archetype	*Key Characteristics*	*Strengths*	*Weaknesses*
Portfolio Divisional Model	This model is characterized by aspects of both the Collaborative Officer and Unit-Based models. It is distinguished by collaboration and the presence of several direct reporting units in a vertically integrated portfolio, creating a dedicated divisional infrastructure.	Establishes a dedicated role to advise on matters of diversity. Enhances capacity to create new diversity deliverables in terms of new initiatives, projects, and events. Enhances capacity to engage in collaborative relationships with others and seed new possibilities. Has ability to leverage current diversity infrastructure. Creates CDO/dedicated diversity capacity and economies of scale. Sends powerful symbolic message of commitment to the campus diversity agenda. Mirrors the divisional structure of comparably titled roles. Is most vertically structured and professional archetype for engaging diversity issues as a strategic priority.	Integrated into the traditional campus structure and may generate organizational conflict on campus. Potential organizational dissonance with dedicated diversity units not in the CDO portfolio. Most cost-intensive model, requiring more resources for staff and other expenses related to hosting another division at the institution. Alignment of campus diversity units in a common portfolio may be perceived as "ghettoizing diversity."

the ability to effect change through personal leadership, and the capacity to offer financial resources to broker new alliances.

Our research found that these officers report being stretched thin because of understaffing and the numerous requests they field to participate in initiatives, committees, social gatherings, position searches, and conferences. In response to these environmental pressures, some CDOs attempt to focus their span of attention on a particular issue, like faculty diversification. Box 4.4 explores a specific instance of faculty leadership in the Collaborative Officer Model.

Although many officers operating in the Collaborative Officer Model discussed areas in which they have influence, they also noted the paradox of being high-ranking officers with no staff or direct reporting units. When the

FIGURE 4.2
Percentage of Chief Diversity Officers Across the Three Vertical Archetypes (N = 110)

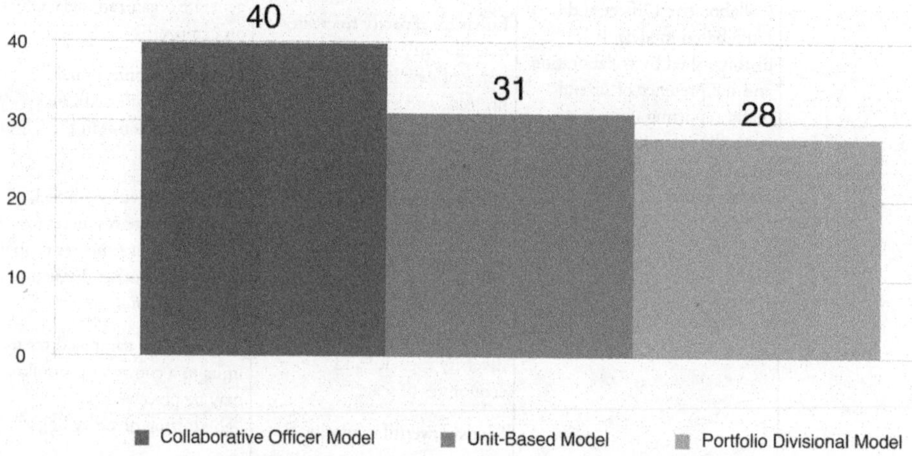

CDO has no staff and few formal resources, institutions often experience a strategic misalignment of dedicated diversity capabilities. This is especially true when institutions create new positions that give a vague description of the officer's role, and then provide no material resources to enable the CDO to carry out his or her duties. Indeed some refer to the Collaborative Officer Model archetype as the "burnout model." As a CDO at a small liberal arts institution in the Midwest told us during a question-and-answer session at a national conference, where we presented findings of our research:

> I just refer to it as the *burnout model* because that is what it does. If you do not have staff or resources, but you do have responsibilities, you just burn yourself out. It does not matter if you are at a large university or a small college. To get your hands around faculty diversification, student achievement, and the campus climate, you need office staff and resources; otherwise, you cannot even get the conversation going.

Although every CDO faces the challenge of coordinating with academic departments and campus-wide units, officers in the Collaborative Officer Model do not possess the ability to provide formal leadership to dedicated diversity units like multicultural affairs, affirmative action offices, intergroup

FIGURE 4.3
Collaborative Officer Archetype of CDO Structure

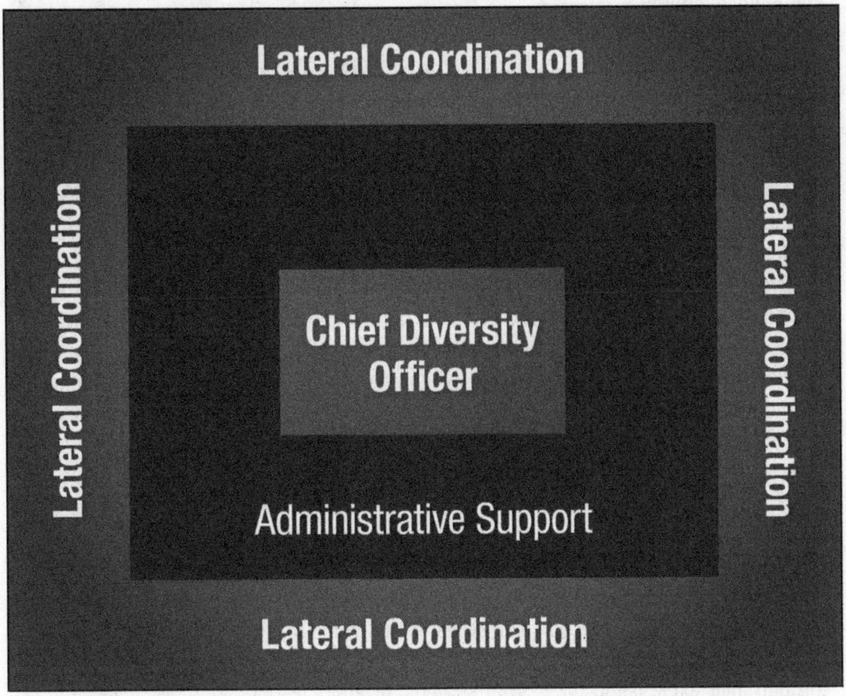

relations programs, and other bodies that address diversity issues. As a result, officers in this archetype must necessarily work to convince dedicated diversity allies to collaborate on a shared vision, just as they must with other campus-wide units. Box 4.4 explores the particular implications of deploying a faculty-appointed position within the Collaborative Officer Model.

BOX 4.4
The Implications of Faculty Leadership in the Collaborative Officer Model

At institutions with strong faculty governance and lean senior administrative teams, it is not uncommon to find faculty-appointed leaders who operate in the Collaborative Officer Model archetype. Although many institutions are moving toward a more professionalized approach, faculty appointees can make effective leaders on matters

(continues)

(continued)

of diversity and other areas like teaching and learning, faculty development, and international affairs.

In many instances, the appointed faculty member serves a three- to five-year appointment before rotating back to his or her primary academic department. The individual is often committed to institutional diversity and a trusted ally on these matters, having served on diversity planning committees and initiatives, or pursued scholarly research on diversity issues. These officers also possess abundant "idiosyncrasy credits," which refers to their ability to amass interpersonal credits or the symbolic capital that comes from being an authentic member of the community (Hollander, 2006).

Over time, faculty-appointed CDOs can accumulate a bank of idiosyncrasy credits, earned through their scholarly research and participation in the policies, programs, rituals, and shared values of the institution. In particular, faculty who have gone through the tenure process and have served in the faculty senate or other governing and administrative bodies may enjoy an advantage in amassing idiosyncrasy credits over either nontenured colleagues or nonfaculty professional administrators.

It is for this reason that some believe that faculty CDO appointments possess particular advantages, allowing the CDO to use his or her banked credits to gain buy-in with individuals who may not be directly engaged on diversity issues. The possession of a faculty rank and the idiosyncrasy credits that come with it may be particularly appropriate when leading in the Collaborative Officer Model, in which charisma, relationships, institutional knowledge, and personal capital are often the officer's only resources.

By contrast, nonfaculty members may possess idiosyncrasy credits earned through their expertise in the field of strategic diversity leadership, their successful efforts at a respected peer institution, or their national recognition as scholars and thought leaders. Hence, no matter how you begin, the process of strategic diversity leadership is transactional, and can be navigated by pursuing a variety of different strategies. The increasing complexity of diversity-related issues in higher education warrants that senior leaders consider carefully the advantages and disadvantages of pursuing a faculty-appointed position as opposed to a professionally trained administrator. We point out these choices not to discourage institutional leaders from appointing faculty members, but to ensure that they consider all of the relevant dynamics when making decisions. In some instances, faculty appointments to the CDO role may make sense even if the faculty member lacks expertise on diversity issues. Clearly there is also a cost implication as institutions weigh elevating a faculty member to the role, perhaps in exchange for reducing the member's teaching load, as compared with hiring a nonfaculty professional.

The Unit-Based Archetype

Like the Collaborative Officer Model, the Unit-Based Model places a premium on lateral coordination and relationship building; however, it is also characterized by a more robust vertical capability. Officers in this model have a core team that may include other diversity officers at a lower rank, administrative support staff, and program and technical specialists. The Unit-Based Model has greater potential to deliver diversity programs and initiatives than the Collaborative Officer Model, although the CDO still has no direct reporting units or offices in his or her direct span of control.

The Unit-Based Model (see Figure 4.4) is a more complete CDO archetype than the Collaborative Officer Model because it is associated with staff and office space, larger budgets, and more complex structural relationships. Indeed, the team's size, experience, and quality play a key role in defining how well the office is positioned to pursue the institution's strategic diversity agenda. The core team for the office may include a range of different areas and levels of expertise that can position the unit-based archetype for success regarding the campus's strategic diversity goals. For instance, if you have an organizational priority to integrate diversity into the curriculum, you may need a strategic diversity specialist who possesses a doctorate in education

FIGURE 4.4
Unit-Based Model of Chief Diversity Officer Archetypal Structure

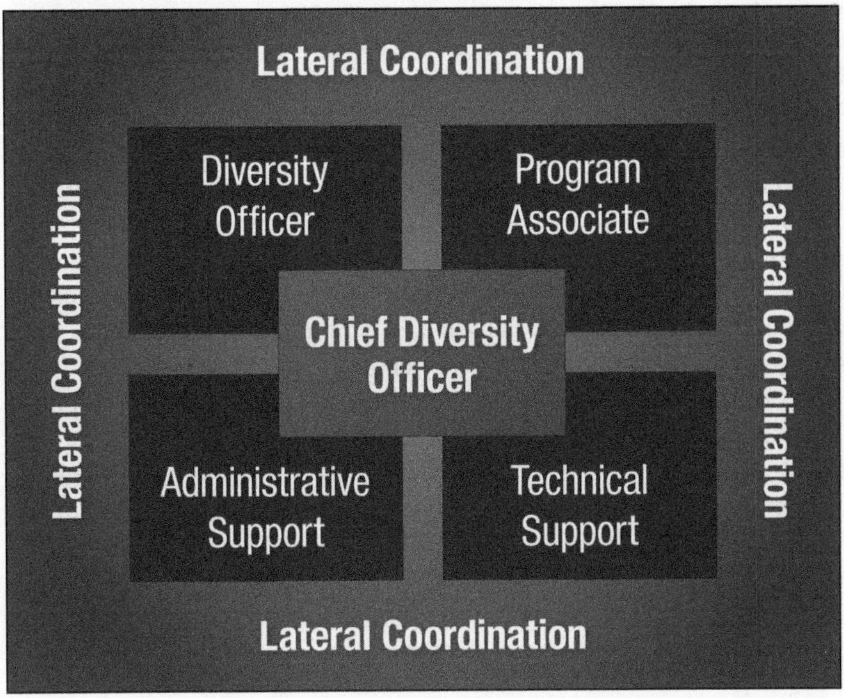

and a background in curriculum design. Beyond curriculum changes, this specialist and the CDO team may then offer workshops as part of new faculty orientation, partner with faculty as they pursue external grants, or provide consulting services to a particular department interested in changing aspects of its curriculum.

Beyond specialized functions, the core team also helps the CDO deliver his or her integrative agenda. Because the CDO is attempting to connect and amplify possibilities through new relationships and strategies, the core team can help execute projects like conferences, workshops, special meetings, retreats, diversity-themed print and online publications, and assisting with correspondence among numerous stakeholder groups, to name only a few possibilities. Team members should possess the background, expertise, and degrees in areas related to deliver the office work product. Core roles might require backgrounds in public relations, digital media, information technology, project management, student development, intergroup relations, change management, legal affairs, community relations, leadership development, diversity education, curriculum transformation, and conflict resolution. At the end of the day, each core team should have unique capabilities that add value institutionally, by providing the CDO with a team that he or she can direct in efforts to create change on campus.

Some officers have seen their roles reframed in the spirit of the Unit-Based Model to raise their profiles and make their positions more relevant. For example, a university in the northwest transformed its Office of Minority Affairs into a Center for Multicultural Excellence, while elevating its CDO position to the associate provost level. The unit's mission acquired a new focus on intergroup relations and dialogue, faculty diversity recruitment and retention, and the academic success of historically underrepresented students. This solution allowed the campus to reframe its diversity capabilities to build on current diversity budgets and staff and give the officer a new structure to guide institutional diversity efforts.

As this example illustrates, one approach to building CDO capability on campus assumes there is a preexisting office, and works to elevate the stature of the office so that it can better fulfill the institution's strategic diversity agenda. This can be a cost-effective approach to building a CDO unit because it leverages existing resources and builds from a point of strength. Campus leaders have pursued this kind of reorganization increasingly, as the diversity debate in our country has moved from addressing past injustices to an effort to embrace a complex, multicultural, and increasingly global economy. A CDO at a large research university in the Midwest explained some of the steps associated with expanding the mission and scope of her office and role, from a Collaborative Officer to a Unit-Based model:

> I talked with the president and the provost and we agreed that my office should not be your grandpa's affirmative action office anymore. We decided to be service oriented; to have proactive initiatives that focus on education; to get involved with community organizations; to build recruitment databases; to connect with students, staff, and faculty; and to support the types of novel initiatives that people want to do on campus through grants, incentives, and innovation funds. Leadership provided the resources and we gradually began changing the mission of the office. Initially, people were slow to embrace our office, but now we get so many invitations to partner that we have trouble keeping up with the requests.

As this passage suggests, senior leaders need to support the reframing effort. It is not enough to lobby for a change in name; institutional leaders must also commit to enhancing diversity capacity. In our consulting work, we have encountered many officers seeking to elevate the rank and capacities of their offices. However, in numerous instances these officers simply had not laid the proper groundwork to take the next step, nor was their leadership prepared to make new investments in repositioning the unit. It is not enough to have specific expertise in affirmative action policies or multicultural student development. Rather, the CDO must be positioned to offer a broad range of support, because elevating the position will bring with it increased demands from the campus community and a greater need for enhanced expertise by the CDO.

The Portfolio Divisional Archetype

The Portfolio Divisional Model is the most vertically integrated of the three archetypes, and the least common (28 percent). It incorporates characteristics of the Collaborative Officer and Unit-Based models, as well as a compendium of direct reporting units within the "line-leadership" portfolio of the CDO. Indeed, it is common for the Portfolio Divisional Model to create space for other senior diversity officers who may directly supervise units in the division, thereby increasing the vertically integrated nature of the division. Even here, however, no matter the size of the vertical portfolio, the

CDO relies heavily on collaboration. Indeed, this collaboration often manifests through the formation of a core team that helps deliver the vision and mission of the CDO, both campus-wide and within individual units that exist within the divisional portfolio. Figure 4.5 depicts the Portfolio Divisional Model archetype of structure.

Among officers in the Portfolio Divisional Model, 42 percent occupied the vice president, vice provost, or vice chancellor rank and 28 percent the associate vice president, associate vice provost, or associate vice chancellor rank. Ninety percent of these officers worked at institutions with at least 10,000 undergraduates. This finding is consistent with the overall tendency of large research universities to employ more vertically integrated structures than smaller liberal arts institutions. Nevertheless, this finding should not preclude smaller institutions from considering a Portfolio Divisional Model if they believe their institution will benefit. Indeed, smaller institutions like Connecticut College, Grinnell College, and Middlebury College have

FIGURE 4.5
Portfolio Divisional Model of Organizational Structure

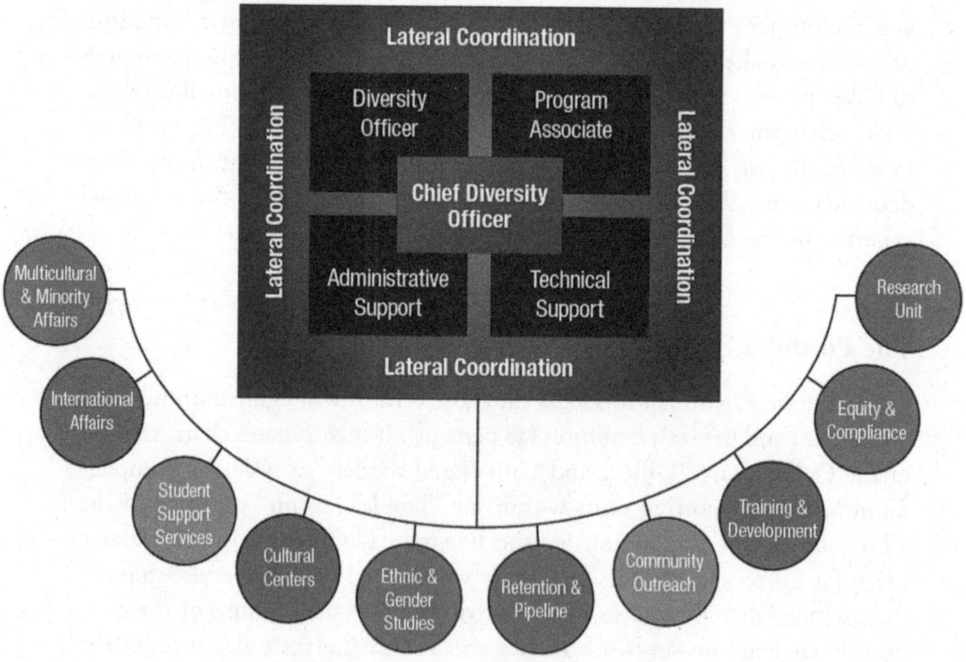

adopted a more vertically integrated CDO portfolio, combining the role with that of the dean of the college in an effort to find new synergies.

Direct Reporting Units

The distinguishing aspect of the portfolio divisional archetype is the presence of direct reporting units within the CDO's span of control. Our research identified 10 potential categories of units falling under the direct supervision of the CDO: (a) minority and multicultural affairs, (b) cultural centers, (c) ethnic and gender studies, (d) retention and pipeline initiatives, (e) community outreach, (f) affirmative action and equity, (g) training and development, (h) general administration student support services (e.g., admissions, registrar), (i) research centers and institutes, and (j) international affairs. Table 4.2 summarizes our research into the Portfolio Divisional models of 34 institutions around the country, capturing the prevalence and characteristics of these divisional units in detail. More specifically, we provide a description of each of the various types of units that may potentially be included in the portfolio and the ratio of their presence in the 34 institutions that qualified for this archetype of structure.

As identified in Table 4.2, the majority of units in the CDO's portfolio are associated with the Affirmative Action and Equity and Multicultural and Inclusion Diversity organizational diversity models. These units included multicultural and minority affairs offices (74 percent), cultural centers (62 percent), community outreach offices (59 percent), retention and pipeline units (57 percent), and affirmative action and equity units (57 percent). The next most frequent group of units was focused on diversity training and intergroup relations (44 percent) and diversity research centers (29 percent), capabilities associated with the Learning, Diversity, and Research Model, which describes efforts to prepare students for a diverse and multicultural global economy.

More than any other model, the Portfolio Divisional Model involves a reframing of assumptions regarding the institution's current organizational structures, taking steps to parallel other high-ranking administrative units with vertical leadership structures. Box 4.5 summarizes several of the advantages of the Portfolio Divisional Model over other structural frameworks.

TABLE 4.2
Potential Supervisory Units in Portfolio Divisional Model ($N = 34$)

Diversity Unit	*Organizational Diversity*	*Description*	*Percentage*
Multicultural/ Minority Affairs	Multicultural and Inclusion Diversity Model	Multifaceted offices focusing on diversity issues and incorporating issues of campus climate, retention, student programming, academic support, and student outreach. The programming is centered on students of color and speakers and lecture series for the broader campus community. Although generally founded to serve the needs of ethnically and racially diverse students, some of these units feature specific programming for the LGBT and international student community.	74 percent
Cultural Centers	Multicultural and Inclusion Diversity Model	Tend to be freestanding with space for student meetings, programs, social events, and computer usage. Whereas multicultural centers tend to focus on a range of groups, cultural centers commonly focus on the particular needs of a specific subgroup, including ethnic and racial minorities, women, members of the LGBT community, Native Americans, students with disabilities, international students, etc.	62 percent
Community Outreach Offices	Learning, Diversity, and Research Model	Provide opportunities for students and others to engage in service learning and community service activities. These units often serve as an institutional gateway for the campus community to engage with the broader community on substantial partnerships and initiatives.	59 percent
Retention and Pipeline Offices	Affirmative Action and Equity Model Multicultural and Inclusion Diversity Model	These programs focus on educational attainment and feature initiatives designed to enhance access and retention programs for diverse students. They may include units with special admissions programs for capable but underprepared students, government programs intended to build the pipeline of talented youth into higher education (including minorities and/or women in the STEM fields), and efforts designed to promote achievement in diverse and first-generation student populations. The retention programs in this area may include a scholarship component, and precollege initiatives may begin as early as elementary school.	57 percent

TABLE 4.2 (Continued)

Diversity Unit	*Organizational Diversity*	*Description*	*Percentage*
Affirmative Action and Equity Offices	Affirmative Action and Equity Model	Affirmative action and equal opportunity offices have responsibility for investigating discrimination, implementing affirmative action policies, and ensuring compliance with all federal and state regulations during faculty and staff searches. Under the rubric of equity, the role of ombudsman may exist to resolve conflicts in the workplace and foster a supportive institutional environment for students, faculty, and staff.	57 percent
Diversity Education, Intergroup Relations; Community Building	Learning, Diversity, and Research Model Multicultural and Inclusion Diversity Model	This category includes centers for teaching and learning; offices of faculty development; and diversity training units; and, in recent years, intergroup relations programs. The focus of these units is to improve intergroup relations, enhance cultural competency, manage institutional conflict, and improve the campus climate for diversity and inclusion from a platform of skill development.	44 percent
Diversity Research Centers	Learning, Diversity, and Research Model	Centers and institutes dedicated to researching and exploring social scientific issues of diversity, community, and difference in both basic and applied research. These centers may feature unique relationships with the institution's administration and focus their efforts at least partially on addressing campus diversity challenges in terms of retention, ensuring continuous quality improvement of diversity efforts, understanding the educational benefits of diversity, and creating collaborative research and scholarly synergies across campus.	29 percent
Ethnic and Gender Studies	Learning, Diversity, and Research Model	Includes academic departments, programs, centers, and institutes that offer specific courses, majors, minors, and scholarship opportunities focused on the concerns of diverse students, faculty, and subgroups. These groups might include both aggregate groups in terms of race and ethnicity, or separate groups like African American Studies, Asian Pacific Islander Studies, Latino Studies, Women's Studies, Queer Studies, etc.	18 percent
International Affairs	Learning, Diversity, and Research Model Multicultural and Inclusion Diversity Model	Areas dedicated to studying international issues, providing students with study abroad opportunities, and handling visa and SEVIS compliance issues. These offices also work broadly on global partnerships, international internships, research agreements, visiting scholar programs, and joint degree programs.	18 percent

TABLE 4.2 (Continued)

Diversity Unit	*Organizational Diversity*	*Description*	*Percentage*
Academic Support Services	None	Units not typically associated with diversity and multicultural affairs focusing on enhancing and supporting the undergraduate experience irrespective of traditional diversity-related issues and identities.	18 percent

SEVIS, the Student and Exchange Visitor Program; *STEM,* Science, technology, engineering, and mathematics.

BOX 4.5
Advantages of the *Portfolio Divisional Model* for Structuring the Chief Diversity Officer Role

1. Developing the CDO capability consistent with other high-ranking administrative officials allows them to provide both coordinating and direct supervising leadership to their institution's strategic diversity agenda.

2. The Portfolio Divisional Model can foster synergies between different areas of diversity responsibility, promoting programming, coursework, and research that might link areas in new and provocative ways, such as pairing race and ethnicity issues with gender concerns, or global issues with domestic diversity concerns, to name only two possibilities.

3. Economies of scale allow disconnected diversity units to pool human, financial, and other resources, allowing institutions to leverage budgets and staff to increase efficiency and strengthen influence.

4. Consistent diversity leadership across an institution's dedicated diversity capabilities allows the officer to act in a more cohesive manner and avoid overlapping or falling into conflict—thus driving accountability and greater alignment in the use of limited institutional resources.

5. The Portfolio Divisional Model creates opportunities for powerfully linking the dedicated diversity areas of the institution to the campus-wide plan for diversity and developing a hub of diversity capabilities for the entire institution.

A Scalable Archetype of Structure

The Portfolio Divisional Model is scalable and can be as small as 1 direct reporting unit and 5 people or as large as 30 units and 300 people. Our research uncovered divisions all along this spectrum and infrastructures constructed in a wide array of combinations. Figure 4.6 presents an organizational framework of the potential components of a Portfolio Divisional Model, both vertically and horizontally.

Figure 4.6 illustrates how the CDO can report to either the president or provost, supervise a core team and other senior diversity officers, work both vertically and laterally with an array of diversity units and resources, and may have an advisory board that plays a key role in strengthening the division in a number of different ways. It also depicts the frequency with which a particular type of unit appears in the CDO's vertical portfolio. These data are provided not only to reflect what we found in our research, but also to provide a rubric for institutional leaders to consider as they look to build their portfolio divisional infrastructure.

The campus lateral infrastructure of relationships and priorities is also illustrated, as the CDO must engage in integrative relationships regardless of title, rank, or vertical portfolio. Even in the presence of a large division and core team, the CDO must collaborate with other diversity units, committees, stakeholders, academic leaders, and the like. We continue to emphasize this point as many mistakenly criticize the Portfolio Divisional Model as a way of exempting other leaders from having any responsibility to advance the campus diversity agenda. In fact, this particular archetype creates greater accountability, is more effective at leveraging existing diversity resources, and helps position the CDO to collaborate with others. This is particularly true when an institution has made major investments in dedicated diversity infrastructures, like those of large research universities in particular. The CDO cannot live in an administrative silo, even if that silo was to include a well-defined and well-resourced vertically integrated structure. The CDO's divisional structure must be porous, allowing the efforts of the CDO to flow into other areas, even as those areas flow into the office of the CDO.

A New Vision of Structure

In our experience, even self-purported diversity champions can be critical of the CDO role. Some argue against having a CDO with a dedicated diversity

FIGURE 4.6
Fully Developed Portfolio Divisional Infrastructure and Campus Lateral Infrastructure

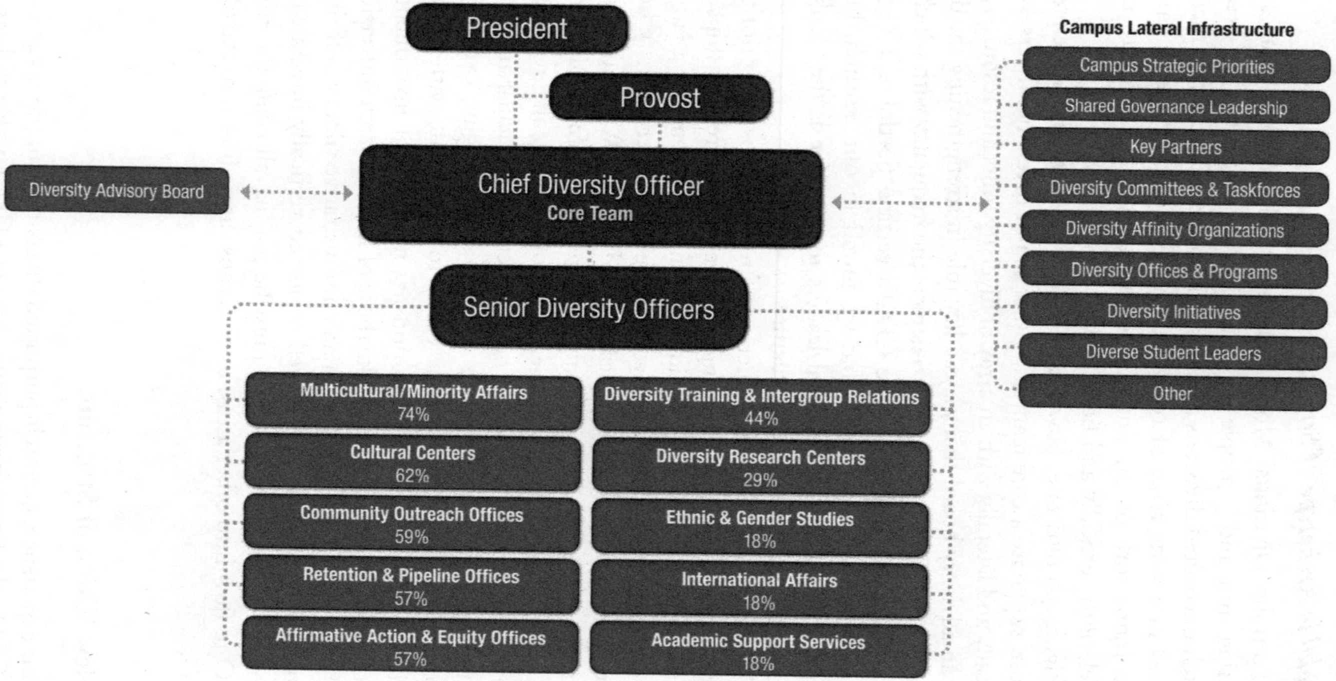

portfolio, whereas others maintain that an officer's portfolio must include general administrative responsibilities in addition to diversity duties, as described in the hybrid CDO role presented in the previous chapter. This dynamic even plays out among diversity officers themselves, as some shy away from communicating their titles and duties for fear of being dismissed as just the "diversity person" by colleagues both on and off campus.

What critics fail to realize, however, is that the strategic diversity leadership movement is responding to tectonic shifts in the global economy, and therefore moving from a mission centered solely on access and equity issues to one that embraces the opportunities and challenges of living and working in a diverse, global society. In this world, diversity issues cannot exist on the margins. To the contrary, issues of access, retention, curricular diversity, and engaged scholarship represent a new "academic diversity canon" that has become fundamental to fulfilling the mission of academia in the new millennium. The Portfolio Divisional Model archetype provides a vision of structure that is best positioned to capture the dynamics of change and brings together units focused on issues of race, gender, sexuality, nationality, and other groups across student, academic, and administrative areas.

Virtually every effort to build diversity infrastructure in the past has begun by challenging the status quo. The Portfolio Divisional Model is no different. The development of a vertically integrated CDO division offers a powerful way of creating a more responsive organizational infrastructure by creating economic, organizational, and strategic effects on campuses where diversity investment is otherwise misaligned or disconnected. Perhaps even more than its companion archetypes, this model represents a new way of thinking that challenges the power base of traditional campus organizational structures. It is a model that, in its most robust expression, embraces the diversity idea with a hopeful purity that our work in diversity, equity, and inclusion will have a shining beacon for us to rally around.

The University of Connecticut: A Decade of Evolution

The first author of this book has had the opportunity to witness firsthand the development and dismantling of an incredibly unique diversity portfolio.[1] From 1999 to 2008 the University of Connecticut reorganized its administrative infrastructure to strengthen and streamline its diversity policies and programs. An essential component of its ability to deliver on its vision resided in its willingness to adapt and evolve its infrastructures in response to a rapidly changing diversity landscape. It was able to create a structure that includes a portfolio of academic, administrative, and student diversity centers, offices, institutes, and programs engaged in both multicultural and international affairs work. But the struggles the division faced after its tenth year, when the divisional leader retired and a relatively new university president and provost made significant structural changes to the division, point to the vital role of senior leadership in providing stability and continuity to the Portfolio Divisional Model.

Launching the Division

The division was launched in 1999 with the appointment of Professor Ronald Taylor, an exceptionally well-regarded faculty member and long-standing departmental and governance leader, to the position of vice provost for multicultural affairs. After chairing an unsuccessful recruiting effort to fill the position, Taylor was personally recruited by President Phil Austin to take over leadership for the newly created role. He accepted the role on the condition that, in his words, "We would be committed to doing something meaningful, and building a campus-wide vision and plan to truly get something done." According to Taylor, "I was happy being a faculty member, and if at any moment had felt that we were not committed as an institution, I would immediately have stepped down and returned to my research and role in the classroom." Taylor's comments clearly illustrate the benefit of having a tenured faculty member assume the CDO role, because he or she has the flexibility to pivot out of the position if there is no institutional commitment in place. Indeed, a tenured faculty member often enjoys a greater degree of political and relational capital than an untenured administrator, and can push against an intransigent culture without fear of losing his or her job.

Taylor's collegial leadership style, impecable scholarly credentials, and strong commitment to the university afforded him a high level of support by the campus community, as well as the backing of the president, provost, and chairman of the board of trustees. Initially, as vice provost he supervised a number of campus cultural centers and ethnic studies departments, and oversaw affirmative action and equity matters. This initial set of units included, among others, the African American Cultural Center, the Women's Center, the Asian American Cultural Center, the Rainbow Center, the Puerto Rican and Latino Studies Institute, and later the Office of Equity and Diversity (Table 4.3).

In 2001, the board of trustees appointed a Diversity Action Planning Committee to develop a campus-wide diversity plan, which was ultimately

TABLE 4.3
University of Connecticut Portfolio Divisional Role Evolution

Timeline	*Unit Title*	*Archetype*	*Major Changes in Vertical Portfolio*
1998	Office of the Vice Provost for Multicultural Affairs	Collaborative Officer Model	A national search is conducted for a vice provost for multicultural affairs, resulting in no hire and an unsuccessful search.
1999	Office of the Vice Provost for Multicultural Affairs	Portfolio Divisional Model	The chair of the failed search committee, Professor Ronald Taylor, is appointed as the inaugural Vice Provost for Multicultural Affairs. The Office of the Vice Provost for Multicultural Affairs (OMA) role is created to lead the university's diversity efforts and manage a new division of units. The original configuration of the division includes the African American, Puerto Rican/Latino, Asian American, and women's centers. It also includes the African American Studies Institute; the Puerto Rican and Latino Studies Institute; the Asian American Studies Institute; Women's Studies; the United Nations Educational, Scientific and Cultural Organization (UNESCO) Chair and Institute of Comparative Human Rights; and the African National Congress (ANC) Partnership.
1999	Office of the Vice Provost for Multicultural Affairs	Portfolio Divisional Model	The OMA assumes supervising authority over the Office of Diversity and Equity.
2001	Office of the Vice Provost for Multicultural Affairs	Portfolio Divisional Model	An interim associate provost for multicultural affairs is hired to assist the vice provost in writing the campus's first diversity plan, with the support of a campus-wide planning committee.
2002	Office of the Vice Provost for Multicultural Affairs	Portfolio Divisional Model	The board of trustees authorizes its Diversity Action Plan, accepting nearly 130 recommendations made by the Diversity Action Planning Committee. The action plan establishes an assistant vice provost to serve in the core team with the vice provost, associate provost, and administrative support personnel. A full-time interim diversity trainer position is added to the divisional portfolio as part of the core team.

TABLE 4.3 (Continued)

Timeline	*Unit Title*	*Archetype*	*Major Changes in Vertical Portfolio*
2002	Office of the Vice Provost for Multicultural and International Affairs	Portfolio Divisional Model	The OMA expands to include the Office of International Affairs, creating the division of the Office of the Vice Provost for Multicultural and International Affairs. This merger offers a means to provide consistent leadership regarding the institution's domestic and international diversity capabilities while building stronger collaboration between the various areas and units conducting research, programs, and scholarship. Units added to the portfolio as part of the International Affairs area include African Studies, European Studies, India Studies, Middle Eastern Studies, the Center for Latin American and Caribbean Studies, the International Student Center, the Department of International Services and Programs, the Global Training and Development Institute, and the University of Connecticut American English Language Institute.
2003	Office of the Vice Provost for Multicultural and International Affairs	Portfolio Divisional Model	The National Science Foundation–funded Louis Stokes Alliance for Minority Participation (LSAMP) project is launched in collaboration with leaders in the College of Agriculture and the College of Liberal Arts and Sciences. The project's program staff report directly to the OMA leadership.
2007	Office of the Senior Vice Provost for Multicultural and International Affairs	Portfolio Divisional Model	The Vice Provost for Multicultural and International Affairs is promoted to Senior Vice Provost for Multicultural and International Affairs and gains additional administrative staff, including a budget officer. The Senior Vice Provost takes on new tasks, working directly with the president as a domestic and global emissary for the university, building new campuses globally.

TABLE 4.3 (Continued)

Timeline	*Unit Title*	*Archetype*	*Major Changes in Vertical Portfolio*
2009	Office of the Associate Vice President for Diversity and Equity	Portfolio Divisional Model	Following the retirement of the Senior Vice Provost for Multicultural and International Affairs, the CDO role is reframed as the Office of the Associate Vice President for Diversity and Equity. Several units are removed from the division, including all ethnic and women's studies units, units within the international affairs area, the office of the UNESCO chair, and the ANC office. These units are placed in the College of Liberal Arts and Sciences. The newly crystallized division includes the aforementioned cultural centers, the Office of Equity and Diversity, and the LSAMP program. The new division also assumes leadership of the Health Center Office of Equity and Diversity. The positions of Assistant and Associate Vice Provost are eliminated from the leadership team and the budgets recaptured back into central administration.

accepted in 2002 (Table 4.3). Under the leadership of the vice provost, and with the assistance of a well-respected faculty member appointed to interim associate vice provost for multicultural affairs, the committee submitted a centralized campus diversity plan that included nearly 140 recommendations. The committee's suggestion to improve staff support ultimately led to the authorization of two new positions at the associate and assistant vice provost levels. Simultaneously, a talented new executive director for diversity and equity was hired from the corporate sector and given a mandate for reframing the capacity and operational procedures of that office.

In 2002, the division of international affairs was merged into multicultural affairs, creating the Office of the Vice Provost for Multicultural and International Affairs. Although the original multicultural affairs division included the African National Congress office, as well as the United Nations Educational, Scientific and Cultural Organization chair for human rights, it did not include other international areas of the campus diversity infrastructure. This expansion brought units like European Studies, India Studies, Middle Eastern Studies, European Studies, the International Student Center, African Studies, the Center for Latin American and Caribbean Studies, the Department of International Services and Programs, the Global Training and Development Institute, and the University of Connecticut American English Language Institute into the division.

Stabilizing the Transition

Tensions existed when the international affairs area was integrated into the Office for Multicultural Affairs as departmental leaders were concerned about the future of their areas. The vice provost and his leadership team were able to stabilize this turbulence by focusing on continuity in leadership, structure, and operations. According to many who were involved in the reorganization, the most substantive shift was in the division's name and the move to give the executive director of international affairs a direct reporting relationship to the vice provost for multicultural and international affairs. Over time, senior leaders within these international affairs units embraced the merger of international and multicultural affairs. As the associate director told us:

> When we were first incorporated into multicultural affairs, we wondered, would we be treated like second-class citizens? Would some of our units collapse or be folded into the ethnic studies areas? We just did not know. But after a couple of years, I began to feel that this really would work. We started to get the conversation going around collaboration, particularly on the academic side of the house, something we did not understand when we thought that we would be in a division with student cultural centers and such. But the vice provost was really understanding and respected our history. For the first time in the 10 years since I started working in international affairs, I felt like someone understood what we were trying to do.

Midway through the division's span of existence, Vice Provost Taylor was appointed to the role of senior vice provost for multicultural and international affairs and given a number of expanded duties in the provost office. Under his successful 10-year tenure, the office initiated several successful campus-wide and unit initiatives, and produced several positive outcomes:

- Historically underrepresented student representation, first-year retention, and graduation rates reached an all-time high.
- Faculty diversification rates increased in response to new resources deployed through the Office of the Senior Vice Provost to drive this change.
- The division was profiled by the American Council on Education, the nation's largest higher education policy organization, as a leader in merging the domestic and international diversity conversations in the academy.

- The division celebrated its 10-year anniversary with an impact report illustrating that during the senior vice provost's tenure, faculty, staff, and others had produced 271 publications, including 112 book chapters, 83 journal articles, and 59 books and monographs spanning a range of topics and disciplines in the multicultural and international affairs areas.
- Several new faculty hires were added across the various ethnic studies institutes. Moreover, departmental tenure review procedures were strengthened. Although ethnic studies faculty were tenured in their home disciplines, the institute director and divisional leader were able to review their tenure applications, because the positions were funded jointly by the division, allowing the ethnic studies directors to have an influential voice in the tenure decision, as never before.
- More than $3 million in new diversity resources were secured for the University of Connecticut in the areas of diversity, equity, and inclusion from the National Science Foundation, the National Institutes of Health, Travelers Insurance, Pfizer Corporation, and the Connecticut Health Foundation, to name a few of the most prominent.

Finally, several peer institutions studied the University of Connecticut during efforts to develop their own diversity infrastructures, including University of California–Berkeley, Clemson University, and Middlebury College. The division's efforts were featured in *About Campus,* the *New England Journal of Higher Education, Inside Higher Education, Diverse Issues in Higher Education,* the *Journal of College and University Personnel Administrators (CUPA),* and other publications.

At its peak, the University of Connecticut Office of Multicultural and International Affairs was one of the most vertically integrated diversity portfolios in the nation, representing a diversity division in its truest form. The division included units that focused on race, ethnicity, gender, sexuality, and nationality. It sponsored cultural, social, and leadership events; hosted international studies conferences; produced cutting-edge scholarship; and developed partnerships for new initiatives around the world. The division represented an unparalleled effort to create new synergies; brand diversity with one unified message; and explore the intersection of culture, experience, and identity from a myriad of perspectives. One of its most promising aspects included an intentional connection among research, student development, and administratively themed diversity units. Unfortunately, its potential was never totally realized.

The Dismantling of the Multicultural and International Affairs Hybrid Model

After roughly 10 years of existence, the division dramatically shifted focus and direction, largely in response to personnel changes both within the division and within the university's senior leadership. First, the original president, provost, and trustee chair stepped down or retired from their positions over time. Second, Senior Vice Provost Ronald Taylor also departed, returning to the faculty. And finally, the core team of associate and assistant vice provosts, who had helped launch the Office of Multicultural and International Affairs, moved on to other roles. Meanwhile, the incoming president, provost, and board chair had a radically different vision for the diversity division, which ultimately led to a dramatically different structure.

These rapid changes destabilized the *Diversity DNA* of the institution, a term explored in *Strategic Diversity Leadership,* the companion volume to this book. An institution's Diversity DNA is composed of the institutional definition of diversity, senior leadership support, diversity infrastructure, diversity planning systems, change activation techniques, and other resources. When any one part of the DNA shifts, other parts will follow. When the senior leadership team changed, the vision and commitment that led to the division's creation was interrupted. While the senior vice provost left his role on the grounds of retirement, not all divisional changes went smoothly, or were welcome. The associate vice provost role was eliminated as she returned to the faculty after a dispute over the direction of the new division and its shift away from an academic focus on multicultural and international matters of teaching, learning, research, and scholarly engagement. The assistant vice provost role was eliminated as the individual in this role left to pursue opportunities at another institution. These changes occurred within less than a year, dramatically destabilizing the division as the three leadership roles in the vice provost core team were left largely unfilled.

Finally, the new president and provost refrained from conducting a national search for a new senior vice provost and instead appointed the executive director of diversity and equity (the campus affirmative action officer) to the role of associate vice president and CDO. They then eliminated several senior staff roles, most notably the assistant and associate vice provost positions. In addition, the ethnic studies, gender studies, and international area studies units were removed from the portfolio and the CDO role was removed from the provost executive team. The new, more conventional diversity division lacked the academic focus and breadth that it enjoyed previously.[2]

Lessons Learned

Perhaps the most powerful lesson to emerge from this transition was that, for better or worse, the entire infrastructure hinged on the personality, charisma, and experience of the CDO. Too many decisions to both build and ultimately dismantle the division were based on personality, rather than organizational best practices. When the senior vice provost retired and his leadership excellence and political capital were no longer associated with the division, the entire system was placed in jeopardy. Moreover, the arrival of a new president and provost meant that the division was necessarily subjected to the scrutiny of two people not involved with its formation. Their alternative vision for structuring diversity efforts met little resistance because there simply was not enough shared buy-in within the division to present a united front, despite its positive outcomes. Put simply, the division was "personalized" and not "institutionalized" as part of the university's infrastructure.

In addition, the division lacked the political support of powerful internal and external stakeholders. In times of transition, powerful alumni, influential faculty, and vocal student leaders, as well as political and corporate leaders, can help educate new administrators about the institutional diversity model and its strengths. In this case, the division lacked a diversity advisory board, which could have proved helpful in finding common ground, keeping attention on the broader issues, and reminding decision makers of the significant contributions made under the Office of Multicultural and International Affairs infrastructure. Box 4.6 provides an overview of the important role that diversity advisory boards may play, particularly in times of leadership transition.

Finally, although the decision to focus on stabilization was the right move early on in the division's development, over time, leadership should have been more demonstrative in creating a shared purpose within the division. Solutions might have included hosting divisional retreats, expanding the leadership team to include members of the international affairs division, changing the titles of international affairs division leadership, giving them an expanded role within the core team, and creating new initiatives that cut across departmental boundaries within the division.

This example is not alone; other ambitious Portfolio Divisional Model offices have been scaled back in response to leadership changes. The more innovative or novel the structure, the more likely that new leaders will not understand or value it. Hence, the CDO must work hard to ensure that his or her office is well positioned, resourced, and effective at communicating its diversity efforts.

BOX 4.6
Role of Diversity Advisory Boards

A diversity advisory board has the potential to provide additional leadership infrastructure on diversity issues. Although the advisory infrastructure can exist with any model archetype, it is most logical to pair it with institutions attempting to move forward in a coordinated and cohesive way. We found that advisory boards often emerge after several years of the CDO's existence and stabilization, paralleling the development of other advisory infrastructures that may exist in the schools, colleges, or divisions that exist across campus. In some instances, however, a diversity advisory board may even predate the emergence of the CDO role. In these instances, the CDO then assumes a leadership role within this committee.

Strategic diversity leadership is a political process and the advisory board is a key tool for helping the CDO to engage leaders who can help sway opinion, introduce diversity into new areas of organizational life, keep diversity on the priority list of busy presidents and chancellors, and overcome obstacles and resistance to change. A number of different types of advisory boards can exist. Some boards are internal and include faculty, staff, and student diversity champions. In other instances, the board might be external and include diversity champions with financial, community, or relational capacity. Boards with strong financial capacity can help lead diversity-themed fund-raising.

Regardless of type, these boards are critical to providing political currency for the CDO. They are ambassadors for the mission of the CDO, helping to raise money, improve public relations, sway key opinion makers, and speak at campus events on behalf of the CDO. They advise the mission and programming of the CDO, while lending their credibility, and at times their organizational assets, to encourage diversity-themed change.

Leading a Divisional Reorganization

As we suggest in our discussion of the University of Connecticut, one of the most powerful levers to achieve diversity-themed change is program reorganization in the spirit of the Portfolio Divisional Model. At its best, this approach can energize the institution with a common sense of purpose, thereby making it easier to implement a new strategy, improve efficiency, and align long-standing diversity units under a shared and unified purpose. But unless they draw on a wealth of practical experience and decades of academic research, reorganizations tend to fail. We argue that by drawing on organizational best practices, including PACE and the CDODF, senior leaders can achieve the kind of vertical integration necessary to advancing a strategic diversity agenda.

Change is difficult for most. Even when people acknowledge that change is necessary and that the end result will be better, the process can be stressful. Box 4.7 outlines several reasons why vertical reorganization is resisted. Opposition from faculty, staff, and students, combined with a lack of clarity about the goals of a reorganization effort, are major reasons for the problems that bedevil so many institutions. The most answerable challenges involve poor communication, heaping excessive pressure on community members, and not creating a context where individuals at all levels are engaged in the change. When moving to reorganize, the CDO and his or her allies must respect and address these concerns if they are to effect the structural changes they seek.

BOX 4.7

Reasons Why Vertical Reorganization Is Resisted

- The purpose of the reorganization is not clear. When community members do not understand why changes are implemented, anxiety and suspicion often fill the information vacuum.
- The campus community members do not see a need for change. Even if community members understand the reasons for change, they may disagree with leadership's perspective.
- The community members are not involved in the planning. People support what they helped create. If community members do not believe they have enough input in planning change, resistance may increase.
- Communication regarding the reorganization is poor. Even if the change affects only one other person, clear and transparent communication is essential.
- Key people in the organization are not seen as really advocating the change. If community members believe that key leaders within their community do not support the change, they will have trouble embracing it.
- The community members perceive a negative effect on their social relations.
- Key job characteristics are changed. Community members will be more resistant to the change if they believe it will decrease their autonomy, the level of challenge the job offers, the type of feedback they receive, or the degree of importance the organization places on their work.
- The community members have been exposed to a long history of poorly executed changes. If the community members believe that the leadership is

(continues)

(continued)

involved in another ill-planned reorganization, their enthusiasm will diminish significantly.

- The community members fear failure. Change involves learning and learning involves mistakes; when people are not given the latitude to learn from their mistakes, they may feel discouraged from participating.
- The community members lack confidence in their capacity to implement the change, or in management's commitment to the training they need.
- Excessive pressure is involved. When community members are already feeling overworked, the additional pressure brought on by the change may create resistance.
- Community members perceive that organizational objectives of the change and their own personal goals are incompatible. Resistance increases if community members believe the change will block or significantly restrict the achievement of their own personal goals.

Retrieved February 11, 2009, from http://hrweb.berkeley.edu/guides/managing-hr/managing-successfully/reorganizations#resistancetoreorg10

A Multidimensional Framework for Achieving Reorganization

It is particularly important that leadership approach the reorganization process as a change journey and not a destination that ends once the decision to reorganize has been made. Educational and business rationales must drive the change. It cannot appear that the change is simply "rearranging the furniture" to satisfy a personal whim; there must be an organizational case that drives the change effort. As such, technological, human resources, financial, and cultural change techniques must be applied to ensure a successful reorganization. Reorganization is easy, but reframing strategy, relationships, roles, culture, and strategic capacity is where the real work begins. Table 4.4 lays out some of the principles and strategic priorities that should guide an institution as it implements a Portfolio Divisional Model.

It is also vital that reorganization efforts happen in an intentional and deliberate way, and are not rushed. It may be critical early on that day-to-day work realities remain the same, as was done at the University of Connecticut. Nevertheless, the change agenda must begin immediately, launched by a series of activities designed to assuage fears and create clarity regarding the reasons for the reorganization and next steps moving forward. As always, this type of change effort is best accomplished through the broad engagement of

TABLE 4.4
Reorganization Principles and Strategic Priorities

Principles	*Strategic Priorities*	*Timeline*	*Description*	*Sample Activities*
• **Reorganization is a journey and not a destination.** Reorganization is easy to conceptualize; reframing strategy, relationships, roles, and strategic capacity is where the real work begins. • **First we try and then we do.** The change effort will take time and provide ample opportunity for trial and error. Leadership must be deliberate and take demonstrative steps without moving too fast. The key is to put something together that makes sense and will provide greater capacity moving forward. • **For the most part, day-to-day activities should remain the same.** Unless specific transitions are vital, leadership should work to preserve continuity in the beginning and communicate any shifts moving forward. • **The process works by consensus, not command.** Time must be spent together taking the first steps as a community by working together collaboratively. • **A respect for history and traditions should be maintained.** Even as change is envisioned, strategy and implementation should happen with a high level of sensitivity and respect for what existed in the past.	**Stabilize the Transition**	Immediate	Immediate and long-term activities to stabilize the transition in terms of human resources, physical space, fiscal infrastructure, communication technology, and other areas	• Senior leadership transition meeting • Communication memo to set the big-picture vision and general expectations moving forward • Central campus communication • Meetings hosted by the president or provost with key stakeholders outlining the goal of the reorganization and affirming the leadership of the CDO • Key stakeholder communication to external partners • Unit directors meetings—regular unit staff meetings • Unit director one-on-ones • Transition advisory team • Develop strategic priorities framework • Hiring of new staff roles • Establishing financial transition protocols • Establishing technology transition plan • Space allocation decisions
	Build the Division	Immediate and Long Term	Long-term activities designed to create a divisional identity, culture, mission, vision, plan, principles of practice, etc.	• Unit directors retreat • All divisional retreat • Community town hall meeting • Establishing advisory board • Regular meeting schedule • Professional development plan • Develop a principles, values, and purpose document; strategic plan; and finalized organizational chart • "Divisional branding activities" • Long-term space utilization plan finalized • Fiscal plan • Technology plan
	Evolve and Optimize Unit Capabilities	Long Term	Immediate and long-term activities designed to strengthen and evolve unit capabilities	• Unit mission reviews and alignment plans • Unit advisory board optimization • Unit hiring • Program redesign efforts • Annual reporting framework • Annual performance reviews • Professional development

numerous participants. This may involve creating a transition leadership team to help define key challenges and strengths and determine the division's overall mission, projects, and branding.

Finally, changes cannot be communicated in a top-down fashion; there must be two-way communication and ample space for campus leaders to ask questions. The CDO and his or her team should help stakeholders see the big picture and the advantages that the reorganization offers them and the broader institution. Such efforts can help create buy-in, particularly among those who are most directly affected by the shift because they have a new reporting relationship directly to the CDO.

Three Types of Reorganization Tactics

Presidents, provosts, and others must recognize that a successful reorganization will require a substantial commitment of time and effort. The CDO cannot simply take over the reins of several disparate units and initiatives and immediately expect a cohesive vision for the new division. To the contrary, this work will take time and necessitates looking at both immediate and long-term goals and challenges. The presence of a reorganization plan can both calm stakeholders and provide a vision for moving forward. Successful reorganizations have a clear set of principles that sit at the center of the reorganization. As indicated by Figure 4.7, senior leaders must put into place three broad reorganizing ideas: stabilizing activities, long-term division development activities, and unit optimization activities.

What are the defining features of each of the three reorganization tactics? As explained in Table 4.4, leaders must stabilize the transition through a number of immediate activities to allow a high level of program continuity through the first four to six months after the reorganization process. At the same time, the CDO must begin cultivating a vision for the division and engaging key stakeholders in defining the long-term mission, priorities, and values of the new aggregate unit. Finally, leaders must think about how they will optimize the various areas that compose the division to ensure synergies, utilization of best practices, responsible financial stewardship, and maximization of program outcomes. These three sets of activities are interrelated: stabilizing activities often help build the divisional identity; activities designed to build a strong strategic vision will ultimately stabilize the reorganization; and, combined, these stabilizing and vision activities will help strengthen the work taking place at the unit level.

FIGURE 4.7
Divisional Reorganization Priorities

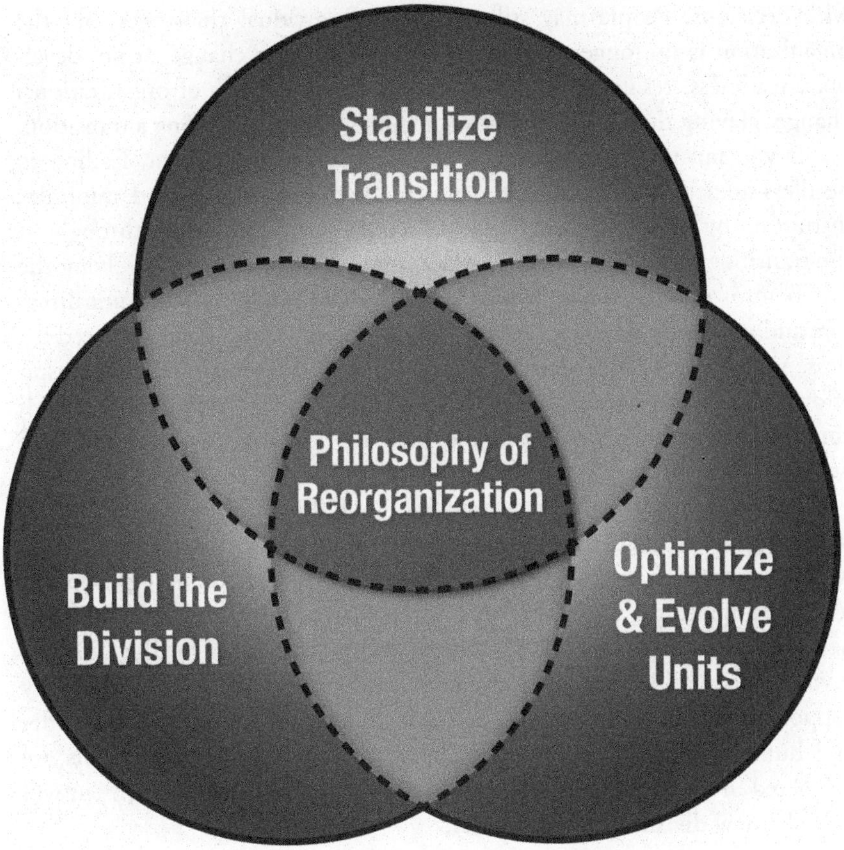

Stabilizing Activities

Stabilizing activities include communication strategies involving members of the various units and the campus community, as well as direct communications with students, faculty, and staff within the various units that are most closely involved in the reorganization. The process of stabilizing may begin before the formal decision has actually happened as it may prove prudent for the CDO and others involved in designing the new division to meet with individual departments affected by the reorganization and engage them in a conversation about priorities, challenges, and organizational possibilities.

When changes inevitably have to be made, the mechanisms must be in place to have the conversations, debate the oppositions, and move forward with decisions. People may still experience individual challenges, but the organization is no longer turned upside down by the change. It has developed readiness, resilience, and competence in the process of organizational change. Having these conversations is the first step in stabilizing a transition.

If you fail to do so, stakeholders might assume the worst, leading to needless anxiety and confusion. You can help raise morale and minimize disruption by providing clear, honest, frequent communication throughout the transition. It is vital to put in place a stakeholder meeting involving the president or provost, during which senior leaders can outline for unit directors and other key partners the goals of the reorganization and the need for those within the CDO's span of relationships to support the reorganization effort. This is also important for illustrating that senior leadership has high confidence in the reorganization and that the CDO is supported in his or her new expanded leadership duties.

In the twenty-first century, transitions of this kind may even involve migrating sensitive student information to a new server, launching a new website and social media tools, establishing a revised technology support plan, or migrating stakeholders to a new e-mail server consistent with their new administrative home. As a result, it will be important for the CDO to involve information technology experts in the transition. A new technology support plan may be required in addition to establishing new budget codes and human resources procedures. The more that administrative units are partnered in leading the reorganization, the better, as their involvement will help the new division launch quickly.

Building the Division

It is also critical for leadership to develop a plan for building the division's identity as a new organizational entity. This effort will require a series of retreats, planning meetings, and perhaps the involvement of outside consultants. A critical part of these activities will be new initiatives that begin establishing new administrative systems, priorities, direct reporting relationships, meeting structures, and a culture within the division. For example, a CDO we spoke with at a midsized institution on the East Coast mentioned establishing an annual holiday party; launching a series of professional development workshops; and developing regular e-mail communications to all students, faculty, and staff in her division.

The CDO should also establish a regular meeting schedule with all unit directors. Although individual meetings with the CDO will prove important to understanding the strengths and opportunities of each unit, group meetings are key to establishing a new culture of collaboration, shared identity, and group problem solving. This staff meeting can provide a creative process for developing solutions to problems that may be affecting multiple areas of the division and indeed the campus. Contributions from the unit directors may lead to improved understanding of the challenges and a shared sense of well-being.

Finally, branding of the new division becomes important. What should the new name of the division be? Should it pivot in a new direction, or simply take on the formal title of a CDO, who is vice chancellor for diversity, equity, and inclusion? Developing a planning group to explore issues such as title, branding, values, and mission is critical as these activities set the stage for building a new and more cohesive identity on campus. As that new identity is developed, revised websites, brochures, newsletters, and mission statements are needed to launch the rebranded division among stakeholder groups both on and off campus.

Unit Optimization

The third dimension of reorganization activities will involve efforts by the CDO and his or her core team to optimize the various units within the division. This may necessitate the CDO calling for an external review of specific units, as well as self-studies and initiatives designed to understand and then formulate a new course of action. In *The First 90 Days: Critical Success Strategies for New Leaders at All Levels,* Michael Watkins (2003) argues that new leaders must adapt their strategy to the situation they inherit. For a CDO in the midst of program reorganization, this means determining if the units involved in the reorganization are, in Watkins's words, "start-ups," "turn-around efforts," "realignment projects," or areas for which the main need is to "sustain success." We turn to these themes in Chapter 8 as a means to focus on helping new officers get off to a fast start, but provide a brief overview here because it is helpful for understanding the process of unit optimization.

In a start-up situation, the new CDO is charged with gathering the necessary human, financial, and technical expertise to launch a new effort. For example, a CDO may be charged with developing a new intergroup relations program as part of his or her activation of a new diversity plan. To get this effort off the ground, the CDO will need to establish a vision for this new unit, as well as hire the appropriate staff and then provide a "business model" for the unit.

In a turnaround, the CDO is taking on a unit that is in trouble and trying to get it back on track. In both the start-up and turnaround scenario, the focus is on creating and assembling a strategy, an operational plan, and a team that can deliver the unit's mission, whether launching a new effort or reframing an existing one. Turnaround efforts are especially difficult as incumbent leaders and staff, long-standing operational plans, and a low-performing or demoralized culture often require a tremendous amount of time and energy to shift. Too often incumbents are resistant to change because they simply do not know how to pull the plug on strategies that have not yielded the desired results.

In situations of realignment, the challenge of the CDO is to revitalize a unit that has drifted into trouble, but is still doing generally well. In a sustain-success situation, the challenge is for the leader to shoulder responsibility not only for preserving the vitality of a successful effort but to take it to the next level. In other words, the CDO has to find ways to challenge a high-performing unit to do even better.

Although leaders must immediately dive into action with start-up and turnaround efforts, the CDO can take more time with units that either need realignment or are performing well. To return to our example at the University of Connecticut, few of the units involved in the reorganization were in a turnaround situation, and none of them were in a start-up situation. Indeed, many were in a sustain-success situation, in which the CDO needed to define new challenges for these units and leverage their strength to find new synergies. One challenge might have been to help them create new interdisciplinary scholarship efforts, collaborate on new grant initiatives across cultural boundaries, and explore the intersectional nature of the student experience as a way of creating new retention and leadership development initiatives.

Understanding the history and current reality of the various units in the new division is essential to situating them in one of these general scenarios. In the absence of a multidimensional plan, many leaders fall back on entrenched politics. Many reorganization efforts fail to begin with a careful analysis of the problem, followed by a systematic analysis of alternatives, and then finally an implementation of new, workable solutions. Institutions seeking to successfully reorganize should be engaged in just such a multidimensional process to stabilize, build the division, and optimize each unit.

Summary

The most politically contested dimension of designing the CDO role on campus centers is vertical infrastructure. Who will report to whom? How high will a role sit in the formal organizational chart, and what is the position's formal rank? And will the person lead in a Collaborative Officer, Unit-Based, or Portfolio Divisional model archetype? Whereas the first three chapters of this book discussed the CDO role generally, this chapter focused on the vertical dimensions of the CDO position. It provided greater depth to our discussion of the CDODF by explaining issues pertaining to formal title and rank, archetypes of vertical structure, the process of reorganization, matrix relationships, and dynamic diversity deployment.

When designing the CDO position, senior leaders must define the formal rank and decide whether the position will carry the CDO designation. According to numerous officers, it is vital to empower this position with stature and material resources to participate at the highest levels of campus leadership. For example, by designing the role at the vice presidential level, this officer should be able to access the strategic plans, priorities, and needs of different job roles as a normal process of leadership at the senior level. That said, we identify several possible ways to configure the CDO position.

Regardless of the CDO's direct span of control, campus diversity units and others must work collaboratively, pooling their efforts around the institution's broader diversity agenda. Although the CDO may have responsibility over some diversity offices and units, this role will not—and should not—have vertical authority over every diversity capability on campus. As we have emphasized throughout, much of the CDO's most important work is accomplished through the institution's lateral diversity infrastructure, including the many individuals and organizations that share the CDO's diversity values. Regardless of whether the CDO has a portfolio of direct reporting units or not, integrative work requires human and financial resources to engage the campus community, whatever its size.

Unless we create new lateral relationships or vertically reorganize diversity offices and divisions, the CDO position often leads to challenges of coordination and control. Organizational dissonance emerges when none of the institution's dedicated diversity capabilities are placed within the direct vertical portfolio of the CDO. This dissonance may take the form of an inconsistent connection between the overall institutional diversity strategy and areas that should be working collaboratively. These conflicts can only be mediated by placing similar programs in a common area, coordinating them through matrix structures of personal relationships, or using tools like the PACE model to overcome institutional complexity.

It is critical for CDO design decisions to be considered in light of a greater infrastructure of complementary offices, units, policies, and job roles. When a new CDO role is created, a series of ripples occurs, causing many individuals to adjust. Thus, campus leaders must focus on creating a position that will allow for the institution to realize its strategic diversity agenda over time. When there is no clear chain of diversity leadership, institutions that have invested in multiple roles, units, committees, and initiatives may find themselves operating in ways that not only lack efficiency and strategic alignment, but that lead to competition over institutional territory and financial resources.

Notes

1. The first author, Dr. Damon A. Williams, served as assistant vice provost at the University of Connecticut between 2002 and 2008, assisting in the development of the Division of Multicultural and International Affairs as a senior officer in the CDO's core team.

2. In June of 2012, the interim provost created a new vice provost for diversity and CDO role organized in a collaborative officer model portfolio, featuring one of the campus's most respected tenured scholars who emerged from a national search to fill the newly designed position. At the time of appointment, the unit featured no direct reporting units and was designed in a pure collaborative officer model. Please see provost.uconn.edu, retrieved from http://today.uconn.edu/blog/2012/06/uconn-names-jeffrey-ogbar-vice-provost-for-diversity/. It remains to be seen if the divisional infrastructure will be reconstituted, or what new initiatives will emerge in this particular structure. Nevertheless, what is clear is that the interruption then the insertion of an academically focused chief diversity officer illustrates the often-random changes that diversity infrastructures can be subjected to as an institution's Diversity DNA shifts.

PART TWO

THE STRATEGIC DIVERSITY LEADERSHIP MOVEMENT

5

ISOMORPHIC DYNAMICS AND PARTNERS

Leveraging External Energy to Drive Change

> To address [today's] meta-problems we must shift from the level of the single organization to a population of organizations that share a concern for a problem. This organizational ecology perspective aims to draw together a wide range of social organizations in order to develop a multi-organizational response to meta-problems. . . . To actively adapt to the turbulent environment, independent organizations [must seek] expertise and capacity beyond what they themselves can produce. The intelligence gathering and sharing of many organizations can provide the additional knowledge needed to produce a more effective response to a set of problems.
>
> —Roberts (2004, p. 17)

Chief diversity officers (CDOs) live in the eye of a "perfect storm," as an emerging knowledge-based, global economy meets the shifting demographics of a more diverse and multicultural population. These individuals are part of a loosely connected transorganizational movement increasingly reliant on a credible and sophisticated body of research addressing diversity, equity, and inclusion issues. These officers shape and are shaped by what we refer to as the "strategic diversity leadership movement," and are at the forefront of defining the diversity profession across all sectors of organizational life.

Whereas the first chapters of this book were focused on defining the CDO role, this chapter seeks to help CDOs connect more powerfully with the strategic diversity leadership movement. More specifically, this chapter lays out the tapestry of this movement in higher education by presenting a conceptual framework that we call "institutional isomorphism," a theory for exploring the key players involved in today's diversity movement and the effort to professionalize the CDO role (DiMaggio & Powell, 1983; Meyer & Rowan, 1977). As part of this discussion we address several organizations that are helping to redefine what it means to lead credibly on diversity, equity, and inclusion issues.

Although many capable CDOs have engaged their work without formal training, there is a growing wealth of research on diversity best practices that we have termed the *artful science* of strategic diversity leadership. CDOs enjoy today an unmatched opportunity to activate their work as part of an evolving community of scholars, higher education policy makers, corporations, and others involved in implementing diversity-themed change. This chapter is aimed at strengthening how CDOs understand and ultimately participate in the growing diversity movement, tapping into a transorganizational dynamic in which possibilities are enhanced by shared learning and partnerships (Roberts, 2004). Although working with campus colleagues is essential to achieving better diversity results, the more CDOs can understand and leverage external relationships to drive change internally, the more powerful their outcomes will be. The research themes, groups, and organizations described here are far from exhaustive, but they help provide a guide to assist CDOs in their effort to activate and sustain diversity policies and programs at their campuses, and beyond.

Key Contributors to the Strategic Diversity Leadership Movement

The companion volume addresses in detail the complex "perfect storm" of social, political, and economic forces driving today's diversity movement. They include (a) the emergence of a knowledge-based global economy; (b) changing demographics; (c) persistent educational inequalities along racial, ethnic, and gender lines; (d) the crystallization of the importance of diverse experiences, both within and outside the classroom, for all students as an educational and workforce imperative; and (e) the legal and political challenges to diversity and affirmative action. To this list, and for the purpose of this book, we can add another vital category: the emergence of a growing organizational network of diversity scholars and champions who are reframing the diversity debate in the United States and empowering campus diversity efforts in new and meaningful ways. All too often, American colleges and universities are defined by a staid and tradition-bound culture, in which governing processes could be described as opaque at best. These processes contrast starkly with the aspirations of our highest diversity values, which center on creating a more open, transparent, and democratic society. Thus, it behooves CDOs to look beyond their campus reality to the scholars and policy makers who have offered the most compelling ideas about how to initiate diversity-themed change.

Over the last several years, we have observed a growing tide of individuals, institutions, and alliances that are increasingly joined in their efforts to create a foundation for college and university leaders to act more strategically around issues of diversity. To paraphrase Jim Collins (2001), many people have boarded the "strategic diversity leadership bus." These individuals form a higher education diversity ecology that has established a growing set of norms and expectations of what strategic diversity leadership should look like, while expanding the diversity conversation to include ideas about academic excellence and organizational performance. We have uncovered six emerging forces that are reshaping issues of diversity, equity, and inclusion: (a) diversity research and theory; (b) diversity officer affinity organizations; (c) diversity management and certification programs; (d) diversity conferences and symposia; (e) higher education policy organizations; and (f) cross-sector partnerships among higher education, government, and the private sector. Figure 5.1 provides a visual representation of these emerging dynamics that are changing the face of diversity work in academia, and Table 5.1 provides a narrative summary, and specific examples, of each.

Institutional Isomorphism

To anchor our discussion of the strategic diversity leadership movement, we turn to "institutional isomorphism," or *institutionalism*, as it is known in sociology (DiMaggio & Powell, 1983; Meyer & Rowan, 1977). Two pioneering theorists, Paul J. DiMaggio and Walter W. Powell (1983), have observed that organizations adopt similar models of structure and strategy, not only because of competitive dynamics and the desire to maximize their performance, but also as a way of legitimizing themselves in the eyes of their peers. Appealing to Max Weber's classic imagery of the "iron cage," DiMaggio and Powell note that environmental pressures interact dynamically, pressuring institutions to respond in similar ways, a phenomenon they refer to as *isomorphic.*

FIGURE 5.1
Dynamics of the Strategic Diversity Leadership Movement

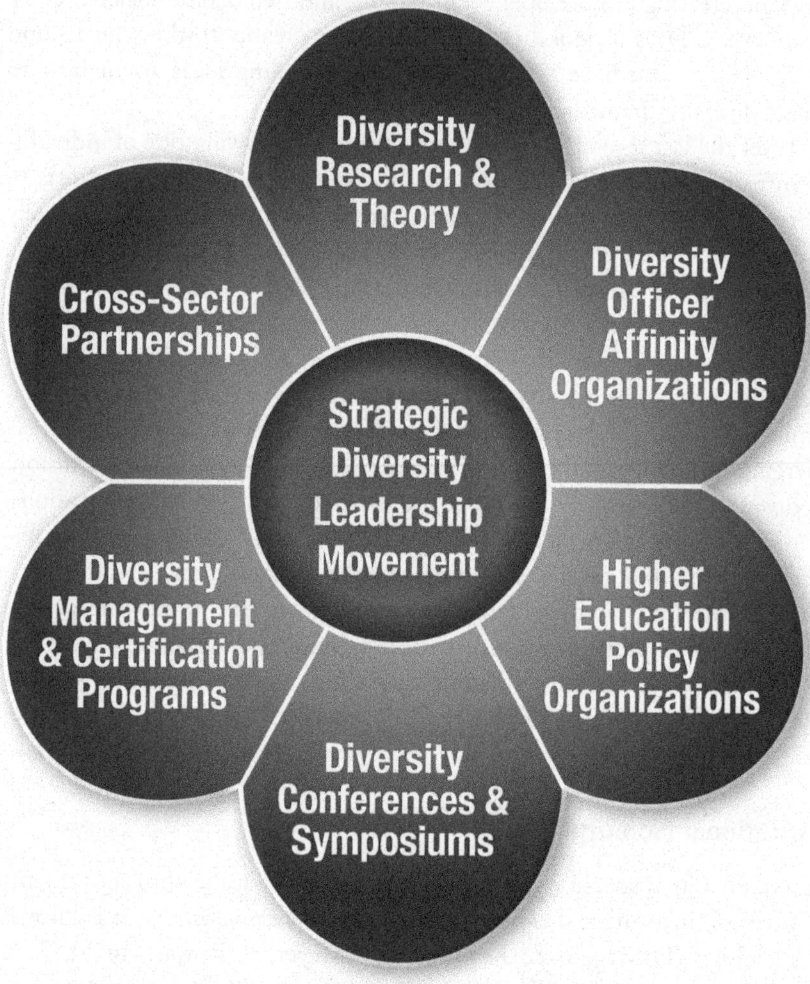

Isomorphic pressures describe the context in which institutions adopt similar strategies, structures, and processes in response to industry standards and professional demands. According to DiMaggio and Powell (1983), three types of isomorphic pressures exist: (a) coercive isomorphism, which relates to political pressure; (b) mimetic isomorphism, when uncertainty leads an organization to imitate successful peers; and (c) normative isomorphism,

TABLE 5.1
Strategic Diversity Leadership Movement Dynamics

SDL Movement Dynamics	*Description*	*Examples*
Crystallization of the higher education diversity research canon	Recent years have witnessed the emergence of higher education diversity scholars providing an increasingly sophisticated body of diversity-themed research to create more diverse, equitable, and inclusive campus learning and work environments.	• Diversity-themed scholarship in traditional academic journals • Prominent faculty exploring diversity issues at top-ranked research universities • Nationally influential diversity-themed research projects • Higher education diversity-themed research centers and institutes
Emergence of diversity officer organizations	Several diversity officer organizations, associations, and alliances have begun pooling their resources to develop best practices and collective solutions to address local challenges and define the diversity profession.	• National Association of Diversity Officers in Higher Education (NADOHE) • Liberal Arts Diversity Officers in Higher Education • Committee on Institutional Cooperation
Emergence of diversity management certification and degree programs	Diversity management certificate and degree programs are beginning to provide the critical certification and credentials that define professional fields of study and work.	• Cornell University Industrial Relations Diversity Management Program • Georgetown University Diversity Management Program • Cleveland State University Diversity Certification Program
Development of higher education diversity conferences and symposia	Higher education diversity conferences and symposia are creating opportunities for collaboration and community.	• National Conference on Race and Ethnicity (American Council on Education [ACE]) • NADOHE National Conference • Association of American Colleges and Universities (AAC&U) Diversity, Learning, and Inclusive Excellence Conference
Influence of higher education policy organizations	Higher education policy organizations are focusing on efforts to help campuses develop strategic diversity leadership programs and policies.	• AAC&U Diversity Initiatives • ACE Diversity Initiatives • National Association of Student Personnel Administrator Diversity Initiatives
Cross-sector partnerships	Powerful strategic partnerships are emerging among nonprofit organizations, foundations, corporations, and the academy designed to diversify campuses and spark a new generation of diversity leaders.	• Higher Education Recruitment Consortium • National Posse Foundation • Management Leaders for Tomorrow • Gates Millennium Scholars Program • Compact for Faculty Diversity

which is associated with building standards of practice, training, and credibility often associated with a field of professional practice.

Coercive Isomorphism

Coercive isomorphism results from formal and informal pressures imposed by an entity or organization that enjoys a degree of influence or power over an institution (DiMaggio & Powell, 1983). A classic example might be a statewide higher education system that requires all institutions to create a diversity plan or strategy. Another example might be the role played by a college's or university's board of trustees similarly demanding a new plan. In both of these examples, a formal, hierarchical power structure requires subordinate structures to advance a plan or an agenda in a top-down fashion. Two additional forms of isomorphic pressure are legislative acts, including affirmative action, immigration, and equal employment opportunity laws; and court rulings, like the Supreme Court's 1954 landmark *Brown v. Board of Education* decision. Colleges and universities can respond to these pressures in a wide variety of ways. For example, when Texas and Florida lost the ability to use race and ethnicity in competitive admissions decisions, both states created new admissions strategies based on accepting the top percentile of their states' graduating high school seniors (Horn & Flores, 2003). Although fraught with controversy and questions regarding its effectiveness, this tactic to accomplish undergraduate student diversity was in direct response to coercive isomorphic pressures requiring institutions to drop race and ethnicity from consideration in their admissions procedures, a reality that many more institutions may be forced to confront depending on the outcome of the Supreme Court's ruling in *Fisher v. University of Texas*, which is expected in mid-2013.

Isomorphic pressures can move from the bottom up as well. As Hurtado and Dey (1997) have noted, grassroots energy by communities of color, women, and others has always been part of the diversity change equation in higher education. For decades now, students, faculty, staff, alumni, and community members have pooled their collective resources to pressure institutional leaders to be proactive in their pursuit of institutional diversity goals. Box 5.1 provides an example of coercive isomorphism helping to drive change in intercollegiate athletics.

BOX 5.1
Black Coaches and Administrators: Applying Pressure to Diversify Intercollegiate Athletics

One example of isomorphic energy powering the strategic diversity leadership movement is the work of the Black Coaches and Administrators (BCA) organization. Founded in 1988, the BCA is a 501(c)3 nonprofit organization dedicated to fostering the growth and development of ethnic minorities at all levels of sport, both nationally and internationally. Throughout its 20-year history, the organization has served as a leader in the strategic diversity leadership movement, continually updating its vision and mission in a rapidly changing world.

Diversity Report Card to Drive Accountability

Among other contributions, the BCA has issued a series of studies to highlight the persistent inequity that exists in intercollegiate athletic hiring. Developed in partnership with researchers at University of Central Florida's (UCF) The Institute for Diversity and Ethics in Sport, the BCA produces multiple report cards addressing minority hiring in men's football and women's basketball. Over the past decade, the BCA has emerged as an important voice in the sports administration landscape, creating engagement around issues of diversity, specifically the lack of diversity in coaching and sports management despite the predominance of African American student athletes in many sports.

The BCA regularly reaches out to colleges and universities to review institutional practices in a variety of categories, including communication, hiring and search committees, candidates interviewed, and reasonable time. Each school is asked specific questions for each of the four categories; responses are then scored and graded for reporting purposes. Schools that hire an ethnically or racially diverse coach receive a two-point bonus added to their final score.

It is important to emphasize that the BCA reports have no formal authority to force colleges and universities to make a specific hire or behave in an equitable and inclusive manner. Those decisions are rightfully left to the governing bodies of the institutions and reflect their standards and priorities regarding diversity, academic excellence, and athletic performance. But because they promote transparency, these reports have received considerable public support (even as some have criticized their confrontational approach). They do, in fact, create heightened awareness that carries with it its own form of isomorphic energy. When an institution receives a grade of "D" or "F," its policies and programs attract the attention of media, alumni, concerned campus leaders, recruits, parents, and other stakeholders. They, in turn, can bring both subtle and direct pressures to bear on colleges and universities, disrupting or redirecting usual patterns of decision making.

(continues)

(continued)

The reports and activities of the BCA and their partners at UCF create an enhanced accountability environment crucial to the evolution of an institution's strategic diversity agenda. Using a combination of direct and indirect pressure, these and other organizations are helping to harness and direct the energy of a sustained diversity movement in higher education.

Source: Lapchick, Benoit, & Morris, 2010.

Mimetic Isomorphism

Colleges and universities often operate in ways that are nonstrategic, merely mimicking the actions of respected peers as a means to define what it means to engage legitimately and authentically in diversity issues. For example, in a scenario that we discuss at length in the companion volume to this book, when senior leadership is faced with a diversity crisis, they often draw from a diversity planning playbook that touts their institutional commitment to diversity while doing little to address the underlying problems that led to the crisis.

In these instances, the president, or some other senior leader, may make a high-profile statement about diversity's importance. He or she might commission a task force; engage in a yearlong process of dialogue and planning; and, at a minimum, roll out a diversity plan for the campus. In these instances, senior leaders often mimic what they have seen at other institutions responding to a campus diversity crisis. Indeed, institutions that routinely compare themselves with one another often have similar infrastructures, plans, and other markers of credibility. To this end, if one were to pick randomly from the diversity plans of several different academic institutions, one would probably see the same types of ideas. This is because to do anything differently is to risk engaging in an illegitimate approach to diversity. The common expectation is that an institution's efforts should be consistent with the canon of diversity-themed action.

One of the primary reasons that this occurs stems from the fact that many higher education leaders are hired from within and rise to leadership based on limited professional experience, often in just one or two institutions. As a result, in some instances their leadership vision can be overdetermined by a narrow range of past experiences. Although these experiences can be valuable in certain respects, problems emerge when leaders are closed to new possibilities. Too often, senior leaders either work with ineffective models or are out of step with the most recent trends in the strategic diversity leadership field. Other times, they may halt progress in a novel campus diversity approach that may point the way toward new and unforeseen possibilities.

Even for effective CDOs, the higher education landscape is filled with threats. We spoke with several individuals who felt that their voices and expertise often fell on deaf ears, particularly when faced by senior leaders who wanted to pursue their own understanding of diversity work. We encountered no fewer than five nationally preeminent institutions where CDO divisional infrastructures were radically dismantled after new leadership came on board, a point that we make in the University of Connecticut case study. In each of these situations, new leadership was not the only common denominator. In addition, each of the institutions was characterized by diversity efforts in which officers led a portfolio of diversity units that featured traditional diversity units (e.g., multicultural affairs offices, cultural centers) and nontraditional diversity units (e.g., honors program, institutional research, etc.). In the words of one vice president for diversity at a large Midwestern institution, "Nearly overnight I saw my shop cobbled up into various pieces as campus vultures took the pieces that they had been coveting for years and left the rest for my successor." When we probed further to find out why this happened, his response echoed the comments of several other diversity officers:

> My structure was different. We had intentionally created a portfolio of diversity and nondiversity units as a way of repositioning the diversity discussion. However, it was nontraditional in many ways. But when the new president came on board, it bothered her from the beginning because it did not look like her previous institutions. The struggle to build something new that was really working at our institution just did not matter to her. What mattered was re-creating what she knew and as a result, she totally ignored the recommendations that I offered as I was leaving. She dismantled over a decade of effort putting together a special situation that, candidly, I believe was working.

Normative Isomorphism

The third type of pressure, normative isomorphism, relates directly to the process of professionalization (Wilensky, 1964). We define *professionalization* as the collective effort of a group to define the conditions and pedagogies of its work, control the means of production within a given domain of work, and define a set of best practices with respect to approaching the work (Larson, 1977). As we discuss here, normative isomorphic energies are at play across all organizational life, as diversity leaders interact with one another to form a more cohesive and evidence-based approach to leading diversity-themed change.

Indeed, we are often asked whether the CDO role is a profession, even though many officers have decades of experience working throughout the educational, government, corporate, and nonprofit spheres. We have already cited H. L. Wilensky's work in the introduction to this book. In a similar vein, DiMaggio and Powell (1983) identified two forces that form the primary origins of normative isomorphic energy: (a) the development of professional training standards, which are anchored in the efforts of colleges, universities, and other training entities; and (b) the emergence of umbrella professional associations and networks that help spread best practices across organizations and entities.

College and university degree programs and certificates are important platforms for the development of professional norms, skills, and expectations among managers and leaders in the emerging diversity field. Such mechanisms create a talent pool of members who share similar skills and are able to draw on proven practices drawn from contemporary theory and scholarship. Box 5.2 provides an overview of Dr. Christopher Metzler's efforts at Cornell and Georgetown University to develop programs that have helped crystallize the strategic diversity leadership profession.

BOX 5.2

Christopher J. Metzler: Developing Certification and Degree Programs to Drive the Strategic Diversity Leadership Movement

As professor and associate dean of human resources at Georgetown University, Christopher Metzler is helping to drive the professionalization of the strategic diversity leadership movement. A longtime leader in diversity management and human resources, Metzler has created two noteworthy diversity credential programs designed to strengthen the ability of diversity leaders to engage on diversity issues in colleges and universities, corporations, and public and nonprofit institutions.

Beginning his work at Cornell University, Metzler established both certification and master's degree programs in the area of diversity management. He also established the "Chief Diversity Officers Roundtable," a series of conferences designed to bring leading officers together to share best practices, establish a support network, and initiate research relevant to their specific work areas. The Cornell program now regularly generates millions of dollars in external funding.

(continues)

(continued)

Since transitioning to Georgetown University, Metzler has created an interdisciplinary diversity management master's degree program in the School of Continuing Studies. The two-year program includes several foundational classes essential to leading as a CDO, as well as courses in strategic planning, organizational development, general business principles, intergroup conflict, international development, and social psychology. Specific program areas include:

- *Introduction to Diversity as Organizational Change* addresses diversity and inclusion efforts in the context of change management, requiring students to develop strategic plans and implementation activities that will create interpersonal, group, intergroup, and organization-wide change. This course also provides the theoretical foundations of diversity-themed change as an applied behavioral science.
- *Fundamentals of Conducting a Diversity Assessment* helps students develop their organizational learning lens by providing them with the practical tools necessary to conduct an organizational needs assessment. The course also provides a foundation in research design, project execution, and results analysis to help meet the policy and program needs of organizations.
- *Facilitating Strategic Diversity Planning and Goal Setting* helps students to develop the type of skills necessary to facilitate and lead diversity-themed change. This course provides participants with a strategic planning model that blends facilitation skills and activities to help organizations develop a mission statement, an organizational vision, specific objectives, and individual employee action plans.
- *EEO Law: The Fundamentals of Compliance* provides students with a foundation in equal employment opportunity law and its relevance to the practice of strategic diversity leadership.
- *Diversity in Talent Management* focuses on helping leaders to understand how to recruit, train, develop, and retain a diverse and constantly changing workforce.
- *Diversity Leadership* helps participants understand how to demonstrate their commitment to diversity. This program emphasizes team building and ways to capitalize on the educational and economic benefits of a diverse working environment.

Dr. Metzler is currently working to help develop similar credentialing programs at other institutions. These efforts are helping the field of strategic diversity leadership to stabilize and gain legitimacy in powerful ways.

Source: Personal interview with Christopher Metzler, May 5, 2009.

Meyer and Rowan (1977) argue that in our age of corporate and institutional mergers, organizational culture is becoming ever more characterized by a focus on best practices. This dynamic can be felt also in the realm of regional and national diversity affinity organizations, including the National Association of Diversity Officers in Higher Education (NADOHE), which is creating a professional community of practice that seeks to nurture the CDO profession in higher education.

As CDOs come to appreciate these forces, they can more effectively access their energies and resources. Change is often about marshaling energy to create new strategies and tactics. The more we generate positive isomorphic energy, the more influence our diversity efforts will have. Isomorphic energy abounds in the academy, and diverse stakeholders should be involved in tapping this energy in an effort to reinforce and steer the strategic diversity leadership movement. In the following pages, we provide an in-depth description of institutional isomorphism and its relevance to college and university diversity efforts.

Crystallization of the Higher Education Diversity Research Canon

According to Andrew Abbott (1988), for any profession to emerge, the skills required to perform that work must be directly linked to a structured body of knowledge. Indeed, the ability of a profession to define and sustain its area of focus is often directly connected to the breadth and depth of its intellectual foundation. Academic scholarship legitimizes professional work by clarifying its dimensions and connecting these dimensions to broader cultural values and schools of thought.

Empirical Foundations of the Strategic Diversity Leadership Movement

Sixty years ago, institutions had very little empirical grounding on which to engage issues of diversity, equity, and inclusion. Today, a robust body of literature exists across a range of fields, providing the intellectual foundation of the strategic diversity leadership movement. These scholarship areas include:

- Enhancing the retention and academic achievement of diverse groups[1]
- Interpreting legal and policy changes to develop institutional policy around the use of race- and gender-conscious admission, financial aid, and employment decisions[2]
- Recruiting and retaining diverse faculty[3]
- Studying and improving the campus climate[4]

- Building high-impact intergroup dialogue programs and initiatives[5]
- Promoting minorities and women to senior administrative roles[6]
- Developing CDO capacity[7]
- Fostering diversity-themed organizational change efforts[8]
- Assessing the educational benefits of diverse experiences[9]
- Strengthening the identity and development of diverse groups[10]
- Assessing diversity and equity progress as a tool to inspire change in higher education[11]

This scholarship has created a powerful evidence-based platform for diversity efforts and constitutes an important tool for overcoming resistance to policies and programs that promote diversity, equity, and inclusion. To be effective in building support for their ideas, CDOs must understand and know how to wield the literature in several different areas. Indeed, this was a workshop topic at the 2009 Association for the Study of Higher Education (ASHE) annual meeting, as CDOs joined with higher education diversity scholars to discuss the myriad ways that diversity officers might apply research to their efforts. Box 5.3 provides a general overview of how diversity research has helped drive faculty diversification strategies across the country.

BOX 5.3

Using Faculty Diversification Research to Encourage Change

Faculty diversification is one of the most pressing challenges facing higher education today. In response, Claremont Graduate University professor Daryl Smith and her colleagues have examined the faculty search processes of several institutions and have developed a sophisticated understanding of critical issues in the diversity hiring process. Their research concluded that achieving a diversity hire often hinges on "interrupting the usual strategies," including such efforts as creating a diversity-themed statement in the position description, leveraging strategic diversity hiring resources, and engaging in special diversity-themed outreach.

The study goes on to highlight a number of myths surrounding faculty diversity, including the notion that prospective faculty will avoid some teaching environments no matter what the job, or that only the wealthiest institutions can win bidding wars for a talented diversity candidate.

The authors have used this research and related scholarship in dozens of conversations to illustrate the myths, challenges, and techniques required to move the faculty diversity agenda on campus. With each presentation, new isomorphic energy is released, creating a shared understanding of how to advance faculty diversity efforts and move beyond the myths that can freeze campus leaders in their tracks.

Source: Smith, Turner, Osei-Kofi, & Richards, 2004.

Diversity Research Centers and Institutes

Where ethnic and gender studies departments have been a powerful force in diversifying the curriculum and research capacities of colleges and universities, new diversity research centers have emerged to add their contributions to driving change at their institutions. A review of university websites and discussions with leaders in the diversity research field have helped us identify several diversity-themed research centers at several institutions (Table 5.2). Although each center is unique, they all have a similar mission to engage research, transform institutional life, and expand the landscape of scholarship that exists around issues of diversity, equity, and inclusion on college and university campuses, the corporate sector, and in other areas of organizational life.

We began our discussion of the higher education diversity landscape with a discussion of research and scholarship because understanding and leveraging evidence-based practice is fundamental to implementing effective diversity change. Strategic diversity leadership must be grounded in the scholarship and guidance of the nation's leading diversity scholars and thought leaders. Yet our discussion should not be mistaken as indicating that this scholarship is automatically finding its way into practice. Although credible research is available, many individuals whom we spoke with felt that it was questionable how well these insights could be translated into practice. As one vice chancellor at a large research university in the Northeast stated:

> The research is out there, but the greatest problem is getting your leadership on board with it. First, you have to make them aware. Next, you have to help them to understand that it is credible and that the people doing it are not simply diversity advocates, but researchers doing peer-reviewed scholarship at the nation's leading institutions. Then you have to translate the research into practice. Unlike 30 years ago, when I started this work, senior leaders can no longer say, "So, where is your evidence?" I have the evidence—the social science foundation is there.

The ability to overcome the distance between research and practice helps determine our ability to create material change in the culture and improve outcomes at our institutions. Some techniques we have encountered include

TABLE 5.2
Sample of Diversity Research Centers and Institutes in Higher Education

Institution	*Center*	*Founding*	*Mission*
University of California, Los Angeles	Civil Rights Project/ Proyecto Derechos Civiles	Founded in 1996 and relocated and renamed in 2007	The mission of the Civil Rights Project/Proyecto Derechos Civiles is to help renew the civil rights movement by bridging the worlds of ideas and action, to serve as a preeminent source of intellectual capital within the social justice movement, and to deepen the understanding of the issues that must be resolved to achieve racial and ethnic equity in the twenty-first century.
University of Southern California	Center for Urban Education (CUE)	1999	The CUE engages in socially conscious research and develops tools for institutions of higher education to produce equity in student outcomes.
University of Illinois	Center on Democracy in a Multiracial Society (CDMS)	2002	A central aim of the CDMS is to promote interdisciplinary approaches for examining issues pertaining to race, ethnicity, gender, class, age, sexuality, disability, religion, and citizenship status. In addition to analyzing the national dynamics of racial divisions and of democratic possibilities, the Center supports transnational and international diversity research.
The Ohio State University	The Kirwin Institute	2003	The Kirwin Institute's mission includes (a) fostering critical and creative thinking on concepts about race and ethnicity; (b) examining hierarchies and systems of control, domination, and oppression; (c) exploring the interrelatedness of race and ethnicity to other foci such as gender and class; (d) examining the cultural, economic, political, and social experiences of racial and ethnic minority groups in the Americas; and (e) interrogating the material conditions of life and achievement among groups who are systematically subjected to systems of domination and oppression.
University of Washington	Diversity Research Institute (DRI)	2004	The DRI focuses on generating interdisciplinary knowledge about diversity, social justice, and institutional transformation. The institute also hosts an annual research conference and lecture series, supports a number of diversity-related events across the university, and works closely with other research centers to encourage and support faculty research on underserved communities.

TABLE 5.2 (Continued)

Institution	*Center*	*Founding*	*Mission*
University of Michigan	National Center for Institutional Diversity (NCID)	2005	NCID catalyzes innovative approaches to diversity opportunities within academia, other major social institutions, the nation, and the world. Addressing diversity in its broadest sense, the NCID launches and advances national exemplars that foster concrete, lasting social change.
Northwestern University	Center on the Science of Diversity (CSD)	2008	The mission of CSD is to promote academic, managerial, and educational research about the social effect of diversity. The center's academic team is composed of scholars from across Northwestern University, with representation from the Kellogg School of Management, the Weinberg College of Arts and Sciences, the School of Education and Social Policy, the School of Communication, and the Medill School of Journalism.
University of Minnesota	Institute for Diversity, Equity, and Advocacy (IDEA)	2009	IDEA convenes scholars from the university and around the world to collaborate across disciplines, departments, colleges, and campuses. In addition to supporting the development of new research, the institute enhances retention and faculty diversity by fostering stronger ties between faculty and the local community.
University of Wisconsin	Wisconsin Equity and Inclusion (WEI) Laboratory	2010	The WEI Lab is dedicated to conducting both basic and applied research on topics of equity and inclusion in education, with a particular focus on higher education. The WEI Lab defines equity and inclusion as efforts taken by organizations to ensure educational success for all their constituents. Researchers partner with the institution's CDO; conduct regular evaluations; assess activities; and conduct studies on various diversity, equity, and inclusion issues.

facilitated dialogues among key leaders, informal discussion groups that work to implement grassroots change, dedicated teams that work to take research insights and turn them into new initiatives and training programs, and taking senior leaders to diversity-themed conferences and trainings. At the heart of this effort is engaging leaders in the change process and helping them to develop or, in some instances, reframe their understanding of the work.

Diversity Officer Organizations, Associations, and Alliances

Diversity affinity networks can serve as innovative hot spots, catalyzing the strategic diversity leadership movement. Among the more prominent include the NADOHE, the Committee for Institutional Cooperation, the Consortium of Liberal Arts Colleges Diversity Officers (LADO), the Central Pennsylvania Association of Liaison and Officers of Multicultural Affairs (PALOMA), the Northeastern Pennsylvania Diversity Educational Counsel (NEPDEC), and the California Council of Cultural Centers (CaCCCHE). There are also several public higher education system-wide diversity organizations, including those within the Minnesota, Pennsylvania, and Wisconsin state systems. Table 5.3 provides an overview of several CDO affinity networks.

Networking Movement

When individuals or organizations realize they have common goals, they tend to form groups that then interact with each other, coalescing around similar challenges, needs, and questions (DiMaggio & Powell, 1983). Both formal and informal diversity networks and organizations have emerged in an effort to help campus leaders become more successful in leading diversity-themed change. According to one officer at a small liberal arts institution in the Northeast, "Just the ability to sit and talk with my colleagues about what is going on is cathartic. This is difficult and stressful work; coming together once or twice a year to share war stories helps me to go home and do what I need to do."

By adopting empirical research findings, engaging in professional associations, and networking formally and informally, diversity leaders are building the connective tissue of the strategic diversity leadership movement. According to DiMaggio and Powell (1983), institutional fields have crystallized in response to

> an increase in the extent of interaction among organizations in the field; the emergence of sharply defined inter-organizational structures of domination and patterns of coalition; an increase in the information load with which organizations in a field must contend; and the development of a mutual awareness among participants in a set of organizations that they are involved in a common enterprise. (p. 148)

Diversity affinity organizations offer great platforms for new ideas and isomorphic energies to emerge. Although on-campus efforts are clearly central, external energy is also important. Too often, campus diversity leaders strive to overcome obstacles that are grounded in decades of tradition,

TABLE 5.3
Sample of Diversity Officer Affinity Networks and Alliances

Organization	*Description*
Committee on Institutional Cooperation (CIC) Senior Diversity Officers	Formed in the early 1990s, the CIC is a consortium of Big Ten member institutions and the University of Chicago. It convenes to provide mutual support, share best practices, and build opportunities for everyone in higher education. Participants include the most senior diversity administrators at their respective campuses. The consortium shares promising practices, provides support around major diversity challenges, and offers a supportive forum for diversity officers.
Liberal Arts Colleges Diversity Officers (LADO)	LADO is a consortium of liberal arts institutions that meets regularly to discuss the particular challenges and opportunities of leading diversity efforts in liberal arts institutions.
Central Pennsylvania Association of Liaisons and Officers of Multicultural Affairs (PALOMA)	PALOMA is a consortium of diversity officers from across Pennsylvania that includes both small liberal arts colleges and larger universities. This group provides professional development and support, and shares best practices across institutions.
Northeastern Pennsylvania Diversity Educational Counsel (NEPDEC)	NEPDEC's goals are to create a more inclusive, dynamic culture in its region and to prepare for increasingly complex and diverse communities and workplaces. To achieve these goals, it (a) provides educational programming, (b) supports member diversity initiatives, (c) organizes networking and social events for relaxed interaction and sharing, (d) builds alliances among historically isolated groups, and (e) uses shared resources more efficiently and effectively.
California Council of Cultural Centers in Higher Education (CaCCCHE)	CaCCCHE affirms the ongoing efforts of existing centers, provides leadership for the establishment of new initiatives, creates opportunities for networking and personal growth in the field, and promotes a philosophy that recognizes the opportunities and benefits of a diverse learning and work environment.
The National Diversity Council (NDC)	The NDC is the first nonprofit organization to bring together the private, public, educational, and nonprofit sectors to discuss the benefits of a multicultural society. The NDC serves as an advocate for the value of diversity and inclusion, supporting statewide and regional affiliates, and fostering an understanding of diversity as a dynamic strategy for business success and community well-being. The NDC seeks to cultivate a nationwide network of affiliated councils to advance diversity by transforming our communities into inclusive environments where individuals are empowered to reach their fullest potential.
National Association of Diversity Officers in Higher Education (NADOHE)	NADOHE supports collective efforts to lead member institutions toward the attainment of their strategic diversity goals. The organization disseminates empirical evidence to inform diversity initiatives, identify and circulate exemplary practices, provide professional development for aspiring diversity officers, inform and influence policy decisions, and foster networking opportunities for diversity professionals and champions.

whether the issue is faculty hiring, performance evaluation, or student advising. To overcome a culture that is resistant to change, diversity advocates need to band together with other leaders at similar institutions. By uniting their voices, CDOs add power and credibility to their arguments. Box 5.4 provides a powerful example of an aligning strategy pursued by the LADO consortium.

BOX 5.4
Building Strategic Relationships and an Action-Oriented Agenda Through the Liberal Arts Diversity Officers Consortium

Although usually composed mainly of senior diversity administrators, diversity affinity organizations regularly invite nondiversity professionals to participate in their discussions and trainings. The LADO consortium illustrates a powerful example of this type of strategic partnership effort. The group emerged to focus on the unique challenges of leading diversity efforts in smaller, usually private, liberal arts institutions. Originally a fairly informal network, they have become increasingly formal in recent years. They regularly gather to collaborate on common initiatives, share best practices, and engage in an action-oriented effort to move the diversity agenda at their respective institutions.

In our research for this book, we talked with several members who played a prominent role bringing LADO to life. According to the dean of the college and CDO at one particular institution, "We wanted to come together and build a mini-movement that would really help us advance the agenda in an organic way. Our focus is not simply to come together and talk, but to be an action-oriented group that mobilizes to get something done."

After a series of organizing meetings, the group decided to hold a conference on the future of diversity initiatives in liberal arts colleges. Williams College and Columbia University's Center for Institutional and Social Change cohosted the conference and Professors Susan Sturm and Lani Guinier served as facilitators. The meeting brought together the presidents, chief academic officers, and CDOs from nine liberal arts colleges to address (a) the frameworks or strategies for advancing diversity as a transformational concept and a core value, (b) how to build collaborations and sustain innovation in difficult economic times, and (c) how diversity efforts can be used to create a strong foundation for advancing the core values of their institutions.

The central theme of this meeting was that campus leaders have to be in conversation with one another if they are going to find a new approach to leading campus

(continues)

(continued)

diversity efforts. Particularly impressive, LADO focused on bringing together leaders who could share their experience and discuss the transformative energy they created within their institutions' most senior leadership. According to the vice president for diversity and strategic planning at a highly selective eastern liberal arts college, the "conversation was only going to matter if we got real decision makers into the room. For this reason, I enlisted my president to attend the meeting. The only way that institutions could attend was if their president, provost, and CDO were all in attendance. If all three could not be in attendance, the institution could not participate."

At the core of the LADO philosophy is the belief that a more dynamic approach to change will only emerge if presidents and provosts take collective ownership of the diversity discussion. The primary purpose of this meeting was to bring powerful decision makers from different institutions together. As a result, the conference created isomorphic energies that helped foster new strategic diversity efforts at various campuses. These leaders realized that it is more productive to discuss new possibilities with a group of their peers than to address these issues in isolation.

The National Association of Diversity Officers in Higher Education

In 2006, the American Council on Education (ACE) helped support the foundation of the NADOHE, which almost overnight registered 150 charter-member institutions. It now serves as one of the nation's largest formal umbrella organizations for CDOs and represents nearly 200 member institutions. The group describes itself as the principal organization of chief and senior diversity officers at institutions of higher education.

In remarks given at the 2009 annual meeting of the ASHE, inaugural president William Harvey stated that NADOHE was founded in response to "the growing need for higher education to leverage and maximize investments in diversity initiatives, provide opportunities for cross-institutional exchange and fertilization of ideas, and to enhance professional standards" among diversity professionals in higher education. Members host their annual meeting during the ACE presidential leadership conference, and have founded, in collaboration with the American Psychological Association, the *Journal of Diversity in Higher Education*. The launching of NADOHE and a peer-reviewed academic journal has empowered the strategic diversity leadership movement and sharpened the ability of diversity champions everywhere to lead change efforts. Box 5.5 provides reflections by William Harvey, NADOHE's inaugural president.

BOX 5.5

Comments by William Harvey on Launching the National Association of Diversity Officers in Higher Education

Quite frankly, what we realized was that the impetus for this change came, to some significant degree, from the corporate world, where these positions were already entrenched in some significant way long before they were well established in the academy. To get a sense of the field, I convened a small group of CDOs in 2003, involving members of the academy and the corporate community. Around 30 people gathered at The Ohio State University; about two-thirds of them were CDOs from the postsecondary world and a third were CDOs from the corporate world.

We wanted to find out what, if anything, were the kind of reference points that individuals used to go about their jobs, and the similarities and differences there. Obviously, we found out that while some of them were easily identifiable and quite pronounced, others were more subtle. Every time we would talk to the corporate CDOs about this thing called "tenure"—you know, lifetime employment without termination—they would say, "What? How does that work again?"

What we realized was that the emerging CDO role was probably going to be extended. And so we began to look for ways to identify members of this group and ways to pull them together into an organization. This was one of the key outcomes of that meeting. We knew we needed a CDO organization in the academic community where we could organize and learn to speak with a collective voice. A couple of years later we got the organization up and running. By then I had left the American Council on Education and was serving as CDO at the University of Virginia.

We spent a lot of time organizing and trying to identify institutions that were interested in having a position of this kind and being a part of our organization. We identified about 120 institutions in 2005. We put out a call to individuals from those institutions to come and meet with us at the *Educating All of Our Nation Conference* in Phoenix, Arizona. We thought we might get 35 to 40 people to come. Well, we had 85 people in the room from institutions around the country. Clearly, people felt very seriously about the need for an organization, and so a year later, we implemented what is now known as the National Association for Diversity Officers in Higher Education. We started out with about 135 members and have been moving along ever since.

Source: Panel discussion, *How Institutional Chief Diversity Officers Use Our Research*, ASHE 2009 transcript.

The presence of higher education diversity officer umbrella organizations like NADOHE is consistent with other infrastructures that we have seen both within and across organizational sectors. Dennis Kennedy, founder of the National Diversity Council, has led the development of numerous diversity councils in states across the country, bringing together diversity champions and leaders in the higher education, corporate, nonprofit, and K–12 communities. His efforts are focused on sharing best practices and creating a more powerful strategic diversity leadership movement.

Professional Development: Diversity Leadership Degree and Certificate Programs

Professional development is an important key to strengthening the strategic diversity leadership movement and legitimizing the role of CDOs. Put simply, professional development is the process of acquiring new skills that relate to one's job responsibilities and work environment (Jasper, 2006). It may include a number of different learning opportunities, ranging from workshops and professional development trainings to structured certification and degree programs that include bachelor and graduate degrees in a particular area of expertise.

Developing CDO Competencies

Our qualitative research uncovered that a majority of CDOs have developed their craft through a confluence of personal experiences, on-the-job training, study and research into related disciplines, and participation in professional associations like those we discussed previously. Very few officers in higher education have participated in structured certification and degree programs in strategic diversity leadership. Indeed, our research into the professional development of CDOs who participated in our national survey revealed that most officers were interested in attending executive education opportunities focused on the various dimensions of the strategic diversity leadership field. As we note in Table 5.4, over 80 percent of CDOs would like to attend a diversity leadership institute centered on assessing campus diversity, developing and implementing campus diversity plans, conducting fund-raising for diversity initiatives, overcoming faculty resistance to diversity, infusing diversity into the curriculum, and managing organizational change. CDOs expressed greatest support for workshops focused on the recruitment and retention of diverse faculty. Even the least frequently supported topic, enhancing minority student success in the science, technology, engineering, and math (STEM) fields, held a strong degree of interest for CDOs, at 67 percent.

TABLE 5.4
Potential Topics for a Strategic Diversity Leadership Institute

Potential Professional Development Topic	*CDO Support*
Assessing campus diversity	82%
Developing and implementing institutional diversity plans	84%
Faculty diversification—recruitment and retention	86%
Building intergroup relations and dialogue programs	70%
Diversity in the wake of legal challenges and attacks on affirmative action	76%
Increasing minority students' success in the STEM disciplines	67%
Fundraising for diversity initiatives	82%
Developing effective diversity task forces and commissions	71%
Overcoming faculty resistance	83%
Forging community collaborations	74%
Infusing diversity into the curriculum	83%
Managing organizational change	80%

STEM, Science, technology, engineering, and mathematics.

Although these strategic management and faculty and curricular diversity topics led the way, it should be noted that officers across the board expressed interest in receiving professional development in all of the areas surveyed. The high level of interest in obtaining additional training is an indication of the need to strengthen this aspect of the strategic diversity leadership movement. Our capacity to produce professionals who have formally studied the strategic diversity leadership literature, and who have obtained a specialized certificate or degree in this area, is essential to the legitimacy of the diversity leadership movement.

College and University Diversity Management Certification Programs

Although the number of for-profit diversity training and credentialing programs is growing, undergraduate, graduate, and executive degree programs are just beginning to emerge on college and university campuses. Consequently, the overwhelming majority of CDOs do not possess a degree or certificate in strategic diversity leadership, even though they may possess degrees in higher education administration, leadership development, organizational behavior and management, industrial psychology, or some other management field.

Like diversity affinity networks, the presence of strategic diversity leadership degree and certification programs is foundational to the strategic diversity leadership movement and the long-term potential of the CDO role to evolve into a fully professionalized position in organizational life. Cleveland State University, Cornell University, and Georgetown University are at the forefront of developing these kinds of programs (Table 5.5). Each of these institutions offers a combination of either a certificate or graduate degree in the general area of diversity and inclusion management. These programs focus on reframing strategic diversity leadership as a process of organizational change and require leadership development, assessment, and an understanding of cultural dynamics. Programs also focus on both theory and practice, providing students with frameworks and tools that they can deploy after graduating from the program. Although not focused specifically on leading diversity and inclusion efforts on college and university campuses, these programs offer powerful learning opportunities for developing a general approach to strategic diversity leadership that can be helpful in corporate, nonprofit, health, and higher education environments.

These programs have served as trailblazers of the strategic diversity leadership movement, providing executive and traditional educational programs designed to strengthen the core competencies of diversity leaders. As noted by DiMaggio and Powell (1983), core degree programs constitute a powerful tool for stabilizing an area of work, rendering it a profession. The diversity certificate and degree movement constitutes another step in the development of the strategic diversity management field. Over time, its emergence as a new area of applied management may prove similar to the development of higher education and student affairs administration, which emerged nearly 50 years ago as individuals in sociology, K–12 education, psychology, and other areas came together to develop what was, at the time, a new field of study and practice.

Diversity Conferences and Symposia

A consistent opportunity for CDOs to strengthen their professional communities occurs at local, regional, and national diversity conferences, symposia, and events. Prominent among these is the National Conference on Race and Ethnicity in American Higher Education (NCORE), which regularly brings together

TABLE 5.5
Sample of Diversity Management Degree and Certificate Programs

Institution	*Description*	*Graduate*	*Certificate*
Cleveland State University	Offered through the Department of Psychology, the Masters in Diversity Management Program is designed to prepare practitioners to meet the challenges of diversity and inclusion. Students develop expertise in the areas of organizational behavior, strategic management, diversity management, diversity and inclusion education, interpersonal relations, change leadership, collaborative conflict management, cultural competency, intergroup dynamics, and human resources management. A master's degree in psychology is granted to those who complete a program focused on the interaction of theory, case studies, and real-world application.	✔	✔
Cornell University	The Cornell Industrial Labor Relations program offers a diversity management certificate focused on helping leaders to manage diversity in the workforce. It also offers a Certified Diversity Professional/Advanced Practitioner program, coaching services, and on-site training for CDOs and other diversity practitioners.		✔
Georgetown University	Georgetown University's Masters Degree of Professional Studies in Human Resources allows for a concentrated major in Diversity and Inclusion Management. Meanwhile, the University's Certificate of Diversity Strategy, granted through the School of Continuing Studies, is a professional development certification program. Both are designed to help individuals gain the skills needed to help organizations implement a strategic, long-term, sustainable approach to diversity and inclusion management. The courses introduce participants to the latest diversity research and provide functional and relevant tools to plan and implement a sustainable diversity strategy.	✔	✔

over 3,000 primarily higher education diversity professionals. The biannual Association of American Colleges and Universities' (AAC&U) Diversity, Learning, and Pathways to Inclusive Excellence meeting regularly brings together nearly 1,000 participants. Finally, the National Association of Student Personnel Administrators' (NASPA) diversity assessment conference and NADOHE's annual conference take place in coordination with the ACE presidential meeting.

In addition, several institutions and public systems of higher education have started hosting regular diversity conferences and meetings. We have uncovered meetings and conferences sponsored by the Tennessee State System Board of Regents, the University of Minnesota, the University of Oregon, the University of Denver, Ohio University, Towson University, the University of Wisconsin, Pacific University, Washington and Jefferson College, the Pennsylvania State System of Higher Education, and The Ohio State University, among others. These meetings have focused on making meaning of the current diversity movement and thinking through the types of strategies and conversations that we must have to move a strategic diversity agenda forward. Perhaps the best aspect of these conferences is the opportunity they afford for developing relationships and collaborations among attendees.

Higher Education Policy Organizations

Higher education policy organizations also play a major role in promoting the strategic diversity leadership movement. Organizations like AAC&U, ACE, the Association of Public and Land-Grant Universities, NASPA, and others represent thousands of institutions working together to advance campus diversity initiatives.

The Association of American Colleges and Universities

For decades, the AAC&U has been a prominent force on organizational diversity issues. Caryn Musil, Mildred Garcia, Yolanda Moses, and Daryl Smith (1995) have articulated one of the first meta-summaries of how diverse experiences affect college students and have done more recent work focused on models of institutional change and transformation (Clayton-Pedersen, O'Neill, & Musil, 2009; Clayton-Pedersen, Parker, Smith, Moreno, & Teraguchi, 2006). Thanks to their efforts, and the work of many, AAC&U has issued guiding principles on diversity efforts in a post-Michigan Supreme Court environment, *Making Excellence Inclusive.*

With funding from the Ford Foundation, AAC&U convened a national conversation with diversity champions and scholars to address the future of diversity, equity, and inclusion in higher education. As part of its efforts, AAC&U assembled three research teams to develop a summary understanding of topics critical to the discussion of diversity and excellence in the new millennium. These research teams produced unique monographs that addressed several key strategic diversity leadership themes, including the importance of diversity to student learning and engagement; the continuing significance of racial and ethnic equity; and the need to tackle diversity issues from an organizational, strategic perspective (Bauman, Bustillos, Bensimon, Brown, & Bartee, 2005; Milem, Chang, & Antonio, 2005; Williams, Berger, & McClendon, 2005).

Since the publication of these monographs, AAC&U has continued to evolve the *Making Excellence Inclusive* agenda, incorporating principles around student learning, racial equity, and organizational change into its conferences, summer institutes, and continuing initiatives. Its vision has seeded inclusive excellence efforts at hundreds of colleges and universities. Some institutions have attempted to develop a policy framework and strategic plan based on inclusive excellence principles, others have attempted to create high-level marketing campaigns centered on the idea, and still others have used the concept as a way of bringing together all of their preexisting diversity efforts under a common organizational umbrella. We believe that all of these approaches have merit as leaders engage these ideas in an effort to promote change in the areas of diversity, equity, and inclusion.

Association of Public and Land-Grant Universities and the American Association of State Colleges and Universities

Similarly, in 2005, the American Association of State Colleges and Universities with the then-named National Association of State Universities and Land-Grant Colleges and Universities[12] published a report on diversity and organizational change after the University of Michigan Supreme Court decisions. Written by a steering committee of senior administrators and faculty from institutions across the country, *Now Is the Time: Meeting the Challenge for a Diverse Academy* offers guidelines designed to help higher education leaders become more sophisticated in leading on diversity issues. *Now Is the Time* poses key questions for leaders in academic affairs, student affairs, and faculty, providing a powerful tool for presidents and chancellors to begin the process of institutional dialogue (Table 5.6). The tool resonates because senior leaders can look at the report and simply ask critical strategic diversity questions of the various dimensions of the institution. Just asking the right

TABLE 5.6
Strategic Diversity Leadership Questions

Domain	*Academic Affairs*	*Student Affairs*	*Faculty*
Recruitment	Do I hold those reporting to me responsible for diversity outcomes in student enrollment, retention, and graduation in faculty hiring and promotion? Does my hiring record demonstrate progress in achieving a more diverse faculty and staff? How do we maximize scholarships and financial aid to enhance the diversity of the student body?	Is racial diversity across staff at all levels of my division? How do I achieve and maintain that diversity? Do our services and programs reach out to all students? How do I reach out to all minority students?	What partnerships exist with K–12 public and private schools? What might I contribute to these partnerships? Do I communicate with my admissions offices about ways to connect my research and expertise with their goals of strengthening diversity on campus?
Retention	How do I support the academic success of all students? Do I monitor the retention, achievement, and graduation rates of students of color? How do I support the retention and success of faculty of color? Do I monitor the retention and promotion rate of faculty of color?	Do I know the retention patterns and trends across all racial groups of students? How do I use that information for setting goals and program development and enhancement? Do I know and incorporate best practices for minority student retention, achievement, and graduation in our programs and services?	How do I create an environment that encourages students to remain committed to completing their college education? What have I done to create a welcoming environment for all students? Have I volunteered to mentor a student, participate in diversity committees, or help with programming? Do I reach out to students who seem to be isolated or struggling at our campus? If not, what keeps me from engaging?
Partnerships	How do I work with K–12 systems in districts with large populations of students of color? Do I promote collaboration with historically Black colleges and universities, or institutions that serve other diverse ethnic and minority individuals and subgroups? Is our institution working to help prepare our students to work in a global economy? Have I established institutional structures to facilitate the success of faculty and students of color?	Do I belong to groups whose members and programs are or historically have been racially exclusive? If so, how have I fostered the value of diversity within those groups? Do I ignore issues of race and treat and serve everyone on the same basis? Do I encourage the creation of diversity activities when I participate with off-campus partners?	How could activities with off-campus partners help elevate our commitment to diversity on campus? Do the businesses and community organizations with whom I work have diversity programs that attract diverse students to our campus? Are scholarships available from my partners that could assist students in navigating career opportunities or internships while they are completing their degrees?

TABLE 5.6 (Continued)

Domain	*Academic Affairs*	*Student Affairs*	*Faculty*
Campus Climate	Is the environment that I control welcoming to all? How do I contribute to a positive campus climate for diversity? Does our institution regularly assess our campus climate for diversity? Have I clearly communicated my expectations that discrimination will not be tolerated?	Do I engage in conversation or difficult dialogues about race? How is diversity reflected as a value across all members of the division? How do I respond when I hear a racially disparaging comment or stereotype from colleagues? Do I respond differently if the individual or group is from a race different from mine? How do I respond when I observe the lack of diversity in major institutional programs, services, and systems of recognition? Do I foster change?	Is the environment that I control warm and welcoming to all students? Do I speak up when those with whom I interact speak hurtful or racist words? Do I notice when students of color are not included in decisions that directly impact them? Have I reached out to include diverse colleagues and students in all my personal and professional activities?
Professional Development	Do I recognize my biases and/or stereotypes and work to challenge them? Do I provide professional development opportunities for faculty and staff in the area of diversity?	How do I foster intercultural student engagement? How often do I do this? How do I foster cultural competence across staff and students in my division? Is leadership development with a diversity focus included in our orientation for new faculty, staff, and students? How do we ensure diversity competence among all of our staff within the division?	Do I participate in conversations that challenge my biases and/or stereotypes? Have I reflected on my policies and programs to examine where I may exclude anyone? What discussions have I participated in at my professional meetings that raise issues about diversity in our profession? Have I examined the content of my curriculum to ensure that it is inclusive to all?
Assessment	How often and to what extent do I evaluate our measurements of diversity-related achievements? Do I have academic success, graduation, and promotion and tenure data for minorities and women in terms of students, faculty, and staff? How do I reward faculty and staff for achieving goals related to diversity? Have I assessed the campus climate and culture of my area?	Do I know what the access and enrollment issues are for students on my campus? Have I assessed the campus climate and culture of my area?	Do I know what the access and enrollment issues are for students on my campus? Am I aware of how financial aid is awarded? Have I conducted research to examine institutional data on diversity? Have I examined campus diversity reports? Do I think about the educational impact of diversity?

Source: Adapted from NASULGC/AASCU Diversity Task Force, 2005.

questions can communicate a great deal in terms of establishing a set of expectations about what should happen on campus.

The American Council on Education

The American Council on Education (ACE), the nation's largest higher education policy and advocacy organization, has been key in advancing an organizational diversity change agenda. In addition to publishing a national status report on minority educational presence and attainment in higher education, ACE regularly publishes guidance for campus leaders. Some notable examples include *Leadership Strategies for Advancing Campus Diversity: Advice From Experienced Presidents* (Kezar & Eckel, 2005) and *Race-Conscious Financial Aid and Other Diversity-Enhancing Programs: Legal Developments for Colleges and Universities* (Michaelson, Meers, & Drier, 2006). Adriana Kezar and Peter Eckel explore the role of new presidents in developing and implementing strategies toward achieving diversity on American college and university campuses. Martin Michaelson and associates address laws pertaining to racially and ethnically conscious financial aid and related programs at colleges and universities, and provide a legal framework for important questions presidents should consider as they develop various strategies to ensure the academic success of students of color.[13]

Another initiative launched in 2007, *At Home in the World: Educating for Global Connections and Local Commitments* (C. L. Olson, Evans, & Shoenberg, 2007), represents the combined efforts of ACE's Center for International Initiatives and the Center for the Advancement of Racial and Ethnic Equity. The focus of this initiative includes regular roundtable discussions and a summer leadership institute for exploring best educational practices in internationalization, access, success, equity, and multicultural education. *At Home in the World* is driven by the premise that synergistic efforts between the global and the local can assist institutions in educating more effectively in the twenty-first century.

Capitalizing on the imminent wave of college presidential retirements and the resulting opportunity to ensure a more inclusive pool of leadership talent, ACE and several others partnered to launch *The Spectrum Initiative: Advancing Diversity in the College Presidency.* This multiyear national agenda is designed to diversify and broaden executive leadership talent in higher education through collaboration with boards of trustees, executive search firms, campus search communities, current presidents, and aspiring leaders (Bridges, Eckel, Cordova, & White, 2008). *Spectrum* reinforces ACE's long-standing commitment to leadership development through its prestigious ACE Fellows Program, which is dedicated to preparing senior leaders to serve in American colleges and universities. The ACE Fellows Program not only places a premium on selecting a diverse group of higher education leaders, but providing these leaders with a range of opportunities and tools that will allow them to lead at our increasingly diverse colleges and universities.

National Association of Student Affairs Administrators in Higher Education

Another influential higher education umbrella organization with a long-standing commitment to institutional diversity is the National Association of Student Affairs Administrators in Higher Education (NASPA).[14] NASPA represents more than 11,000 members at over 1,400 institutions around the world, and is particularly influential among those in higher education who work in student affairs.

As a leader in shaping the practice of student development on college and university campuses, NASPA is uniquely positioned to engage diversity in all of its complexity, reinforcing for its membership the importance of valuing diversity and equity from a personal, interpersonal, institutional, and global perspective.[15] NASPA includes diverse voices and topics in its publications and supports the Multicultural Institute, which focuses on diversity issues in student affairs and among higher education administrators and scholars. Finally, NASPA maintains a network of "Knowledge Communities" that provide an opportunity for NASPA members to access information in a specific area. The "Knowledge Communities" support the NASPA mission, vision, and goals, elevating the diversity conversation in a myriad of ways.

Specific diversity-themed communities include African American, Asian/Pacific Islander, disability, LGBT, Latino, and Indigenous People. These communities provide a powerful space for learning through workshops, presenting new research, and mentoring. One of the greatest benefits of these communities is that they provide an entry point into the broader NASPA organization, creating a forum for new professionals to connect, collaborate, and learn from their colleagues.

Finally, NASPA's Undergraduate Fellows Program, formerly the Minority Undergraduate Fellows Program, constitutes a leadership development effort that the authors have participated in directly. This program is a semi-structured mentoring program for undergraduate students wishing to explore the field of student affairs or higher education. Students and mentors apply as a pair, and if selected are provided support in establishing a mentoring relationship at their institution. Members of the program participate in internship opportunities, including a national conference and a Summer Leadership Institute. Although diversifying the ranks of the student affairs field is a long-range objective of the effort, its most important goal is to ensure that each fellow enhances his or her writing, presentation skills, and cultural competencies, and develops a better understanding of the process of ethical decision making.

The higher education policy organizations that we have focused on here represent only the tip of the iceberg; other organizations making a difference include the College Board, American Association of Universities, and higher education accrediting organizations. Indeed, national accrediting agencies like the Middle States Commission on Higher Education, the North Central Association of Colleges and Schools, and the Higher Learning Commission have continued to strengthen their requirements that colleges and universities develop strategic diversity leadership agendas as part of their accreditation process.

Through their fellowships, conferences, and symposia, the organizations and institutes discussed here have helped create a context for diversity change across multiple institutions simultaneously. By publishing research, providing strategic guidance, creating expectations, and helping to shape the agenda, their collective efforts are quickening the pace of change on campus. In higher education, new approaches to structure, strategy, and change often emerge in response to broad environmental shifts or after institutions come to similar conclusions about how to respond to a given challenge. Through their individual and collective efforts, these organizations help validate new ways of thinking and move senior leaders from merely exploring best diversity practices to implementing them.

Cross-Sector Strategic Partnerships

The last driver of the strategic diversity leadership movement that we would like to highlight is the burgeoning group of nonprofit, government, corporate, and philanthropic organizations partnering with colleges and universities to advance diversity (also see Table 5.7). Over the years, these partnerships have emerged as a powerful force for change, particularly as affirmative action policies and financial supports have weakened. Although the United Negro College Fund (UNCF) has been engaged in this work for nearly seven decades, others are new. Prominent examples include the Higher Education Recruitment Consortium (HERC), the Consortium for

Graduate Study in Management (the Consortium), the Compact for Faculty Diversity, the National Posse Foundation, the Gates Millennial Scholars (GMS) Program, and Management Leaders for Tomorrow (MLT).

Although there are other programs in the strategic diversity leadership movement, we have chosen these organizations because of their relevance to CDOs and their focus on some of the most difficult diversity challenges. All are dedicated to creating a new community of leaders who will not only possess the requisite academic credentials to create change, but also the social, political, and relational capital required for success in today's knowledge-based, global economy. Although each has its own distinct agenda, all of these organizations are masters at marshaling financial resources from numerous sources, and forging strategic alliances to pursue new possibilities around diversity issues. It is common for these organizations to bridge the gap between the academy and the private sector by bringing in financial support and helping student leaders gain valuable experience partnering with mentors who are national leaders in their fields of expertise.

The Higher Education Recruitment Consortium

Founded in 2000, HERC's mission is to advance the efforts of its member institutions to recruit and retain outstanding and diverse faculty and staff and to assist dual-career couples (J. Hogan, personal communication, January 10, 2012). Its online listings are available at no charge to anyone seeking employment in higher education. HERC is a powerful player in the strategic diversity leadership movement because it helps CDOs and other senior leaders find diverse talent. In particular, HERC can help with what is referred to in the recruitment literature as "strategic sourcing" (Davenport, Leibold, & Voelpel, 2006), serving as a platform for building relationships, establishing referral possibilities, and finding talented employees. Effective sourcing is a critical element of the recruiting process. In addition to the job board, HERC helps remove common barriers to recruitment and retention by fostering a collaborative model in which members share costs, information, professional development opportunities, and resources. HERC works to improve the diversity of applicant pools by engaging in national advertising, facilitating strategic partnerships with women- and minority-serving organizations and publications, and promoting minority conferences. HERC is also focused on dual-career academic couples, helping candidates to find jobs within a commutable distance.

The Consortium for Graduate Study in Management

The Consortium is one of the oldest alliances in the strategic diversity leadership movement. Its mission is to enhance diversity in business education and

TABLE 5.7
Cross-Sector Strategic Partnerships Advancing the Strategic Diversity Leadership Movement

Organization	*Overview*	*Focus*
Higher Education Recruitment Consortium	Founded in 2000, HERC's mission is to advance the efforts of its member institutions to recruit and retain outstanding and diverse faculty and staff and to assist dual-career couples. Today, it is active in 12 regions across the nation and includes a national HERC office (www.hercjobs.org). With over 17,000 faculty and staff jobs on any given day, HERC is the largest nonprofit higher education job board in the world.	Faculty and administrative diversity
The Consortium for Graduate Study in Management	The mission of the Consortium, an alliance of leading American business schools and some of our country's top corporations, is to enhance diversity in business education and leadership by helping to reduce the serious underrepresentation of African Americans, Hispanic Americans, and Native Americans in both member schools' enrollments and the ranks of management. We believe this mission can be achieved by recruiting for graduate business education–qualified U.S. citizens and U.S. permanent residents who can demonstrate a commitment to the Consortium's mission and can best assist the Consortium in pursuing this mission.	Graduate student diversity Diversifying corporate leadership
Management Leaders for Tomorrow	MLT begins with the premise that there is great talent in the minority community that needs to be exposed and groomed for leadership in all aspects of organizational life. Working with African American, Latino, and Native American students, MLT is a premier career development organization focusing on helping high-achieving minority students to unlock their career potential.	Undergraduate and graduate student diversity Diversifying corporate leadership
National Science Agencies	The National Science Foundation (NSF), the National Institutes of Health (NIH), the National Aeronautics and Space Administration (NASA), and the U.S. Department of Energy (DOE) all provide major funding designed to enhance racial and gender diversity in the STEM fields. These organizations are key leaders in the strategic diversity leadership movement and in enhancing a diverse scientific and technical workforce for the new millennium.	Graduate student diversity STEM student success Faculty diversity
Compact for Faculty Diversity	The Compact for Faculty Diversity mission is to increase the number of minority students who earn doctoral degrees and become college and university faculty. The Compact includes a number of strategic partners in the philanthropic, educational, and government communities.	Graduate student diversity STEM student success Faculty diversity
National Posse Foundation	Working with nearly 40 colleges and universities, the National Posse Foundation has three goals: expand the pool from which top colleges and universities recruit outstanding young leaders from diverse backgrounds, help these institutions build more interactive environments so that people from all backgrounds feel welcome on campus, and ensure that Posse Scholars thrive in their academic studies and then assume leadership positions in the workforce.	Undergraduate student diversity STEM student diversity

TABLE 5.7 (Continued)

Organization	*Overview*	*Focus*
Gates Millennium Scholars Program	GMS promotes academic excellence and provides an opportunity for outstanding minority students with significant financial needs to reach their highest potential by reducing financial barriers for racially and ethnically diverse students with high academic and leadership promise who have significant financial need; increasing the representation of these target groups in the disciplines of computer science, education, engineering, library science, mathematics, public health, and the sciences; developing a diversified cadre of future leaders by facilitating successful completion of undergraduate and graduate degree programs; and providing significant support from undergraduate through doctoral programs for students selected as Gates Millennium Scholars.	Undergraduate student diversity Graduate student diversity STEM student diversity

leadership by helping to increase the representation of diverse leaders in the nation's top business schools and in the corporate sector.[16] Through an annual competition, the Consortium awards merit-based fellowships that cover tuition costs at the nation's top MBA programs.

The Consortium began in 1965 against a backdrop of civil unrest.[17] Over the years, participation in the Consortium has grown, even as the organization itself has expanded its definition of diversity. Initially conceived as a way to assist African American men in developing the skills necessary to compete for entry-level positions in American business, the program broadened its scope in 1970 to include women and Hispanics. With shifts in the legal, political, and demographic landscape around issues of diversity, the Consortium's mission evolved again in 2004 to include U.S. citizens and permanent residents of all races and ethnicities who demonstrate a commitment to the Consortium's mission. Since its inception, the Consortium has increased the number of annual fellowships it awards from 21 to over 350. These fellowships are funded by some of the nation's top businesses and participating universities.

Management Leaders for Tomorrow

Launched in 1994, MLT is quickly gaining traction, serving as a powerful leadership development platform for African American, Native American, and Latino/Hispanic students throughout the course of their careers.[18] The vision for MLT developed out of an independent study project conducted by the organization's founder, John Rice, while a second-year MBA student at Harvard University's Business School. He noticed that the most talented minorities from some of the nation's leading institutions did not even consider going to business school. In response, he created MLT, an organization that now helps direct diverse students directly into the nation's top 20 business schools. In 2005, over 40 percent of all Harvard Business School MBA students were MLT alums and 55 percent of MLT applications to the top 10 business schools were accepted.

Like the efforts by the Posse, Consortium, and GMS programs, MLT is focused on "cracking the code" on career potential and developing the next generation of minority leaders in the corporate, nonprofit, and entrepreneurial sectors. MLT rightly recognizes that career success takes more than classroom education. It takes having the relational and cultural skills required to recognize and leverage early opportunities, navigate difficult choices, build relationships with the right people, and unlock the hidden vault of leadership that many minorities are not even aware exists. Although many organizations focus on providing minorities with access to educational opportunities, MLT prides itself on delivering concrete skills that are critical to success. MLT has formalized the delivery of these principles across its Career Program, MBA Prep, and Career Advancement and Alumni programs. Beginning with the Career Program, MLT works with undergraduates in their junior year, helping to fast-track them into their first professional leadership roles both during and immediately after college. The program focuses on intensive one-on-one coaching, leadership and analytical skill development workshops led by corporate partners, leadership conferences, and access to recruiters at sought-after firms.

MBA Prep picks up a couple of years after the Career Program concludes and guides early career professionals through the application and interview process, showing them what it takes to be successful in business school and beyond. The MBA Prep curriculum focuses on career coaching, the graduate application process, preparing for interviews, and helping MBA fellows to build early relationships with corporate partners and nonprofit organizations. The newest MLT offerings are the Career Advancement and Alumni programs, which focus on creating networks of diverse leaders and helping historically underrepresented minorities to move into executive leadership positions within their organizations.

National Science Agencies

Some of the most prominent organizations driving the strategic diversity leadership movement are federally funded and focus on diversifying the STEM disciplines and the undergraduate, graduate, and faculty health fields.

These federal agencies have joined long-standing leaders in the strategic diversity leadership movement like the Department of Education's federally funded TRIO programs to provide critical resources to colleges and universities in their efforts to develop new strategic alliances and ultimately diversify their student and faculty ranks.

Yet the influence of these leading organizations goes beyond a simple focus on enhancing the demographic diversity of our institutions. Over the past several years, there has been increasing recognition in federal science organizations and funding agencies that more research scientists should be directly involved in education and public outreach. Some U.S. agencies, including the National Science Foundation (NSF), are now insisting that all scientists describe how their proposed research will have "broader impacts." That is, even if the grant will not focus specifically on issues of diversity, researchers are expected to answer how their studies will affect the public good, including implications for community outreach, public engagement, learning, and the general welfare. Thus, each grant author must identify the following:

> How well does the activity advance discovery and understanding while promoting teaching, training, and learning? How well does the proposed activity broaden the participation of underrepresented groups (e.g., gender, ethnicity, disability, geographic, etc.)? To what extent will it enhance the infrastructure for research and education, such as facilities, instrumentation, networks, and partnerships? Will the results be disseminated broadly to enhance scientific and technological understanding? What may be the benefits of the proposed activity to society?[19]

The broader effects of a proposed activity are central to the NSF's mission to promote the progress of science; to advance the national health, prosperity, and welfare; to secure the national defense; and for other purposes (downloaded from www.nsf.gov/nsf/nsfpubs/straplan/mission.htm March 1, 2013). Hence, the NSF is challenging researchers and creating a system of accountability in its efforts to enhance issues of diversity. Because of the centrality of scientific discovery and the long-standing resistance of many within the scientific community to recognize the relevance of diversity issues to their fields of study, these agency efforts are vital to changing the institutional and educational culture of the math and science fields. The scientific community is a powerful group and its engagement in the movement is a boon to its long-term potential for change in the academy.

The Compact for Faculty Diversity

The challenge of diversifying the faculty ranks is one of the most difficult in all of academia, requiring success at all phases of what is an invariably leaky higher education pipeline. The Compact for Faculty Diversity is dedicated to increasing the number of minority students who earn doctoral degrees and become college and university faculty.[20] The Compact is composed of a number of higher education associations and federal programs. They include the Southern Regional Education Board (SREB); the Western Interstate Commission for Higher Education; the National Institutes of Health (Bridges to the Professoriate); the NSF (Alliance for Graduate Education and the Professoriate); the Alfred P. Sloan Foundation; and the Office of Federal TRIO Programs, and the United States Department of Education Ronald E. McNair Program.

Since its founding in 1993, the SREB's Doctoral Scholars Program has supported more than 900 scholars at 83 institutions in 29 states and has helped produce over 500 graduates in partnership with academic institutions. In 2010, the program received the prestigious John Hope Franklin Award from the magazine *Diverse: Issues in Higher Education*. The program currently assists more than 300 scholars actively pursuing doctoral degrees. More than 80 percent of its graduates have begun academic careers in higher education.

The Compact for Faculty Diversity also hosts annually the Institute on Teaching and Mentoring, a gathering that brings together over 1,000 doctoral students, mentors, and faculty. Now in its seventeenth year, the Institute exposes minority scholars to research and teaching workshops and leadership activities designed to help them thrive in graduate school, earn doctoral degrees, and position themselves for success in academia. CDOs across the country attend this meeting annually with faculty from their institutions to find and recruit diverse faculty.

The National Posse Foundation

The National Posse Foundation is another influential partner advancing the strategic diversity leadership movement, and recently received a contribution from President Obama's Nobel Peace Prize award. Posse has partnered with academic institutions to help support and graduate thousands of scholarship recipients and is creating a national network of diverse leaders. Founded in 1987, the program has grown exponentially with offices in seven major cities and 39 academic partnering institutions. The Posse program has three primary goals: expand the high school talent pool from which top colleges and universities recruit outstanding diverse talent, help academic institutions build more interactive and welcoming campus environments, and assist Posse scholars during their college years and beyond.

Posse not only partners with academic institutions, it facilitates collaboration and support systems among small cohorts of students who attend an institution together and assist one another in achieving academic and leadership success. Each "posse" engages in an intensive pre-collegiate training experience and later in leadership activities designed to help it make the transition to higher education environments. Many Posse Scholars are minority and first-generation college students. The Posse Scholarship program boasts a graduation rate of more than 90 percent.

Gates Millennium Scholars Program

Launched in 1999 with a $1 billion gift from the Bill & Melinda Gates Foundation, the GMS Program provides full funding for college tuition, fees, books, and housing to high-achieving, low-income minority students.[21] The goal of GMS is to provide an opportunity for outstanding minority students with significant financial need to reach their highest potential by:

- Reducing financial barriers for African American, American Indian/Alaska Native, Asian Pacific Islander American, and Hispanic American students with high academic and leadership promise and significant financial need
- Increasing the representation of these target groups in the disciplines of computer science, education, engineering, library science, mathematics, public health, the sciences, and areas where these groups are traditionally underrepresented
- Developing a diversified cadre of future leaders for America by facilitating successful completion of bachelor's, master's, and doctoral degrees
- Providing uninterrupted support from undergraduate through doctoral programs for students selected as Gates Millennium Scholars entering target disciplines

The UNCF administers the GMS Program in partnership with the Hispanic Scholarship Fund, the Asian and Pacific Islander American Scholarship Fund, and the American Indian Graduate Center Scholars. GMS annually selects 1,000 talented students who are provided with personal and professional development assistance throughout their college career. The GMS award has enabled thousands of young Americans to attend undergraduate and graduate institutions of their choice, launching them on a trajectory to assume important roles as leaders in their professions and in their communities.

Summary

Taken collectively, the efforts of the aforementioned higher education associations, diversity officer umbrella groups, research centers, nonprofit organizations, and emerging diversity degree and certificate programs have established a strong institutional and financial support system for the strategic diversity leadership movement. Our hope is that CDOs will tap these isomorphic streams to advance their diversity efforts. This movement is anchored in an emerging body of scholarship and the work of higher education policy organizations and foundations. These entities represent the best of what we know about intentionally managing diversity and inclusion efforts, not only in higher education, but in the corporate, government, and nonprofit sectors as well.

Rather than struggling toward solutions in isolation, CDOs should seek to leverage diversity-related research and professional networks to create a more evidence-based and data-driven platform for their policies and programs. A more proactive approach that is consistent with an emerging body of best practices could have far-reaching implications for a broad range of diversity activities, including curriculum reform, intergroup relations, strategic planning for diversity, building systems of accountability, and diversity plan implementation.

The more that CDOs understand about the isomorphic forces outlined in this chapter, the better they can draw from them to create stronger support systems at their institutions. As we emphasize throughout this book, change is often about marshaling energy to create new opportunities and outcomes. The resources explored in this chapter are primarily normative and mimetic in nature, and lack the intrusive force that characterizes coercive isomorphic energy, including policy shifts or changes in the law. As a result, CDOs should view these programs and initiatives as part of an intricate exchange of resources subject to the motivating energy and direction of the CDO. Interactions between and among college and university leaders, higher education governing bodies, credentialing entities, leadership institutes, degree-granting programs, and legislative and judicial systems form what we call the "institutional ecology" of higher education. Thus, it is imperative that CDOs participate in national diversity discussions and engage their institutions in competitive benchmarking, the application of evidence-based practice, and other activities that can move their institutions into a dynamic, even competitive context.

But even as we champion the normative and mimetic isomorphic energies presented here, leaders must be ready to seek new and innovative ways to advance our shared diversity values. Too often, institutions back away from bold ideas for fear of being attacked by conservative organizations and the right-wing media. Many senior leaders are unable to think outside the box because their professional experience is limited to just one or two institutions. Thus, we encourage senior leaders—whether or not their work domain includes diversity issues—to consider pursuing the opportunities explored in this chapter.

Understanding and leveraging the emerging resources of the strategic diversity leadership movement is fundamental to positioning academic institutions to thrive in today's diverse, global marketplace. For CDOs working in the slow-moving and tradition-bound culture of academia, their best chance at creating change is to tap into the resources outlined in this chapter. Although many of these institutions and research centers are in dialogue with each other, until a large enough community of higher education leaders embraces new ways of thinking, standard models will persist. There remains a tipping point on higher education's horizon: the more that chief diversity officers engage with the resources that we have outlined here, the more they will be able to embolden their change efforts.

Notes

1. For example, see Harper, Patton, Wooden, 2009; Hurtado & Carter, 1997.

2. For example, see Alger, 2009; American Association for the Advancement of Science, 2010; Coleman & Palmer, 2004.

3. For example, see Moody, 2004; Smith et al., 2004; Turner & Myers, 2000.

4. For example, see Hurtado, Milem, Clayton-Pedersen, & Allen, 1998; Matlock, Wade-Golden, & Gurin, 2002, 2010.

5. For example, see Nagda & Gurin, 2007; Nagda, Gurin, Sorensen, & Zúñiga, 2009; Sorensen, Nagda, Gurin, & Maxwell, 2009; Zúñiga, Nagda, Chesler, & Cytron-Walker, 2007.

6. For example, see Jackson, 2006; Jackson & O'Callaghan, 2009.

7. For example, see Leon, 2010; Pittard, 2011; Williams & Wade-Golden, 2007, 2008.

8. For example, see Clayton-Pedersen et al., 2006; Kezar & Eckel, 2008; Smith, 2009; Tierney & Sallee, 2008; Williams & Clowney, 2007; Williams et al., 2005.

9. For example, see Gurin, Hurtado, & Gurin, 2002; Matlock et al. 2002, 2010; Milem et al., 2005.

10. For example, see Antonio, 2004; Kuh, Cruce, Shoup, Kinzie, & Gonyea, 2008; Sellers, Smith, Shelton, Rowley, & Chavous, 1998.

11. For example, see Bensimon, 2004; Bensimon, Hao, & Bustillos, 2003; Bensimon & Malcom, 2012.

12. On March 30, 2009, the National Association of State Universities and Land-Grant Colleges and Universities changed its name to the Association of Public and Land-Grant Universities.

13. These issues have also been explored by the College Board, the NAACP Legal and Educational Defense Fund, the Mexican American Legal Defense Fund, the American Association of University Professors, and Education Counsel. Each of these organizations and numerous others have contributed scholarship and guidance to help institutions navigate the current threats to their diversity efforts. Although not directly addressed in this chapter, these organizations are key players in the higher education diversity movement.

14. National Association of Student Affairs Administrators in Higher Education was renamed the National Association of Student Affairs Administrators in Higher Education, but still continues to use the acronym NASPA. For more information about NASPA please visit www.naspa.org/about/history.cfm.

15. Retrieved September 30, 2011, from www.naspa.org/about/diversity.cfm

16. Retrieved May 10, 2010, from www.cgsm.org/about-us/

17. The first institutions to participate in the Consortium were Washington University, Indiana University–Bloomington, and University of Wisconsin–Madison. In its first three years, the Consortium only provided fellowships to Black men. The first class consisted of 21 Black men.

18. Retrieved May 1, 2010, from www.ml4t.org/

19. Retrieved May 1, 2010, from www.nsf.gov/pubs/policydocs/pappguide/nsf08_1/gpg_3.jsp#fn33

20. Retrieved May 2, 2010, from www.instituteonteachingandmentoring.org/Compact/index.html

21. Retrieved May 10, 2010, from www.gmsp.org/

6

STRATEGIC DIVERSITY LEADERSHIP

Activating Change and Transformation in Higher Education

> You have to develop a long-range vision and plan for change that is more than just paper. It has to be real. I have been at the university for more than 20 years and plans come and go, but to make it real, you have to have the support of the president, resources, build accountability, and help people to do the right thing. If you do not, nothing changes.
>
> —A vice president for diversity and equal opportunity at a large university in the Southeast

Fostering an institutional environment that truly embraces diversity takes years of conscious effort. Thus, it is vital that we neither become impatient in our quest for results nor lose focus, shifting our attention to other issues. Instead, chief diversity officers (CDOs) must leverage what we refer to as a *strategic diversity leadership approach* to implementing their diversity, equity, and inclusion efforts. Traditionally, diversity efforts have rightly been characterized in terms of our moral and social responsibilities. But in today's changing world, diversity has a vital and positive role to play in creating a more robust, competitive, and engaged society and economy.

Understanding the critical principles of strategic diversity leadership is key for leading successful diversity initiatives, and is the focus of the companion volume to this book. In this chapter, we present 10 themes associated with strategic diversity leadership, and then address the extent to which they have been applied at institutions that have CDO roles. Drawing on our national survey of more than 700 institutions, we explore strategic diversity leadership at both the macro and micro level, presenting several concepts that are vital to activating change and transformation at colleges and universities. What follows in this chapter is a primer on the subject of strategic diversity leadership, providing an overview of concepts discussed across multiple chapters in the companion volume to this book.

Strategic Diversity Leadership

The Strategic Diversity Leadership Model frames the diversity and inclusion journey as an intentional effort to change institutional culture and move diversity issues from the periphery to the center of institutional life. It is a philosophy designed to activate a combination of principles for changing organizational structure, strategic plans, reward systems, and accountability processes. Successful diversity strategy means more than having a well-written diversity plan or assembling a loose and haphazard network of policies and programs over a couple of years.

The overarching diversity strategy must be crafted through dialogue and the creation of a shared understanding among many stakeholders. Although not every member of the campus community will share the same level of commitment or concern, it is best to cast the net widely and capture the ideas and priorities of as many participants as possible. For a diversity agenda to be effective, it must be relevant to every member of the campus community, not just minorities, women, or other traditionally disadvantaged individuals and groups. The same can be said of implementation. If the strategic diversity agenda is confined to diversity professionals, it will gain little traction among other members of the campus community. The role of the CDO is to enable and facilitate this process, setting the conditions for a productive conversation, followed by an effective implementation.

At its core, therefore, strategic diversity leadership involves CDOs, diversity champions, senior leaders, and others actively working to change the culture of their institutions to maximize the educational and cultural benefits of diversity. CDOs must be able to read the external and internal environment, navigate treacherous organizational politics, and leverage the best of what we know about change management science. In the companion volume to this book, this approach is outlined in great depth, beginning with a discussion of strategic diversity goals before moving to an overview of key leadership competencies that strategic diversity leaders need to master.

We have identified four overarching diversity goals: (a) increase access and equity for historically underrepresented groups, (b) create a multicultural and inclusive environment for every member of the campus community, (c) develop curricular and cocurricular initiatives to prepare students for a diverse and global world, and (d) advance diversity-themed research to expand our understanding of diversity issues at the domestic and global levels. These goals address the traditional equity and social justice arguments for promoting diversity, as well as newer trends in social psychology and organizational behavior and management that underscore the benefits of diversity (Milem, Chang, & Antonio, 2005). The goals can be reached, in part, through a CDO's concentrated efforts to develop different leadership frameworks, or lenses, for approaching his or her diversity efforts. Box 6.1 provides a primer on the strategic diversity leadership lenses that a CDO must command.

BOX 6.1
Five Leadership Lenses Essential for Chief Diversity Officers

A Multifaceted Strategic Diversity Leadership Lens

More than that of most executive leadership roles, the power of CDOs is as much grounded in their structural position within the organization as their ability to lead through influence, relationships, symbolism, and the political dynamics of their institution (Leon, 2010; Williams, Berger, & McClendon, 2005). CDOs should therefore develop a multifaceted leadership lens to leverage what Lee Bolman and Terence Deal refer to as the "power of organizational reframing" (Birnbaum, 1988; Bolman & Deal, 2003). We present a brief overview of five essential leadership frameworks to guide their efforts.

1. **Organizational Learning Leadership Lens**
   Organizational learning refers to the ability of an organization to learn and adapt. CDOs must be able to bring about the conditions of organizational learning by helping their institutions learn from past mistakes and break the reactive cycle of diversity crisis incidents that too often characterize institutional diversity efforts. An effective CDO needs to build efforts that are intentional, evidence-based, and grounded in best practices. These best practices include developing strategic diversity leadership scorecards, campus climate studies, program evaluations, diversity audits, performance reviews, learning forums, and collective decision-making processes to define new organizational possibilities and approaches to leading change and transformation.

2. **Structural Leadership Lens**
   Structural leadership refers to the formal administrative structure and policies of an institution (Bolman & Deal, 2003). The CDO's structural authority

(continues)

stems from his or her placement in the formal hierarchy and the budget, staff, direct reporting units, diversity plans, and policies that he or she controls directly. The more formal authority that the CDO has around issues of diversity, the more empowered he or she is to lead on campus. At the same time, even CDOs with well-resourced and -structured positions must work collaboratively. As a result, change is also determined by the CDO's ability to shift the formal bureaucratic structures and make diversity a key priority in the strategic plans, budget allocations, hiring decisions, admissions processes, annual reports, performance reviews, strategic hiring efforts, and other aspects of the formal organizational reality of the institution.

3. **Political Leadership Lens**
   Political leadership is determined by one's ability to navigate the competing interests, priorities, coalitions, and power dynamics that exist on campus (Bolman & Deal, 2003). So much of a CDO's work happens in this realm, and the best officers must possess a savvy ability to bargain, negotiate, jockey for position, build allies, and cultivate partnerships both on and off campus. Although political acumen is not usually included in the CDO job descriptions, it is one of the competencies that we highlighted previously, and having a deft political touch is fundamental to leading in often contested and volatile situations.

4. **Symbolic Leadership Lens**
   CDOs are also required to lead through symbols and demonstrate an ability to establish a compelling narrative that legitimates diversity as an institutional priority (Bolman & Deal, 2003). The symbolic frame of leadership defines organizational life as theater, where leaders are constantly sending verbal and nonverbal messages to an audience that forms its own impressions of what it sees on the institutional stage. One of the refrains that we hear most often from CDOs is their unflagging effort to reframe diversity as a strategic priority. CDOs must know how to leverage key events, frame issues and ideas in their speeches and public forums, and wield the power of symbols as another tool in their leadership arsenal.

5. **Collegial Leadership Lens**
   Collegiality is the final leadership frame that CDOs must master (Birnbaum, 1988). The collegial lens is defined by collective decision making and implementation activities that bring together individuals and groups. Collegial leadership assumes that academic institutions make decisions through an open and democratic process. Because colleges and universities are highly collegial cultures, CDOs find that the most critical diversity initiatives require the buy-in and involvement of faculty and other leaders. CDOs must ensure that this

(continues)

(continued)

open and more flexible process does not leave diversity issues out of the discussion. To be effective, CDOs must demonstrate outstanding skills; build relationships; establish rapport with colleagues; and understand how to leverage collegial decision making by collaborating with governance leaders, student organizations, community stakeholders, diversity communities, alumni communities, corporate leaders, and others.

Strategic diversity leadership more resembles an improvisational jazz ensemble than a soloist's controlled performance. As a result, CDOs should never rely on leading purely through their formal role and rank. CDOs must be able to pivot between different leadership styles, leveraging structural, symbolic, political, and collaborative relationships in their efforts to lead on diversity issues, a point that Raul Leon (2010) concluded in a case study of CDOs at multiple institutions.

In the sections that follow, we outline 10 strategic diversity leadership themes essential to activating change that can be both incremental and transformative in nature. The companion volume to this book goes into depth regarding each; here, Table 6.1 offers an overview of these 10 themes, providing a broad framework for examining the extent to which they are in place at institutions with CDO roles. They also set the stage for elaborating best-practice techniques for tackling key diversity issues.

Theme 1: The Critical Role of Senior Leadership

CDOs cannot be seduced into thinking that just because they help generate the diversity vision for their institutions results will follow. Only the president, provost, faculty, and other senior leaders can prioritize diversity in a manner sufficient to create deep institutional change (Cox, 2001; Loden, 1996; D. A. Thomas, 2004; Williams, 2006). Senior leaders can make diversity a strategic priority by redirecting resources necessary to implement the vision, protecting diversity efforts during difficult budgetary times, and requiring plan development and accountability from individuals at multiple institutional levels. As James Duderstadt, president emeritus of the University of Michigan, observed in an interview, "You [the president] have to carry the flag on these issues and get out in front of the institution. You cannot lead these efforts from the rear, and you cannot assign them over to anyone else" (Duderstadt, personal communication, February 27, 2004). CDOs can provide point leadership and strategic thinking, but final responsibility for guiding the change rests squarely with senior leaders.

TABLE 6.1
Themes of Strategic Diversity Leadership

Theme	*Description*	*Examples*
The Critical Role of Senior Leadership	Placing a premium on senior leaders guiding the change journey	• Identifying diversity as an institutional priority • Ensuring that resources are allocated to support diversity • Keeping diversity on the radar of other senior leaders • Protecting diversity budgets in difficult economic times
Building Dedicated Diversity Capacity	Leveraging organizational capacity perspectives in galvanizing often disparate campus diversity efforts	• Recognizing that diversity efforts must be defined in a holistic and comprehensive way • Strengthening affirmative action and equity; multicultural and inclusion; and learning, research, and diversity efforts on campus • Working across silos to create core competencies and tackle difficult institutional diversity challenges
Collegial Engagement of the Campus Community	Engaging the campus community in the process of leading change	• Developing shared understanding of the campus's diversity agenda • Leveraging forums, retreats, symposia, and other relationship-building strategies to create diversity agenda alignment
Focus on Transforming Institutional Culture	Focusing on transforming institutional culture	• Appreciating the multiple overlapping cultures of organizational life • Developing change techniques at every level of culture, from the geospatial to the deeply embedded mental models and assumptions that leaders hold • Cultivating a spirit of innovation and experimenting with new efforts
Strategic Planning for Diversity	Applying a number of strategic planning techniques to drive change	• Infusing diversity into the mission statement and academic and strategic plans of the institution • Developing dedicated, centralized, and decentralized diversity plans to accommodate the overall institutional vision for change
Developing Diversity Leaders	Establishing diversity hiring, training, and leadership development efforts	• Building highly relevant diversity education platforms for students, faculty, and staff that embrace issues of cultural competence and leadership development • Prioritizing hiring individuals with strategic diversity competence to help guide the change effort
Building Accountability Techniques	Establishing accountability strategies to drive change	• Connecting diversity efforts to the financial systems of the institution in terms of merit, annual budgets, strategic priorities, cost-cutting scenarios, and hiring and promotion decisions
Developing Incentives to Encourage Change	Creating entrepreneurial and motivational strategies to encourage change	• Creating challenge grants, financial and nonfinancial incentives, and other technology to create buy-in and engagement

TABLE 6.1 (Continued)

Theme	*Description*	*Examples*
Establishing a Strategic Diversity Leadership Scorecard	Using scorecards to track change and enhance organizational learning	• Establishing multidimensional scorecards to track diversity progress across the related domains of access and equity, campus climate, learning and diversity, and research and scholarship • Establishing complementary diversity scorecard perspectives around fund-raising for diversity, marketing, and other areas of key concern to leaders on campus
Communicating the Institutional Diversity Brand	Communicating campus diversity efforts effectively	• Establishing diversity websites, newsletters, blogs, e-mail networks, and other channels to drive campus diversity efforts • Infusing diversity goals, accomplishments, and continuing challenges into the remarks of senior leaders across the organization

The active involvement of senior leaders is therefore a key tenet of effective strategic diversity leadership, and perhaps the most powerful change lever at their disposal is financial support. A college's or university's budget plays a dominant role over all aspects of campus life. Hence, budgetary decisions are vital to advancing and solidifying a strategic diversity agenda. CDOs must be able to work effectively with senior leaders in developing ways to allocate financial resources that help galvanize new diversity possibilities.

Theme 2: Building Dedicated Diversity Capacity

Over the years, institutions have invested billions of dollars in developing campus diversity policies, programs, and offices. We define these campus diversity efforts as dedicated diversity capabilities because leaders in these areas generally pursue diversity-related efforts as their first institutional priority. Although most campuses have invested in dedicated capabilities that focus directly on diversity, for broader efforts to succeed, many people outside of these areas must collaborate. CDOs must help their campuses to consider these efforts as more than a number of disconnected offices, programs, initiatives, and plans. They must help their institutions to conceptualize their intergroup dialogue programs, general education diversity requirements, LGBT centers, dual-career development programs, diversity-training efforts, international affairs offices, and other diversity capabilities to collectively add up to more than the sum of their parts.

As also noted in the introduction to this book (see Figure I.2), Figure 6.1 provides a conceptual framework for categorizing college and university diversity efforts as part of three primary diversity models: the Affirmative Action and Equity (AAE) Model; the Multicultural and Inclusion Diversity (MID) Model; and the Learning, Diversity, and Research (LDR) Model. These models help to answer the following questions: What goals and dynamics differentiate diversity models? What core organizational technologies are required to accomplish the goals of each model? What limitations

FIGURE 6.1
Three Primary Models of Diversity in Higher Education

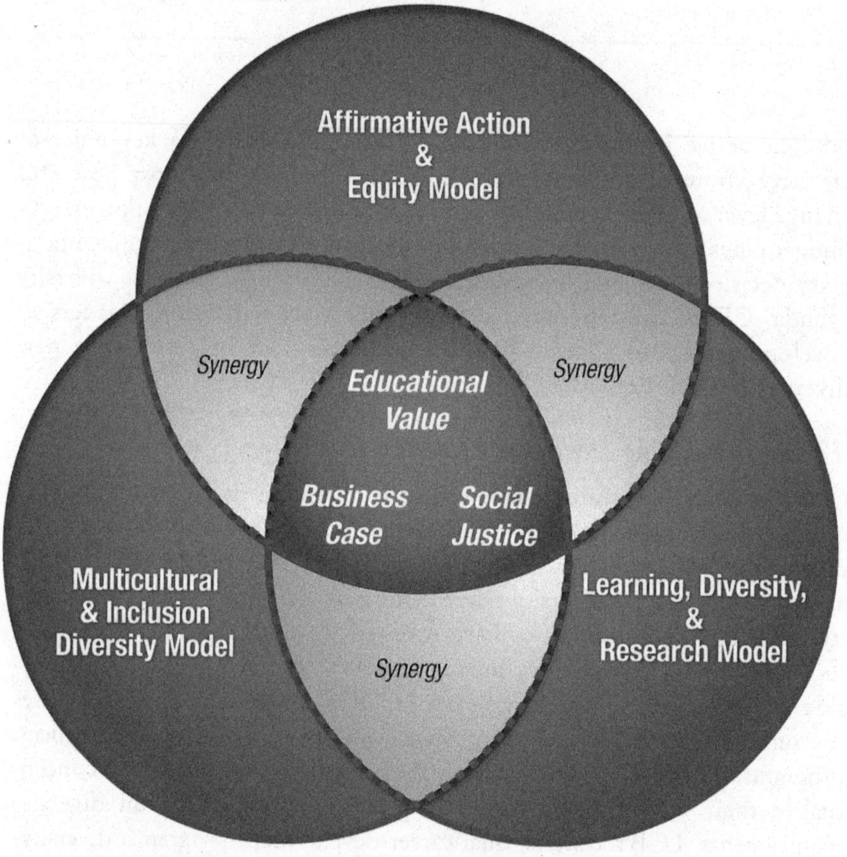

Source: Williams, 2012.

are associated with various models in terms of promoting organizational change on college and university campuses? As Figure 6.1 demonstrates, these models are both distinct and interconnected. Although each is rooted in its own orientation toward particular diversity outcomes, they share important synergies and areas of overlap.

The AAE Model was developed to eliminate overt barriers of exclusion to higher education and increase the numbers of minorities, women, and other protected groups enrolled and working on college and university campuses (Washington & Harvey, 1989). Affirmative action officers, policy statements of nondiscrimination, targeted recruitment initiatives and hiring programs, holistic admission and financial aid programs, outreach initiatives, and race-attentive admissions and financial aid programs are the primary organizational tools through which the diversity capabilities of the AAE Model are realized.

The MID Model evolved out of the cultural politics of the 1960s and 1970s and empowerment campaigns like the Black Power, Chicano, Native American, and feminist movements (Hale, 2004; Ogbar, 2005; Peterson et al., 1978; Smith & Wolf-Wendel, 2005; Wilson, 2005). These movements embraced racial-, ethnic-, gender-, and identity-specific values, politics, and traditions (Ogbar, 2005). The MID Model is motivated by a commitment to capitalize on the richness of different cultures and helping those cultures to thrive within a broad institutional environment that may, actively or passively, resist their presence on campus (Fleming, 1984; Gurin & Epps, 1975; Peterson et al., 1978).

First, to overcome embedded forms of resistance, institutions should look to develop services, programs, student organizations, affinity organizations, and offices designed to nurture student success on campus (Fleming, 1984; Gurin & Epps, 1975; Peterson et al., 1978). Second, the model emphasizes exposing people to diversity in ways that enhance mutual understanding, respect, and openness to difference (Loden, 1996). The third priority of the MID Model aims to advance research of previously ignored communities of women, minorities, and others. This priority is synergistic with the LDR Model. Common institutional capabilities of this model include cultural centers; multicultural affairs offices; culture-specific student organizations; and diversity-themed events, such as February's Black History Month or the fall's National Latino Heritage Month, which takes place in the months of September and October.

Today, the LDR Model is at the forefront of efforts by higher learning institutions to broaden their diversity efforts to all areas of university life. It is coming into full crystallization with the emergence of social science research touting the educational benefits of diversity, as well as responding to policy shifts that emerged after the 2003 University of Michigan decisions decided by the U.S. Supreme Court (Milem et al., 2005). The LDR Model recognizes the educational and social benefits of a diverse student body, as well as the importance of advancing research around issues of diversity, equity, and inclusion. At its heart, the LDR Model explicitly links diversity efforts with the academic programs of the institution. It thereby moves the diversity debate from the margins to the center of the academy in terms of teaching, learning, and research. Capabilities include diversity-focused general education requirements, major and minor degree programs, service learning and study abroad programs, living-learning communities, initiatives focused on intergroup relations, diversity-themed research centers, and ethnic and gender studies departments that live in synergy between the LDR and MID models (Humphreys, 1997, 2000; Laird, Engberg, & Hurtado, 2005).

Part of the value that CDOs must bring to their institutions is an ability to organize how campus leaders conceptualize their institutions' diversity capabilities. The three-part organizational diversity framework offers a tool to help leaders stop thinking of campus diversity efforts as disparate capacities sprinkled across campus and begin thinking of them as a connected network of capabilities that, if deployed in a more cohesive manner, could lead to even greater levels of diversity-related change. We should therefore work to clarify and strengthen the connections between and among our various diversity efforts, using divisional reorganizations, committees and task forces, and new strategic partnerships that transcend institutional silos and politics.

Theme 3: Collegial Engagement of the Campus Community

To effectively implement broad-based diversity changes, CDOs must broadly engage the campus community, particularly when changes will affect the institution's academic domains (Rowley & Sherman, 2001). Hence, CDOs must help the campus community understand the rationale for change and build broad support for implementing diversity policies and programs. This demands honest and open communication with campus constituencies. Faculty, staff, and students care about their institutions and are more favorable to change if they are invited early to participate in the process (Birnbaum, 1988; Rowley & Sherman, 2001).

The most powerful strategies create the opportunity for dialogue between the campus community and institutional decision makers. Successful dialogue efforts include hosting conversations with key institutional stakeholders; town-hall meetings with faculty, students, and staff; and regular meetings with shared governance committees. Although some of these avenues provide the opportunity to garner an explicit vote of confidence or endorsement, such as a resolution of support from a faculty senate assembly, most efforts are more informally structured around fostering understanding and awareness. It is vital that the CDO avoid implanting a policy behind closed doors or in a top-down fashion. By creating an open and consensus-based approach, the CDO will honor an important ideal of academic institutions, giving the community a chance to guide the change journey (Birnbaum, 1988).

Theme 4: Focus on Transforming Institutional Culture

But even as CDOs work toward building informal, collegial networks of support, they must also aim toward systematically interrupting traditional processes of institutional culture (Smith, Turner, Osei-Kofi, & Richards, 2004). Noted organizational theorist Edgar Schein (1985) has observed that institutional cultures have multiple layers. The surface or geospatial layer is the easiest one to manipulate, as institutions have little difficulty making superficial changes, like adding diversity to their promotional brochures and magazines.

The more challenging changes take place at the core of institutional culture and involve the embedded values, beliefs, and assumptions guiding the behavior of students, faculty, staff, and administrative leaders (Schein, 1985). It is at this level where diversity efforts most often meet resistance, as many community members stubbornly view themselves as part of a sacred academic tradition that must be protected at all costs (Rowley & Sherman, 2001). For example, CDOs frequently encounter resistance when encouraging academic diversity competencies like effective teaching of diverse audiences, mentoring diverse students, and embracing multicultural perspectives in the curriculum as part of every faculty job description. If each candidate had to illustrate these competencies as part of his or her selection process, regardless of discipline, it would require a deeper level of cultural change and alignment at the level of shared values and beliefs about what is important academically. This new way of thinking is much more difficult to accomplish than hanging a mural of diverse students in the alumni office, or putting diverse images on the homepage of the college's website.

The long-term success of this model centers on the capacity of senior leaders to unfreeze, move, and reset the campus culture (Schein, 1985). Whether the change involves developing new diversity recruitment and retention processes, supporting ethnic-specific faculty affinity organizations, or hosting a diverse faculty development conference, the overarching goal of these efforts is to open the institution to academic and social practices beyond a traditional focus on the needs and interests of majority White culture. Diversity leaders must think about their work as part of an integrated whole and activate efforts at multiple levels of the institution's culture. This will require plans, accountability, incentives, training systems, and the investment of new resources if change is truly to emerge.

Theme 5: Strategic Planning for Diversity

Planning strategically for diversity begins by writing diversity into the formal mission statement of the institution and developing policies and programs that can be implemented locally at the school, college, or divisional level. Given the permanence of the institutional mission statement, referencing diversity in this document is an important building block for other campus diversity efforts. These statements should provide a clear definition of diversity and its benefits to student learning and meeting the educational mission of the institution. By making the mission prioritize diversity, senior leaders can create a more permanent and visible justification for investing energy, resources, and time into their diversity planning efforts.

Activating these priorities is most effectively accomplished by developing a strategic diversity plan. Authorized at the highest levels of the institution, a comprehensive plan constitutes the superstructure on which an institution's efforts are grafted. Our research uncovered three types of strategic diversity plans: centralized diversity plans, decentralized diversity plans, and integrated diversity plans. In the companion volume to this book, we discuss these plans in detail. Though no panacea, campus diversity plans provide a beacon for the institution to follow.

Centralized diversity plans are generally called for by the president, board of trustees, or regents, and entirely focus on the topic of diversity. They provide vision statements, set broad goals, and make recommendations for change in a variety of diversity areas, generally over a 5- or 10-year span.

Widely different academic institutions around the country have deployed these plans to address issues like staff and faculty professional development, faculty research, student and faculty recruitment and retention, support services for diverse communities, and issues related to campus climate. To achieve maximum effectiveness, centralized diversity plans should be accompanied by decentralized diversity plans, which help define the scope of diversity work at the school, college, unit, and department level. By requiring diversity plans across campus in a decentralized and local way, specific units and departments can "own" their own diversity efforts.

An integrated diversity plan, by contrast, seeks to integrate diversity efforts into preexisting academic and strategic plans. Although integrated diversity plans lack a singular focus on diversity concerns, they still offer an opportunity to enhance and promote diversity efforts. Indeed, by integrating or infusing diversity as a major action item within an institution's broader priorities, senior leaders can organically place diversity near the center of discussions about budget allocations, faculty hiring and retention, and curriculum decisions. The key is to create mechanisms for addressing the diversity aspect of integrated plans at formal governing meetings, like trustee and faculty senate meetings. The challenge is to ensure that diversity priorities are meaningfully integrated into an institution's broader strategic priorities and do not simply end up functioning like window dressing, serving a merely symbolic function instead of building capacity over time.

Theme 6: Developing Diversity Leaders

An institution's human resources, including its faculty, staff, and administrative leaders, offer a powerful lever for changing institutional culture. From this vantage, institutional leaders have three options for developing a team of diversity leaders:

1. Remove people from office who no longer meet the expectations of an institution's emerging diversity agenda, and hire those who do.
2. Bolster the efforts of those already involved in campus diversity efforts by enhancing their ability to do their work.
3. Cultivate knowledge, skills, and attitudes in those currently employed in administrator, faculty, and staff roles.

Removing people from positions is inevitably rare; instead, senior leaders will have to focus their efforts on enhancing existing staff capacity. CDOs will need to partner with different parties to develop human performance enhancement strategies and diversity educational programs, and to help faculty, staff, administrators, and students develop the abilities required to help advance the diversity change process. We use the term *education* rather than *training* to suggest that leadership development is best accomplished through a confluence of learning pedagogies and not simply through diversity-training "workshops" (Cox, 2001).

Strategic diversity leadership requires more than basic training on interpersonal dynamics, sexual harassment, and the legal context of diversity. Rather, it requires creative leadership development designed to facilitate new skills, abilities, and understanding among all members of the campus community. This might take the form of semester-long diversity leadership courses or targeted retreats to explore a particular theme like diversity and communication. It also involves informal conversations designed to create a forum for presidents, provosts, deans, and vice presidents to engage in working meetings around diversity topics.

Theme 7: Building Accountability Techniques

Establishing accountability processes is essential to strategic diversity efforts. At the most general level, *accountability* is defined as creating transparency and visibility around campus diversity efforts and outcomes in the form of reports, presentations, and forums. The most intensive forms of accountability connect campus diversity efforts to the financial systems of the organization, including budget allocations, performance reviews, bonuses, and merit decisions (Rowley & Sherman, 2001).

For institutions serious about implementing their strategic diversity goals, tying merit and budgets to strategic objectives offers a powerful way of rewarding individuals and providing a human performance driver to get members of the campus community engaged. The challenge is that aggressive strategies often meet with resistance. It will require a senior leadership team that is deeply committed to achieving its institutional goals and is willing to experience the discomfort that this type of change may incite. CDOs should proactively introduce these strategies but use extreme caution in navigating the political dynamics associated with activating accountability strategies, because they require the strong support of senior leaders.

Theme 8: Developing Incentives to Encourage Change

Along with accountability measures, CDOs should aggressively work to establish "pull" strategies and incentives to encourage involvement in the diversity change process. In an environment characterized by shared governance and collegiality, motivational energy and entrepreneurial strategies are particularly vital. Moreover, in an era of stretched resources, not all rewards can be monetary. Other incentives and rewards, such as release time, program and individual recognition, and special perks like a privileged parking space should be considered. The progress made by individuals, schools, and departments should be recognized and rewarded (Cox, 2001). For example, the president might host a campus-wide recognition banquet attended by trustees or regents, senior leaders, alumni, and other institutional stakeholders. This type of event sends a powerful message to the campus community regarding diversity's importance and establishes new traditions that help to further embed diversity in the campus culture.

Although central funding of diversity is critical, another strategy is to have relevant leadership structures (e.g., school, college, department, etc.) contribute a portion of their annual budget, or carry forward monies left over from the previous year, toward a central strategic diversity account. By placing diversity change efforts in the competitive space that exists between deans and other senior leaders, we may create new motivating energy for academic leaders to own and activate the campus change process. A final pull strategy is to make a portion of these funds available as competitive grants accessible to students, faculty, staff, and departments. These competitive funds offer financial incentives to encourage new diversity initiatives bubbling up from the institutional community. Funded initiatives then might contribute to a special report, conference, or presentation that could be used to communicate both internally and externally the institution's efforts toward its diversity goals.

Theme 9: Establishing a Strategic Diversity Leadership Scorecard

Strategic diversity leadership is about more than simply increasing the numbers of minority students and women on campus. Colleges and universities must embrace comprehensive performance measurement indicators that connect back to our discussion of organizational diversity capacity. The Strategic Diversity Leadership Scorecard is a multidimensional tool that can simultaneously drive and assess change in four areas: (a) access and equity, (b) campus climate and inclusion, (c) learning and diversity, and (d) domestic and international diversity research and scholarship. These areas, along with sample indicators of progress listed in Table 6.2, can help guide the construction and assessment of campus diversity plans.

TABLE 6.2
Strategic Diversity Leadership Scorecard Perspectives, Description, and Sample Indicators

Perspective	*Description*	*Sample Indicators*
Access and Equity Perspective	To achieve access and equity for historically underrepresented minorities and women, boosting attendance, retention, graduation, and promotion rates, and achieving academic outcomes that match the performance of the majority population	• Six-year graduation rates for minorities and women, students with disabilities, first-generation students, Pell Grant recipients, and others • Graduating minorities and women in the professional schools commensurate with their representation on campus • Graduating minorities in the STEM majors commensurate with their representation on campus • Minorities and women in significant leadership positions at all levels • Minorities and women advancing to full professor at rates commensurate with all faculty members • Minority and female tenure rates • Percentage of minorities and women graduating with a 3.0 GPA or higher • Percentage of minorities and women, students with disabilities, first-generation students, and Pell Grant recipients in the honors program
Multicultural and Inclusive Campus Climate Perspective	Establishing campus climate of inclusion, in which every member of the institution feels a sense of belonging and is able to participate fully in the life of the institution	• Levels of use and participation in diversity and campus-wide activities and initiatives (e.g., high-impact learning experiences) • Perceptions of belonging, engagement, satisfaction, the campus climate, and the work–family environment • Number of lawsuits and settlements • Number of sexual harassment cases • Number of racial discrimination cases • Structured employee feedback
Learning and Diversity Perspective	Ensuring that students, faculty, and staff are prepared for a diverse, knowledge-based, global economy	• Social and emotional intelligence indicators • Democratic outcomes such as the ability to take the position of the other, look at the world from multiple perspectives • Measures of cognitive complexity • Measures of essential learning outcomes • Fulfillment of general education diversity requirements
Diversity Research and Scholarship Perspective	To advance scholarship and research around domestic, international, and intersectional diversity issues	• Total number and value of grants designed to drive research and scholarship in the areas of diversity, equity, and inclusion • Research and scholarly output (e.g., articles, books, chapters, etc.) • Presentations at national and international meetings focused on issues of diversity, equity, and inclusion

Scorecards are powerful tools for helping institutions align their change vision with administrative structures, day-to-day operations, and overarching organizational processes (Bensimon, 2004; R. S. Kaplan & Norton, 1992). They can also communicate progress to institutional stakeholders. Such a tool, when constructed as the guiding vision of your diversity plan, can enable the campus to move from simply "checking off" diversity outcomes (usually represented by the compositional diversity of the student body) to managing a comprehensive plan to reach diversity and educational quality goals and to place these goals at the core of institutional planning and action.

Theme 10: Communicating the Institutional Diversity Brand

In today's competitive environment, higher education leaders need to think about their diversity capabilities in the context of developing a competitive advantage. To accomplish this goal, institutions must communicate their diversity vision, strategy, and outcomes consistently and with conviction. Diversity can play a positive role in building an institution's "brand equity" as it positions itself in relation to peer institutions. In other words, diversity can play a positive role in promotional efforts, just like building a new football stadium, opening a new life sciences center, or recruiting a Nobel Prize laureate to the faculty. The key is to be open in acknowledging continuing challenges and to express authentically the new efforts and commitments being dedicated to the campus's diversity goals.

To keep diversity on the campus radar, progress reports must be given regularly to the board of trustees, faculty senate, donors, and alumni associations. One of the most powerful ways for leaders to move their institutional diversity agenda forward is through storytelling. It is in this context that the president should give an annual "state of diversity address" to discuss major milestones and next steps. These presentations are necessary not only because they communicate what is happening but also because they position efforts within the evolving myths, symbols, and rituals of the institution. Leaders must tell the story of campus diversity efforts to provide a narrative that helps institutional stakeholders to make sense of where the campus is on issues of diversity. These stories assist leaders with "sensemaking" and "sensegiving," as leaders draw on the raw materials of narrative to construct new organizational sense of what should be done to advance campus diversity efforts (Gioia & Chittipeddi, 1991). Indeed, it is this focus on "sensemaking" and "sensegiving" that rests at the core of leading in college and university environments, where perception and symbol are so important.

Higher Education Diversity Capabilities: A Comparison of Institutions With and Without the Chief Diversity Officer Role

Using data from our national survey of diversity officers at over 700 academic institutions, we compared the strategic diversity leadership capabilities of institutions with CDO positions with those that lack them. Although not a direct comparison of the officers' personal backgrounds and abilities, the data do allow us to understand the capabilities—diversity planning and accountability systems, faculty diversification policies, and so on—of institutions that have the CDO capability as opposed to those that do not. This comparison is critical for understanding whether institutions with a CDO role were more likely to have a strategic diversity leadership focus as defined by their institutional diversity capacity.

It is important to remind our readers that this discussion relies on an operationalization of the CDO role, for which we drew out 110 officers based on their responses to a series of questions. Similar to our data reporting in previous chapters, these individuals were selected for inclusion in our analysis on the basis of four criteria: (a) self-classification as a CDO; (b) a direct reporting relationship to the president or provost of the institution; (c) institutional rank of either special assistant/senior advisor to the president, vice president/provost/chancellor, associate vice president/provost/chancellor, assistant vice president/provost/chancellor, or dean, reflecting the institutional titles that most frequently populate the "chief" designation nationally; and (d) a diversity element in their title. Other respondents to the survey were determined to be lower ranking diversity officers because they did not satisfy these four criteria. Nevertheless, many are diversity officers who play a key role in leading diversity, equity, and inclusion efforts at their campuses, and are certainly aware of the various capabilities that exist institutionally.

Before delving into a discussion of several of the strategic diversity leadership themes presented earlier, we begin with a general discussion of what the data revealed about whether diversity was a priority or not at CDO and non-CDO institutions.

Diversity as an Institutional Priority

Although diversity was identified as a priority among a majority of institutions, we observed important differences. Though 81 percent of CDOs responded that diversity was a major institutional priority at their institution, only 54 percent of diversity leaders without the CDO status indicated the same. At least in regard to perceptions, diversity leaders at institutions with a CDO felt more positive about diversity efforts than those leaders at institutions without a CDO. We found a similar response when we asked respondents specifically about the importance of increasing the demographic diversity of the campus community. Respondents at institutions with a CDO overwhelmingly agreed (88 percent) that increasing the number and retention of minority and underrepresented students was a major institutional priority. By comparison, 68 percent of respondents at institutions without a CDO felt that increasing the number and retention of minority and underrepresented faculty was a major institutional priority.

As we examined the capabilities of the institutions with a CDO position, we saw further evidence of investments in various diversity technologies. To uncover these diversity resources, we asked the following: What types of diversity plans are colleges and universities developing? How are institutions creating accountability among faculty, staff, and administrators? Are institutions focused on developing initiatives to prepare students, faculty, and staff for a knowledge-based, global economy? What differences exist between institutions that have the CDO capability and those that do not? From this analysis, we uncovered five capabilities that are particularly important for advancing a strategic diversity agenda: (a) strategic diversity planning systems, (b) diversity accountability systems, (c) diversity research and assessment initiatives, (d) diversity training and educational efforts, and (e) faculty diversification. As we have emphasized throughout this chapter, these five capabilities are essential to implementing a strategic vision for diversity and are discussed here through a comparative treatment of institutions that have a CDO versus those that do not.

Table 6.3 provides an overview of higher education diversity capabilities that we uncovered through our research. More specifically, we identify both general diversity capabilities and those systems that are more intensive in nature. Generally, the more intensive strategies put a premium on engaging diversity issues in a proactive and intentional manner. They often cut against the grain because they require the institution to engage diversity as a high-level strategic priority backed by financial resources, rigorous accountability, and involvement from faculty and administrative leaders not usually involved in diversity efforts.

Capability 1: Strategic Diversity Planning Systems

For campus diversity efforts to be successful, there needs to be a road map for success. Diversity plans help provide direction and focus for the entire

TABLE 6.3
Higher Education Diversity Capabilities Overview

Capabilities	*Description*	*Items*
Strategic Diversity Planning Systems	Planning systems designed to advance institutional diversity efforts across the various campus planning systems	• Official mission statement that addresses diversity • Diversity addressed in institution's academic plan • Strategic and academic planning documents that contain goals for diversity—integrated diversity plans • Existence of an official definition of diversity • Presence of a campus-wide diversity plan • Decentralized diversity plans for schools, colleges, divisions, and departments • Existence of campus-wide plans for international affairs (e.g., study abroad, global research partnerships, international student recruitment, faculty exchanges, etc.)
Diversity Accountability Systems	Intentional systems to drive the institutional diversity agenda	• Institution formally reports on campus diversity plans, including successes, challenges, and ongoing opportunities • Diversity goals and achievements discussed annually at board of trustees or regents meetings • Diversity leadership is assessed as part of the merit review of administrators and faculty
Diversity Research and Assessment Systems	Intentional capacity exists to assess campus diversity progress	• Institution assesses the educational implications and benefits of diversity • Institution uses a diversity scorecard system or other measurement to assess diversity progress • Institution regularly assesses the campus climate for diversity
Diversity Training and Education Initiatives	Formal systems designed to prepare entire campus community to engage with issues of difference, enhancing abilities to thrive in a diverse campus environment and world	• Presence of diversity training and education program for faculty and administrators • Presence of diversity training and education program for students and staff • Existence of diversity course graduation requirement for students
Faculty Diversification Efforts	Intentional capacity to advance faculty diversity on campus	• Key diversity personnel sit on search committees to ensure diversity perspectives • Institution has a formal minority or diversity faculty recruitment initiative • Key diversity staff are an integral part of the tenure and promotion process • Resources are available to partner with academic departments on new faculty hires

institutional community. They establish goals and a course of action for achieving them. A diversity plan also helps departments, faculty leaders, student organizations, and others to align their efforts with common institutional diversity goals. For this reason, we think strategic diversity planning systems are essential to activating a broad-based institutional commitment to diversity.

Figure 6.2 illustrates the variation in strategic planning activities between institutions that did and did not have a CDO. Across each of the six indicators presented here, CDO institutions reveal a greater level of commitment to diversity activities than non-CDO institutions. Not surprisingly, the most prevalent diversity capability at both CDO and non-CDO institutions was more general planning efforts like infusing diversity in the overall institutional mission statement (89 and 82 percent) and creating an integrated diversity plan (91 and 85 percent) where diversity was included as part of the academic or strategic plan of the institution. These were the most prevalent diversity planning tactics across the entire battery of strategic diversity planning systems reported here.

Despite the high percentage of both CDO and non-CDO institutions that include diversity in their mission statements, both institutional types slipped slightly when it came to developing a formal institutional definition of diversity, with 79 percent of CDO institutions and 62 percent of non-CDO institutions reporting a formal institutional definition of diversity. Similarly, 80 percent of CDO and 74 percent of non-CDO institutions have developed strategic diversity goals. By taking the time to create a shared and formal institutional definition of diversity and strategic diversity goals, campus leaders create a context that is essential for accomplishing change. Without clearly delineated diversity definitions and goals, it is difficult for an institution to illustrate how diversity is a strategic priority.

Integrated, Centralized, and Decentralized Diversity Plans

As we looked at more intensive diversity planning activities, two overall findings emerged. First, CDO institutions again evidenced a greater commitment than non-CDO institutions to developing the most meaningful strategies that are associated with delivering a long-term institutional diversity change agenda. Second, our research also revealed that as both types of institutions approach the more difficult work of implementing diversity at the local level, efforts tend to weaken.

CDO and non-CDO institutions were less likely to develop centralized and decentralized diversity plans when compared with less intensive diversity

FIGURE 6.2
Strategic Diversity Planning Systems

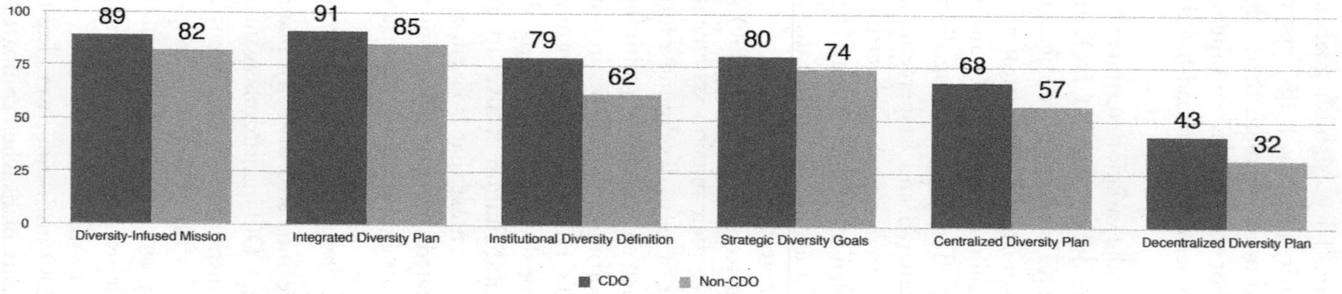

planning activities like infusing diversity into the academic or strategic plan (integrated diversity plans). Sixty-eight percent of CDO institutions had a centralized diversity plan as compared with only 57 percent of non-CDO institutions. CDO institutions were also more likely to engage in decentralized planning processes that reached across schools, colleges, divisions, and departments on campus, by a margin of 43 to 32 percent.

We find that when institutions develop centralized and decentralized diversity plans, it often indicates a more robust strategic diversity planning effort than if they rely solely on integrated diversity plans. Although integrated diversity plans have an important role to play in establishing the strategic framework for diversity efforts, the process of implementation often does not reflect the plan's lofty goals. Indeed, in some cases the integrated diversity plan acts as a smokescreen, allowing campus leaders to avoid developing more direct and resource-intensive centralized and decentralized diversity plans. Diversity efforts thereby end up grafted onto planning documents as an afterthought, rather than as an integral value-added component driving the institution's excellence agenda.

Centralized and decentralized diversity plans allow institutional leaders to focus on a number of different priorities, including providing a powerful educational diversity rationale, outlining clear goals, and assigning key leaders and resources necessary for activating the plan. This is not to say that these plans do not have their flaws. For example, the centralized approach to diversity planning also poses obstacles to achieving broad engagement with the process. In particular, deans and department chairs are less apt to feel ownership over goals that they did not help formulate or that seem poorly aligned with the specific challenges of their units. Hence, it is vital to sustain a local and inclusive planning process across campus. Decentralized plans have their own set of challenges, as uneven implementation results in some schools and colleges taking the challenge seriously whereas others simply go through the motions, doing little of value.

Strategic Diversity Planning Limitations

One of the greatest limitations associated with strategic planning—whether integrated, centralized, or decentralized—is that few institutions have mechanisms for monitoring whether leaders follow through on their commitments. Too many institutions undertake diversity planning efforts sporadically or in response to crisis incidents. Efforts driven by crisis make it difficult to build momentum, because it takes a stable, proactive approach to develop an effective, sustainable diversity plan. And yet despite these challenges, campus diversity plans are an important aspect of strategic diversity leadership and are essential to activating an institution's big-picture diversity agenda. CDOs must understand the strengths and weaknesses of each and should advocate for integrated, centralized, and decentralized plans, depending on what fits best with their institution's vision for diversity. It is for this reason that three chapters are dedicated to discussing why diversity plans fail, best practices for developing diversity plans, and scorecards and accountability techniques in the companion volume to this book.

Capability 2: Diversity Accountability Systems

Our research also examined diversity accountability. We asked about reporting issues at the board level as well as more individually defined accountability mechanisms, including faculty and administrative performance reviews. Overall, CDO institutions were more engaged in all aspects of diversity accountability as compared with non-CDO institutions. Figure 6.3 illustrates the differences between CDO and non-CDO institutions, revealing that 66 percent of CDO institutions confirmed efforts to report regularly on diversity efforts, with 55 percent presenting diversity achievements at annual meetings of their boards of regents or trustees. Meanwhile, only 54 percent of non-CDO institutions confirmed that they reported regularly on diversity efforts, and only 45 percent presented diversity achievements at their annual board meetings.

An annual diversity report can help highlight accomplishments, cultivate new partnerships, and reward the people and initiatives making a difference on campus. Campus stakeholders not only want to know critical diversity outcomes, but why the institution chooses one course of action over another. What were the results of the year's actions? How were resources allocated and to what end? What other opportunities should the institution consider? A report should connect the institution's everyday activities to its mission statement and diversity plans. A report becomes even more important when findings are presented at the highest institutional levels. A presentation before the board of regents draws attention to diversity efforts not only for the board, but also for legislators, alumni, parents, corporations, nonprofit organizations, and the media.

Depending on media efforts, these reports can find their way into newspaper and even television coverage. CDOs should use media coverage to help facilitate further discussions on campus. By increasing public understanding and appreciation, a CDO can promote diversity values "above ground" in the strategic imagination of the institution. As diversity becomes

FIGURE 6.3
Strategic Diversity Accountability Systems

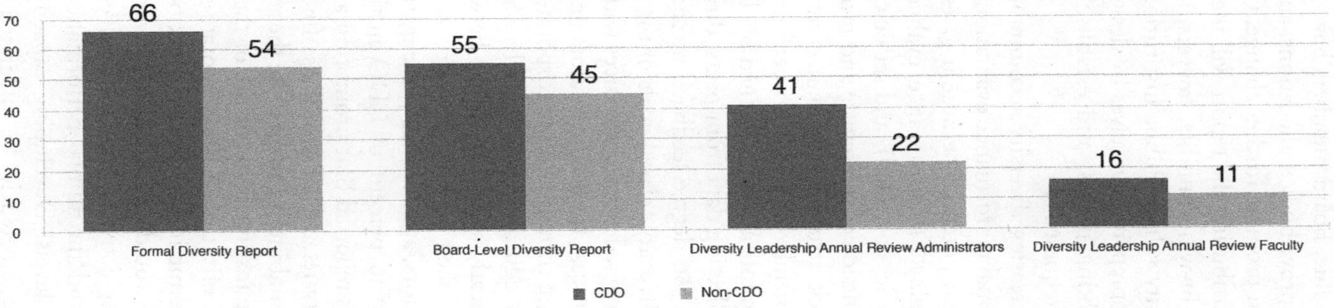

an assumed cultural value, board members have the space to authorize new diversity priorities, approve budget allocations, and create the type of institutional context that can promote further change. CDOs should also be aware that publishing or distributing the report will inevitably elicit questions and even attacks from right-wing pundits, lawyers, and even outside organizations hostile to diversity values. Public institutions are especially vulnerable to attacks and should prepare themselves by designating a dedicated spokesperson, preparing talking points, and establishing a detailed process for responding to media requests.

Another way of creating diversity accountability is to connect diversity leadership to professional performance evaluations. The formal performance review process has great potential because it gives a supervisor the opportunity to address an employee's performance, evaluate whether goals have been met (and any deficiencies corrected), and set new goals for the coming year. Generally speaking, outside of the tenure and promotion system for faculty, many institutions lack strong performance review processes. Moreover, diversity issues are generally absent from performance evaluations for staff, faculty, and administrators alike. As defined by Taylor Cox (2001) this process might include collecting data from peers, direct reports, customers, and supervisors through a 360-degree feedback mechanism regarding a person's contributions to the diversity-related goals of the institution.

Our research uncovered sharp differences with respect to diversity issues in the merit review process for administrators and faculty. Again, although performance reviews are common in the corporate sector, they are not nearly so common in higher education, particularly when it comes to matters of diversity. There was nearly a 20 percent gap between CDO and non-CDO institutions when we asked whether diversity was part of the merit review process for administrators, at 41 and 22 percent, respectively. Among faculty member reviews, only 16 percent of CDO institutions and 11 percent of non-CDO institutions reported that promotion and compensation included recognition of diversity-related efforts. These findings are not surprising as individual-level accountability strategies like these are the most intrusive and counterintuitive to the institutional culture of the academy. However, these measures have proven effective in the corporate sector, and should at least be considered by academic institutions (Cox, 2001).

At their best, this would mean infusing diversity competency questions into the annual faculty activities report, the five-year review of deans and other senior leaders, and the annual performance review of administrators and staff at multiple levels. Developing capacity in this area would also require that diversity competencies be integrated into the search, interview, and screening process of new hires; the assessment of experiences and skills with diverse groups and establishment of the needs of an inclusive work and learning environment should be fundamental expectations for every employee. Finally, this technique would also require institutions to formally infuse diversity and inclusion responsibilities into the job descriptions of leaders across campus, such that this area of competency is formally integrated into the definition of successful leadership institutionally for faculty, staff, and senior leadership.

Capability 3: Diversity Research and Assessment Systems

With respect to the presence of diversity research and assessment systems at CDO and non-CDO institutions, the results were mixed. Our survey asked respondents to identify if their institution assessed the educational benefits of diversity, collected data on the campus climate, or used a diversity scorecard of some kind (Figure 6.4). These three types of research and assessment capabilities allow for senior leaders to understand their institutions' diversity efforts in a number of different ways. First, they help to identify specifically where efforts should be focused to improve overall quality and performance. Second, they allow the institution to benchmark institutional performance with other institutions. Third, they allow the campus community to evaluate performance and monitor the effect of improvement efforts. Fourth, they can provide evidence of how campus diversity efforts contribute to the fulfillment of the institutional mission. And fifth, they inform the context for organizational learning and improvement to help guide future campus diversity efforts.

We were surprised to learn that 62 percent of CDO institutions and 57 percent of non-CDO institutions reported assessing the educational implications or benefits of diversity. Although we caution against drawing too many conclusions from these responses, it is heartening to see that at the very least, survey respondents generally assessed diversity programs and efforts on their campus and found them to be beneficial. Going forward, we hope to access more quantitative and qualitative data that illustrate how diverse interactions lend themselves to different types of cognitive, academic, and democratic outcomes (Milem et al., 2005). This emerging focus marks a welcome trend in higher education. Indeed, our general experience previous to this study had suggested that institutions paid little attention to understanding the effects of diversity on student experiences.

Our research also indicated that campuses are doing more to assess the campus climate. As Figure 6.4 shows, 61 percent of CDO institutions and

FIGURE 6.4
Diversity Research and Assessment Systems

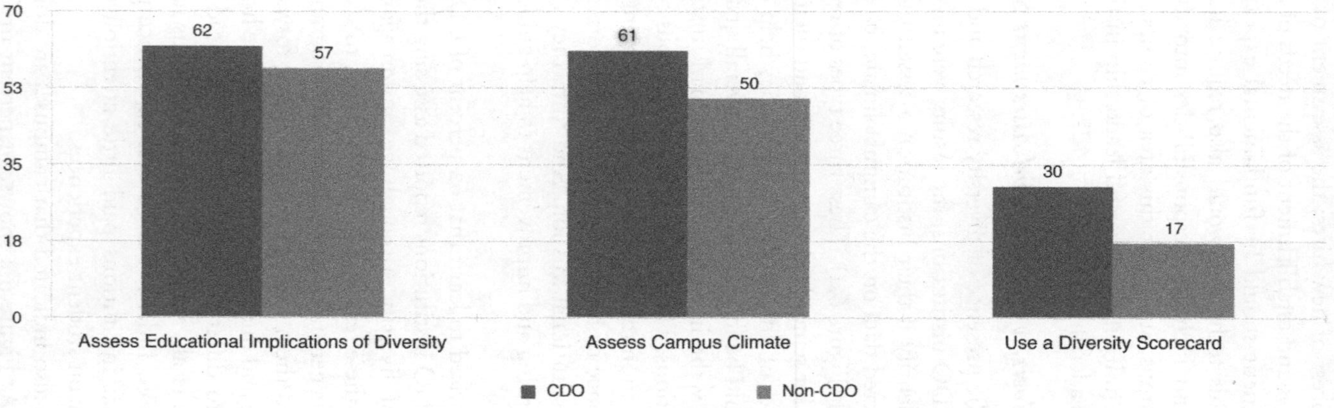

50 percent of non-CDO institutions confirmed that they regularly assess the campus climate. The least frequently cited diversity assessment capability at both CDO and non-CDO institutions was the presence of a diversity scorecard or measurement system to assess diversity progress on campus, at 30 and 17 percent, respectively. As explored in the companion volume to this book, scorecards generally include a balanced and carefully selected set of performance data that helps leadership to understand how their actions ultimately drive their institutions' big-picture strategic diversity plans. More than a simple amassing of data, the scorecard is intended as a tool to identify key performance measures and align the institutional change vision with the formal day-to-day realities of the institution. If designed well, scorecards can provide an accurate and ongoing assessment of an institution's diversity efforts. We encourage institutions to deploy scorecards as a means of taking subjective and speculative elements out of their diversity assessments.

Capability 4: Diversity Training and Education Initiatives

Diversity education and training programs provide an important means of helping students, faculty, and staff to develop the types of leadership skills that are necessary to thrive in a diverse campus community and world. These can take myriad forms, including interactive training sessions, professional development seminars, semester-long courses, and innovative educational activities that encourage a deeper understanding of diversity issues. Our study specifically probed diversity officers to learn more about the general diversity capabilities on their campuses in terms of general education diversity distribution requirements and diversity training and education programs for students, faculty, staff, and senior administrators. As Figure 6.5 shows, CDO institutions were more likely to report engagement in all forms of diversity education/training efforts than non-CDO institutions.

At both CDO and non-CDO institutions, diversity education programs were offered most frequently for staff, followed by students, faculty, and senior administrators. However, although 66 percent of CDO institutions offered diversity training and education programs for staff, fewer than half (48 percent) of non-CDO institutions offered these resources. With regard to cocurricular diversity education and training programs for students, 60 percent of CDO institutions and 48 percent of non-CDO institutions provided programming. And in terms of faculty, 51 percent of CDO institutions and 41 percent of non-CDO institutions offered diversity education and training programs for this community on campus. Among all groups,

FIGURE 6.5
Diversity Training and Educational Systems

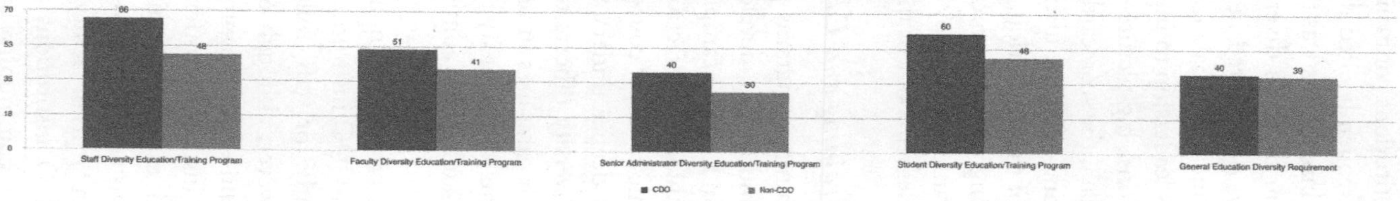

administrators received the least amount of diversity education and training: only 40 percent of CDO and 30 percent of non-CDO institutions offered diversity education programs for their leadership.

Faculty-driven diversity initiatives, especially through curriculum efforts, are essential to advancing the campus diversity agenda. One of the most important diversity capabilities that an institution can pursue is a general education diversity requirement. Although these requirements can take numerous forms, they are essential to moving campus diversity efforts from the outer margins to the inner walls of the classroom. Roughly 40 percent of all officers at colleges and universities in our study reported that their institution had some form of diversity requirement in place (Figure 6.6). This relatively low number was surprising because most institutions endorse the idea that domestic and global diversity issues rank near the top of their academic priorities. Given this rhetoric, we would have expected more institutions to demonstrate their commitment through a course requirement. After all, our diverse, global economy is only becoming more prevalent.

Capability 5: Faculty Diversification Efforts

As we explore in the next chapter, the slow process of diversifying our faculty ranks has been critical to the broader diversity strategic goals of colleges and universities. In our research, we asked respondents about the degree to which they employed four different faculty diversification techniques: (a) possessing an overall faculty diversity effort, (b) ensuring a diversity perspective on search committees, (c) possessing resources to partner with academic units to advance faculty diversity, and (d) participating in tenure and promotion decisions by diversity personnel.

CDO institutions were again more likely to have dedicated faculty diversity capabilities in place, although it would be premature to say how well developed these capabilities were. As Figure 6.6 shows, roughly 50 percent of CDO institutions boasted a faculty diversity recruitment program or initiative, as opposed to 44 percent of non-CDO institutions. It was most common for both kinds of institutions to attach faculty diversity personnel to the search process to ensure that the committee had a diversity perspective. Sadly, both CDO and non-CDO institutions reported that they had not developed or deployed the most aggressive approaches to diversify their faculty. That said, CDO institutions were more likely than non-CDO institutions to indicate that they had offered resources to seed or partner with academic units to spur new faculty lines, by a margin of 42 to 32 percent,

FIGURE 6.6
Faculty Diversification Systems

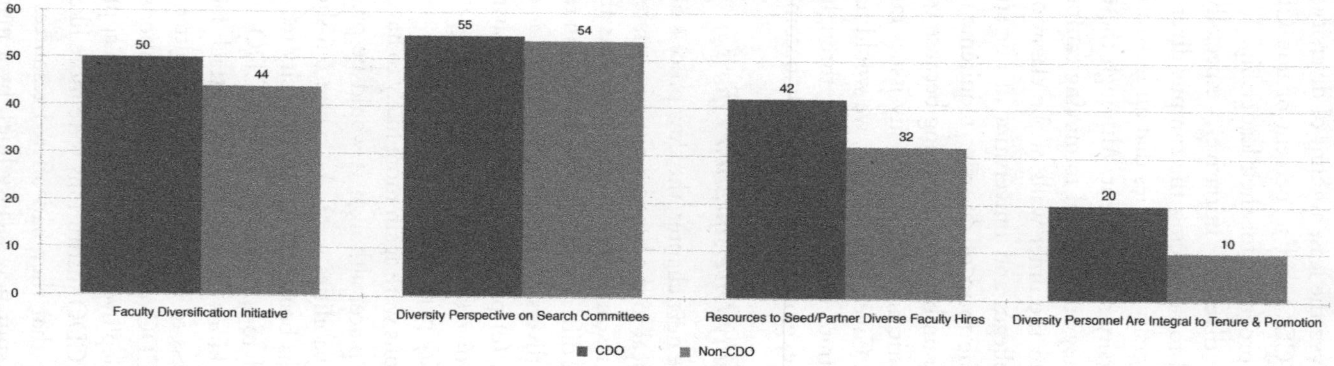

respectively. Finally, CDO institutions were twice as likely as non-CDO institutions to include diversity personnel in the tenure and promotion process than non-CDO institutions.

To serve current and future student populations, diverse perspectives are needed in the classroom. The greater the faculty diversity, the more likely all students will be exposed to a variety of ideas drawn from different life experiences. Because women and minority faculty are also more likely to engage in diversity research, their presence can help transform an institution's pedagogical, research, and curriculum priorities. As our data reveal, most institutions are not pursuing aggressive faculty diversification practices with respect to hiring or the tenure process. Meanwhile, our survey of CDOs discovered that 86 percent of respondents listed attending a faculty diversity strategy workshop as the most important to their professional development. In other words, there is a disconnect between what CDOs see as essential to the strategic diversity movement—diversifying our faculty—and the capabilities that are put in place to accomplish this goal. The next chapter investigates these concerns in detail.

Summary

Today it is rare to find an academic institution that is not, at some level, engaging with issues of diversity, access, and inclusion. But just because diversity is on their radar does not mean that senior leaders are fully dedicated to creating a strategic diversity agenda. A strategic diversity agenda is built on the best of what we know about organizational strategy and change management. Addressing critical topics like racism, sexism, homophobia, classism, access, equity, power, and privilege is vital if we are to build a competitive, culturally intelligent workforce.

In this chapter we laid the foundation for CDOs to develop a strategic diversity agenda at their institutions. We provided a brief overview of the key techniques associated with strategic diversity leadership and discussed the degree to which institutions that have a CDO role have built these capabilities at their institutions. Without question, institutions that have invested in the CDO capability have more institutional diversity capabilities than institutions that have not developed formal diversity leadership at the executive level.

When it comes to implementing a modern-day campus diversity agenda, there is no single solution. Instead, senior leaders should appreciate that there are multiple institutional levers at their disposal. Unlike some change efforts, which can take shape in the minds of only a few people, a strategic diversity agenda needs to reflect the voices if it is going to prove successful. This chapter lays out 10 strategic diversity leadership themes that can help guide either the CDO or an institution's senior leaders in developing their diversity policies and programs. As our research clearly demonstrated, those institutions that have invested early in a dedicated CDO role have a leg up in pursuing the kinds of policies that lead to robust and sustainable diversity change. A qualified CDO appreciates how to lead the diversity effort, drawing on institutional, political, collegial, and symbolic relationships and messaging. Working collaboratively and creatively, he or she can build effective partnerships both on and off campus to help advance our diversity values.

7

BEST PRACTICES FOR IMPROVING FACULTY DIVERSITY RECRUITMENT AND RETENTION

> It is no longer the case—if, in fact, it ever was the case—that a department can simply write an ad, place it in its professional publication, and wait for the hundreds of qualified candidates to submit applications. Attracting a strong and diverse pool of candidates requires both time and hard work, and the entire department must be engaged in attracting candidates.
>
> —Academic dean in a major research university[1]

In the last 20 years, many colleges and universities have touted the importance of faculty diversity. Yet most institutions remain culturally, racially, and ethnically homogenous, and men still predominate in positions of authority. Moreover, as Caroline Turner (2002) points out in *Diversifying the Faculty: A Guidebook for Search Committees,* policies to diversify faculty are among the least successful diversity efforts in higher education. For a majority of institutions, progress has been glacial and the struggle to increase historically underrepresented minority and women faculty, especially in the science, technology, engineering, and mathematics (STEM) fields, continues (Moody, 2004; G. A. Olson, 2007; Smith, Turner, Osei-Kofi, & Richards, 2004). For this reason, this chapter argues that chief diversity officers (CDOs) should make increasing faculty diversity one of their central goals.

Although some CDOs emerge from the faculty ranks and thus possess direct personal experience with the challenges of faculty diversity, others do not. Regardless of background, every CDO must possess a strong understanding of faculty diversification strategies. It is paramount that the CDO navigate the institution's academic culture and be able to collaborate with provosts, academic deans, department chairs, and search committees to develop strategies to recruit and retain a more diverse faculty.

This chapter does not engage in an extensive overview of pipeline issues central to the faculty diversity challenge. Issues like national initiatives for improving minority access to higher education, K–12 disparities, and disparities in the number of women completing undergraduate or graduate STEM degree programs certainly warrant specific and detailed focus. However, our explicit focus here is helping CDOs by presenting several strategies for improving their faculty diversification efforts. To be effective in the area of strategic diversity leadership, CDOs must understand the barriers to faculty diversity, the legal issues associated with faculty diversity efforts, and the best practices associated with hiring and retaining diverse talent. We also offer a case study of one institution that implemented a highly successful faculty diversification program. More than a comprehensive overview of the faculty diversity challenge, this chapter provides CDOs with key techniques for overcoming challenges that have traditionally confronted historically underrepresented faculty. Indeed, the strategies offered here are relevant for achieving faculty diversity among women and members of the LGBT, disabled, veteran, and other communities.

Barriers to Faculty Diversity

In conducting research for this book, we examined diversity scholarships, spoke with key leaders across the country, and reflected on our own experiences working directly on these issues. The barriers to faculty diversity are complex. Our research suggests five primary impediments: (a) the pipeline challenge, (b) outdated faculty recruitment and retention practices, (c) faculty diversity myths that abound in higher education, (d) the decentralized administrative culture of the academy, and (e) the view that faculty diversity is incompatible with academic excellence. Finally, to overcome these obstacles, our efforts must focus as much on retention as on recruitment. What follows is a brief discussion of each of these barriers.

The Pipeline Challenge

Although colleges and universities have experienced growing racial and ethnic diversity, and women are now the majority of students, the faculty ranks remain homogenous. Despite efforts by many institutions, women and minorities make up only 14 percent of the total instructional faculty nationwide (Knapp, Kelly-Reid, & Ginder, 2012). The U.S. Department of Education's latest annual status report illustrates the lack of diversity among full-time faculty: 4.9 percent are non-Hispanic African American, 2.8 percent are Hispanic, 5.8 percent are Asian American/Pacific Islander, and 0.4 percent are American Indians (Knapp, Kelly-Reid, & Ginder, 2012). Women represent only 25 percent of instructional faculty in higher education (Knapp et al., 2012).

The need for a diverse faculty has become even more pronounced in the face of challenges presented by an increasingly multicultural student body pursuing opportunities in a knowledge-based global economy. However, despite an expressed desire to diversify their faculty, most institutions have struggled to make significant progress. Part of the problem is that there are insufficient numbers of women and minorities on the educational pathway entering the professorate. Leaks in the educational system at the K–12, undergraduate, and graduate levels have caused a "pipeline problem" in the upper reaches of many academic disciplines.

Although concerns about the pipeline are legitimate, this rationale should not serve as an excuse for inaction. The common stereotype that a qualified pool of diverse applicants does not exist or is difficult to access encourages search committees to pursue "business as usual" in their hiring efforts, ultimately perpetuating existing inequalities. The deeper challenge is that many diverse candidates simply are not aggressively recruited (Smith et al., 2004). To address this challenge, it is important for academic institutions to employ best practices to hire, promote, and retain the diverse faculty talent that does exist. Institutions that are serious in their desire to enhance their faculty diversity can do so, but they must be aggressive, intentional, creative, and focused on creating change over time.

A Need for "Interrupting the Usual"

There are undoubtedly challenges to recruiting and retaining a more diverse faculty, but it is not an unattainable goal. What it involves, at its core, is what Daryl G. Smith and colleagues have referred to as "interrupting the usual" (2004, p. 153). Departments must move beyond the self-fulfilling prophecies about the difficulty of hiring underrepresented faculty and approach recruitment with rigor and creativity.

Effective recruitment requires commitment, diligence, and innovation. Institutions must establish a complex web of partnerships based on open communication and mutual accountability, and establish external strategic partners who can help develop aggressive and effective strategies. To build outstanding and diverse departments we need to take a page from competitive athletics and the world of business by aggressively pursuing the best and the brightest candidates. Indeed, we might have to help in developing these candidates when the potential is there.

The literature on faculty diversification notes that many institutions fail to interrupt the usual way that they approach the goal of diversifying their institutions and, as a result, miss diversity hire opportunities (Bilimoria & Buch, 2010; Smith et al., 2004). Active recruitment goes beyond simply writing and posting a job description. Institutions have to recruit if they want to achieve diversity. Too often, departments and search committees assume that they can simply place a job advertisement and wait to see which applicants emerge. Time and again the literature suggests that passivity will result in neither a diverse pool of applicants nor a diverse hire (Jackson, 2006; Smith et al., 2004). The successful recruitment of historically underrepresented faculty only happens when institutions employ a multidimensional faculty diversification strategy (Moody, 2004; G. A. Olson, 2007; Smith et al., 2004).

Moreover, many institutions do not even have a faculty diversity strategy in place. Basic procedures are absent, such as requiring search committee training, building an understanding of the pipeline of diverse talent, developing targeted efforts to build personal relationships with diverse candidates, or requiring that a search committee stay in the field until it assembles a diverse candidate pool (Bilimoria & Buch, 2010; Moody, 2004; G. A. Olson, 2007; Smith et al., 2004). Rather, many academic departments use a laissez-faire approach to faculty recruitment. Typically, search committees place the job ad based on a previous faculty member's research and credentials, post the jobs in the traditional venues, receive nominations from trusted colleagues at other institutions, review and rank candidates, develop the short list, interview top candidates, and ultimately make the job offer (Bilimoria & Buch, 2010). The problem with this approach is that it generally fails to result in a diverse applicant pool, let alone a diverse hire (Smith et al., 2004; Turner, 2002).

Daryl Smith and colleagues (2004) examined nearly 700 searches to determine whether specific interventions resulted in the hiring of African American, Latino, and Native American faculty at three large American Association of Universities institutions when one of three conditions was met: (a) the job description explicitly engaged diversity at the department or subfield level; (b) an institutional "special hire" strategy, such as waiver of a search, target of opportunity hire, or spousal hire, was used; and (c) the search was conducted by a diverse search committee. The results demonstrated that using one or more of these three techniques often led to a diverse hire. Among those faculty hires, 86 percent of African American, 100 percent of Native American, and 57 percent of Latino faculty were hired through a search that used one or more of the diversity-enriched search processes. Unfortunately, only 26 percent of the searches included in the study used these more targeted faculty search techniques. The sad reality is that if the search did not use a diversity-intensive strategy, a diversity hire did not take place.

Engaging Faculty Diversity Myths

Another barrier to faculty diversity are the persistent myths surrounding the faculty search process (Moody, 2004; G. A. Olson, 2007; Smith et al., 2004; Turner, 2002). Among the most prevalent is the notion that institutions cannot compete for candidates who are highly sought after by the corporate sector. Another stereotype is that faculty of color do not want to come to a particular campus or a region of the country because it is not diverse or urban enough. Other departments fail to recruit diverse faculty because they believe that minority faculty will ultimately leave for a more desirable position as soon as they make tenure. Finally, still others believe that a strategic effort to recruit more faculty of color perpetuates "reverse discrimination," undermining efforts to hire the best candidate for the job.

All of these claims are either false or grossly exaggerated. The simple fact remains, many well-prepared minority faculty candidates are not actively recruited and do not have the luxury of considering multiple job offers (Moody, 2004; Olson, 2007; Smith et al., 2004; Turner, 2002). In her study of labor markets, Daryl Smith and her colleagues (2004) found that only 11 percent of the scholars of color within a sample of approximately 300 interview participants were "sought after" by institutions of higher education. Other findings included the following: (a) scientists of color were often found in postdoctoral positions and were not being pursued for faculty positions; (b) scholars were interested in working in a wide range of institutional settings, despite a common myth that they are exclusively interested in well-known institutions; (c) when diverse faculty transferred to another institution, they were often motivated by personal rather than financial incentives; (d) the choice to leave academia was often a function of specific criticisms of academia rather than the irresistible temptations outside of academia; and (e) White scholars still enjoyed a consistent advantage in finding faculty positions.

The Decentralized Nature of the Academy and the Key Role of Senior Leadership

Marjorie Fine Knowles and Bernard W. Harleston (1997) examined the faculty diversity efforts of 11 highly regarded research universities. Their American Council on Education report, "Achieving Diversity in the Professoriate: Challenges and Opportunities," concluded that the decentralized nature of academic institutions was a significant barrier to increasing faculty diversity. Senior leaders have little ability to directly influence hiring decisions, although they can create a context for faculty diversity to emerge. Most policy decisions about hiring are made at the departmental level, where considerable power resides with chairs and their hiring committees. Department heads and senior faculty develop recruitment plans and decide what constitutes quality, including how scholarship quality is measured, how publications and research are credited, and the areas of scholarship to be emphasized. Commitment to diversity must therefore take place concurrently at departmental and senior administrative levels. If institutions are going to be more successful in the future, we must integrate our departmental and central diversification efforts.

Research by Knowles and Harleston (1997) found that many faculty members did not know about existing diversity resources and were confused by current legal and institutional policies regarding diversity. Because faculty tend to lack expertise in these areas, CDOs need to educate academic deans and department chairs about the resources available for promoting diversity. This means making faculty diversity part of new faculty orientation events, new department chair training workshops, annual retreats, and other events where faculty hiring and retention issues are raised. The more prevalent faculty diversity efforts become, the more they enter an institution's day-to-day culture.

When talking to senior leaders, Knowles and Harleston (1997) found that many campus presidents and provosts saw themselves as having a limited ability to influence faculty hiring decisions. This is a major barrier to faculty diversity as the support of top leaders is essential to creating a broad institutional context for promoting faculty efforts. Senior leaders can prioritize diversity in campus strategic and academic plans, authorize specific financial resources (e.g., target of opportunity hires, targeted recruitment funds, etc.), and develop accountability strategies that convey an institution's commitment. In 2005, Columbia University President Lee C. Bollinger implemented a $15 million faculty diversity effort that featured on-the-ground leadership of a CDO, search committee education, proactive recruitment efforts, and a host of other techniques designed to make a measurable difference in the composition of faculty, and by extension the research and learning environment (Freudenberger, Howard, Jauregui, & Sturm, 2009).

CDOs can embolden senior leaders to understand that investing in faculty diversity efforts is foundational to expressing an institution's commitment to core values of inclusion and academic excellence. Even though their decision-making culture is usually decentralized, most institutions cannot deter the efforts of intentional, determined presidents and provosts. However, just because senior leaders publicly declare their support for hiring diverse candidates does not mean that there will be success on the ground. Faculty diversity efforts must have top-level support and on-the-ground engagement by faculty, departments, and search committees. To this end, it is important for faculty and department chairs to understand how to access the various faculty diversification tools that may exist on campus.

The Compatibility of Diversity and Academic Excellence

CDOs will inevitably encounter faculty members who view diversity as ancillary with academic excellence (Knowles & Harleston, 1997). Indeed, many faculty fail to recognize that departmental hiring decisions are connected to the broader campus's educational priorities. This is something that needs to change.

Clearly, every faculty member must have the requisite competencies and expertise required to fulfill the teaching, scholarship, and service requirements of his or her position. At the same time, it is important for provosts, deans, department heads, and search committee chairs to emphasize that campus search committees represent the interests not only of their school or department, but the entire academic community. For CDOs and others working directly with search committees, this means helping committees to understand the role they can play in shaping the campus's diversity agenda.

The unfortunate reality is that many who serve on faculty search committees have never even discussed the cultural and academic advantages of promoting a diverse faculty and staff. CDOs must be able to discuss the educational and organizational benefits of diversity. In many instances, this involves leveraging recent research and educating leaders about the importance of diversity in promoting cross-cultural understanding and breaking down stereotypes, essential skills for the workforce and society of tomorrow.

CDOs must rely on research demonstrating that a diverse student body promotes better learning outcomes and provides for more enlightening classroom discussions (Gurin, Dey, Hurtado, & Gurin, 2002; Milem, Chang, & Antonio, 2005). Another tactic includes finding faculty members willing to share their personal experiences with faculty colleagues and serve as diversity champions. Their participation adds an important qualitative element as they can share their experiences in the classroom, mentoring diverse students and engaging in diversity issues and topics. The insights of these trusted scholars can help create support among other faculty (Brown-Glaude, 2009). By engaging faculty diversity champions with strong academic credentials and a history of institutional leadership, a college or university can create support for its diversity efforts from within (Freudenberger et al., 2009).

The support of the administration is crucial to reaching out to diverse candidates. Such support includes providing resources like funding for travel to conferences that facilitate exposure to more diverse candidates, sponsoring presentations by faculty members who have led candidate searches, and providing class buyouts for those leading the effort to diversify the candidate pool. In short, the pursuit of faculty diversity goals must be more than an unfunded mandate.

A Focus on Recruitment and Retention

Finally, institutions must invest in both recruitment and retention activities if they are going to successfully diversify their faculty. Even richly diverse institutions struggle to retain their minority faculty and staff (Moreno, Smith, Clayton-Pedersen, Parker, & Teraguchi, 2006; Turner & Myers, 2000). Put simply, recruitment does not guarantee retention, so any faculty diversification effort that does not address mentorship, improving the institutional culture, or attending to dual-career needs may end up fueling a "revolving door" with respect to new minority hires.

A study of 27 colleges and universities funded by the Association of American Colleges and Universities found that the turnover rate for ethnically and racially diverse faculty is higher than among majority faculty. Looking at a five-year period, the study found that one of every two minority faculty hires constituted a replacement for a previous minority hire who had left the institution (Moreno et al., 2006). One reason for this high rate of attrition is what the American Federation of Teachers Higher Education (2010) refers to as a "culture that sometimes breeds a sense of isolation and exclusion, creates confusion about how to meet job responsibilities and

advance professionally, and imposes unreasonable work
from racially and ethnically underrepresented groups" (
their strategic diversity agendas, CDOs must partner w
and department heads not only to recruit diverse facult
promote them.

Legal and Statutory Support for Faculty Diversification Efforts

As we point out in the companion volume to this book, the legal framework surrounding race-conscious diversity efforts is constantly shifting, with the Supreme Court poised to rule on the ability of colleges and universities to use race in admissions far sooner than most would have anticipated when Justice O'Conner suggested that the *Grutter v. Bollinger* (2003) ruling might last for at least 25 years. The *Fisher v. University of Texas* (2012) case is just another illustration of how the past decade has witnessed growing legal and legislative challenges to traditional diversity policies. Indeed, the lead general counsel at a large research university in the Southwest told us, "Most of the time we are our own worst enemy in terms of rolling out our diversity strategy. We are too scared to act; in order to ensure that we stay in the safe zone of not getting sued, we do too little."

Right-wing organizations like the Foundation for Individual Rights in Higher Education, the Center for Equal Opportunity, and the National Association of Scholars have often succeeded in reframing the diversity debate around claims of reverse discrimination, even though the statistics clearly demonstrate that our higher learning institutions are largely homogenous and lacking in racial and ethnic diversity when one looks at the demographic profile of our faculty. As Ann Springer notes in a report by the American Association of University Professors, the vast majority of discriminatory claims are made by minorities, women, and others in protected categories (Springer, 2006). For an academic institution, there is not only a risk of discrimination lawsuits, but a missed opportunity: a multiplicity of perspectives and lived experiences is essential to a twenty-first-century education (Springer, 2006). These lawsuits are expensive and have a negative effect on an institution's resources, brand, and morale (Springer, 2006). A diverse faculty supported by robust and effective diversity policies is less likely to engage in the kind of discrimination that creates legal risk for the institution (Springer, 2006).

To build a winning faculty diversity strategy, senior leaders must aggressively and creatively address faculty diversity issues (Alger, 2009; American Association for the Advancement of Science, 2010; Coleman & Palmer, 2004; Springer, 2006). This means being careful to respect the law, but also to pursue a set of strategies that will result in significant change. In the legal community, this is often referred to as leading in the "yellow zone," in which leaders, while cautious, work to advance a meaningful diversity strategy. To help their institutions lead in the "yellow zone," CDOs must understand the legal and policy issues surrounding faculty diversification. Although courts have recognized that student body diversity constitutes a "compelling state interest," our capacity to create race-conscious employment practices for faculty and staff is more tenuous (Alger, 2009). At the same time, the constitutional and statutory foundation for advancing an intentional faculty diversification effort is sound (Alger, 2009; American Association for the Advancement of Science, 2010; Coleman & Palmer, 2004; Springer, 2006). Because the Supreme Court has yet to rule on the ability of colleges and universities to develop race-conscious recruitment and hiring programs, there are no definitive answers.

Diversity as a Compelling Interest in Employment

The ability of colleges and universities to use race in admissions decisions will receive further review when the Supreme Court issues its decision in *Fisher v. University of Texas* in mid-2013. This decision will have implications for university efforts to create race-conscious employment strategies as well. Indeed, the present support for race-conscious employment policies in higher education lacks clarity as the legal rationale is grounded in interpretations of case law from other contexts (Alger, 2009; American Association for the Advancement of Science, 2010; Coleman & Palmer, 2004; Springer, 2006).

From the perspective of many legal scholars, a primary rationale for faculty diversification efforts flows out of the race-conscious admissions decisions rendered in the University of Michigan cases, particularly the *Grutter v. Bollinger* (2003) decision (Alger, 2009; American Association for the Advancement of Science, 2010; Coleman & Palmer, 2004; Springer, 2006). In that case, the Supreme Court affirmed the educational benefits of diversity, building on its 1978 ruling in *Regents of the University of California v. Bakke.* Admissions strategies to promote diversity were sanctioned as long as they were narrowly tailored and did so for the purposes of achieving educational goals, not as an "end" in themselves (Coleman & Palmer, 2004). In a

2004 manual on how to develop race-conscious programs in higher education, Arthur Coleman and colleagues noted:

> Diversity for diversity's sake serves no educational purpose and, undirected toward any educational purpose, likely will be viewed by courts as impermissible racial or ethnic balancing. Consequently, the term "diversity" is not, in the first instance, one to be defined by lawyers or judges—or, for that matter, one that can be explained in some formulaic or standardized way. It is a term that should derive its meaning from its institutional or programmatic origins. It may, therefore, relate to (and be defined according to) programs and practices that are as varied as the institutional missions and goals that comprise the higher education community. As a result, this Manual does not attempt to offer a definition of the term. To do so would be to ignore the very academic foundations from which the concept has evolved. (Coleman & Palmer, 2004, p. 2)

The court affirmed that the social context matters when determining how race and ethnicity are to be used in accomplishing campus educational goals (Alger, 2009; American Association for the Advancement of Science, 2010; Coleman & Palmer, 2004). Hence, a wide range of issues including how diversity is defined, the institution's mission, and the techniques used to accomplish diversity goals are all vital to establishing the framework for diversity hiring practices. A critical aspect of the Supreme Court's rationale is its deference to the missions of educational institutions, allowing them to make decisions that determine the overall social and educational context of their learning environments.

Key Principles to Applying Grutter

The Supreme Court's decision to hear the case of *Fisher v. University of Texas* (2012) is likely to have important implications for the future of affirmative action in higher education. It is quite likely that the four conservative justices will vote to strike down at least some aspects of the University of Texas's admissions program. Much depends on the court's "swing vote," Justice Stephen Kennedy. It is an open question as to whether a majority of the court will overturn the *Grutter* decision entirely and conclude that diversity is no longer a compelling state interest that can be furthered by the consideration of race in admissions decisions.

Although the court's 2003 decision in *Grutter* applied only to student admissions, the court did receive a number of briefs filed by corporations, the military, and health fields that validated the importance of diverse experiences as critical preparation for leadership in a global economy. Each of these briefs emphasized the special role that colleges and universities play in preparing the next generation of leaders. In defining how colleges and universities can pursue this compelling educational interest, the *Grutter* decision was clear about the need for institutions to create strategies that were narrowly tailored, thereby setting the parameters for today's diversity policies in admissions, financial aid, and employment (Alger, 2009; American Association for the Advancement of Science, 2010; Coleman & Palmer, 2004).

Although there is clearly a need to proceed with caution in constructing an institutional strategy aimed at diversifying the faculty, there is every reason to believe that such an effort can be implemented while still conforming to today's legal precedents (Alger, 2009; American Association for the Advancement of Science, 2010; Coleman & Palmer, 2004; Springer, 2006). Jonathan Alger (2009), a leading scholar and president at James Madison University, offers guidance that upholds existing laws and shields the institution from allegations of "reverse discrimination":

- **Diversity should be defined broadly.** Institutions that are pursuing an interest in diversity must be able to demonstrate that they are considering a wide range of attributes, not just race or national origin. There should be a wide range of other characteristics that contribute to an educational environment's diversity. Other factors include socioeconomic background, geography, first generation in a family to attend college or graduate school, special skills and talents, unique life experiences, and so on.
- **Each applicant must be able to compete against the entire pool.** Applicants must be reviewed on a holistic basis. Everyone must be able to compete against the entire pool; there should be no separate tracks, committees, or processes based on race or national origin.
- **Quotas are forbidden.** In other words, admissions offices cannot set a predetermined, specific number of openings for minority applicants. Race can be considered a "plus" factor in the admissions decisions, but cannot be used in an automatic or overdetermined way.
- **Race-neutral alternatives must be considered.** Race-neutral alternatives, such as developmental policies to strengthen the pipeline of diverse applicants, must be seriously considered, and should be considered in combination with more direct race- or gender-conscious measures.

- **Majority candidates cannot be unduly burdened.** In any program in which race is taken into account, the burden on members of racial groups that do not receive a "plus" factor must be minimized so that these groups are not harmed.
- **Diversity efforts must not be permanent.** Programs should not be permanent, and should be reviewed periodically.

Race-Conscious Employment Policies

Although the Supreme Court has not specifically ruled on race-conscious hiring policies in higher education (Alger, 2009; American Association for the Advancement of Science, 2010; Coleman & Palmer, 2004), the lower courts have issued decisions in ways that help colleges and universities use race and ethnicity in their employment practices. As Alger (2009) notes, in *Petit v. City of Chicago* (2003) the courts upheld a race-conscious affirmative action plan in the Chicago Police Department, citing a compelling need to have a diverse police force to protect and secure the trust of a diverse community. The court ruled further that this was particularly important at the rank of sergeant to establish a particular tone of leadership in the department and build trust in diverse communities. This particular argument could clearly be extended to campus police who support a diverse campus community.

In the *University and Community College System of Nevada v. Farmer* (1997) the Nevada Supreme Court cited the educational benefits of diversity in upholding a race-conscious hiring decision that led to the hire of an African American scholar, even though both he and a female White candidate were deemed equally well qualified by virtue of their teaching, publications, and areas of specialization. More specifically, the court noted, "We also view the desirability of a racially diverse faculty as sufficiently analogous to the constitutionally permissible attainment of a racially diverse student body countenanced by the *Bakke* decision" (*University and Community College System of Nevada v. Farmer*, 930 P.2d at 735 as cited by W. A. Kaplan & Lee, 2007, p. 212). Here, the court found that diversity was a compelling interest in a faculty hire, just as it is with student admissions (Alger, 2009).

Although more research is needed on the educational benefits of diverse faculty, organizational diversity research by individuals like Scott Paige, author of *The Difference: How the Power of Diversity Creates Better Groups,*

Firms, Schools, and Societies (2007), convincingly explores diversity's importance to organizational performance. Paige found that talented and diverse groups achieve stronger outcomes than homogenous groups in terms of complex problem solving and creativity. The more research that CDOs can invoke about the educational benefits of faculty diversity, the more their perspectives can serve college and university diversification efforts.

Statutory Context

In addition to the diversity rationale established by relevant case law, faculty diversification has been supported by affirmative action policies and case law covered by Title VII of the Civil Rights Act and enforced by the Office of Federal Contract Compliance Programs (OFCCP) (Alger, 2009; American Association for the Advancement of Science, 2010; Coleman & Palmer, 2004). Title VII prohibits policies and practices that have a disproportionately negative effect on minorities. In cases in which there is strong evidence of prior intentional racial or gender discrimination, the employer can pursue policies that take these issues into account to remedy past discrimination.

In a related fashion, if "underutilization" of women and minorities can be demonstrated in the workforce, employers can establish efforts to increase their presence under the OFCCP. Generally, underutilization exists when fewer women or minorities are employed in job groups than expected given their availability in the relevant labor pools (Alger, 2009; American Association for the Advancement of Science, 2010). Institutions that are federal contractors may use underutilization as a rationale to justify their faculty diversification efforts. In these situations, an institution can apply good-faith efforts to expand outreach to women, minorities, persons with disabilities, and certain groups of protected veterans. Over time, the hope is that an institution's workforce—in this case, its faculty—will reflect the candidate pool from which it draws its workforce.

Recommendations for Recruiting Diverse Faculty

If we are to build an outstanding and diverse faculty, we need to take a page from competitive athletics and the world of business by aggressively pursuing the best and the brightest candidates. Effective recruitment begins with a broad institutional commitment that empowers academic departments and search committees to make diverse hires (Moody, 2004; Olson, 2007; Smith et al., 2004).

In developing a strategy that balances the need to foster a more diverse faculty with the legal obligations outlined previously, we have focused on measures that intervene as early as possible in the hiring process (Alger, 2009). These "upstream" recruitment efforts are less risky because the initial effort identifies as many diverse and qualified candidates as possible. That said, we also examine "downstream" approaches that depart from traditional recruitment and hiring processes, such as target of opportunity hiring initiatives. Table 7.1 outlines several critical techniques for developing faculty diversity recruitment strategies.

Diversity Definition and Rationale Statement

A first priority in developing a faculty diversification strategy is to write a faculty diversity rationale that defines *diversity* and its value to the institution. As with student admissions efforts that take race and ethnicity into account, faculty diversity should be defined broadly and address more than increasing racial and gender diversity (Alger, 2009; American Association for the Advancement of Science, 2010; Coleman & Palmer, 2004). As we discussed at length in the companion volume to this book, *diversity* should be defined in broad terms that embrace multiple facets of social identity. It is also important that diversity be presented as fundamental to creating the type of educational experience that enriches the learning environment, rather than as an end in and of itself.

The courts have been very clear that racial balancing does not represent a compelling interest, but that the educational benefits of diversity do (Alger, 2009; American Association for the Advancement of Science, 2010; Coleman & Palmer, 2004). Hence, our recommendation is to develop a faculty diversification definition and rationale that is consistent with this theme. Even if your faculty diversity effort is emerging in a context in which affirmative action is called for because of a ruling of discrimination or underutilization of the workforce, the presence of an educational rationale as part of your framing only strengthens the foundation of why faculty diversity is important in an educational context.

Additional diversity dimensions include religion, political perspectives, socioeconomic or cultural backgrounds, geography, and special talents. Indeed, these various dimensions of "social diversity" can spark new research questions, and even new fields and subfields. It is too simplistic to reduce the shape of research questions, field interests, or interpretive lines of analysis

TABLE 7.1
Strategic Faculty Recruitment Strategies

Recruitment Strategy	*Description*	*Key Themes*
1. *Diversity* Definition and Rationale	An institutional definition and rationale for diversity that is broadly defined and anchors the educational benefits rationale for having a diverse faculty on campus	• Broad definition of *diversity* • Aligned to institutional mission, plans, strategies • Focus on creating a diverse learning environment and rich context for diverse scholarship
2. Diversity Recruitment Plan	A plan that outlines the techniques that a search committee will use to ensure that it casts a broad net and maximizes the likelihood of achieving a diverse applicant pool, possibly including committee training, targeted advertising, special recruitment trips, and other activities	• Plan to cast a broad net • Plans required of every search committee • Professional development around cultural bias in search, selection, and outreach efforts • Identifying a search committee member to serve as the faculty diversification lead
3. Diversity-Enriched Position Descriptions	Position descriptions designed to reinforce the departmental and institutional commitment to diversity	• Standard statement illustrating that diversity is a valued part of hiring, reappointment, tenure, and promotion portfolios • Requesting diversity- and inclusion-related skills and experiences as part of selection criteria • Focus on individuals who can expand scholarly possibilities of the department to be more inclusive and engage diversity issues in the curriculum
4. Multicultural Marketing & Outreach	Marketing and outreach efforts designed to maximize the likelihood that diverse faculty will become aware of and attracted to the potential job opportunity	• Advertisement in diverse publications • Targeted outreach to leading minority scholars in a particular discipline requesting referrals • Strategic partnerships with diverse organizations
5. Creating Diversity-Ready Search Committees	Building diverse search committees that include leaders with an understanding and commitment to diversity	• Creating diverse and inclusive committees • Establishing dedicated faculty diversification roles on the committee • Inclusion of minorities and women
6. Bias Education & Professional Development for Search Committees	Professional development activities designed to help search committees to understand how cultural bias influences the search and selection process	• Targeted professional development efforts • Required training for all committees • Creating continuing educational efforts

TABLE 7.1 (Continued)

Recruitment Strategy	*Description*	*Key Themes*
7. Future Faculty Recruitment & Professional Development Symposia	Proactive recruitment and professional development events designed to engage historically underrepresented minority faculty and women as a way of building a pool of potential faculty diversity job candidates	• Targeted recruitment events to create pre-engagement with diverse candidates • Opportunity to groom the next generation of faculty on campus • Proactive and intentional strategy • Database development • Brand building as an inclusive and intentional institutional diversity goal
8. Accountability	Requiring every search committee to submit a recruitment plan that is reviewed and accepted prior to search authorization; deans and department chairs might also require every search committee to participate in some form of faculty diversification training prior to launching their search	• Requiring search plans • Presidents, provosts, and deans can require diversification efforts as a criteria of launching searches, bringing candidates to campus, and making hires • Regular reporting on faculty diversification efforts at the search and departmental level
9. Strategic Faculty Diversification Infrastructure	Centralized office that plays a key role on faculty diversification initiatives, potentially including oversight of centrally accessible diversity travel, hiring, and recruitment tools that are available on a limited basis at the discretion of central leadership, as well as having full-time faculty diversity recruitment specialists who recruit, conduct professional development, and partner with deans and academic departments	• Faculty recruitment and retention specialists • Travel recruitment grants • Visiting scholar resources for potential candidates • Target of opportunity hiring funds • Cluster hiring funds • Dual-career funds • Retention funds

to the social backgrounds of scholars. A male medical researcher may be profoundly interested in women's health. White historians have made important contributions to African American history. But it is also simplistic to suppose that individual life experiences, and a social and campus climate open to more diverse influences, have little or no influence on the intellectual questions we ask or the new knowledge fields we create (Stern & Williams, 2009).

The faculty diversity definition and rationale statement should connect to a campus-wide commitment to diversity that is embedded in the institution's overall mission and strategic and academic plans. At the University of Wisconsin–Madison, faculty diversity was identified as a major priority of the 2009 academic plan, which led to a three-year pilot initiative supported by a $1.7 million investment (Stern & Williams, 2009). As demonstrated by Box 7.1, the University of Wisconsin–Madison's definition of *faculty diversity* is broad, including not only a focus on social diversity, but also how generational diversity, field and subfield diversity, interdisciplinary diversity, and diversity of institutional type contribute to the university's ability to advance original scholarship and inquiry.

BOX 7.1
Faculty Diversity and Its Connection to the Research Mission at the University of Wisconsin–Madison

A great public university must take seriously the mission of research—the production of original knowledge that moves academic fields forward by extending established ideas, by unsettling or revising once accepted wisdoms, and by placing new research questions on the intellectual table. To accomplish this task, universities recognize the value of diversity, and the interplay of its intellectual and social aspects, in several ways. Examples include:

1. *Generational diversity.* Universities seek a generational balance that ensures an infusion of emerging scholars who are less tied to established research ideas or dependent on a cadre of senior scholars. Generational mixing helps spark new questions and fields of inquiry.
2. *Field and subfield diversity.* Universities benefit when different subfields of knowledge interact. We seek a balance between "building on strength" and avoiding narrow specialization. Too much homogeneity within a narrowly defined range of fields carries a cost. Cross-field dialogue sparks the unexpected question, juxtaposition, or association—in a word, *creativity.*
3. *Interfield and interdisciplinary diversity.* Universities possess the resources to hire in knowledge fields that cut across disciplines or departments. Programs that promote cluster (or theme) hires and federal Title VI centers (area studies) can build a critical mass of interfield and interdepartmental research and scholarship.
4. *Institutional diversity.* Research universities limit the extent to which they hire their own graduates to avoid intellectual stagnation and nepotism. They value recruiting faculty trained in other institutional cultures, or who built careers in a different institutional environment.
5. *Social diversity.* Bringing together faculty of distinct backgrounds and experiences, like generational and field diversity, positively affects research. Social diversity includes not only racial and ethnic variables, but also socioeconomic, gender and sexual, international and linguistic, and disability-related diversity.

Source: Stern & Williams, 2009.

Some diversity champions will undoubtedly be concerned that this broad definition obfuscates the pursuit of greater levels of racial and ethnic diversity. However, the development of such a broad and inclusive diversity definition is essential to withstanding legal challenges in the twenty-first century. More importantly, diversity constitutes the lifeblood of intellectual debate and is critical to driving the creative process of teaching, learning, and research. The diversity definition presented here capitalizes on the increasing emergence of interdisciplinary, global, and comparative research, and even community-based research that is so essential to tackling contemporary educational, economic, and health-related challenges. By creating its institutional diversity rationale in this way, the University of Wisconsin–Madison has established a faculty diversity strategy that is powerfully anchored in its educational and scholarly mission.

In framing the institutional case for faculty diversity, academic leaders must think about the expertise and talent that institutions need to be credible and effective in an increasingly diverse and global society (Smith et al., 2004). This means developing a philosophical rationale for faculty diversity that champions its importance to enhancing scholarship, bringing multicultural ideas into the curriculum, and building partnerships with diverse communities on and off campus. Faculty diversity is also essential to creating administrative diversity, as a lack of diverse faculty translates into a lack of administrative diversity. Finally, faculty diversity provides a role model for undergraduate and graduate students, helping them to see themselves in roles of authority and leadership.

Developing a Strategic Recruitment Plan

The time to discuss diversity is at the beginning of the search. It is too late to address the issue when you are asked, "Why is the finalist list so homogenous?" Search committees have to promote the institution and the job as desirable to diverse candidates and recruit them into the applicant pool. This will require a more proactive approach than some committees may be expecting, especially if they mistakenly believe that if people are interested in the position, they will automatically apply. A passive approach will not attract diverse candidates.

Faculty searches must create a strategic recruitment plan that casts a broad net and makes significant efforts to seek out and evaluate qualified diverse candidates. This might include generating a position description and selection criteria that value diversity, establishing a targeted outreach campaign to access diverse audiences, and requiring committee members to attend a workshop for exploring cultural bias in the search and hiring process.

Although CDOs should help develop the search plan, and can sometimes provide additional resources—including travel funds and special training—it is the obligation of the search committee to demonstrate that a search has made a determined effort to locate and consider diverse candidates. Just as active outreach is generally required as part of the process of recruiting senior faculty, search committees must become equally aggressive in their pursuit of junior faculty appointments. Department chairs and deans have immediate responsibility to create a culture of accountability that ensures that these obligations have been fulfilled. Indeed, they may seek to review the faculty search plan prior to authorizing the search, as a way of enhancing the potential to achieve diversity in the applicant pool.

Developing a Diversity-Enriched Position Description

Once diversity is integrated into an institution's definition of academic excellence, search committees should find creative ways to infuse this focus into the position description and seek candidates who illustrate demonstrated success in these areas. For example, the position description might include demonstrating the ability to work with and mentor diverse students and colleagues, understanding retention issues in higher education, and possessing a variety of teaching methods or curricular perspectives that embrace interdisciplinary research. Box 7.2 provides guidance by the American Association for the Advancement of Science that addresses the inclusion of diverse learners, interdisciplinary research that connects to diverse areas of study, and community-based research focused on broader societal challenges. These race- and gender-neutral qualities are instrumental to creating a robust learning environment by engaging in diverse teaching, learning, research, and mentoring communities.

BOX 7.2

American Association for the Advancement of Science Statement on Diversity for Job Descriptions

The American Association for the Advancement of Science (2010) *Handbook on Diversity and the Law* offers instructive guidance for designing a faculty job description:

(continues)

(continued)

The University seeks to increase the diversity of its professoriate, workforce and undergraduate and graduate student populations because broad diversity—including a wide range of individuals who contribute to a robust academic environment—is critical to achieving the University's mission of excellence in education, research, educational access and service in an increasingly diverse society.

Therefore, in holistically assessing the many qualifications of each applicant, we would factor favorably an individual's record of conduct that includes experience with an array of diverse perspectives, as well as a wide variety of different educational, research or other work activities. Among other qualifications, we would also factor favorably experience overcoming or helping others overcome barriers to an academic career or degree.

This workplace conduct of inclusion and experience provide opportunities to enhance educational, research, and other work outcomes by increasing opportunities for participation of a broad range of individuals and the potential to expand issue identification, collaboration, and problem solving. *Broad diversity* refers to all the aspects of an individual's background and experiences that contribute to a robust academic environment, including perspectives, disciplines, geographic background, talent, family socioeconomic background, disability, ethnicity, race, gender, and other characteristics. Some aspects of broad diversity have been easily achieved, whereas others—including racial and in some disciplines gender diversity—have been more elusive and require focused efforts.

Source: American Association for the Advancement of Science, 2010, p. 35.

In the specific case of STEM faculty, position descriptions might require candidates to outline how they have been able to accomplish "broader societal impact" in their research, leveraging the parameters required in many grants through the National Science Foundation (NSF) and the National Institutes of Health that have placed a premium on involving historically underrepresented groups and making scientific contributions that have relevance in numerous contexts.[2] By infusing these symbolic markers of diversity's importance in the job description, departments send a clear message that they hope to attract diverse talent into the applicant pool, and by association that they value this diversity in the department.

It is also important for search committees to ensure that the position description does not needlessly limit the pool of applicants (Moody, 2004; Turner & Myers, 2000). Some position descriptions may exclude female or minority candidates by focusing too narrowly on subfields in which few specialize. Academic departments should expand how they think about the job description as a tool to attract talent (Moody, 2004; Turner & Myers,

2000). This means looking at more than immediate teaching needs, or replicating the exact qualifications or experiences of those who have filled the position in the past. Although a humanities faculty candidate may have a particular area of expertise in hip-hop culture, he or she may also be perfectly capable of teaching a foundational course on nineteenth-century Western literature. Narrow and rigid job definitions discourage anyone other than the ideal candidate from applying. The job description should be designed in a way that will capture what the department must have in the position, but allow for other qualifications to emerge, thus maximizing the potential to attract a diverse applicant pool and expand the academic reach of the department into new and underrepresented study areas.

Another important way to accomplish this goal is to include interdisciplinary or interdepartmental work as a priority, which creates a broader applicant pool and validates the importance of having faculty members who embrace creative and diverse ways of engaging in academic research (Moody, 2004). Creating opportunities for potential faculty to employ a variety of pedagogical techniques and approaches is not only more likely to bring in a greater variety of candidates, but also encourages a greater variety of students and learning styles.

Multicultural Marketing and Outreach

Multicultural marketing implies applying marketing strategies and programs to reach a particular segment of the market that is defined by one or more cultural identities (Schreiber & Lenson, 2001). For the sake of this discussion, it is about creating advertising and outreach efforts that connect specifically with diverse faculty prospects. Developing a diversity-enriched position description is key to a department's multicultural marketing and outreach efforts, although the position description should not be viewed as enough by itself.

Building a solid relationship with diverse faculty candidates requires a targeted approach. Campuses must make commitments to specific events and pursue electronic and print media that provide access to diverse faculty candidates. This might include advertising in publications like *Diverse Issues in Higher Education* or *Hispanic Outlook in Higher Education.* It might also include posting announcements at identity-themed professional organizations like the Association of Black Sociologists, the National Association of Hispanic Nurses, and organizations like the Southern Regional Educational Board (SREB). It also means cultivating relationships through organizations like the Higher Education Recruitment Consortium (HERC) and using these connections to advertise jobs and connect with diverse faculty audiences.

Search committees should announce open positions to targeted faculty members or graduate students at minority-serving institutions, as well as through organizations that work on minority issues, affinity groups within organizations (such as minority caucuses in national scholarly associations), and historically Black colleges and universities, among others. New positions can also be posted on disciplinary electronic discussion lists.

Another important technique is to connect with diverse social networks in a particular discipline. Often job information is shared as part of regular contact and communication, and those who find out about jobs through these methods are in the best position to have the time and connections to prepare competitive applications (Moody, 2004). By contrast, diverse candidates who are not part of the traditional communication networks of senior faculty and administrators often miss out on the advantage this kind of networking and recruiting provides. Thus, departmental policies and practices need to be aimed toward supporting the expansion of these networks. These policies should recognize that expanding networks must be an ongoing activity, not just something done at the time of a search.

Creating Diversity-Ready Search Committees

The composition of the search committee and its charge have consequences for the outcome of the search (Moody, 2004; Turner & Myers, 2000). It is important that issues of composition and charge be addressed deliberately and early. Creating diversity-ready search committees means more than having minorities and women on the search committee. It also means choosing active and dynamic committee members, creating search committee training programs, and providing best-practice tools and general information about the institution's priorities regarding diversity.

The process of recruiting a diverse candidate pool begins with having a diversity-ready search committee chair. Whatever can be done to strengthen the chair's understanding of diversity is important. Having a meeting with a knowledgeable expert on diversity search dynamics, attending a relevant conference the semester before the search launches, and beginning an independent reading program in this area are just some of the techniques that can assist search committee chairs. To maximize the likelihood of attracting a diverse applicant pool also requires an active and engaged search committee willing to go above and beyond the call of duty to recruit a diverse and talented candidate pool. Faculty members who actively attend professional conferences are more likely than others to have encountered minority faculty in their areas of study. The more active and intentional the committee, the more likely it will yield a diverse candidate pool.

Most departments have few diverse faculty members and it is simply too much for these individuals to serve in every capacity where diverse perspectives are desired (Moody, 2004; Turner & Myers, 2000). In other scenarios, there simply may be no minorities or women in the department. Hence, search committees may choose to bring a diverse perspective to the committee by inviting a nondepartmental member to join the committee. This individual must have a keen understanding of academic talent, a strong perspective on diversity issues, and a high level of respect for the search process. Although this tactic is not often embraced, it does offer a viable option to increase the diversity of the search committee.

The Dangers of Search Committee Bias on Hiring Efforts

The misconception that members of search committees, by virtue of their academic credentials, do not introduce bias into the search and hiring process has played a role in hindering the hiring of historically underrepresented faculty (Moody, 2004; Turner & Myers, 2000). The results from controlled research studies demonstrate that people often hold implicit or unconscious assumptions that influence their judgment (Dovidio, Glick, & Rudman, 2005). Examples range from assumptions about physical or social characteristics associated with race, gender, and ethnicity, to assumptions associated with certain job descriptions, academic institutions, and fields of study. As a result, much of the research on diverse hiring indicates a need for professional development for all those involved in the search and hiring process (Turner & Myers, 2000). Such trainings and workshops are essential to helping committee members become aware of how their biases might undermine the hiring process. Hence, it is critical to require that every search committee enlist members who have gone through a specific training program that explicitly discusses the myths and biases associated with faculty diversification.

Ideally, every committee would engage in a training workshop prior to launching, although this is not always possible. At a minimum, the chair and at least one committee member should undergo a training program to ensure that they understand the process of casting a broad net, how bias operates in selection, and how to execute a fair and inclusive diversity strategy. Some committees may even designate a strategic faculty diversity specialist for the committee who can execute a number of the committee's diversity strategies and coordinate the group's overall approach to enhancing diversity in the applicant pool.

Some of the best trainings that we have encountered have emerged out of NSF Advance Grant projects focused on achieving gender diversity in the STEM faculty. In terms of developing search committee training efforts, research suggests that faculty members respond best to other faculty in their particular area. At the University of Wisconsin–Madison, the Women in Science and Engineering Leadership Institute has created several dynamic trainings that leverage the scholarly literature in the area, feature interactive case studies, and create campus-based research. The trainings are facilitated by seasoned faculty and administrative leaders who have specific expertise on diversity issues. Although early efforts focused on increasing the representation of female faculty in the STEM areas, the program has recently begun addressing the issues of historically underrepresented minorities as well.

Though not required, these trainings have become part of the faculty culture and are widely viewed as a proactive strategy for academic departments to leverage their efforts to advance diversity. This particular approach is particularly important when working with scientists who are more receptive to information that has been introduced by respected researchers and colleagues.

Future Faculty Recruitment and Professional Development Symposia

A valuable extension of an institution's approach to multicultural marketing and outreach is to create a future faculty development recruitment and professional development symposium. A number of institutions have conducted these symposia to build relationships with emerging diverse scholars and help them to develop their careers. Rochester Institute of Technology (RIT), the University of California–Santa Cruz, and the University of Tennessee–Knoxville have all developed symposia that foster relationships among advanced doctoral students, postdoctoral research fellows, and non-tenure-track junior faculty. The symposia are organized around the research agendas of participants and feature opportunities for participants to take part in faculty-led workshops, address their research agendas, explore the unwritten rules of faculty culture, and get a better sense of the institution and the job search process as a whole. The goal is to help diverse faculty candidates develop both a formal and informal understanding of institutional culture.

Developing Diversity Accountability Systems

To truly transform our institutions, senior leaders must develop multiple diversity accountability systems. Although we recognize that the broader campus community must eventually embrace campus accountability systems, institutional research and planning professionals can play a key role by helping to develop solid plans grounded in research and best practices.

Every school, college, or divisional area should develop an institutional diversity report that documents the entity's diversity goals, strategies, successes, and continuing challenges. This report should be presented annually to senior leaders. Each year, a high-profile committee of faculty, staff, and diversity champions should evaluate and comment on the plan for internal planning purposes, thereby helping the dean or divisional leader to improve institutional diversity implementation efforts. Every two or three years, a summary plan should be submitted that evaluates the progress and outcomes of the implementation effort. At this point, the institution might publically rank each diversity plan and connect its contents to decisions about merit for deans and divisional leadership, budget allocations, and the ability to tap into diversity incentive resources.

At a more local level, institutions may create a system that would allow them to evaluate each search and screen committee, developing a summary report that identifies whether that committee cast a broad net, leveraged diversification best practices, achieved a diverse applicant pool, leveraged inclusive interview techniques, and made recommendations consistent with the hiring goals of the institution. This summary report might provide data used in the dean or divisional leader's annual report on diversity. Departments with a strong track record in this area could be eligible for certain diversity incentives, including the ability to tap into strategic hiring resources, winning an annual diversity award, obtaining tickets for sports events and concerts, parking privileges, or any number of benefits to reward diversity-related success. These data might also become relevant when making budget decisions and granting special requests for support on non-diversity-related strategic agenda items.

Our experience has found that most institutions do little in the area of accountability and diversity beyond reporting on campus diversity processes, challenges, and outcomes. Thus, they often fail to connect these reports in ways that have direct implications on the financial reward systems of the institution. To implement the more aggressive ideas outlined here will require senior leaders with a deep commitment to change and to pursuing rigorous accountability measures.

It is also important to hold the search committee accountable for casting a broad net. This strategy might draw on an institution's affirmative action office or some other entity that would require each search committee to submit a faculty search plan that accounts for maximizing diversity in the applicant pool. No search should be allowed to move forward until the plan can demonstrate how it will maximize the potential for achieving diversity in the applicant pool. Leadership support is critical to leading change; institutions that have gone in this direction have done so with the support of strong senior leaders who required that their institutions embrace diversity as a fundamental priority.

A final accountability strategy stems from requiring departments and search committees to participate in faculty diversity development activities as a condition of their ability to tap into additional resources to drive faculty diversity efforts. Hence, if a department wants to access target of opportunity funds, cluster hires, provost discretionary resources, or additional travel funds, the department might go through a certification process involving workshops centered on faculty diversity, equity, and inclusion. The more that accountability techniques can be woven into the financial systems of the institution in this way, the more effective they ultimately become in helping to create new behaviors on campus.

Strategic Faculty Diversification Infrastructure

Institutions should look toward developing a strategic faculty diversity infrastructure that can help coordinate initiatives (Moody, 2004; Turner & Myers, 2000). Many institutions already distribute this work across human resources, affirmative action, chief diversity, and academic affairs officers who work specifically on faculty diversity matters. Depending on how it is structured, it may make sense for this infrastructure to have a primary or direct reporting relationship to the CDO.

A key component of this infrastructure is the presence of dedicated recruitment and retention specialists who can serve as talent scouts and faculty diversity recruitment managers (Moody, 2004; Turner & Myers, 2000). Although faculty hiring usually occurs at the department level, a dedicated faculty diversification office can play an important supporting role. Indeed, our survey found that CDOs identified developing this specialized leadership role as a key recommendation for enhancing the overall efficacy of the institution. An option for institutions interested in moving in this direction includes hiring or appointing someone with a specialized background in diversity issues and human resources. Ideally, the institution should work toward establishing an office that makes faculty diversification its top priority.

Another component of this infrastructure is to establish strategic faculty hiring funds (Moody, 2004; Turner & Myers, 2000). These funds are often used to support the recruitment and retention of historically underrepresented minority faculty, women in STEM disciplines, faculty with a diversity-themed research agenda, and other hiring priorities. Moreover, institutions should consider a wide range of creative funding programs, including target of opportunity hires, financial incentive or bridge programs, visiting scholar appointments, postdocs, or even resources to assist with bringing potential faculty candidates to campus when departmental resources are stretched thin. The most effective CDOs enjoy wide latitude in their ability to access and administer these kinds of funds, working with deans and department heads to boost the opportunities for bringing diverse faculty candidates to campus.

Target of Opportunity Initiatives

Target of opportunity funds allow an institution to allocate resources to target highly qualified individuals who can also contribute to an institution's strategic diversity priorities and goals (Alger, 2009; Moody, 2004; Turner & Myers, 2000). Target of opportunity programs are especially powerful because they give an institution the leeway to hire an exceptional candidate when a faculty line might not otherwise be open. In the words of a former president at a large research university in the Midwest, "These programs give the institution an opportunity to hunt without a license."

Although these programs have traditionally prioritized historically underrepresented minorities and women, they are less susceptible to legal challenge when they are not race or gender exclusive (Alger, 2009). Hence, the guidance offered from *Grutter* is important (Alger, 2009). By activating a broad definition of diversity in its target of opportunity efforts, an institution can support many different types of hires that contribute broadly to diversity. Sexual orientation, disability status, national origin, and veteran status are only the most obvious relevant variables. Indeed, we recommend that institutions consider including majority individuals whose research focuses on diversity issues. For example, a White male candidate who focuses on health disparities in underserved and minority communities may, under the right conditions, qualify as an ideal target of opportunity hire. The key is to deploy the target of opportunity program in ways that serve the institution's overall strategic diversity agenda.

Reconfiguring target of opportunity hiring programs along these lines departs from precedents set during the early years of affirmative action; however, it allows institutions to become more creative in their efforts to find and recruit top diversity talent. One effective strategy for protecting the viability of target of opportunity programs has been to ensure that when someone recruited through this mechanism retires or leaves the institution, the line returns to a central administrative office with jurisdiction over redeploying it. In other words, the line should not become absorbed into the receiving department's permanent budget.

Faculty Hiring Bridge Programs

Financial incentive or bridge programs constitute another important faculty diversification tool (Alger, 2009; American Association for the Advancement of Science, 2010). As their names imply, these programs are less concerned with creating new faculty lines than providing additional resources to "bridge the gap" when hiring top diversity talent. As before, creativity plays a key role. It is not simply about offering an additional incentive to attract a prospective candidate. For example, consider the situation of a department with two highly qualified underrepresented minority candidates in its final pool, but funding for only one position. Through creative fund allocation, the dean may be able to find enough resources for half of the position's salary. Meanwhile, the CDO's or the provost's designee may have the resources to cover the other half. As a result, the department is able to make two hires as the funding for the second hire is bridged into the department. In other instances, the central funds may be leveraged to pay the entire salary for a predetermined period of years, until a full-time equivalent position opens in one of the dean's departments that is then allocated to cover the cost of the new faculty member.

Principles should be established to strengthen the legality and legitimacy of both target of opportunity and bridge hiring initiatives. A standard should be put in place to determine if a department is eligible to access the funding. For example, senior leaders in the department should have participated in a special training on faculty diversity issues. It is also important that the department complete a comprehensive diversity plan before being eligible for funding. To strengthen their legality, these kinds of programs should also be subject to periodic review (Alger, 2009; American Association for the Advancement of Science, 2010). Every time the funds are allocated, the managing office or department should provide a detailed rationale. Scholarship, teaching excellence, and service should remain the key criteria, so that the qualifications of eligible candidates are never in question.

Cluster Hiring Efforts

Cluster hires constitute efforts to bring in two or more appointments together, allowing a department or unit to build faculty capacity in a particular area of strategic priority (Alger, 2009; American Association for the Advancement of Science, 2010). This approach can be useful in developing, comprehensively and holistically, a particular scholarly area, such as disability studies, LGBT studies, and others. Rutgers University established a President's Faculty Diversity Cluster Hiring Initiative that sought out "interdisciplinary proposals for faculty clusters that would strategically and significantly increase the diversification of scholarship and pedagogy at the institution" (Alger, 2009, p. 12). The goal is to create a flexible strategy that allows the institution to build capacity. Although the cluster should not focus exclusively on race or gender, it can entertain these characteristics as an additional objective in the hiring process.

Dual-Career Hiring Programs

Recognizing the needs of dual-career couples is essential to diversifying our faculty (Wolf-Wendel & Ward, 2006), leaders deeply committed to diversity will work creatively to respond to these needs within the context of the institution's mission and goals, strategic plans, and available resources. An important way to increase faculty diversity, enhance career flexibility, and improve work–life balance is to assist faculty partners and spouses in identifying positions within either the institution or the neighboring community. To assist dual-career spouses, institutions should consider establishing a "Faculty Dual-Career Development Initiative." By using a multidimensional approach, an institution can play an important role in helping domestic partners and spouses through limited and part-time appointments, adjunct faculty positions, postdoctoral fellowships, strategic job creation, and priority interviewing. The most advanced programs focus not only on helping prospective candidates find jobs, but helping them to enhance their skills through career coaching and counseling, continuing education, and networking. This may also involve strategic partnerships with local companies, academic institutions, nonprofits, and government agencies. Once the institution has its program in place, search committees should add the following statement to their position ads: "The college is responsive to the needs of dual-career couples."

Although helping in dual-career situations is important, committees must also be aware that it is inappropriate for an individual's marital or partner status to affect his or her application. In other words, although the diversity and human resources offices can and should play a role in facilitating dual-career opportunities, an individual search committee should be careful to avoid even the appearance of preferential treatment during the candidate selection process. Among the committee chair's responsibilities is the duty to ensure that these personal considerations do not inappropriately influence the hiring process and that the dual-career program comes into play only after the top candidate has been identified based on the merits of his or her application.

Rochester Institute of Technology: A Case Study of Interrupting the Usual

RIT boasts a highly successful faculty diversity recruitment effort. Between 2002 and 2008, RIT more than doubled its ranks of historically underrepresented minority tenure and tenure-track professors, from 35 to 78 (June, 2010). After reviewing several strategic documents and talking with key leaders, we identified five key factors associated with RIT's successful strategy:

1. Strong diversity leadership and accountability at the presidential level
2. The development of a strong strategic faculty diversity recruitment infrastructure
3. An aggressive focus on recruitment
4. The establishment of a signature future faculty recruitment symposium
5. Faculty diversification efforts being a cultural norm, not an exception

Strong Presidential Leadership and Accountability

Finding RIT's level of success in faculty diversity recruitment to be "unacceptable," President Albert J. Simone launched a faculty diversity initiative in 2002, nearly a decade into his tenure as president. Working collaboratively with diversity leaders in the campus and corporate community, President Simone called for an intentional faculty diversification strategy (June, 2010). With his leadership, RIT developed an overall plan, new faculty diversification roles, and new signature initiatives. RIT then committed significant financial resources and developed a strong culture of faculty diversity accountability. In the words of one insider, the president's and provost's efforts were vital to success:

> The president made it happen. He engaged the community, wrote editorials, and pushed the work forward. More than simply talking the talk, he put himself on the line for the effort's success. Moreover, we were fortunate to have a supportive provost who really wanted to see RIT develop better processes around searches and bias. Early on, the president and provost aligned their efforts and were willing, when needed, to send working groups back to the drawing board. In order to push the envelope, the president would simply tell them, "We want to see more."

As noted by Kezar and Eckel (2008), presidential leadership is critical to institution-wide progress. Proactive presidential leadership is essential for generating the type of visibility, energy, intentionality, and resources that are required to move an institution into action. As CDOs look to embolden diversity on their campuses, educating and inspiring presidents and provosts is critical to establishing a platform for institutional change.

Building a Faculty Diversification Infrastructure

RIT's strategy was grounded in establishing a dedicated staff position that made faculty diversification its number one priority. President Simone appointed Renée Baker in a faculty diversity recruitment role that eventually evolved into the position of Executive Director of the Office of Faculty Recruitment and Retention (OFRR). Nested in the provost's office with a matrix reporting relationship to the CDO, the OFRR occupies an integral role in academic affairs. Between 2002 and 2008, OFRR had a dual reporting relationship on faculty diversification issues that included both the provost and President Simone. The office is staffed by the executive director, a recruitment specialist, and a faculty recruitment assistant.

In her role as executive director, Renée Baker works directly with faculty search committees to review their recruitment plans, connect them with potential faculty candidates, and proactively develop recruitment activities both on campus and around the country. If a search committee's plan is insufficiently outlined, Baker has the ability to require additional information. As she told us in an interview, "It was essential to our early efforts to really let people know that the president was serious. I had to have that support, so that it was not simply one person trying to get our faculty going in another direction. The support and commitment began at the top with President Simone."

The OFRR's initiatives are informed by Baker's background in leading recruitment and human resources activities in a number of different capacities. She emphasized this background in our discussions, noting, "Some people were really shocked with the approach that I thought we needed to take because it was not consistent with academic culture. But we had to get out there and employ some real recruitment techniques, like those that corporate headhunters use to proactively seek out talent, whether we had a search going or not. This spirit drives the work of our office."

Developing an Aggressive Recruitment Focus

Unlike many institutions that simply post job descriptions and wait for diverse candidates to appear in the search process, RIT is constantly in a proactive search mode—"beating the bushes for diverse talent," according to Baker. A key component of RIT's effort has been to establish an online faculty diversity recruitment system. This system allows department chairs, faculty members, members of the OFRR, and others to constantly expand the candidate pool that may be contacted in the recruitment process.

OFRR staff contact diversity offices, multicultural associations, and department chairs at historically African American– and Hispanic-serving institutions with doctoral programs to ask for help in promoting Rochester to prospective candidates. Baker and her staff also mine the Internet year-round for potential doctoral and postdoctoral candidates, and then alert promising minority and female scholars of positions at Rochester in their fields. The office also sifts through scholarly journals and conference programs in search of relevant researchers and scholars. At present, over 3,000 diverse faculty job candidates are in the RIT faculty diversity recruitment database. Resources exist for travel to conferences and events like the SREB Compact for Faculty Diversity, where diverse candidates can be actively recruited into the RIT pipeline.

A key component of the recruitment process is having discretionary resources that exist in the provost's office to assist in developing competitive offers that attract top diverse talent to campus. These resources are used to strengthen offers and to assist with target of opportunity hiring opportunities.

RIT's Annual Future Faculty Development Symposium

RIT's annual Future Faculty Development Symposium constitutes a signature multicultural engagement and recruiting event. Attracting more than 200 applicants annually, this event brings two dozen graduate students and postdocs to campus for an in-depth look at professional and community life at RIT. This event does more than simply post an advertisement in an academic journal, instead taking a long-term view toward cultivating relationships with prospective minority faculty candidates who may eventually become new hires at RIT.

Faculty leaders play a key role in the selection of participants in the symposium. According to Baker, "Faculty involvement is key. Having faculty intimately involved in the process allows them to be a part of what we're doing and establish a sense of buy-in. At the same time, my office is able to do the lion's share of the logistics and really ensure that we have an administrative focus on making the event happen at a high level." The symposium requires participants to attend workshops, give talks, join mentoring meetings with faculty, and engage in conversations about the realities associated with life as a diverse faculty member at RIT.

A Culture Where Faculty Diversification Efforts Are the Norm

At RIT, a culture is emerging where faculty diversification efforts are the norm and not the exception. Because of their intensive outreach and professional development efforts, many faculty leaders now appreciate how to "interrupt the usual" and cast a broad net in their search-related activities. Also, because they are intimately involved in the Future Faculty Recruitment Symposium selection process, as well as external recruitment activities, there is a growing cadre of faculty diversity champions who play an increasingly important role in driving campus diversity efforts.

RIT's faculty diversity success serves as a powerful example of what can happen if an institution becomes dissatisfied with its levels of faculty diversity success and launches a collaborative, comprehensive process. By leveraging the will of committed senior leaders, partnering with deans and faculty search committees, establishing a dedicated faculty diversity infrastructure, building a culture of accountability, engaging in strategic and innovative recruitment strategies, and establishing long-term relationships with graduate schools and other organizations, RIT has created a culture of success.

Retaining Diverse Faculty

Recruitment, however, is only half of the challenge when it comes to faculty diversification; CDOs must also be proactive in their efforts to help *retain* diverse faculty. Even as they pursue efforts to recruit qualified diverse faculty, CDOs have the duty of advancing and retaining current faculty. Box 7.3 provides several recommendations adapted from Stanford University's Office of Faculty Development and Diversity.

BOX 7.3
Recommendations for Retaining Diverse Faculty

1. The institution should develop practices to examine data on faculty transactions (i.e., appointments, promotions, and resignations) by gender, race, and ethnicity and, together with the relevant school and department, make good-faith efforts to evaluate and address any apparent racial-, ethnic-, or gender-associated disparities. The CDO should develop a regular report on these data in collaboration with institutional research units, human resources, and academic affairs.
2. The institution should periodically assess faculty quality of life through surveys and focus groups, examining results within minority subgroups and across departments, schools, and divisions. These anonymous surveys should be sensitive to the inherent concerns felt by minority subgroups regarding whether or not to participate in surveys.
3. Department chairs and deans should be vigilant in identifying potential retention risks, including circumstances and issues that may lead to the departure of valued faculty, including those who contribute to faculty diversity.
4. It should be recognized that faculty from underrepresented groups may face special challenges with respect to the service component of their position. Whether overburdened by committee work or student advising requests, many faculty members carry an added burden when implicitly selected to serve as the "face of diversity" at their institutions. Others may feel that they are left out of informal department activities on the basis of race, ethnicity, gender, sexual orientation, or some other category of difference. Department chairs and faculty should be welcoming, supportive, and sensitive to the different experiences of faculty from underrepresented groups.

(continues)

(continued)

5. The institution should provide appropriate support and recognition of individual faculty members. Outstanding performances should be recognized through merit raises, awards, and advancement opportunities, including specific initiatives of interest to the faculty member.
6. Schools should reward faculty appropriately for their productivity and contributions, regardless of whether they might be considering outside offers. Schools should strive for a faculty culture where members feel appropriately valued.
7. Schools should conduct periodic salary reviews to ensure that faculty compensation levels are merit based. If improper disparities are identified, the institution should act to adjust salary levels to reflect legitimate academic considerations. If a problem area is identified, appropriate actions should be taken.
8. Similarly, nonsalary forms of compensation and support should be monitored periodically for appropriateness and equity.
9. Both junior and senior faculty should have opportunities to voice concerns and receive feedback through annual or biannual meetings with their department chair or college dean.
10. The institution and schools should provide information and guidance about benefit programs, including programs for new faculty parents, housing assistance, research support, and teaching buy-out opportunities, especially those that either may not always be clear in their application in particular circumstances or may be subject to a dean's or chair's discretion.
11. Deans and department chairs should be knowledgeable about the institution's policies concerning leaves, accommodations for faculty with parenting responsibilities, childcare, and maternity or disability-related needs.

Source: Adapted from the Stanford University Faculty Development and Diversity Office. Retrieved February 5, 2012, from https://facultydevelopment.stanford.edu/main/retention-strategies.

In many ways, retention best practices are difficult to standardize because so many faculty interactions happen informally. Nevertheless, the following tips can assist schools and departments in advancing and retaining a diverse and excellent faculty: (a) welcoming newcomers before they arrive in the department, (b) developing a campus orientation program, (c) building mentoring initiatives, (d) balancing committee work and tenure expectations, (e) building strategic partnerships, and (f) leveraging strategic faculty retention funds. This list is not meant to be comprehensive, but rather to serve as a guide to assist senior leaders as they develop their departmental inclusion and retention efforts.

Welcoming Newcomers

After accepting a job offer, candidates are usually eager to join a department and start their academic careers. The process of welcoming these individuals should begin before they arrive on campus (Moody, 2004). Box 7.4 provides a striking success story drawn from a book by Tierney and Bensimon (1996) on faculty culture and socialization.

BOX 7.4

A Welcoming Beginning for a New Minority Member of the Faculty

Some institutions can maintain the positive tone established during the interview process by preparing for the newcomer's arrival on campus. One Native American woman related the following story, telling us, "I can't tell you how impressed I was by how well they took care of me from the moment I arrived. I was able to obtain one of the university houses. I arrived in the afternoon. One of the classes was just letting out, and most of the students just came over and moved my things out of the moving van into the house. It was very hot and the neighbors brought over some drinks. It was just a very, very good welcome."

Two days later, she went to her office for the first time: "When I got to my office, my name was on the door, and I already had name cards on my desk, as well as a whole array of office supplies that were ordered before I came. I have a beautiful office with a beautiful window. I was given a brand new big computer. I did not request or demand these things. My chair made it happen."

In seeing how much work and thought had been put into making her office ready, the Native American newcomer noted that it made her feel proud, positive, and welcome. In the case of minority faculty, particularly in departments and more broadly institutions where they are low in numbers, such welcomes can dispel the discomfort of being a conspicuous newcomer.

Source: Tierney & Bensimon, 1996, p. 107.

Optimizing the Start-Up Package and Early Communication

As a matter of retention, institutions should guard against the financial shortchanging of women and minority faculty members at the junior and senior levels. Because start-up packages often hinge on a host of variables, including nuances in the market, research specialties, and negotiating skills, departments should be aware of how their incentive and signing packages may be perceived by different faculty members. Departmental leaders should keep in mind the following considerations:

- A lack of uniformity among start-up packages and unclear procedures for resource allocation at the time of hire can generate perceptions that some individuals are valued more than others. The implications can be particularly damaging for minorities and women who may not have received the same level of mentoring as their peers. It is in a department's own best interests to ensure that new faculty candidates receive the mentorship and support necessary to negotiate a fair compensation package, whether in terms of salary, teaching load, or service requirements.
- If any of the equipment or support promised to a newcomer fails to materialize, the chair or a designated senior faculty member should immediately inform the new member and correct the oversight. Doing so will help to avoid an omission that might be construed as a personal or professional slight by the new colleague.
- The department should inform newcomers in advance about their teaching requirements, and any research, administrative, committee, or service requirements. Sending the newcomer sample syllabi, course descriptions, a new hire or faculty handbook, and the contact information of potentially helpful colleagues can help mitigate any confusion about departmental expectations.
- The chair of the department should provide details to the dean and department colleagues demonstrating how valuable the newcomer is to the department. The dean and department chair should hold informal meetings with the new faculty member at regular intervals throughout his or her first year.

Productive Conversations Within the Department

Several months before a new minority or female colleague arrives on campus, faculty members should address any explicit or implicit dynamics within the department that might hinder the new hire's professional development and sense of belonging (Tierney & Bensimon, 1996). This discussion might involve hosting a workshop led by an external facilitator with direct expertise on inclusion and diversity issues. The department as a whole needs to be aware that the experiences of historically underrepresented minorities and women may differ significantly from those of their majority peers and that accumulating the professional and personal capital necessary to be successful in the department is often easier for members of the majority group. The key outcome of these conversations is for each individual faculty member to understand how he or she can work to create an inclusive department.

One strategy is to develop case studies that highlight both positive and negative departmental practices that can arise during a range of social encounters, including department meetings, tenure review and search committee procedures, as well as social interactions between senior and junior faculty. After members identify any negative practices, they should brainstorm positive solutions that the department might seek to adopt. This type of strategy is important for addressing dysfunctional situations and practices *before* they can detract from efforts to create a collegial, supportive community.

It is important to recognize that even minor social slights can fester and undermine a newcomer's morale. Because one's feelings of inclusion or exclusion can be dramatically influenced by what happens during the first semester and year, a department and its faculty would be wise to "frontload" attention and support for a new colleague and then work to maintain a line of connection and community after this positive start is established. To heighten a newcomer's sense of belonging, the chair or a designated senior faculty member might visit the new faculty member's classes on the first day of the semester to briefly welcome and introduce the new member to his or her students. This will help students better appreciate, understand, and respect the new faculty member. New women and minority hires often particularly appreciate these overtures, since they traditionally face more challenges to their authority than their White male peers.

Developing a Campus Orientation and Professional Development Program

A comprehensive campus orientation plan should be developed for all newcomers that goes beyond enrollment into the institution's pension and health insurance plans (Tierney & Bensimon, 1996). Orientation sessions should begin before the newcomer's first semester and then recur every couple of months throughout the academic year as a way of creating a consistent connection between new and senior faculty. Although departmental and college or unit orientation programs are important, we recommend that institutions provide a campus-wide program as well. New faculty orientation programs are especially beneficial to junior faculty, but they also benefit established faculty members—and may involve distinctive elements that can speak to the different needs of individual community members.

Faculty orientation and professional development programs are just one of the many ways that institutions can invest in the long-term success of their faculty. Although the initial launch will introduce faculty to critical information, resources, and support, it should not stop there. Professional development should not stop with summer programming but continue throughout the year. Luncheons and roundtables provide faculty members with opportunities to network with their colleagues and gain additional information important to their success.

Specific sessions might focus on campus services and how to create powerful learning environments for all members of the campus community. By focusing on time management and stress-reduction strategies, the department can provide practical, useful advice and support. Extra attention should be paid to helping newcomers network and build community across disciplines and departments. Other valuable workshops might focus on issues of particular relevance to tenure, including "managing your lab" and "meeting the requirements for tenure." Finally, institutions should consider ways to connect new faculty to teaching and learning resources on campus, as well as specific grant and research opportunities. At many colleges and universities, teaching and research resources go underutilized. A proactive department can consider ways to help new faculty promote active learning in the classroom, whether by developing learning contracts with students, measuring learning outcomes, restructuring test methodologies, managing technology in the classroom, or running group mentoring sessions with students.

These kinds of programs not only benefit historically underrepresented minority and female faculty, they help both new and established faculty members across the board. Faculty development efforts are essential to helping new faculty build their competencies and understand how to achieve success in the classroom and across campus. Indeed, case study research with untenured faculty members at Columbia University found that many were not "adequately informed about tenure standards or about how the tenure process works, that they sometimes receive little official feedback on their scholarship, research, and teaching from senior colleagues except at the moment of the tenure decision, and that they [were] not all included in the informal mentoring networks that faculty naturally establish with some of their junior colleagues" (Freudenberger et al., 2009, p. 261). Although these findings applied to untenured faculty generally, they represent the kinds of challenges that can be felt acutely by new minority and female faculty members. Orientation sessions and mentoring initiatives are critical to helping new faculty understand committee service, the importance of saying no to service requests, and even how to navigate written and unwritten expectations around family obligations (Freudenberger et al., 2009; Moody, 2004; Turner & Myers, 2000). Box 7.5 provides an overview of several diverse faculty and tenure questions.

BOX 7.5

Promotion and Tenure Questions and Issues

Undoubtedly, a critical quality of good leadership in terms of minority and female faculty retention hinges on providing new members with a thorough understanding of the tenure and promotion process and the benchmarks they need to meet to reach these requirements. Invariably, a tenure-track faculty member asks, "What do I have to do to be promoted to tenure?"

One beginning tenure-track Latina professor told us, "I wish someone would tell me what exactly I need to do. What we get told is that we need to publish in the highest quality journals [and] that our research needs to make a contribution to the discipline." Clearly, there is a great deal of ambiguity in research requirements framed this broadly. As an African American faculty member admitted, "I have been here for two years and I am still trying to figure out what is going on and how I fit in."

What does it mean to be published in a tier-one journal? How do departments rate tier-one journals against tier-two or tier-three journals? What is the correct mix? How is influence determined? And how are primary and secondary authorship issues handled? How vital is a book publication for tenure, especially if the scholar's research is more appropriately geared toward publishing articles? What are the exact requirements of a department and how do they differ across institutions?

These issues and others are of concern not only to faculty members who focus on diversity issues, but to tenure track faculty in all fields. The opaque nature of the tenure review process can only foster confusion and anxiety among faculty members, especially newcomers.

Source: Tierney & Bensimon, 1996, p. 107.

Building Mentoring Initiatives

It is not enough for a department chair or senior faculty colleague to state simply, "I always have an open door. Do not hesitate to ask questions." Many new faculty members either are unsure what questions to ask or lack the confidence to ask them. Knowing what questions to ask requires a clear understanding of a particular situation, which for new faculty members is often contingent on the mentoring they received in their graduate programs (Turner & Myers, 2000). Even within enlightened and proactive departments, members of the majority group often receive more informal and formal mentoring and support than do minorities and women. To counteract this tendency, departments should engage new faculty, particularly minorities and women, in mentoring relationships.

One approach is to develop a mentoring committee that works directly with a new faculty member. To maximize the potential for positive relationships, at least one member of the mentoring committee should come from outside the newcomer's department. Because he or she will not be involved in contract renewals or tenure decisions, this member can provide a more independent and objective perspective. Another approach is to involve retired faculty who can help new colleagues understand the protocols and idiosyncrasies of the department. Whatever its composition, the committee can help junior members as they work to meet their teaching, research, and service requirements.

Working together, the mentoring committee and new faculty member can prepare a three- or five-year plan that sets goals and can be used to help evaluate, and reevaluate, progress. The committee can then determine what departmental resources, including money, administrative help, research resources, or pedagogical tools, can best support the plan's execution.

Each pretenure faculty member should receive an annual job performance review as well as details about tenure requirements. Nothing can be as bewildering for a new faculty member as wondering, "How am I doing?" and "What are the tenure goals I should be focused on?" These questions must be answered early in the process so that new faculty members do not encounter problems during critical interim evaluations. The committee should coach new faculty members on ways to remedy any teaching difficulties or concerns raised by student evaluations, while also helping them understand how to navigate the challenges of revising and submitting academic manuscripts. A schedule of regular conversations between mentors and newcomers should be set, with costs underwritten by the dean's office. In addition to professional development, these meetings provide an opportunity to build community and share insights.

CDOs can assist deans in developing faculty mentoring workshops and trainings that draw on the established leaders in the campus community. These individuals could share their personal experiences, along with best practices drawn from the literature, as a way of building mentoring capacity. It is particularly helpful when senior faculty take the time to critique the scholarly work of junior faculty, nominate them for career-enhancing awards, include them in valuable networks, collaborate with them on research or teaching projects, and assist them to become lead and chair sessions at conferences. Mentors must also help new faculty understand the unspoken assumptions that define department culture.

Finally, informal mentoring can occur at various levels and on virtually any occasion. Invitations to lunch, early morning coffee, and a host of other venues are essential for newcomers to learn how things get done within the department and more broadly on campus. Smaller departments that function informally and on a more personal level have an even greater responsibility for orienting newcomers than larger departments, which can rely on the formal administrative structure and extensive human resources offices to facilitate procedures.

Strategies to Balance Teaching, Research, and Service

New faculty members must have a clear sense of how to balance their teaching, research, and service responsibilities. In particular, service responsibilities can potentially overwhelm a new faculty member. CDOs, deans, and department chairs must make an intentional effort to protect junior faculty, especially women and minorities, from excessive committee, advising, and service assignments.

A chronic challenge is that minority and women faculty are asked to serve as the "diversity" member for both departmental and campus-wide committees. The department chair and mentoring committee must be cognizant not only of committee work but also of student advising. Minority students often understandably gravitate to new minority faculty for personal mentorship, independent study, and thesis or dissertation committee leadership. It may not be possible to meet all these demands and fulfill the department's scholarship requirements. A healthy balance must be maintained to ensure that all expectations are met. One recommendation is to provide new faculty with software that helps them to track and monitor their committee work, advising duties, and other service responsibilities. The department should also work to acknowledge and reward new faculty for their service accomplishments, especially during the tenure and promotion review process. Indeed, although it is rare, some particularly innovative departments give special consideration to the especially heavy advising and service load that some faculty carry during tenure, promotion, and merit decisions.

With a desire to get faculty off to a strong start, departments might work collaboratively with the CDO to set aside resources for a "fellowship" semester in the first years of the tenure process that allows new faculty to focus aggressively on their research. This fellowship could take the form of limiting the number of courses the new member teaches or providing grant and travel stipends to promote his or her scholarly activities. These efforts can help newcomers avoid a frenetic and stressful beginning to their careers, and demonstrate the institution's commitment to the success of minority and women faculty members. Using the same standards and definitions that guide incentive and target of opportunity hiring efforts, these fellowship resources can cast a wide net when it comes to helping diverse faculty members.

Strategic Partnerships

Finally, CDOs should help their institutions develop strategic partnerships to advance faculty diversity. Although the ideas mentioned previously focused on the internal mobilization of financial and human resources, CDOs should also explore the possibility of establishing strategic partnerships with peer institutions, minority-serving institutions, and others. For example, the Committee on Institutional Cooperation (CIC) regularly publishes a directory of all of the doctoral students at CIC-membership institutions. This publication allows search committees to recruit doctoral students at institutions like Northwestern University, the University of Michigan, the University of Chicago, the University of Illinois, the University of Minnesota, Iowa University, and others in the CIC. Partnerships with peer institutions like these can help institutions develop a competitive advantage in terms of building peer-to-peer relationships, aiding recruitment and retention efforts. For example, the University of Minnesota regularly hosts an annual "Keeping Our Faculties" conference that focuses on faculty recruitment and retention issues. National and campus participants come together to share best practices, build new partnerships, and create new possibilities around faculty diversity and retention.

Partnerships are also now emerging with external nonprofit organizations that have established a strategic focus on faculty diversification, including Sisters of the Academy (SOTA) and the National Center for Faculty Development and Diversity (NCFDD). Founded in 2001, SOTA works to facilitate the success of African American women in higher education, focusing on teaching, scholarly inquiry, and community service. SOTA also facilitates collaborative scholarship and professional development opportunities. Signature efforts include a researchers' boot camp that connects senior and junior scholars in an intense, one-week program designed to help doctoral students and junior scholars develop sound research agendas. SOTA also holds regular writing retreats designed to help emerging scholars apply the latest research techniques and sharpen their grant-writing skills. Institutions can capitalize on SOTA's resources by partnering on events that involve senior scholars, emerging faculty, and advanced doctoral students.

The NCFDD is a professional development, training, and mentoring community focused on enhancing faculty diversity across the board. Offering institutional memberships, NCFDD's mission is to help new faculty members make a successful transition from graduate student to professor through a number of online and on-site training workshops, leadership development programs, and institutional enhancement efforts. The NCFFD's signature effort is its Faculty Success Program. This program helps emerging faculty members align their personal and professional duties through a 15-week intensive professional development and life-coaching system. The program is for advanced graduate students, postdocs, tenure-track faculty, and even tenured faculty who are looking to improve research productivity while balancing their personal and professional lives. The program features intensive personal coaching, community building, and workshops centered on the most promising techniques for achieving success in the academy.

Other organizations abound, including SREB's Compact for Faculty Diversity Institute on Teaching and Mentoring, the HERC, and Brothers of the Academy. These organizations present new opportunities for CDOs to connect with a growing and dynamic national faculty diversification infrastructure. These partnerships can serve as a critical supplement to campus initiatives by tying individuals and institutions to a broader conversation on the hiring, promotion, and retention of diverse faculty. CDOs, more than any other role on campus, are poised to create these types of synergies and partnerships.

Strategic Faculty Retention Funds

Among the most important tools that institutions can deploy for retaining diverse faculty are strategic retention funds, which can be used to match offers made by other institutions to lure talented faculty away. In these instances, CDOs and their colleagues in academic affairs must have financial tools that they can put into play to retain talented faculty members, whether the situation involves offers from other institutions or dual-career possibilities. The ability of CDOs and senior leaders to make counteroffers and even anticipate competing bids can make the difference between retaining and losing talented and diverse faculty.

Summary

Diverse scholars bring new intellectual interests and backgrounds and can often occupy a unique mentoring role with both minority and majority students. They can also help expand an institution's network into new communities, both on and off campus. Unfortunately, too many departments fail to capitalize on these benefits. By failing to take a robust and proactive approach to faculty diversity efforts, many of today's academic institutions risk becoming a revolving door for minority and female scholars. This reality suggests that CDOs and senior leaders must consider diverse faculty needs from the beginning of their careers all the way to retirement. In other words, the challenge is an institution's recruiting *and* retaining policies. A theoretical commitment to diversity means little without well-articulated and well-funded programs that take an intentional, strategic approach on everything from creating a diverse applicant pool to making a new faculty member feel welcome and empowered to clearly articulating teaching, research, and service responsibilities. These kinds of professional development and advancement possibilities will motivate diverse faculty members to make a lasting commitment to the institution.

If colleges and universities are serious about their commitment to faculty diversity and want to move from symbols to action, they will have to take coordinated and concerted action. CDOs can be catalysts in this transformation, helping to foster a strong faculty culture that removes the intrinsic barriers to recruiting and retaining diverse faculty. Presidents, provosts, deans, department chairs, and faculty champions also need to be willing and able to "interrupt the usual." Developing a faculty diversity recruitment and retention strategy requires a long-term commitment to the best recruitment and retention techniques, as well as a nuanced understanding of the legal policies and rulings that authorize them.

In this chapter, we presented several recommendations to help CDOs build their institution's faculty diversification strategy. Although some of these strategies are designed to help CDOs develop campus-wide initiatives, most are geared toward activities that CDOs can implement in partnership with academic deans and department chairs locally. Most important is that the CDO help his or her institution understand its options and then work collaboratively with the president, provost, academic leaders, and both campus and national organizations to launch intentional and evidence-based practices that increase faculty diversity and strengthen the sense of community on campus.

Notes

1. Bilimoria & Buch, 2010.
2. For example, see the NSF at www.nsf.gov/pubs/2002/nsf022/bicexamples.pdf.

8

THE FIRST 100 DAYS AND BEYOND

Guidance for New Chief Diversity Officers and Institutional Leadership

When I first began in my new role there was a title wave of interest. Students, faculty, community members, alumni, everyone wanted a piece of me. I can remember sitting back and telling myself, okay, take a deep breath and figure out a plan of attack. I knew that I had to create a way of engaging the campus community and working my way through all of the new relationships that I needed to cultivate. I knew it was important for me to get a sense of where they saw the campus currently and where they envisioned it ultimately going, and just to learn the political landscape relative to the definition of diversity, the definition of excellence, and the overall mission of the institution.

—Associate vice chancellor for diversity at a large research university in the Southwest

Many chief diversity officers (CDOs) enter new leadership roles each year. Whether their assignments involve managing a one-person unit or taking over a major division, they face similar risks and challenges during their first critical months on the job. Leading organizational scholars often tout the importance of new leaders getting off to a fast start in their first 100 days (Hargrove, 2011). Harvard University Business School Professor Michael Watkins notes that transitions are periods of opportunity, offering a chance to start fresh and make needed changes in an organization (Watkins, 2003). But transitions are also periods of vulnerability, and new CDOs must give special consideration to their first months on the job.

A new CDO usually lacks established working relationships, political capital, and a detailed understanding of his or her institution's history, culture, and the demands of the new role. This is particularly true for CDOs who are hired from without or who are the first to occupy a newly designed CDO position. New officers will spend at least the first year of their tenure "under the microscope," as other campus stakeholders try to uncover their plans and motives. A CDO's performance during this transition phase is vital, as many interested parties, including both friends and adversaries, will be watching for signs of long-term success or failure. Savvy new officers can use this transition to their advantage, but only if they are operating from a sound foundation (Arnold & Kowalski-Braun, 2011). Actions or decisions taken in this period can have far-reaching consequences and in many ways establish the foundation of their work for years to come.

Although every transition is both complex and unique, there are some approaches that deliver higher probabilities of creating CDO success than others. How presidents and senior leadership set their new CDO up for success, and how new officers navigate their transition months and first year are important factors in their ultimate success or failure. In this chapter, we present proven strategies for moving successfully into a new CDO role, regardless of the size of the institution or other factors that may influence where a CDO is in his or her career. This chapter takes readers through a range of different factors, from the role of senior leaders in creating a supportive context, to developing a transition framework to help new leaders get off to a fast start. This chapter is designed to help new CDOs and their colleagues in senior leadership develop a plan and overcome potential challenges that new officers may experience in their roles across campus.

Establishing a Context for Success: The Role of Senior Leaders

Throughout this book, we have been careful to frame the CDO position as a point leadership role that should complement other units, committees, leaders, and campus priorities. Ideally, institutions should lay the appropriate groundwork before hiring a new officer, because the goal of the CDO is to enable new capacity through greater coordination and collaboration. To ensure a long-term commitment, the president and others must align resources and shape policy in such a way that students, faculty, and administrators become involved in campus diversity initiatives. We have explored these resources and policies in great detail in the companion volume to this book and as part of the holistic design process that we present in exploration of the Chief Diversity Officer Development Framework (CDODF) in Chapter 3.

During the early stages, the challenge of developing a strong CDO position rests squarely on the campus community. A CDO entering a position only to operate in isolation is doomed to failure. The entire campus community must be involved in the change process, and presidents, provosts, and other senior leaders are essential to helping the CDO off to a fast start. Enabling a powerful diversity infrastructure that has centralized diversity capabilities and a shared commitment among faculty, staff, and students will require new investments by the entire campus community.

Presidents must serve as an active part of the diversity change journey. A key component is for the president to provide clear support to the CDO, ensuring that this person gets off to a good start and that momentum can be sustained over time, particularly after the initial excitement of the new hire has expired (Arnold & Kowalski-Braun, 2011). The president is critical for establishing a tone for the CDO that centers on tackling difficult diversity issues, embracing new opportunities, and establishing a tone for the campus that centers on evolving the institutional culture. The president has to send the message that the appointment of the new CDO is not an opportunity for business as usual, but that this critical leadership appointment constitutes a serious step toward galvanizing a deeper shared commitment to diversity, not simply adding a new officer or program.

Although it is important to tout the new CDO as providing integrative point leadership, it is equally important to champion long-standing advocates who have led campus diversity efforts over the years. Finding creative ways to recognize and elevate the work of faculty, staff, and student champions is a great way to mitigate some of the inherent tensions between long-serving diversity leaders and a new CDO. Senior administrators must appreciate the delicate diplomacy required to introduce new leadership while simultaneously recognizing the preexisting capacities designed to promote and sustain diversity. Numerous internal and external stakeholders will challenge the validity of the office, its value to the institution, and the expense of hiring top-tier talent. To ensure that the CDO rises to these and other challenges, we offer a number of recommendations. Box 8.1 offers a case study of the transition plan put into place at Grand Valley State University (GVSU).

BOX 8.1
Grand Valley State University: A Case Study in Transition Planning

Leveraging the scholar practitioner model, Jeanne Arnold and Marlene Kowalski-Braun provide an excellent case study of the process that senior leaders used to develop and implement a new CDO leadership position at their campus at GVSU in Grand Rapids, Michigan. Their case study outlines key steps that they took prior to the search process and then the formation of a vice president for inclusion and equity and CDO role (Arnold & Kowalski-Braun, 2011). We assisted this group early in their efforts, as they were determined to create a CDO infrastructure and transition plan that could set their officer up for a fast start and long-term success.

Pre-Efforts to Launching the Chief Diversity Officer Role

The vision for a campus CDO was established by President Thomas Haas and supported by the GVSU Board of Trustees. President Haas viewed this role as integral to his institution's strategic plan of satisfying its mission of creating a diverse and inclusive environment for all students seeking a liberal education. With the support of GVSU's provost, a team of faculty and staff members drafted a written proposal describing the position that led to the contracting of an executive search firm that assisted with a search and screen process and the eventual hire of inaugural CDO Dr. Jeanine Arnold.

Recognizing the need for a solid foundation on which to build the new CDO role, leadership leveraged campus climate research, campus-wide forums, national benchmarking, and discussions with sitting CDOs in a coordinated effort to implement an organizational design process. As part of these considerations, leadership was clear that they must define more than the title and rank of the role. As such, their design efforts considered budget allocations for the new CDO, departmental reorganization, and branding the role for success, thereby working to counterbalance any common misperceptions that the new officer would only be charged with leading on diversity issues. Understanding the collegial nature of the academy, they took a multifaceted approach to the design process and researched the institutional mission, vision, strategic plans, and other documents; examined institutional demographics; explored the campus history of exclusion and inclusion; and conducted personal interviews with community leaders.

Developing the Chief Diversity Officer Infrastructure

A careful consideration of the campus diversity infrastructure led to the establishment of a division that included the Office of the Assistant Vice President for Affirmative Action, the Office of Intercultural Training, and the Director of Disability Services,

(continues)

(continued)

which had been previously housed in Academic Affairs. These offices were charged to work collaboratively with faculty, staff, students, and others in the broad activation of GVSU's diversity commitment. The goal was to give these units structural legitimacy and support by providing them with an institutional home where they could grow stronger and more effective.

Leadership also recognized that the division might need to grow over time, and many of the campus's diversity units were vetted for consideration in the inaugural portfolio. This divisional infrastructure and the messaging behind its launch were part of the institution's commitment to create a sold infrastructure for the CDO and to dispel the myth that diversity efforts belong solely to the CDO.

Transition Team and Roll Out

A two-person transition team was appointed by the president to assist the new CDO in acclimating to her role on campus. One person was responsible for logistics, and the other assisted with orientation and relationship building. One tool that the group developed was a transition guide that included written summaries of every diversity office, group, and unit, highlighting their missions, goals, and key challenges. This guide was instrumental in steering the first set of join-up and relationship-building meetings that the CDO hosted. To assist in the relationship-building process, senior leaders hosted a series of receptions involving both campus members and off-campus leaders, including the mayor, chief executive officers from health care organizations, lawyers, human service agency representatives, and small business leaders.

In an effort to fully embrace the leadership of the CDO, senior leaders reassigned office space to ensure that the CDO was geographically positioned near the president. At the same time, the CDO was given a start-up budget and presented to the community through a series of press releases, newspaper articles, and media interviews.

The GVSU community was highly effective in its effort to engage the structural, collegial, and symbolic aspects of the new CDO's leadership potential. Early on, senior leaders demonstrated their personal support in helping the new CDO build capacity, navigate institutional politics, connect diversity to key strategic priorities, and build relationships. These steps illustrate exactly the type of thoughtful, proactive leadership that is required to position new officers to be successful over time.

Source: Arnold & Kowalski-Braun, 2011, pp. 1–10.

Ten Questions the Chief Diversity Officer Must Ask the President

Depending on the institutional context, there are 10 initial questions that a new CDO should ask his or her president or provost. Some of these questions should be asked before the position is actually accepted, because they are key to understanding how the role is positioned. CDOs should be prepared either to reconcile themselves to their president's response or to advocate for immediate adjustments. These questions can help set the stage for a long-term relationship between key leaders who must be in synch if campus diversity efforts are to flourish. The questions include:

1. What does my being CDO mean to you?
2. As CDO, am I a member of your executive leadership team?
3. As CDO, if I should report to someone other than you, will this person report to the president?
4. As CDO, will I be a staff or a line executive[1]—and can that change?
5. As CDO, what types of decisions will I be responsible for?
6. What kind of resources are you prepared to invest into my role, office, or division?
7. Are you prepared to support a broader campus diversity infrastructure?
8. Looking ahead, what would you like to see in three months, one year, and three years from now?
9. What are you looking for from the diversity planning committee or group?
10. What is the greatest diversity challenge that our institution faces and what is my role in addressing that challenge?

Because these are all open-ended questions, a CDO can expect a nearly endless variety of responses. Moreover, the president's answers can take both verbal and nonverbal forms, and be both specific and open-ended. CDOs should look for any information that provides insight into whether the president has committed himself or herself to situating the CDO as a meaningful senior leader on campus. A key outcome of these questions is to gain an understanding of whether your vision for taking the position matches the president's vision in creating it. If you report to the provost, who reports to the president on your behalf, these same questions should be asked of the provost. Asking for either the president's or provost's perspective on these matters should give some indication as to whether the CDO role is actually valued by the institution. If it is, the CDO can expect to be included in the decision-making process on matters of diversity planning and strategy, as well as on general administrative issues. Conversely, if the president does not view you as part of senior leadership, you might be forced to conclude that the position is more symbolic than material, and that the "C" and "O" matter very little. The choice you face is whether to decline the position, or accept it knowing that you will need to invigorate the position from within.

General Action Steps for a Powerful Chief Diversity Officer Launch

The process of establishing CDO readiness begins before the new officer is hired. Throughout the search process, the campus community should be educated to correct flawed assumptions that this new officer will operate as the campus "diversity police" telling people what to do. Faculty, administrators, and staff should understand that the new officer is being hired to improve institutional effectiveness, not act as a "diversity watchdog." Techniques for helping with this goal include distributing campus literature on the CDO role, hosting an educational session featuring diversity consultants and scholars, and engaging in listening and feedback sessions to learn more about the community's perspective on diversity issues.

At a minimum, the president should establish an initial strategic diversity initiatives budget to ensure that funding is in place to launch the new unit before the officer is hired. These initial resources should be permanently allocated to the CDO as part of his or her base budget. Although the CDO may inherit several legacy budgets, programs, units, and initiatives, these new initial resources can help as CDOs begin their work on campus. These funds allow the officer to mobilize consultants, visit benchmark institutions, and attend relevant conferences. Because the CDO's work centers on encouraging others to become involved, possessing discretionary resources is critical to encouraging buy-in from colleagues and other strategic partners. By developing an initial budget before hiring, institutions demonstrate their commitment to attracting the most talented diversity officers.

Most experienced leaders in transition rely on a "kitchen cabinet" of trusted advisors for advice and counsel. We recommend that the president jump-start this process by appointing a transition team to assist the new officer in meeting key stakeholders, learning the institutional culture, and developing a better sense of institutional norms. Several people on the transition team may emerge from the search committee. Having some members of this group ready in a formal transition role is key to helping new officers navigate institutional politics, build new relationships, and understand infrastructures that may already be in place.

The president should charge the CDO with drafting a strategic plan that elaborates the resources required to develop the office. The initial CDO strategic plan is vital to the officer's first year on campus, helping to set priorities and integrate efforts into institutional budgets for the upcoming fiscal year. Furthermore, this initial plan can help both the CDO and senior leaders establish key indicators for determining the CDO's success as he or she works to deploy the institution's more long-range strategic diversity plan.

The CDO's strategic plan should specifically speak to his or her office and its evolution over time, rather than the broader campus diversity plan, which must be developed through a campus-wide planning process. By comparison, the CDO's strategic plan will speak more narrowly to the development of an initial staff for the office and a marketing and communication plan, establishment of a website and digital footprint, and launching of new initiatives that will emerge directly out of the CDO's office. This plan may also allude to the campus's overall needs and set a context for a campus-wide planning process and the development of a campus diversity plan. In the companion volume to this book, *Strategic Diversity Leadership,* we discuss three types of diversity plans that may emerge institutionally: (a) decentralized diversity plans that are developed in the schools, colleges, and divisions of the institution; (b) integrated diversity plans that are part of the campus's overall strategic or academic plan; and (c) centralized diversity plans that provide an overall vision and action steps for the entire campus community. Each of these plans can be developed to provide a formal blueprint for guiding the campus's diversity efforts.

As part of this commitment to developing a strategic plan for the CDO's office, the president should be open to designing a CDO structure that will allow for maximum institutional gains, even if it means undertaking conversations about realigning historic offices and role responsibilities to create a unit-based or portfolio divisional CDO structure. In Chapters 3 and 4 of this book, we present the CDODF and discuss the critical role of vertical structure in developing a highly effective CDO capability. Again, it is important to draw a distinction between the CDO's initial strategic plan for his or her office or unit, and the institution's diversity plan, which sets the big-picture vision for diversity efforts. The CDO's strategic plan is intended to strengthen his or her office's ability to add value over time, and ultimately contributes to the formation and implementation of the broader campus strategic diversity plan. The CDO's strategic plan is separate from the campus's strategic plan for diversity, particularly if it is a brand new role. Careful planning and new resources must go into building CDO capacity as a function of developing and delivering the institution's big-picture strategic goals.

And in situations in which there is a brand new CDO position, having a multiyear strategic plan to launch the office makes good sense.

Creating a Supportive Context for the New Chief Diversity Officer

The president must communicate his or her vision for diversity and convey that the CDO is the senior-most point person for activating this vision institutionally. This communication sends the message that the CDO has the president's strong support and that the two are working in lockstep to advance the campus diversity agenda. This message has to be communicated early and often in public and private settings to establish a shared understanding, or social contract, that the new CDO and diversity are important priorities. The president should work from talking points that capture campus diversity goals, priorities, accomplishments, and support for the new CDO's leadership. By drawing on the help of the institution's communications team, the CDO, and the campus diversity planning committee, the president can deliver a clear and consistent message of support, whether before public and private gatherings or in written documents.

Early in the new CDO's tenure, the president should dedicate a leadership team meeting to addressing the CDO's and president's respective visions for promoting diversity and ways to involve the campus community in future efforts. As we noted previously, CDOs must speak with the authoritative backing of the president. By engaging on these issues directly with other senior campus leaders, the president can set expectations and hold people accountable for pursuing diversity policies and programs. Some presidents may wish to consider hosting a senior diversity leadership retreat in the first months of a new CDO's tenure. A diversity leadership retreat provides an ideal setting for updating the CDO on campus diversity efforts, sharing national best practices, and beginning the type of shared dialogue that sets a positive context for the CDO's future endeavors.

We also recommend that the president ensure that the institution's central communication team is fully prepared to support the new CDO. Simply put, diversity communication should not end with the press release announcing the CDO's appointment. Instead, the president should consider finding ways to deploy his or her central communication resources in ways that support the CDO's leadership and the strategic diversity plan. Options include articles or videos that feature an extended interview with the new

CDO that might then appear in the main campus magazine, alumni magazines, student media outlets, and on the institution's website. For institutions involved with the corporate community, a targeted letter provides another vehicle for promoting the CDO's efforts. The key is to begin framing diversity efforts early and often, and to maintain consistent and pervasive support for diversity efforts across multiple media platforms. Box 8.2 provides recommendations for senior leaders in launching a new CDO role.

BOX 8.2

Recommendations for Senior Leaders to Assist the Chief Diversity Officer With a Powerful Launch

Senior leaders should proactively partner with the new CDO as he or she develops new initiatives and programs. Recommendations for assisting the CDO with getting off to a fast start include:

- Send a communication welcoming the new CDO to campus and offering to meet with him or her to discuss efforts in the particular department, unit, college, or division.
- Invite the CDO to a relevant staff or committee meeting to learn more about what is going on in a particular area and introduce his or her vision or philosophy of diversity.
- Develop a packet of materials about diversity efforts in different areas and send them to the CDO. This may take the form of a brief diversity report that highlights successes, continuing challenges, infrastructure, and new initiatives.
- Host a dinner, reception, or special event to welcome the CDO to the community.
- Volunteer to be an early partner or first adopter of innovative new diversity leadership development and training opportunities, accountability considerations, campus climate projects, or other efforts.

A Strategic Transition Framework

A new CDO at the senior level can sometimes mistakenly indicate to the campus community that transformation has already arrived and that infinite new possibilities are now on the table. Our research tells us that many new CDOs feel a need to respond to these feelings and have an immediate effect.

However, often the most appropriate place for a CDO to start rests less with launching new initiatives than with learning about existing efforts. CDOs must understand all they can about the new institution *before* they undertake ambitious projects. Indeed, they must create a formal, even rigorous, method of listening and learning about the institution. By listening and learning first, they can establish a foundation for their role's strategic mandate to accomplish diversity-themed change—that is, to influence existing institutional diversity priorities and establish new ones.

As an integrative leader, the CDO should not go behind a closed office door and simply emerge with a campus strategy for change, however thoughtful and effective his or her recommendations. As we often explain to new officers, it is less about what they know, and more about the relationships they need to cultivate. A vital component of any CDO's work is building relationships across campus, fostering conversations between groups that may be working at cross purposes, and engaging issues with groups and individuals that may not be talking at all. This style of leadership must begin immediately during the new CDO's tenure on campus. To accomplish this goal, a transition framework is essential.

A transition framework outlines initial goals and the techniques needed to launch them. It also provides clarifying guidance around the CDO's big-picture vision of diversity leadership. The framework helps cultivate understanding, foster relationships, and clarify the institution's most immediate diversity priorities. We prefer to use the term *framework* over *plan,* as it connotes a broader and more fluid vision of the transition than a plan, which may be anchored in a particular timeline. By developing a transition framework, institutional leaders can establish a clear set of goals and techniques without committing themselves to an immediate timeline. Although the first 100 days are essential, we believe that the first year is required for most institutions, because the decentralized, collegial, and politicized nature of academic culture requires an even greater emphasis on relationship building, cultivating allies, and understanding the unwritten rules of engagement and interaction.

Learning, Relationship Building, and Prioritizing

Upon arrival at the University of Wisconsin–Madison, the first author of this book began a multidimensional transition strategy process of collegial engagement as part of his transition efforts. The transition framework

"Learning, Relationship Building, and Prioritizing" was produced in both digital and hard copy; then 15,000 copies were distributed to stakeholders both on and off campus. Throughout its life, the framework underwent three revisions, each one updated to reflect the progress that had been made and the number of groups and individuals participating in its activation over the first nine months of the CDO's appointment.

The framework was written to communicate both the material and symbolic importance of diversity and how the new CDO was attempting to both engage and understand the culture as part of an intentional transition strategy. The framework also defined the role of the CDO for the campus community in new ways, emphasizing that even though the office was to play a point leadership role on diversity, the new CDO would be functioning in an integrative leadership role and working to define diversity broadly as more than just race and ethnicity. An early transition framework allows the CDO to define diversity in a broad and inclusive way, thereby preempting opponents who will invariably argue that diversity efforts are about providing special preferences.

Although new CDOs will inevitably become involved with several initiatives that are outside of the framework, the framework helps give order to a transition process that can be overwhelming at first. It is not uncommon for students, faculty members, school superintendents, alumni, concerned citizens, presidents of various civic organizations, and minority stakeholders to overrun a new CDO with requests for time. Because the CDO is in a diversity-related position, many will view this person as the only voice that they can turn to with their project or concern. It is for this reason that the CDO needs a big-picture strategic framework to guide his or her work in an intentional way, so that he or she does not get lost in the weeds of meetings, conferences, projects, and personal requests.

A major focus of the "Learning, Relationship Building, and Prioritizing" framework was to activate a campus-wide conversation of students, faculty, staff, administrators, and community members. No matter the context, this conversation focused on mapping the institution's diversity investments; seeking out hidden gems of diversity innovation and creativity; assessing the influence of promising activities; defining campus diversity priorities; and seeking new ways to collaborate across campus units, departments, initiatives, and agendas. The plan featured four major goals:

1. To have the new CDO become an engaged member of the University of Wisconsin–Madison campus community

2. To develop a clear understanding of campus diversity capabilities and dynamics
3. To build the organizational identity of the newly reframed Office of the Vice Provost for Diversity and Climate and CDO
4. To clarify priorities and an action platform for developing a new strategic diversity plan, building on lessons gained from prior efforts

Figure 8.1 depicts the six key strategies that were used to engage the campus community to accomplish the CDO's transition goals. These activities were the following: (a) transition roundtables with key individuals and offices; (b) diversity capabilities retreats with individuals and teams working on similar issues like diversity communication, retention, and graduation challenges for diverse groups, intergroup relations, and campus climate; (c) campus-wide diversity audit and program reviews of key diversity initiatives and offices; (d) external campus reviews involving leading diversity stakeholders; (e) targeted communications to various groups about the transition and new leadership on campus; and (f) individual and unit join-up meetings with administration, student, and faculty governance leaders.

Six Strategies to Power the Transition

We offer this framework in Figure 8.1 as a way to help new officers get their hands around diversity infrastructures that can be large and unwieldy. Responding to the civil rights movement and the feminist and other social justice movements of the 1960s, institutions have developed multiple plans, initiatives, committees, and offices to promote and preserve diversity. New CDOs need to find ways to understand this history and the various capabilities that have emerged on campus. These strategies are intended to help the new CDO to mine stories of success, capacity, unrest, and failure that may not have been formally captured in a report, but that tell the story of inclusion and exclusion in ways that are critically important for engaging the politics and history of a particular institution. Table 8.1 provides a narrative overview of each transition strategy noted in Figure 8.1.

Transition Roundtables

Building on the long-standing tradition of shared governance and collaboration, transition roundtables offer an initial opportunity for the CDO to connect with relevant constituencies and learn more about campus governance, offices, policies, diversity successes, opportunity areas, synergies, and

FIGURE 8.1
Strategic Transition Framework Impact Model

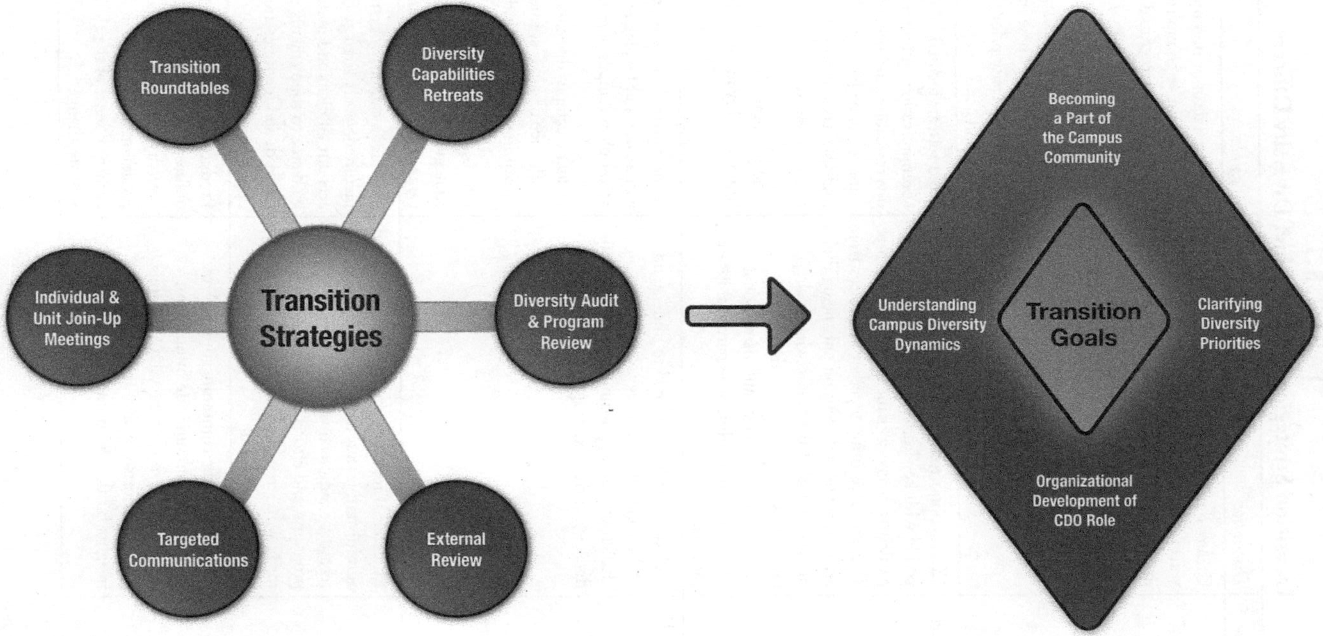

Source: Williams, 2008.

TABLE 8.1
Transition Strategies for New Chief Diversity Officers

Transition Technique	*Description*	*Examples*
Transition Roundtables	Creates opportunities to bring together key voices from a range of different spaces to discuss diversity issues on campus, often from a particular organizational perspective.	Convert a dean or presidential cabinet, faculty executive committee, or other regular meeting into a structured opportunity to discuss diversity issues on campus. Conduct a targeted meeting of key off-campus community leaders or corporate partners, bringing these individuals together to discuss diversity priorities, the role of the CDO, and action steps moving forward.
Diversity Capabilities Retreats	Creates opportunities to spend an extended period with key leaders focused on a particular diversity challenge or opportunity. These sessions bring together key voices from across campus and focus on enhancing their understanding of the issues, what is already taking place on campus, national best practices, peer and aspirant institutional activities, and building new partnerships on campus.	Hold retreats focused on diversity communication, graduation rates, faculty diversification, and other key topics. These retreats can be half day, all day, or even multiple days, depending on the level of commitment required. Produce summaries and takeaway reports that summarize key insights gleaned from the day.
Diversity Audits and Program Review	Include initiatives designed to understand and document the strategy, outcomes, challenges, and opportunity areas of campus diversity initiatives, programs and units.	Review how diversity is used in the admissions and financial aid process to accomplish campus diversity goals. Evaluate campus diversity programs using a confluence of surveys, interviews, and institutional database studies. Fill requests for reports that outline the strategy, structure, and process of various campus diversity offices and initiatives.
External Review	An external review is conducted by respected administrative, research, and policy experts regarding campus diversity strategies, programs, and efforts, resulting in guidance for how to strengthen the campus's diversity commitment overall.	Conduct a campus-wide review of the big-picture diversity strategy that takes into account all plans and metrics; provides guidance to supplements the strategy going forward; and identifies areas of strength, opportunity, and risk.
Targeted Communications	Includes specific communication efforts designed to communicate information specific to the role of the CDO, campus diversity efforts broadly, and important insights for the community.	Produce targeted articles, press releases, and online social media to frame the campus diversity discussion, the commitment of the president, and the role of the CDO to give an authentic sense of the challenges required to activate change.

TABLE 8.1 (Continued)

Transition Technique	*Description*	*Examples*
Individual and Unit Join-Up Meetings	Incorporates outreach efforts by the CDO to connect with key leaders and their teams in one-on-one or group settings. Frequently this involves the CDO hosting a private meeting with the leadership of a school, college, department, division, or committee, and then developing a broader relationship with the unit.	Hold informal meetings designed to establish personal rapport and relationships, and share inside information regarding past history, culture, challenges, and relationships, which are the keys to understanding the unwritten culture of the institution. Hold formal meetings with offices and various leadership teams to gain greater understanding of how a particular area is pursuing diversity, the role of the leadership, the vision of the president and role of the CDO, and the important goals and parameters being set institutionally.

potential areas for collaboration. They should feature a cohosting office, unit, or point person with specific knowledge, background, networks, and institutional memory in a particular area. The roundtable discussions are organized around different professional and social identities to facilitate understanding of key issues among constituencies related to the work of the CDO.

Although each group ideally has a target audience determined by the CDO and the partnering lead, each roundtable group should be open to anyone who would like to attend. Potential campus roundtable topics include the following: (a) disability and accessibility issues, (b) race and ethnicity issues, (c) gender issues, (d) international issues, (e) LGBT issues, (f) diversity in the curriculum, (g) retention and academic advising, (h) faculty diversity, (i) community engagement and precollege initiatives, and (j) evaluating and assessing campus diversity efforts. Although other roundtable topics are possible, these provide a well-rounded assessment of campus diversity themes that the new CDO should mine.

Transition roundtables are ideal in the first 100 days of a CDO's tenure but can take place throughout the academic year. More than a simple "meet and greet," transition roundtables should draw on successful facilitation techniques to draw key insights into the campus culture. The hope is that many of these sessions will build on previous interactions with members of the campus community and others. Each roundtable should result in a brief summary document detailing major ideas that emerged as part of the discussion.

Diversity Capabilities Retreats

A primary thrust of the CDO is to build the institution's "lateral diversity infrastructure"—in other words, those offices, units, and initiatives that fall into a number of different supervising portfolios but in many ways define an institution's access and equity, multiculturalism and inclusion, and learning and diversity capabilities. A key item that may emerge for many is a need for greater coordination, assessment, and interaction across the myriad of programs and offices that exist to activate diversity. Diversity capabilities retreats are an important tool for accomplishing this goal both during the transition year and beyond. This is particularly true as these conversations can help to foster a discussion that will eventually lead to a greater understanding of shared norms, challenges, priorities, and ways to amplify and enhance diversity efforts by creating economies of scale, common systems, and more intentional and strategic collaboration.

Each diversity capabilities retreat should have a targeted participation group identified by the CDO. Table 8.2 explores several potential topics for diversity capabilities retreats, including (a) CDO organizational development; (b) recruitment and retention of historically underrepresented students of color; (c) recruitment and retention of historically underrepresented faculty of color and women in the STEM fields; (d) learning and diversity initiatives for employees; (e) learning and diversity initiatives for students; and (f) diversity assessment and analyses. Whereas roundtable discussions should be open to anyone who wants to participate, diversity capabilities retreats center on gathering key stakeholders together to discuss and develop a shared understanding of key diversity issues.

Although time constraints always necessitate flexibility, the hope is that each retreat will last several hours and begin with a brief presentation from a member of the campus community who can help frame the discussion. Depending on the subject matter and format, other retreats might last the entire day or be broken up over several days, allowing for multiple extended sessions. Each retreat should produce a brief concept paper summarizing major ideas and action steps to be taken moving forward. Continuing meetings, recommendations, and actions can build on the work completed during the retreat. These concept papers should be posted electronically and be available for individuals not participating in these discussions.

Diversity Audits and Program Review

Diversity audits can be very helpful in establishing a clear understanding of an institution's diversity capabilities, challenges, successes, and opportunity

TABLE 8.2
Targeted Diversity Capabilities Retreats

Potential Retreat Theme	*Priority Areas for Discussion*
CDO Organizational Development	Facilitate focused discussion to further develop the organizational identity and mission, role, and focus of the CDO. Some specific areas for discussion include the mission, title, branding, vision, internal diversity grant-funding protocols, campus-wide diversity communication strategy, and immediate priorities.
Recruitment and Retention of Historically Underrepresented Students of Color	Facilitate focused discussion regarding the recruitment and academic achievement of historically underrepresented students. Launched from a discussion of what we know about recruitment, retention, and achievement of underrepresented students, this retreat focuses on understanding how institutions can positively respond to this challenge. Some specific areas for discussion might include the role, focus, and return on investment of numerous campus programs and initiatives, aligning programmatic efforts, establishing a standing retention and graduation task force, and creating more strategic implementation activities.
Recruitment and Retention of Historically Underrepresented Faculty of Color and Women in the STEM Fields	Facilitate focused discussion regarding the recruitment, retention, and promotion of historically underrepresented minority faculty and women in the STEM fields. Launched from a discussion of what we know about historically underrepresented faculty, this retreat focuses on understanding how we can positively influence our current outcomes. Some specific areas for discussion include the return on investment of past and current strategic hiring programs and efforts; promising recruitment practices and strategies; strategic relationships with minority-serving institutions; and the presence of any gender-equity themed grants or projects, such as NSF Advance, among others.
Learning and Diversity Initiatives for Employees	Facilitate focused discussion of programs and initiatives that center on creating an inclusive environment by providing learning moments for faculty, staff, and administrators to explore broadly defined issues of diversity. Inevitably, this discussion will involve leaders from major initiatives, such as campus diversity-training programs, sexual harassment training, search committee training, human resources training, and other programs and offices dedicated to social justice, diversity, intergroup relations, and equity. Some specific areas for discussion include common challenges, strengths, areas for cooperation, the development of multimedia deployment strategies, and ways to strengthen the influence of these initiatives both individually and collectively.
Learning and Diversity Initiatives for Students	Facilitate focused discussion on those programs, offices, policies, and initiatives aimed at preparing students for a diverse, global economy. Inevitably, this discussion will involve major curricular and cocurricular efforts focused on intergroup dialogue, social justice education, the work of teaching and learning offices in the provost's office, diversity distribution requirements, service learning, and study abroad. Some specific areas for discussion include common challenges, strengths, areas for cooperation, the development of multimedia deployment strategies, and ways to strengthen the activation potential of these efforts both individually and collectively.

TABLE 8.2 (Continued)

Potential Retreat Theme	*Priority Areas for Discussion*
Diversity Assessment and Analyses	Facilitate focused discussion of the different types of diversity data that are required to lead diversity planning and implementation activities going forward. Potential topics include a systematic assessment of the educational implications of undergraduate student experiences with diversity, the minority faculty turnover quotient, gateway course analysis data for the historically underrepresented, campus climate research, development of a longitudinal study of the student experience, use of the National Study of Student Engagement, Cooperative Institutional Research Project Surveys, and other related discussions. A key group in this conversation is the office of institutional research, which guides institutional research efforts and is a key player in interpreting data collected by the institution and translating this information into key insights for practice.

NSF, National Science Foundation; STEM, science, technology, engineering, and mathematics.

areas. The best audits will be multitiered and involve cataloging the campus diversity infrastructure, developing a data-driven understanding of where the campus is on several strategic diversity indicators, mining relevant campus climate reports, and conducting self-reporting and external evaluations of key diversity programs and efforts.

One of the first steps for any new CDO is to develop a comprehensive understanding of a campus's previous and existing efforts. This means carefully reviewing every diversity office, initiative, committee, report, policy, and program. The goal is to gain a sense of the mission, location, priorities, and key challenges of campus diversity programs and initiatives. These data might be gathered using a combination of online survey tools, interviews with key leaders, report requests, and the individual analysis of websites and other information. At some institutions, hundreds and even thousands of efforts may exist.

One of the most important plans to search for is any recent accreditation report. These reports often require a description of campus diversity efforts and can provide a rudimentary snapshot of strengths, limitations, and opportunities. Of course, it is vital to review all campus strategic diversity plans, as well as any affirmative action policies and position papers that may have been drafted to assist in CDO role design.

Another component of the audit may involve intentionally mining the institutional data on campus demographics, campus climate, and programs. As we discuss in the companion volume to this book, many institutions have a wealth of data that often goes ignored during times of diversity leadership transition or when developing a new diversity plan and accountability strategy. A review of campus data systems is a good way of involving institutional research colleagues in your transition process. Efforts might include analyzing the institutional database; examining levels of demographic diversity among students, faculty, and staff; and reviewing retention, graduation, and promotion patterns. Institutions should be well positioned to examine whether students are taking advantage of various high-impact learning experiences, including general education diversity requirements, service learning opportunities, and study abroad programs. Whether looking at campus demographics or climate survey data, it is critical to disaggregate the data in terms of race, ethnicity, gender, national origin status, and other relevant diversity dimensions whenever possible.

In addition to cataloging campus diversity efforts, new officers may consider conducting a more specialized and detailed review of diversity offices, programs, committees, and policies. This review might include some combination of directed self-study, environmental benchmarking, or an internal review conducted by a campus-wide committee. These types of reviews can be helpful in terms of understanding influence, operational efficiency, and strategic needs.

As Table 8.3 demonstrates, diversity program reviews can be especially helpful for understanding whether a particular diversity program is race and ethnicity conscious, exclusive, or neutral (Alger, 2009; American Association for the Advancement of Science, 2010; Coleman & Palmer, 2004). As we discuss in Chapter 1 of the companion volume, racially and ethnically conscious diversity efforts can be quite confusing as federal and regional legal and policy dynamics are constantly shifting. New CDOs need to understand the legal risk associated with campus diversity programs and work effectively with their president, legal counsel, and external scholars to gain valuable perspective regarding the legal context of diversity-conscious financial aid, admissions, and employment efforts. The insights of an external review can help a new CDO and his or her colleagues understand whether their institution is being overly risk-averse or reckless, or are appropriately proactive and grounded in current legal policy, when the external team brings a broad-based perspective that can take into account not only relevant case law, but how other institutions are interpreting that case law, as well as national policy guidance in this most contentious of areas.

External Review

One powerful way to provide additional perspective to the process of setting campus priorities is to engage an external review team that can provide

TABLE 8.3
Race-, Ethnicity-, and Gender-Conscious, Exclusive, and Neutral Policies

Program or Policy Type	*Description*	*Example*
Race and Ethnicity-Conscious Policies	Policies that reflect and express racial, ethnic, or gender preferences, with corresponding effects	Race-conscious policies may include explicit racial classifications, such as the University of Michigan Law School's admissions policy, in which race is one factor used in evaluating applications. Another policy might include a scholarship program that considers race as one factor in eligibility, even though all students are eligible for the scholarship.
Race- and Ethnicity-Exclusive Policies	A subset of conscious policies in which eligibility is restricted to a particular race, ethnicity, or gender	In this instance, the scholarship is restricted to a particular group, although multiple academic factors may be considered as part of the ultimate decision to make an award. For example, an institution might consider a race-exclusive scholarship for which only African Americans may apply.
Race- and Ethnicity-Neutral (Facially Neutral)	Policies that do not include an express preference on the basis of race, ethnicity, or gender in an individual decision, but generally use proxies that, although apparently neutral, encourage results that benefit applicants of historically disadvantaged groups	Such policies have aims apart from racial, ethnic, or gender diversity, such as socioeconomic or geographic diversity or the need to attract individuals who have strong records of inclusive conduct and multicultural skills. Such policies may contribute to racial, ethnic, or gender diversity, but their aim is distinct. Inclusive outreach and recruitment policies that expand efforts to generate additional applicant interest are typically considered to be neutral as long as they do not confer material benefits to one individual or group over another. Percent plans, like those in use in Texas, are often described as "race neutral" because race and ethnicity are not taken into account in the actual process of rendering an admissions decision, at least under the aspects of admissions that are governed by the Top Ten Percent law.

Source: Alger, 2009; American Association for the Advancement of Science, 2010; Coleman & Palmer, 2004.

another lens of analysis. The best teams bring together a diverse group of administrators, scholars, and thought leaders who can provide particular expertise on issues of diversity, organizational strategy, change management, and relevant diversity policy and legal issues. The group should have impeccable credentials, high standards for the review, and operate in a transparent way so that many parties are aware and can potentially participate in some part of the review.

It is common for the review team to spend multiple days on campus, talking with numerous groups and leaders, reviewing documents and reports, and conducting targeted focus groups. These activities should result in a major report that is then presented to campus leaders. Although the institution may desire to have the report issued publically, this comes with some degree of political risk. If some aspects of the report unearth sensitive legal issues, it may be better to be more circumspect and judicious in its distribution.

Although the external review is an excellent tool for gaining an external perspective regarding what exists across campus, it is no replacement for the learning that comes through conversation with knowledgeable students, faculty, and staff community members.

Targeted Communications

In a new CDO's first several weeks on the job, it is difficult to make a measurable difference in the strategy and tactics of the institution, but it is easy to build personal credibility with key audiences. These early actions are important to determining how the new CDO is perceived. New CDOs have to determine how they will get "connected to their organization" (Watkins, 2003, p. 88). This means defining the key messages that they want to communicate to different audiences, and tailoring those messages to fill the needs of a particular group.

In an effort to accomplish this goal, targeted communication letters should be developed for all of the various parties that the CDO wants to engage with. This might include community organizations, faith-based organizations, K–12 school leaders, corporations, alumni groups, and others with a vested connection to the institution's diversity interests. The goal is to introduce the CDO as a campus resource, capitalize on preexisting relationships, and build new ones. This strategy might also include launching new social media tools for the office and developing a series of intentional messaging strategies to communicate the institutional vision for diversity and the role of the CDO.

Individual and Unit Join-Up Meetings

Throughout the year, the CDO should engage in a series of ongoing join-up meetings with key stakeholders on campus. Inevitably, these groups will include individual leaders, offices, divisions, committees, students, and student organizations. These meetings might even take the form of a campus-wide town-hall forum as the CDO joins up with the entire campus community presenting opportunities for questions, insights, and discussion about campus diversity goals, priorities, and the role of the CDO. As more and more meetings take place, it is important for new officers to test the insights and theories that they gain from various interactions with leaders, whether they take place in a one-on-one meeting, structured retreat, or through informal conversations. These activities are key to the sensemaking process and engaging in them will allow the CDO to develop a solid working theory of his or her organization.

These meetings also help new CDOs establish a rapport with stakeholders so as to understand what they care about, and to signal a sense of the CDO's values and working style. We often tell new CDOs that by the end of these meetings they should understand the stakeholders' key objectives and major concerns, and be ready to support their interests.

CDOs should avoid the phrase, "We did it this way at my previous institution," because many in the community will grow tired of hearing about how it was done at another institution. Most students, faculty, and staff have a deep regard for their institutions. The last thing they want to hear is how much better the CDO's previous institution was, or how they should try imitating another school. At the same time, strategic comparisons that point to general best practices can prove quite helpful in efforts to unleash isomorphic energies that legitimize new approaches.

Why the Transition Framework Is Important

There are no universal rules for success in transitions. New CDOs need to diagnose the institutional situation accurately and clarify its challenges and opportunities. The transition framework provides a big-picture road map for the new CDO early on and is key to getting off to a strong start. Although it will not lead to immediate change, this strategy of joining up, or becoming connected with the campus community, shows a healthy respect for the collegial nature of the academy, as well as the highly politicized and contested nature of diversity issues in higher education. It also sets a template for the type of integrative and collegial leadership that the CDO will need to provide throughout his or her tenure on campus. A new CDO may find that prior to his or her arrival, these types of discussions may not have ever occurred. We believe that this type of interactive change strategy is essential to sparking the type of organizational sensemaking that is foundational to shaping how campus leaders define and ultimately become involved in the change journey (Kezar & Eckel, 2008).

Because the framework focuses on program review and external and internal audits, it also establishes an expectation that the CDO will have a strong voice in determining what diversity efforts are sound, what adjustments need to be made, and where investments might need to be placed in the future. Setting a culture of program review and critique is essential because it allows us to take a hard look at what we are doing and potentially alter long-standing efforts. Because program reviews and audits are sometimes intrusive and focused on accountability, they are often resisted. In these moments, the president's authority is essential and explains why the CDO unit should report at the most senior levels. The full support of the president allows the CDO to more easily move across the dynamic boundaries of his or her role as he or she is inevitably guided into conversations that may traditionally exist in the purview of student affairs, enrollment management, human resources, and other departments. Again, this is a good reason for leaders to proactively use the PACE tool that we outlined in Chapter 3.

Finally, the transition framework provides the new CDO with a window of time to begin establishing the type of collegial network that will be required to launch a powerful campus-wide diversity agenda. The new CDO often encounters unreasonable demands and is expected to launch new initiatives while resolving issues that have troubled an institution for decades. No CDO is going to magically transform the campus climate overnight. It takes the committed work of many leaders. A clear framework helps establish networks, open new possibilities, and lay a foundation for the CDO's strategic plan.

Matching Strategy to Situation

Many of the transition techniques that we have presented focus on big-picture diversity challenges, goals, and opportunities. New CDOs must also diagnose the CDO role, unit, or division itself, depending on the nature and archetype of the CDO position. Although we outlined a process for determining where an institution is with respect to its stage of diversity maturation—understanding its *Diversity DNA*—in the companion volume to this book, similar questions must be asked about the CDO role specifically. In his research on organizational transition, Michael Watkins (2003) theorizes that most units are in one of four circumstances of transition: (a) start-up, (b) turnaround, (c) realignment, or (d) sustaining success. This four-part framework is helpful whether the incoming CDO is the first at that institution, or assuming a second- or third-generation role that has existed and evolved for several years. Leaders who do a poor job of diagnosing their situations will have a difficult time getting off to a fast start.

Although the framework has campus-wide utility for thinking about the campus diversity infrastructure as a whole, it is intended to help CDOs understand the vertical and in some ways lateral structures that they lead in terms of their core team, direct reporting units, and the committees they chair or sponsor. For the most part, those entities in a CDO's span of control include the individuals they have the ability to hire, fire, oversee, and administer. We address this aspect of the transition in this way because CDOs can lead differently in those units that report directly to them as opposed to units where they must share leadership, or facilitate the shaping of new initiatives, because they do not have formal authority.

Drawing from Watkins (2003), we present an outline of the characteristics associated with each situation in Table 8.4. Because of a general lack of infrastructure or supporting resources, start-ups and turnarounds usually require a significant investment of resources. By contrast, a CDO entering a realignment or sustaining-success situation has certain automatic advantages because he or she is building from a position of strength; capacity; and, in some instances, positive outcomes. To help CDOs diagnose their situations and tailor their strategies accordingly, we offer a brief overview of each.

Start-Up

In a start-up situation, everything is new and at times the general mood is one of excited confusion (Watkins, 2003). The CDO must channel this energy in a positive direction, securing the initial budget, hiring staff, finding office space, developing marketing and media strategies, and establishing a mission and inaugural strategic plan. The great thing about a start-up is that it allows the CDO to establish a culture, process, and staff consistent with developing a twenty-first-century diversity organization that aligns with the big-picture diversity goals of his or her institution. Because there is no prior existing officer, the CDO has a chance to work with his or her colleagues to establish new relationships, expectations, and partnerships that may not have existed in the past. It is also a powerful opportunity to leverage relevant strategic diversity leadership theory, best practices in the field, and innovative approaches that may not be as possible if there was a CDO infrastructure in place previously.

The challenge in a start-up situation is that the new CDO lacks a preexisting framework to draw from. In addition, the new CDO may meet resistance as faculty, student affairs, alumni relations, and human resources

TABLE 8.4
CDO Challenges and Opportunities by Transition Type

Transition Type	*Challenges*	*Opportunities*
Start-Up	• No history or understanding of the CDO role • Political dynamics associated with turf issues • Acquiring the resources necessary to enable the CDO role	• Opportunity to build guided by theory and best practices • Stakeholders are energized by new diversity leadership • Chance to hire competent diversity professionals • Build new relationships and identity for diversity leadership
Turnaround	• Giving hope to demoralized stakeholders • Quickly diagnosing the challenge and areas for change • Following an unpopular leader • Making difficult decisions in the face of history and legacy roles, initiatives, and relationships • Acquiring the resources necessary to enable the CDO role	• Many recognize that change is needed • Chance to acquire early wins • External stakeholders may offer support for the turnaround that can be helpful • Existing resources potentially eligible for redistribution • Small victories may shape opinion positively
Realignment	• Legacy roles, initiatives, and relationships • Enough success for leaders to believe no change is necessary • Restructuring the team and refocusing the organization	• The organization has pockets of strength • People want to continue to see themselves as successful • Existing resources potentially eligible for redistribution
Sustaining Success	• Following a revered leader • Creating a culture of innovation • Legacy of success	• A strong team may be in place • People have a history of success • Successful foundation to build on

offices seek to protect their turf. This is particularly true as the new officer may identify a number of departments, roles, and projects that need to be realigned into the direct supervising portfolio of the CDO. As we have noted, academic institutions are resistant to change, which underscores the need for the CDO to have the staunch support of senior leaders. Because many will have a flawed assumption of what the new CDO's role should be, it is critical to create awareness using listening sessions, town-hall meetings, consulting visits, and messaging about the CDO role in clear terms.

Turnaround

In a turnaround situation, the CDO is often dealing with stakeholders who may be upset or jaded by previous diversity leaders or efforts (Watkins,

2003). The CDO has to get his or her hands around this negative energy and create a sense of hope within the department or unit. As with start-ups, the CDO may still need to secure operational capital and staff, build a positive identity on campus, and develop new partnerships and relationships. The challenge here is that these efforts are taking place in a context still recovering from past or present failures and disappointments. In these situations, new officers must find ways to build a new team while continuing on the journey. As Watkins (2003) notes, "Molding a team is like repairing a team in midflight. You will not reach your destination if you ignore the necessary repairs. But you do not want to crash the airplane while trying to fix it" (p. 160).

One of the positives associated with a turnaround scenario is that many stakeholders may at least recognize that change needs to happen. The question remains, do they have the courage, integrity, and will to support a new officer in creating a vision and bringing these changes to life over time? There is generally a reason diversity efforts stagnate or falter. It may stem from the leadership deficiencies of the former CDO. It may reflect a lack of resources. The problems may lie deep in the nested politics of an institution's history of race, gender, and sexuality. Regardless, the CDO must find a way to reenergize demoralized employees and stakeholders, create new energy under the bright glare of expectations, and make difficult choices while lobbying for new resources and support. Again, this is why it is so important for the CDO to get a commitment from senior leaders that he or she will be allowed to transition into the institution and ultimately have a conversation regarding new resources as the vision for change and the CDO infrastructure becomes clearer.

A positive aspect of this circumstance is that the CDO has a chance to diagnose areas in which he or she can find early wins that can make an immediate difference. These early wins can be instrumental in helping a new CDO acquire the political capital necessary to develop more aggressive change efforts down the line. Officers should recognize that some of their most powerful allies may be people who work outside their span of control, but may serve as key strategic partners who can be enlisted in shaping the turnaround effort. Some specific techniques to help with turnaround situations are external reviews and program evaluations by third-party consultants, task forces designed to identify problems and benchmark other organizations, and strategic planning activities led by the CDO, where it is clear that a bold new vision may emerge. CDOs in a turnaround situation must be willing to make tough calls, but they should take care to do so in a way that is fair.

Realignment

In realignment, the primary challenge is to revitalize a unit, process, or project that may be drifting into trouble (Watkins, 2003). This can often mean redirecting existing resources, including offices, units, staff, and budgets, toward new strategic priorities. At many institutions, legacy infrastructures have existed for 30 years or more. Although campuses must look to invest new resources into their diversity efforts, change also hinges on reframing and deploying current diversity capabilities. This may require reviewing a mission, new training, establishing new budget priorities, and at times hiring new leadership. During any realignment, the supervising CDO must work to match the resources and infrastructure to the strategic goals of the institution. This type of change is often easier said than done, as many diversity champions will often toil for years, under the radar, with little or no formal support from the institution. As a result, their contributions must be engaged with great care as new CDOs look to innovate and realign current capacity to new and emerging needs and priorities. To realign, CDOs must address diplomatically the need for change and new expectations.

Sustaining Success

In a sustaining-success situation, the challenge is a bit different. The CDO may be following in the footsteps of a well-loved leader. Here, the constant standard of measurement will be to determine if the new CDO measures up to the departed CDO. When inheriting a high-performing team or operation, it is not the CDO's job to make radical changes but to look for ways to refine and enable new possibilities. This may involve making minor adjustments or adapting processes in ways that may be imperceptible to those within the system. It usually does not involve radically remaking the unit. Here the greatest challenge is to shoulder the responsibility for preserving the excellence and success of a long-standing operation that may have very powerful allies and supporters. In realignment, the CDO has to reinvent the core operating processes and technologies, whereas in a sustaining-success context, he or she works to uncover and address new challenges. For example, if one inherits a student retention and academic success program with a 90 percent graduation rate for historically underrepresented minority students, the goal is not to reinvent how the program approaches graduation success overall. The program is successful in that regard. Rather, the goal may be to define the challenge in new ways, perhaps setting new goals to increase the average GPA of students; improve the number of science, technology, engineering, mathematics, and professional school graduates; or increase the number of students who go on to graduate school.

Summary

It is unlikely that the CDO's first 100 days will guarantee either wild success or dismal failure. However, it is during the first months and year that opinions about the new leader begin to crystallize and feedback loops are established. Significant missteps can lead to downward spirals that are hard to interrupt. So it is far better for new leaders to get early wins that build personal credibility and political capital, rather than dig themselves into holes that they then have to scramble out of.

Success will depend on the CDO's ability to influence people outside his or her direct line of control. Supportive alliances, both internal and external, will be vital to achieving ambitious goals. New CDOs cannot define their ability to lead change solely on the basis of their positional authority. Although some CDOs will have a large staff and perhaps even a division to lead, all CDOs must be able to build effective collaborative relationships and lead with others.

Note

1. Staff executive roles generally operate in a collaborative officer model archetype with little or no professional staff and no direct reporting units. By comparison, line executives are most often associated with leadership in a portfolio divisional structure and have one or more units within their span of supervision.

9

HIGHER EDUCATION AND CORPORATE CHIEF DIVERSITY OFFICERS

A Preliminary Comparison

> Diversity is no longer merely an issue of equity in hiring but of strategy in the marketplace. Companies that are unable to communicate with or win over diverse markets domestically and globally will see their market share erode and financial performance suffer. Leading companies that understand these dynamics have accordingly evolved the role of the diversity officer from its earlier incarnations in equal opportunity and compliance to that of a change agent. In this demanding new role, the diversity officer must be able to help guide the company through major cultural transformation in order to harness the business value of diversity as a core competency of the company.
>
> —Billy Dexter, Partner, Heidrick and Struggles

Up to this point we have focused our discussion on the chief diversity officer (CDO) role in higher education, giving only passing attention to its connection to the CDO role in the corporate and nonprofit worlds. Yet diversity professionals and others often ask us how the role of a corporate CDO compares with the role of a higher education CDO. Are the roles structured differently? Do they manage similar resources? How do their backgrounds compare? What does the compensation package look like across sectors? How does the process of strategic diversity leadership differ depending on the environment, whether corporate, educational, nonprofit, or governmental? Although we are just beginning to formulate detailed answers to these questions, we feel that the conclusion of this book offers an inviting opportunity to entertain some initial responses. Though there are many gaps in the current literature, this chapter also seeks to elaborate several areas for future research.

Because so much confusion exists regarding the CDO position, we need to clarify our understanding of the CDO role. Consistent with our grounded definition, this chapter focuses on executive-level CDOs. Our research is grounded in a confluence of sources, including our direct interactions with 110 higher education CDOs (Williams & Wade-Golden, 2008), interviews with leaders across dozens of different classifications, and a careful utilization of the strategic diversity leadership literature on CDOs in the corporate sector (Dexter, 2010; Diversity Best Practices, 2005; Metzler, 2008). By combining these data, we are prepared to offer the first ever comparison of different CDO roles.

We begin this chapter by offering a comparative framework that contrasts directly the higher education and corporate CDO roles. Although we provide some insights into the nonprofit and government CDO role, our primary focus is on the higher education and corporate CDO roles. We chose to examine these roles not because they are more important than the others, but because at present they are more prevalent and mature than their nonprofit and governmental counterparts. This prevalence allows us to construct a relatively clear picture of how these roles compare.

A Chief Diversity Officer Comparative Framework

Establishing a high-ranking CDO role often indicates that senior leaders at least formally acknowledge the importance of diversity and the need for executive leadership in this area. Some of the nation's leading higher education institutions have established CDOs, as have organizations like the Democratic Party;[1] the American Tennis Association; Teach for America; and Fortune 500 companies like Starbucks, Walmart, and IBM.

Table 9.1 applies aspects of the Chief Diversity Officer Development Framework described in Chapters 3 and 4 of this book. More specifically, we present a comparison of the higher education and corporate CDO in terms of their historic roots, strategic diversity platform, vertical structure, and officer background and characteristics. Our sources include data collected from our national study of 110 CDOs in higher education; in-depth interviews with leading CDOs in both educational and corporate fields; data reported in the 2005 Diversity Best Practices Report (a study of 177 CDOs);

TABLE 9.1
CDO Comparative Matrix

Dimension	*Description*	*Higher Education CDO* (N = *110)*	*Corporate CDO* (N = *177)*
Historic Roots	Early Precursors to the CDO Role	AA and EEO Academic Support Services Minority Student Affairs	AA and EEO Human Resources Purchasing
Strategic Diversity Platform	Primary Rationale	Educational Benefits of Diversity Social Justice Rationale	Business Case for Diversity Corporate Responsibility
	Strategic Diversity Leadership Focus	Access and Equity Creating a Multicultural and Inclusive Campus Climate Preparing Students for a Diverse and Global World Fostering Diversity-Themed Domestic and International Research and Scholarship	Recruiting, Retaining, and Developing Diverse Human Talent Creating an Inclusive Organizational Culture Marketing to Diverse Domestic and Global Markets Enhancing Supplier Diversity
	Target of Efforts	Students Faculty Staff Administration Alumni	Leadership Staff Diverse Suppliers
Vertical Structure	Executive-Level CDO Title and Rank	Vice President, Provost, Chancellor: 33 percent Associate Vice President, Provost, Chancellor: 22 percent Assistant Vice President, Provost, Chancellor: 6 percent Special Assistant to the President: 36 percent Dean: 4 percent	Vice President: 64.7 percent Chief Diversity Officer: 23.5 percent Senior Vice President: 8.8 percent Director: 17.1 percent Executive Vice President: 2.4 percent Manager: 4.7 percent
	Staff Size	Divisional Model: 28 percent Unit-Based Model: 31 percent Collaborative Officer Model: 40 percent	More Than 21 Staff Members: 30 percent Staff of 4 to 20 Staff Members: 58.7 percent Staff of Fewer Than 4 Members: 11 percent
	Budget Ranges	More Than \$1 Million: 16 percent \$300,000–\$1 Million: 25 percent \$100,000–\$300,000: 26 percent Less Than \$100,000: 32 percent	More Than \$3 Million: 16 percent \$1 Million–\$3 Million: 41 percent Less Than \$1 Million: 43 percent

TABLE 9.1 (Continued)

Dimension	*Description*	*Higher Education CDO* (N = *110)*	*Corporate CDO* (N = *177)*
Officer Backgrounds	Key Competencies of the Role	Ability to Cultivate a Common Vision In-Depth Perspective on Organizational Change Politically Savvy Results Orientation Sophisticated Relational Abilities Technical Mastery of Diversity Issues Understanding of the Culture of Higher Education	Ability to Influence Change Management Skills Building and Maintaining Credibility Results Orientation Leadership Skills Commitment to Diversity Business Acumen
	Pathway to CDO Leadership	Faculty with Diversity Research Agenda Track General Administrative Track AA and EEO Compliance Track Diversity-Themed Student Affairs Track Strategic Diversity Leadership Track Other	Line Business Track AA and EEO Compliance Track Diversity-Themed Human Resources Track Strategic Diversity Leadership Diversity-Themed External/ Community Relations Track Diversity-Themed Procurement Leadership Track Other
	Personal Compensation	Over $200,000: 12 percent $100,000–$200,000: 57 percent $50,000–$100,000: 30 percent Under $50,000: 2 percent	Over $300,000 and bonus of More Than $100,000: 23 percent $200,000–$300,000, With a Bonus in the $75,000 Range: 46 percent $100,000–$200,000 With a Bonus in the $50,000 Range: 30 percent
	Race	African American: 74 percent Asian American: 3 percent Hispanic, Latino: 10 percent White: 13 percent	African American: 37 percent Asian American: 2 percent Hispanic, Latino: 4 percent White: 19 percent Unknown: 39 percent
	Gender	Female: 58 percent Male: 42 percent	Female: 65 percent Male: 35 percent
	Education	Bachelor's Degree: 2 percent Master's Degree: 22 percent Law Degree: 9 percent Doctoral Degree: 67 percent	Bachelor's Degree: 40 percent Master's Degree: 48 percent Doctoral or Law Degree: 12 percent

AA, Affirmative action; *EEO,* equal employment opportunity.

and finally a review of current research, including Christopher Metzler's 2008 report on the role of the CDO and Billy Dexter's 2010 report on CDO competency areas.

Historic Roots of the Role

The historical development of the CDO role follows a similar track for the corporate and higher education sectors. Both roles emerged from precursor positions that focused on classic affirmative action, equal employment opportunity (EEO), and minority affairs issues (Metzler, 2008; Peterson et al., 1978). At the time of their emergence, the meaning of a diversity officer, director, or manager was not framed in terms of achieving the organizational bottom line, or in terms of enhancing organizational excellence. Instead, these roles were framed in response to a changing legal and political context and the need to avoid claims of discrimination and expensive lawsuits.

It is also important to note that early roles focused largely on the needs of African Americans and women. Only recently has the cultural framework of diversity expanded to include other historically excluded or marginalized groups, as well as a new appreciation of the inherent benefits of inclusion and diversity in a knowledge-based, global economy. However, understanding this historical context is important to appreciating the rise of the modern executive-level CDO role in higher education and corporate America.

Higher Education

As we have noted, as the civil rights movement and the struggle of African Americans to enter higher education began to transform college campuses in the 1960s and 1970s, academic institutions had to adjust. Thanks to landmark Supreme Court victories, executive orders, and the demands of emerging national groups and their allies, academic institutions adopted affirmative action policies and opened their first minority affairs offices. Often, shifts in the student and faculty population led to the development of at least three diversity role categories focused on diversity issues and priorities: minority student affairs specialists, ethnic studies faculty, and EEO leaders.

Among the earliest diversity leadership roles were positions focused on minority student issues. These early leaders were usually found in admissions offices, financial aid offices, student centers, or in some instances as special assistants to the president (Peterson et al., 1978). They were concerned with the academic, financial, social, and cultural well-being of African American students, and by extension newly emerging minority faculty and staff members. These positions provided the first leadership opportunity for minorities to participate in higher education outside of historically Black colleges and universities.

The activist energy of diverse student leaders and their White allies pressured colleges to create the first ethnic area studies, including African American and Black world studies, Chicano and Latino studies, and Asian American studies. These early ethnic studies programs provided the model for women's studies, which sought to advance feminist theory and gender issues while diversifying the curriculum and faculty ranks. These early pioneers offered the first consistent efforts to diversify the college curriculum, while simultaneously focusing on supporting diverse students and creating bridges to local communities (Peterson et al., 1978).

These student and academic roles were complemented by workforce development positions that emerged in the late 1970s and early 1980s. These positions played a key role in ensuring that institutions actually moved forward with desegregation plans, complied with guidance from the Office of Civil Rights, and followed regulations established by the Department of Labor's Office of Federal Contract Compliance Programs. These affirmative action and EEO roles ensured institutional compliance with state and federal laws and regulations regarding equity, affirmative action, nondiscrimination policy, and workplace dynamics.

Corporate Sector

In some ways, the development of corporate diversity capacity tracked a path similar to higher education, particularly in terms of workforce development. In the 1960s and 1970s, a number of federally sponsored equal employment laws were put in place to prohibit workplace discrimination based on age, color, disability, Vietnam-era veteran status, national origin, race, religion, and gender. To address discriminatory patterns in the workplace and in business development and procurement, businesses sought to establish human resources positions that functioned like an early precursor of the CDO role (Metzler, 2008).

These roles were predicated on the belief that simply lifting barriers of access to opportunity would not create a level playing field for members of diverse groups to compete for opportunities. A more proactive and intentional organizational change model was required to pressure organizations to change. Out of this context, companies created affirmative action, EEO, and minority business development roles to help change the demographic profile of their organizations to reflect that of the external labor; consumer; and, in some instances, vendor pools (Metzler, 2008).

These early roles were focused on satisfying legal requirements and ensuring compliance with federal and state regulations. As opposed to the modern-day CDO, the primary responsibility of these individuals "was to police the very ones who hired or appointed them" (Metzler, 2008, p. 12). The implications of this leadership model should be obvious: relationships between early diversity officers and their employers were often awkward and sometimes hostile. Metzler (2008) argues that

> organizational productivity suffered because of the amount of time these individuals spent reviewing hiring and promotion rates and developing lengthy documents to chastise management and meet compliance requirements. . . . This type of exercise only served to create deeper tensions and divisions amongst blacks and whites, as well as the compliance officers. (p. 12)

Early diversity officer roles were nearly exclusively located in human resources and buried beneath several layers of administrative hierarchy (Dexter, 2010; Diversity Best Practices, 2005; Metzler, 2008). That said, these officers did play an important role in monitoring compliance and disseminating information about the institution's affirmative action policies. They also helped to ensure that search, selection, and other employment activities fulfilled the institution's stated commitment to affirmative action and EEO. Finally, they helped to drive minority business development by advancing efforts to help minority- and women-owned businesses apply for contract opportunities.

Building the Case for Diversity: The Legitimating Diversity Narrative

In the companion volume to this book, *Strategic Diversity Leadership,* we argue that the best leaders have the ability to "frame" organizational possibilities from a number of different diversity perspectives. No communication skill is more critical to the CDO role than the ability to frame effectively issues of diversity. Both higher education and corporate CDOs spend a considerable amount of time demonstrating the strategic advantages of diversity. Enough research now exists demonstrating diversity's importance to top leadership, subordinates, colleagues, strategic partners, the media, and others. In the corporate sector, this means talking about the "business case for diversity," whereas in higher education, it usually means focusing on the "educational benefits rationale for diversity."

The Educational Case for Diversity

In higher education, the primary frame for diversity has emerged out of the social scientific rationale about diversity's educational importance, a point we have made throughout this book and in its companion volume. As such, college and university CDOs emphasize the importance of creating diverse learning environments that benefit all students. According to this rationale, the presence of a diverse student body, particularly an ethnically and racially diverse student body, helps to create the type of rich learning environment that colleges and universities need to prepare students for a diverse and global world.

Granted, many academic CDOs also point out that the work of the civil rights movement remains unfinished and that the cause of advancing diversity remains an important social justice issue. However, the social justice rationale has become less prominent in the face of legal challenges that have gradually chipped away at the strength and variety of affirmative action and EEO policies.

One of the main reasons that higher education focuses so heavily on the educational benefits of diversity rationale is the powerful way that the legal and policy environment has shaped the concrete policies and programs of diversity in the academy. Indeed, the isomorphic energies that emerged from the Michigan decisions have shaped the way that most institutions are framing diversity on their campus. In the companion volume to this book we discuss not only the educational benefits of diversity, but shifting demographics, workforce needs, persistent educational and societal inequities, and even the business case for diversity as key drivers legitimating diversity as a strategic priority for colleges and universities.

The Business Case for Diversity

By comparison, corporate CDOs constantly emphasize how diversity is fundamental to the financial bottom line of their organizations (Dexter, 2010; Diversity Best Practices, 2005; Metzler, 2008). In the words of an officer at a Fortune 500 company, "The only way to make meaningful and sustained change, and to make progress on diversity, is to fully link our efforts with those of business."

Corporate CDOs define the business case for diversity in a number of different and complementary ways that illustrate a broad-based and multidimensional argument for why diversity matters (Dexter, 2010; Diversity Best Practices, 2005; Metzler, 2008). Most emphasize the importance of capitalizing on demographic changes and the increased purchasing power of diverse consumers, highlighting the importance of multicultural and cross-consumer marketing. Others focus their attention on the importance of hiring, retaining, and engaging diverse talent as a way of enhancing the organizational creativity and strategic thinking potential of their companies. Finally, they understand that a positive, inclusive working environment provides a measure of protection against more overt forms of discrimination, which inevitably lead to lost worker productivity and even expensive lawsuits.

Although the language of social responsibility has existed in the management lexicon since the 1970s, companies are increasingly seeking proactive outreach activities to express their diversity values. The social responsibility rationale argues that corporations have a responsibility to be good neighbors and help communities deal with major social challenges, including poverty, education, diseases, environmental degradation, natural disasters, and other challenges. This perspective has led companies to create and fund nonprofit foundations and to focus on building community outreach vehicles that leverage the core competencies of the company in efforts designed to serve the public good.

Validating Diversity Work

In both the academic and corporate worlds, CDOs are essential to framing diversity efforts. In addition to engaging in research and policy work, CDOs help establish the broader narrative framework about why diversity matters. The more that officers can articulate these issues, the more legitimating energy they can create. Narrative frameworks establish coherent systems of interrelated and sequentially organized stories that contextualize diversity in ways that are helpful for understanding its definition, value, and legitimacy. Establishing the master diversity narrative helps to resolve conflicts by presenting a rationale for why diversity is important and worthy of organizational attention and support.

To build this support, CDOs must rely on personal influence and authority, sound arguments, and compelling messaging. Moreover, the more a CDO can leverage external dynamics to help build credibility and understanding of his or her internal efforts, the better. Truly embedding diversity values in an organization cannot simply be the work of the CDO. It requires senior-level support, as well as involvement by stakeholders up, down, and across the organization using a systems approach to change. The more that senior leaders successfully leverage the critical diversity resources of their organizations, the better they can help to create a broader cultural understanding of the value of diversity. Without this type of master narrative, it is difficult for diversity champions to establish an expectation of what is valued and the direction that the organization should take going forward. Box 9.1 examines a corporate diversity ranking system as a driver of legitimating isomorphic energy.

BOX 9.1
DiversityInc's Corporate Diversity Ranking System

As we noted in Chapter 5 of this book, the more that CDOs can tap into isomorphic energies of change, the more they can validate the approach and techniques used to drive their diversity agendas. One important area of distinction between higher education and the corporate sector hinges on the various ranking systems that many companies use as a way of publically touting where they stand with respect to their corporate commitment to diversity. Magazines like *DiversityInc, Fortune,* and *Working Mother* issue rankings that have become vital to companies seeking to publicize their commitment to diversity. These publications rank companies in terms of their policies toward minorities, women, and members of the LGBT community, while also ranking how well companies implement their strategic diversity leadership efforts.

Perhaps the most prominent ranking system belongs to *DiversityInc. DiversityInc* was founded in 1998 as a web-based publication and launched its print version in 2002. The publication features more than one million unique monthly visitors at DiversityInc.com, and boasts a circulation of over 340,000. DiversityInc.com also publishes DiversityIncBestPractices.com, a website dedicated to diversity management and best practices, and hosts monthly webinars and national events.

Using a range of different indicators, *DiversityInc* works to identify the most diversity-friendly companies in America. Each year it sends a survey to companies with over 1,000 employees. Each survey consists of more than 300 empirical questions, each weighted appropriately to reveal the strength of each company's diversity programs. *DiversityInc* then examines a range of issues, including the connections between and among workforce and managerial diversity and rates of promotion. The survey also explores four key areas of diversity endeavor: chief executive officer (CEO) commitment, human capital, corporate and organizational communications, and supplier diversity. Companies must score above average in these four areas and demonstrate a strong commitment to their diversity-management initiatives to earn a positive rating.

(continues)

(continued)

These rating systems create validating isomorphic forces. Understandably, companies want to see themselves on the *DiversityInc* list, because a favorable rating tends to garner the interest of diverse job candidates and improves the morale of existing employees. Despite some criticisms of its methodology, *DiversityInc's* importance to helping legitimate organizational diversity efforts cannot be denied as an isomorphic change energy (Metzler, 2008). By comparison, institutions of higher learning are not subject to a similar external ranking system with respect to their diversity capacity broadly defined.

Source: http://diversityinc.com/the-diversityinc-top-50-companies-for-diversity/diversityinc-top-50-methodology-2/

A Strategic Leadership Diversity Focus

The CDO position is multifaceted and faces challenging demands and expectations. One of the most important distinctions between the higher education and corporate CDO is how diversity is defined organizationally in terms of big-picture goals and priorities, and how CDOs collaborate with others to build strategic capacity to pursue these goals. Our research identified four major priorities guiding the work of each sector's CDO, or eight total. Several of these priorities relate very closely. For example, there are particularly close areas of correspondence between a higher education CDO's efforts regarding "fostering access and equity" and a corporate CDO's efforts regarding "valuing diverse human talent." Similarly, the middle sections of each pyramid—"multicultural and inclusive campus climate" and "inclusive corporate culture"—share vital connections. It is for these reasons that we have arranged these priorities at the top and middle portion of each pyramid in Figure 9.1.

In other areas, however, the work of the higher education CDO and corporate sector CDO diverge markedly. As our individual treatment of each sector advances, these differences in priority will become clearer. That said, CDOs in each sector have much to learn from each other. We hope that by exploring the chief characteristics of each overarching principle, we can locate other potential areas where the sectors might eventually inform and improve the diversity efforts of the other.

Higher Education

As Figure 9.1 demonstrates, CDOs in higher education are principally concerned with four objectives: (a) fostering access and equity for historically

FIGURE 9.1

Higher Education and Corporate Chief Diversity Officer Capabilities

underrepresented groups; (b) creating a multicultural and inclusive campus climate for the entire institutional community; (c) enhancing domestic and international research and scholarship around issues of diversity; and (d) preparing all students for a knowledge-based, interconnected, and global economy and society.

If you spend time conversing with campus diversity leaders or reviewing the various diversity capacities on campuses, you will find that most aspire to meet the four overarching goals described in Figure 9.1. Indeed, it has been our observation that most initial conversations about diversity invariably center either on trying to define a diversity rationale, or elaborating the big-picture goals of the strategic diversity agenda. This is particularly true when the groups included in the conversation represent a range of different constituencies, including communities characterized by differences in race, ethnicity, gender, sexual orientation, veteran status, and national origin. There are also distinctions between and among faculty, staff, alumni, senior leaders, students, and community members. Within the context of these four big-picture priorities, the issues of every member of the institutional community are potentially embraced and defined.

Figure 9.1 places access and equity at the top of the model because CDOs spend a considerable amount of time focusing on the historic and still incomplete goal of achieving access and equity for racially and ethnically diverse groups, women, and other traditionally disadvantaged communities. In higher education, this aspect of the model could also be extended to issues of vendor relationships and strategic sourcing, ensuring that minority- and women-owned companies are treated fairly in an institution's procurement process. Granted, this priority is generally higher for corporate CDOs than for CDOs in higher education.

The presence of a diverse faculty, staff, administration, and student body enhances the potential of the institution to accomplish the two strategic goals placed at the base of the pyramid: (a) preparing all students for a diverse and global world, and (b) pursuing areas of diversity research and scholarship. Although many have begun talking about the diverse educational needs of all students as part of their institutional diversity agenda, they have not similarly embraced the need to support faculty in ethnic studies, gender studies, and others engaged in scholarship that is so critical to understanding the diverse and multicultural world that we live in today. We placed these goals at the two corners of the pyramid because they are foundational to higher education and its focus on teaching, learning, research, and service.

Engagement in these areas is a place for growth for CDOs as they focus on these and other academic issues.

What holds the model together is the vision of fostering a multicultural and inclusive campus climate in which every student, staff member, faculty member, and administrator can thrive. This means eliminating overt acts of discrimination and prejudice while promoting identity-themed organizations and initiatives designed to create an inclusive experience for diverse groups. Some examples might include establishing an affinity organization for women faculty members, creating an international student center, or even establishing a dedicated prayer and reflection area for students of faith to use for spiritual purposes.

There are many stakeholders involved with higher education in the twenty-first century, and contemporary diversity efforts must be robust enough to handle this complexity. To make diversity a matter of excellence, the campus diversity agenda must simultaneously expand access and equity, create inclusive environments, and build the academic diversity capabilities of our institutions. Within the strategic diversity goals framework offered here, institutional leaders have to fully conceptualize the breadth of diversity issues that exist on today's campuses.

Corporate Sector

Like their higher education counterparts, corporate CDOs recognize that increasing the representation and success of diverse employees, and creating an inclusive culture where people feel welcome, is vital to institutional and economic success. However, CDOs in the corporate sector have a different set of tools to draw from, and, as a consequence, their objectives shift as well. As illustrated in Figure 9.1, the four guiding objectives in the corporate sector are (a) recruiting, retaining, and developing diverse human talent; (b) creating an inclusive and supportive work environment; (c) enhancing supplier diversity; and (d) capitalizing on diverse domestic and global markets.

As with the higher education strategic diversity pyramid, the corporate pyramid centers on the classic diversity issues of representation, achievement, and success in the workplace and valuing diverse human talent. Corporate CDOs are concerned with finding, retaining, and developing top-tier diversity talent. Within this framework, racial and gender diversity remain key, with many corporations having diversity recruitment teams, internship programs, and strategic partnership with national diversity affinity organizations. Although the language is different in higher education and the corporate sector, officers in both realms focus their efforts not just on recruiting diverse communities, but also retaining, promoting, graduating, and developing diverse talent, whether the focus is on students, faculty, and staff in academia, or workers, managers, and senior leadership in corporate America.

Many companies continue to focus on a definition of diversity largely limited to race, ethnicity, and gender, but many others are broadening their diversity definition significantly. For example, many companies now are promoting policies to recognize and respect the rights of their LGBT members. Other corporations are making intergenerational diversity a priority. Although generational diversity exists in higher education, academic institutions tend not to think as consciously, or as strategically, about the characteristics, needs, and aspirations of senior citizens, baby boomers, members of Generation X, and Millennials.

Another important area of distinction between the higher education and corporate CDO hinges on the constituents that they serve. Although corporate CDOs have to focus on entry-level, middle manager–level, and executive-level roles, they do not have to focus on the unique challenges of diversifying and retaining students and faculty. Businesspeople may occupy different roles and face a complex set of both diffuse and specific job expectations, and their responsibilities and concerns depart significantly from the priorities and realities of students and faculty in an academic setting. The challenge of tenure and its influence on everything from claims of discrimination to issues of retention and promotion adds another complex layer to higher education culture. There is also more complexity in the policy environment of higher education, as legal guidance regarding Title IX enforcement in sports, combined with the legal and policy terrain regarding race-conscious scholarships, admissions, and outreach processes, combined with the already great complexity involving workforce compliance, Student and Exchange Visitor Information System (SEVIS) visa compliance issues, and disability policy, means that diversity efforts are even more complex in higher education.

But as in higher education, the corporate diversity model is centered on establishing an inclusive corporate culture. Corporate CDOs are concerned with more than head-count diversity. These officers spend a considerable amount of energy developing training programs, affinity organizations, celebratory events, and diversity-friendly workplace policies designed to create a welcoming and inclusive culture. Indeed, corporate sector CDOs more prominently use the language of inclusion than higher education CDOs, and in many ways have more broadly deployed technology to accomplish goals in this area.

Whereas higher education has done a good job building capacity in the form of diverse student organizations and cultural centers, it has not done nearly enough to create powerful leadership development systems to help faculty and administrators teach and work in more inclusive ways. By comparison, corporate CDOs have developed more intentional and consistent approaches to diversity leadership development. More than simply raising awareness, corporate CDOs have invested in approaches that feature external consultants; multimedia tools; consistent off-site training events; customized learning packages; and workshops that focus on cultural differences, communication styles, role playing, and structured relationship-building methodologies between and among peers, subordinates, and supervisors. Although higher education diversity-training programs exist for low-ranking staff, the majority of faculty and senior leaders often go through the majority of their careers without ever participating in a diversity-themed workshop. Thankfully, the same cannot be said about corporate leaders. Corporate CDOs have not only implemented robust training programs, they have helped systematize diversity and inclusion efforts, increasing accountability and integrating diversity efforts into the overall performance management culture of many companies.

At one corner of the corporate pyramid's base is the importance of capitalizing on diverse domestic and global markets. As the general population in the United States continues to become more diverse, with non-White populations now making up around 30 percent of the population—and growing—the days of one-size-fits-all marketing are gone forever. Today, marketers are much more aware of the significant opportunity that these varying demographic groups present. With increasing frequency, CDOs are partnering with brand management teams, helping them to develop this strategic business priority. It would be incorrect to say that CDOs are as involved in this area as they are in the human talent dimensions of the corporate strategic diversity goals pyramid, but their participation is growing. For many years, the focus was on the importance of having a diverse workforce to serve increasingly diverse consumer markets. This dynamic was especially relevant for industries like retail, hospitality, food service, consumer packaging, and other industries that directly interface with diverse consumers.

Finally, corporate CDOs focus their energy on supplier diversity. Supplier diversity emerges out of the EEO context and is a business program designed to encourage the use of minority-, female-, veteran-, and veteran disabled–owned businesses. Supplier diversity goals focus on increasing the number and volume of procurement and business opportunities that go to diverse businesses of all sizes. This is a major part of the portfolio of many corporate CDOs as they identify, review, and manage the supplier diversity program, holding considerable sway in determining vendor contracts. Although supplier diversity is a challenge in higher education, it rarely appeared in our interviews with leading CDOs as a top priority. When procurements issues were a priority, it was generally at large public institutions that had a number of ongoing construction projects.

Globalization as an Emerging Priority

The need to compete in a global marketplace—particularly in new or emerging markets—will force more organizations to pay attention to how diversity and cultural intelligence figure into their business models, and develop career trajectories in which exceptional global leadership traits are not optional but essential. As globalism grows more pervasive in all aspects of the economy, chief executives will depend on the CDO's expertise about new markets and cultures. This will demand an astute understanding of both management and leadership. In our conversations with corporate CDOs regarding emerging priorities, this was a consistent theme. According to Billy Dexter (2010), a former higher education leader and CDO at MTV Global Network and Monster, and now a management consultant and partner at Heidrick and Struggles, the global dimension of diversity and inclusion work is an area in which the modern CDO must develop competency. As companies place talent in diverse communities across the world, develop international partnerships with key business partners, and manage the complexities of mergers and acquisitions, they will encounter cultural obstacles every bit as challenging as their most complex computations regarding labor markets, production costs, and distribution.

In higher education, a similar convergence of domestic and international diversity issues is underway. Organizations like the American Council on Education have elevated the conversation about the intersection of multiculturalism and internationalization in the academy. With increasing frequency, higher education CDOs are becoming more involved in these conversations. Emerging issues include whether the presence of international students removes the incentive, and even the responsibility, of colleges and universities to recruit diverse domestic students; whether international and study abroad offices are doing enough to increase the number of diverse students who study abroad; whether academic institutions should be exploring new synergies among ethnic, gender, and international area studies; and whether and how academic institutions should seek global partnerships with institutions in developing countries like China and India.

Size and Capacity

Our research suggests that in both academia and the corporate sector, large organizations are more likely to have infrastructures in place to support diversity initiatives. Infrastructure in this instance means training programs, diversity councils, affinity groups, diversity consultants, and other diversity programs. According to research into the diversity capabilities of more than 200 institutions by the Institute for Corporate Productivity, as companies increase in size, so does the likelihood of their offering diversity training.[2] Of organizations with more than 10,000 employees, 75 percent offer some type of diversity training (Oakes, 2008). Our examination of American colleges and universities found that more than 70 percent of institutions with more than 20,000 students have diversity-training programs in place for staff. The Institute for Corporate Productivity also found that size mattered when it came to sponsoring diversity councils and affinity groups. Whereas just 34 percent of all companies report having diversity councils in place to provide feedback on issues such as race, gender, and sexual orientation, more than two-thirds of larger companies (more than 10,000 employees) report such councils (Oakes, 2008). This was the same for affinity groups; 61 percent of large organizations report having invested in building this capacity. Although direct comparison data do not exist for colleges and universities, the general trend is for larger organizations to have more dedicated diversity capacity, a point we substantiate in Chapter 8 of *Strategic Diversity Leadership.*

Vertical Structure

In our research into vertical structures, we were able to focus on three key concepts: rank and title, vertical structure, and the budgetary resources of the CDO role. Rather than treat these structures in isolation, we found it more revealing to discuss their relative features in higher education and the corporate sector in an integrated way. This approach allows for a more fine-tuned comparison of the two sectors.

Title and Rank

Executive-level CDOs possess a high rank regardless of organizational context. As we pointed out in Table 9.1, a study of 177 CDOs by Diversity Best Practices (2005) found that roughly 65 percent of corporate CDOs carried the title of vice president, and almost 24 percent carried the title of CDO as their primary working title. By comparison, our 2008 national survey found no officers that held CDO as their formal title (Williams & Wade-Golden, 2008), a trend that has changed as officers at Harvard University, Clemson University, and several others have adopted the CDO title as their formal rank. Our survey found further that 33 percent of officers hold the formal rank of vice president, vice provost, or vice chancellor.

Generally, we define the CDO nomenclature as a designation rather than a title, preferring to see individuals carry titles like "Vice President for Global Diversity Initiatives and Chief Diversity Officer," rather than just "Chief Diversity Officer." When there is a definitive declaration of rank, the CDO knows exactly where he or she stands organizationally from a formal structural perspective. At the same time, the use of the CDO nomenclature as a formal title may be particularly appropriate in the corporate sector, given the widespread use of the "chief" designation as a formal title of the CEO, chief operating officer (COO), and chief financial officer to describe senior executive roles. Generally, however, we recommend that the CDO should have a rank, such as senior vice president or vice provost, along with the CDO designation in higher education.

Ideally, the CDO will report to the CEO, president, provost, COO, or other senior-most leader in the executive suite of his or her respective organization. Although it is difficult to define the most optimal direct reporting relationship, a general rule of thumb is that the better aligned the CDO is with the CEO or president, the more effective he or she will be positioned to have influence. In cases in which the COO or provost leads the day-to-day operations of the organization, it may make sense to have the CDO report to one of these leaders. The only hard-and-fast rule is that the CDO must report at a level elevated enough to allow for serious engagement on issues of diversity. This is a persistent theme in nearly every report and article on the role of the CDO, with some scholars definitively recommending that the CDO must report to the president or CEO (Dexter, 2010; Diversity Best Practices, 2005; Metzler, 2008).

The Hybrid Versus Dedicated Diversity Model

As we pointed out in Chapter 3, the CDO role can either take a hybrid or dedicated diversity form. The hybrid CDO role focuses on diversity and other organizational areas, whether academic affairs in higher education, or sales or human resources in the corporate sector. Using this general filter in our examination of the corporate sector, we notice a trend toward developing hybrid CDO roles. Although still preliminary in nature, our research, summarized in Table 9.2, indicates that corporate sector CDOs often operate in overlapping areas like talent development, external affairs, sales, business development, and human resources.

The hybrid approach to the CDO is not nearly as prevalent in higher education. This absence is not necessarily negative and may merely indicate that higher education is a better fit for establishing a dedicated CDO approach than the corporate sector, where the hybrid approach is vogue.

TABLE 9.2
Comparison of Corporate and Higher Education Chief Diversity Officer Titles

Corporate	*Higher Education*
Senior Vice President, Talent Development and Diversity	Chief Diversity Officer and Special Assistant to the President
Senior Vice President, Talent Development and Chief Diversity Officer	Dean of the College and Chief Diversity Officer
Vice President, Diversity Sales and Business Development	Vice President for Diversity and Community Engagement
Vice President of Diversity Initiatives	Vice Provost for Multicultural and International Affairs
Vice President, Diversity and Inclusion Development	Vice President for Diversity and Equity
Global Diversity and Inclusion Executive	Vice President for Strategic Planning and Diversity
Vice President of Global Diversity	Vice Provost for Strategic Diversity Initiatives
Senior Vice President of External Affairs and Global Chief Diversity Officer	Vice President for Campus Life and Senior Diversity Officer
Vice President, Global Diversity and Inclusion, and Chief Diversity Officer	Vice Provost for Equity and Inclusion
Senior Vice President and Global Chief Diversity Officer	Vice President for Inclusion Diversity and Equal Opportunity
Vice President, Corporate Responsibility and Diversity	Associate Provost for Equity and Diversity
Vice President, Executive Succession and Diversity Strategies	Vice Provost for Diversity, Equity, and Educational Achievement
Vice President, Talent Management and Chief Diversity Officer	

Through the years, colleges and universities have developed more dedicated diversity technology than in the corporate sector. In addition to commonly shared technologies—including workforce development, diversity-training units, and affirmative action offices—academic institutions also boast a range of student affairs and other academically themed diversity efforts. These roles fall across the Access and Equity, Multicultural and Inclusion, and Learning, Diversity, and Research models of organizational change that we explore at length in the companion volume to this book.

Although a typical company may have a CDO role and core team associated with supporting his or her efforts, a company's dedicated diversity capacity often does not go beyond a diversity committee, a healthy budget for an external consultant, and a series of affinity organizations. By comparison, a large research university may have hundreds of diversity-themed units and initiatives, including racial, ethnic, and gender studies departments and other pedagogical and research areas and units. This dedicated diversity infrastructure is often complemented by dozens of diversity committees and student organizations. In addition to their work partnering with various allies, CDOs must attend to this wide spectrum of diversity infrastructures and initiatives. As the dedicated diversity capacity of colleges and universities has increased, developing a dedicated CDO role increasingly makes the best sense.

As we illustrate in Table 9.2, no clear consensus exists in the nomenclature for the CDO role other than the use of the term *diversity* as a general descriptor. It is also common for "inclusion" to be part of the CDO title in the corporate arena, and many in higher education are moving in this direction. As mentioned earlier, the language of equity has nearly vanished from the corporate landscape. By comparison, higher education CDOs still use the equity language in their title, mission, and discussions of their work. The continuing use of equity language to describe the CDO role in higher education is a clear indicator of how issues of access and equity remain prevalent, even as colleges and universities move to frame diversity efforts in the context of their educational benefits.

Budgetary Resources

The comparative data that exist between higher education and corporate CDO budgets must be interpreted with caution; nevertheless, the data presented in Table 9.3 illustrate that the corporate CDO has a much larger budget than his or her higher education counterpart. More specifically, only

TABLE 9.3
Budget Resource Overview: Higher Education Versus Corporate Sector CDO

	Higher Education (N = *110*)	*Corporate* (N = *177*)
Annual Budget	More than $1 Million: 16 percent $300,000–$1 Million: 25 percent $100,00–$300,000: 26 percent Less than $100,000: 32 percent	More than $3 Million: 16 percent $1 Million–$3 Million: 41 percent Less than $1 Million: 43 percent

16 percent of higher education CDOs reported managing a budget of greater than $1 million, compared with 57 percent of corporate officers, with many managing over $3 million annually. Indeed, 32 percent of higher education CDOs reported having a budget of less than $100,000. Although these data are preliminary, the magnitude of differences cannot be avoided and suggests that corporate CDOs have more substantial resources than their higher education counterparts.

The discrepancy between higher education and corporate CDO budget resources may serve as another example of different cultural and administrative contexts. Although there is generally a breadth of capacity in higher education, these resources are often outside of the supervising portfolio of the CDO. Colleges and universities are generally decentralized and loosely coupled structures. Even though the higher education CDO may have a dedicated role, he or she may not lead in a portfolio divisional infrastructure. Indeed, our research suggested that only 28 percent of CDOs lead this kind of more vertically organized structure.

As a result, many higher education CDOs simply do not have ultimate authority over the various diversity budgets and resources at their institutions. By comparison, the corporate CDO may control nearly all of the dedicated dollars associated with diversity. However, although corporate CDOs tend to lead a larger unit (often more than a division), the diversity management function is often consolidated within their unit, whether they have hybrid responsibilities for another functional area or not. Consequently, the differences that we see between the higher education and corporate CDO may be attributed to differences in scale of resources, as well as a difference in the culture and design decisions that go into constructing the different types of roles. (See Box 9.2 for a discussion of these dynamics for CDOs in academic health centers.)

BOX 9.2
Mapping the Role of the Chief Diversity Officer in Academic Health Centers

The Chief Diversity Officer in Academic Medicine Forum

Although not the primary focus of this chapter, one of the trends that we see at the intersection of higher education and the corporate health care sector is the increased emergence of CDO roles in academic medicine. In response to this changing reality, the lead author of this book partnered with leaders at the Association of American Medical Colleges (AAMC) and the American Hospital Association Institute for Diversity in Health Management to write *The Role of the Chief Diversity Officer in Academic Health Centers* (Williams, 2012).

This monograph grew out of a daylong CDO forum convened by AAMC and moderated by Dr. Christopher Metzler, senior associate dean at Georgetown University School of Continuing Studies. The CDO forum was complemented by a series of interviews with participants from the meeting and others with expertise about the CDO role in academic medicine.

Strategic Diversity Foci of the Chief Diversity Officer in Academic Health Centers

Officers discussed the complexity of their work generally, outlining six overall areas that frame the strategic diversity foci of CDOs in academic medicine. They are:

Academic Diversity Engagement

Officers located in medical schools and colleges often focused their work on issues of academic diversity, particularly as it relates to increasing the diversity of the faculty and student bodies of their organizations, diversifying the learning experience of students, embedding cultural issues into the classroom and clinical experience, and promoting health equity research.

Supplier Diversity and Business Development

Different from CDOs in medical schools, officers working in hospitals and broad-spanning health care systems often prioritize the importance of sourcing diverse vendors for their organizations operating diversity procurement programs. These programs focus on expanding the number of certified minority, women, and other diverse business relationships that may have contracts with their organization.

(continues)

Community Engagement and Partnerships

Officers were involved with a number of community engagement efforts that allowed them to expand the reach of their organizations into diverse communities. Some major initiatives included community health fairs, health equity campaigns, K–12 partnership programs, faith-based community partnerships, and other efforts designed to create a deeper relationship between their organization and diverse communities in their area.

Creating a Climate of Inclusion and Support

A number of officers talked of the important work that they lead in creating inclusive and supportive work and learning environments. Common efforts included the development of onetime workshops, ongoing leadership development credentialing programs, and other efforts designed to enhance the diversity and inclusion abilities of clinicians, faculty, graduate students, and employees within their respective organizations. Officers also touted the importance of supporting affinity groups of minorities, women, and members of the LGBT community as a way to engage in the needs, priorities, and challenges of these groups.

Affirmative Action and Compliance

Although affirmative action and compliance is a less dominant narrative of diversity and inclusion efforts in most organizational sectors, a number of officers talked of the need to keep their organizations compliant with federal offices and relevant employment, admissions, and financial aid case law regarding issues of diversity and inclusion, illustrating how many CDO roles are rooted in legacy diversity positions with EEO roots.

Addressing Disparities in Care and Outcomes Within the Patient Experience

At the core of the leadership tasks provided by CDOs is improving the patient experience, which includes concepts of quality, safety, and effective communication. It also concerns reducing inequities in all aspects of organizational functions including such practices as promoting patient access, staff recruitment, employment, and satisfaction.

These areas of engagement are similar to the strategic diversity foci of CDOs in higher education and the corporate sector. Probably the key area of difference in terms of both mission of the role, and the key competencies of leaders, was the realities of the academic medicine cultural context, with its focus on culturally competent health care, the persistence of racial and ethnic health disparities, hospital and medical school culture, and the need to prepare the next generation of diverse health care providers. These realities informed the areas of engagement of leaders and the types of skills necessary for leaders to be effective in their roles, further illustrating

(continues)

(continued)
the contextual nuance of the CDO role for a particular organizational and cultural context. This finding is unsurprising given the premium that the CDO role plays in boundary spanning and relationship building, a finding that holds true for CDOs in the education, government, and nonprofit organizational sectors as well.

Chief Diversity Officer Leadership Competencies

As we note in Table 9.4, CDOs need a remarkably similar set of leadership competencies, regardless of whether they work in a higher education or corporate context (Dexter, 2010; Diversity Best Practices, 2005; Williams & Wade-Golden, 2007). As we analyzed several overviews of the CDO role by higher education and corporate researchers and consultants, we began to find some broader trends that could be combined into a set of leadership skills and competencies that hold true for both higher education and the corporate community. These competencies include (a) possessing a deep technical mastery of best-practice diversity, equity, and inclusion techniques broadly defined across an array of strategic diversity leadership areas of engagement; (b) intimately understanding the process of change management and the dynamics of organizational culture; (c) having a generalist leadership perspective regarding the big-picture challenges, priorities, competitors, and opportunities of their respective fields; and finally (d) possessing sophisticated relational abilities that allow them to inspire others, build relationships, navigate organizational politics, and lead individuals who may not report directly them.

Industry and Organizational Acumen

CDOs must understand the core mission of their organization and have a sophisticated ability to navigate its culture. This means connecting with the organization's leaders and communicating why diversity is part of their organizational imperative. Research by Diversity Best Practices (2005) argues that "an individual in a top diversity role needs to have a good functional understanding of [human resources] and legal, but in addition they need to understand how the business works. If they have some functional expertise in marketing, finance or supply chain, then it can help them to be more effective" (p. 119).

TABLE 9.4
Chief Diversity Officer Competencies Across Sectors

CDO Competency	*Description*	*Characteristics*
Industry and Organizational Acumen	The CDO must have an intimate understanding of his or her organization's core mission and an advanced ability to navigate its culture. Today's CDOs must master the big-picture issues of their organizations and possess the ability to connect key threats, opportunities, competitors, and priorities to the strategic diversity agenda of their organization.	• Ability to understand the organization's core mission and culture • Ability to leverage industry language to discuss key issues • Ability to develop diversity priorities and metrics that connect to the organizational bottom line
Change Management Expertise	The CDO is able to develop a collaborative vision for change and provide integrative leadership that results in tangible results. The ultimate goal is to develop new strategies, structures, processes, reward systems, and initiatives that make diversity a high-level priority, however an organization's diversity goals are defined. But beyond their technical acumen leading change, the best CDOs have the willpower to overcome setbacks and organizational resistance.	• Ability to build a collaborative vision for change • Ability to develop and implement diversity plans and strategies • Ability to manage the change journey as a process of building systems, capacity, and new behavior • Focus on change goals even in the face of resistance • Focus on change that is both incremental and transformative
Relational Abilities and Political Savvy	The CDO must have the ability to articulate a clear vision and persuade others of its value while navigating competing interests, entrenched politics, and resistance to change. The best CDOs are able to work across departmental and other boundaries both internally and externally, shaping the diversity agenda for individuals at all levels.	• Ability to persuade others • Ability to frame diversity issues in ways that multiple audiences can understand • Skill working across boundaries, building new relationships
Cultural Intelligence and Technical Mastery of Diversity Best Practices	The CDO must have an in-depth understanding of the issues and full spectrum of strategic diversity leadership best practices as it relates to recruitment and retention, creating an inclusive organizational environment, creating diversity-themed learning and leadership platforms, and assessing diversity.	• High degree of cultural intelligence • Knowledge of different social identity groups • Knowledge of diversity best-practice strategies • Ability to develop new diversity best practices
An Innovator's DNA	Because the field of strategic diversity leadership is still evolving and change always takes place in a particular organizational context, the CDO must possess the DNA of an innovator. This means that CDOs must have a number of different skills that enable them to question the status quo, observe what is and is not working, build networks that open new possibilities, and experiment with new initiatives.	• Ability to associate across contexts • Ability to question their organization on issues of diversity • Ability to observe and define new ways of doing things • Ability to network and learn from others • Focus on experimenting and trying new ideas to spark change

The more that the CDO understands the core organizational mission, the more effective he or she will be at communicating diversity's relevance. Hence, the CDO at Procter & Gamble should understand the packaged goods industry and the critical role of marketing as a source of competitive advantage. The CDO working for Major League Baseball should understand the professional sports industry and the unique history of this venerable institution in American life. The CDO for a large school district should understand the pressure that teachers face to achieve national standards, as well as the pedagogical issues surrounding educational disparities in test scores and graduation rates. Effective CDOs understand the core culture and history of their organizations, whether dealing with tenure and promotion at colleges and universities, or the critical role of marketing in food service industries like McDonald's and Coca-Cola, for which African Americans and Latinos are an important segment of the consumer population.

Effective CDOs become so by studying their organizations and learning their cultures. As we have emphasized, clearly the CDO in the investments industry must know the history, structures, and policies of his or her bank. Beyond this, however, he or she must also understand the culture, which is to say the collective norms, values, beliefs, and assumptions that provide a frame of reference for individuals within the organization. A key building block for CDOs is to develop an ability to apply the language of the industry in ways that illustrate competency, as well as to be fully invested in the corporate and educational mission of their organizations. As such, CDOs need to be able to outline diversity priorities and metrics in terms of this mission, whether the focus is on teaching, learning, research, services, or products.

Change Management Expertise

Another competency across CDO roles is the ability to provide integrative leadership in accomplishing diversity-themed change. CDOs should work collaboratively to develop a change vision, interfacing with senior leaders in both sectors and with shared governance bodies in higher education. CDOs must be able to develop new strategies, structures, processes, reward systems, and initiatives that make diversity a high-level priority, however an organization's diversity goals are defined. But beyond their technical acumen leading change, the best CDOs have strong wills, which allows them to overcome setbacks and organizational resistance.

Nearly every leader that we interviewed for this project spoke of the need for CDOs to have a sophisticated understanding of change management, strategic planning, and leadership development. Although officers were clear about the significant challenges associated with leading cultural change, they also recognized that this was a fundamental aspect of their roles as CDO. For example, in the higher education arena, cultural change could take the form of helping the student affairs division to recognize the need to create more culturally relevant approaches to student orientation. In the corporate sector, CDOs often need to work with the marketing department to recognize the importance of winning with diverse consumers domestically and globally. According to Billy Dexter (2010):

> As leading companies realized the business relevance of diversity and inclusion, their stance gradually changed. Those who early on saw the demographic writing on the wall understood that their workforce should look like their customer base, not only out of fairness but because they believed that from a brand perspective such policies might improve business results. Eventually some began to see that diversity wasn't simply a numbers game but a matter of bringing diverse ideas and perspectives into the company in such areas as marketing, product development, and the like. Today, the leaders in diversity have taken it several steps further. They value diversity of perspective and know how to put it to work in a business context. (pp. 3–4)

Thus, CDOs in both worlds are engaged in the business of change. It is therefore common for higher education CDOs to talk about developing a new diversity plan for their institutions, complete with recommendations, a vision for change, and role assignments. Specific diversity plans are less common among corporate CDOs, but many reported having a "diversity change framework" that expressed their priorities and values around issues of diversity.

Indeed, in all of our interviews and review of data, having the ability to create change was perhaps the most highly valued skill trait possessed by CDOs. No CDO was hired to maintain the status quo; by definition, CDOs are focused on leading change, building new capacity to advance diversity, and partnering with others to help their organizations become more diverse, inclusive, and strategically engaged on issues of diversity.

This may mean partnering with the human resources to develop a new leadership program to groom the next generation of women to assume a senior level of corporate leadership. Or in terms of higher education, it may mean assisting a senior faculty member with a research grant by helping the faculty member fulfill the National Science Foundation's requirement specifying that funded research efforts lead to broader impact and in some ways engage issues of diversity. Whether incremental or transformative,

CDOs focus their efforts in ways that help to activate change energy within their organization.

Relational Abilities and Political Savvy

CDOs, by definition, are often required to work with people from diverse backgrounds in various functional areas across the organization. For this reason, the role of CDO requires highly developed relational abilities and political savvy. As we noted previously, officers rarely have the power to make sweeping organizational changes on their own. In practical terms, this means that CDOs are often called on to lead in an integrative way, by collaborating, seeding, catalyzing, and nurturing change through relationships with many others. This is true whether the CDO is in higher education or the corporate sector.

The CDO must have the ability to persuade others of diversity's value, while navigating competing interests, entrenched politics, and resistance to change. Because their work spans different boundaries, the best CDOs have strong communication skills and are able to frame their organization's diversity agenda for numerous constituencies, whether delivering a prepared presentation or helping colleagues negotiate the best way to move ahead on a particularly thorny diversity initiative. In higher education this means interacting with students, faculty, staff, alumni, members of the media, elected government officials, corporate partners, and community members. Similarly, corporate CDOs interact with their boards, media, external communities, and organizational leaders. When talking with the best of the CDO ranks, one finds leaders who are confident, verbally gifted, and capable of resonating with small and large groups.

Lastly, CDOs need to prove that if their insights are followed, the organization will reap rewards. To make their case, CDOs need to draw on the best and most recent diversity research. Both academic institutions and corporations can be resistant to change, especially if proposals do not come grounded in compelling evidence. For this reason, a CDO often occupies dual roles, on the one hand the ambassador who negotiates with established political hierarchies, and on the other the advocate who champions diversity as a new means of adding value within the organization. Persuasion is important to both organizational contexts, as is the related ability of being able to synthesize information about diversity, the company's core industry, and social trends. CDOs must also be able to identify the internal and external politics that affect the work of their organizations. Hence, it is important to approach each situation with a clear perception of organizational and political reality and the effects of alternative courses of action. In Chapter 5 of *Strategic Diversity Leadership*, we explore five key diversity leadership models.

Cultural Intelligence and Technical Mastery of Diversity Best Practices

Effective CDOs must have a deep personal commitment to issues of diversity that is complemented by an exceptional level of cultural intelligence that allows them to interact in diverse cultural environments, see the world from multiple perspectives, and build relationships across a number of different social and cultural markers (Ang, Van Dyne, & Koh, 2005; Earley & Ang, 2003). More than any other role, CDOs must engage diversity issues across multiple groups, avoiding the identity politics that can at times pit minorities, women, members of the LGBT community, and others at odds with each other over limited resources. As a part of their core knowledge base, CDOs must have a strong grasp of the core issues confronting these groups and others.

Effective CDOs will understand best-practice techniques for engaging issues of diversity in their respective industries. Generally, this means understanding diversity-themed procurement, building multicultural affinity organizations, infusing diversity into the teaching and learning curriculum, eliminating disparities between diverse groups, creating inclusion initiatives, and building diversity training and leadership development initiatives. In an interview with a corporate consultant with deep insight into higher education and the corporate sector, he noted that:

> Chief diversity officers must have an understanding of the full spectrum of diversity issues defined from a recruitment, retention, inclusion, marketing, and strategic perspective. This work has to live at the forefront of our organizations. This is the reason that the CDO has become so important as one of the top leadership roles in corporate America, because we need that visible, day-to-day leadership at the strategic level helping to set the agenda and mobilize the work with the same level of operational discipline and focus that we do everything else in the business world. And while I have not worked in higher education for years, I would argue that the same is true in that arena as well.

A vice president for diversity and dean of the college at a small liberal arts institution in the Southwest made a similar point:

> The role of chief diversity officer has expanded. If you want to be effective in this role, you have to know something about the recruitment and retention of faculty, issues of identity and the campus climate, and how to talk with faculty about what is going on in the classroom with respect to inclusion and learning. In order to do the diversity piece, and have broad credibility, a strong platform of knowledge is critical.

Although very few spaces exist for leaders to receive training in how to engage in the process of strategic diversity leadership, officers whom we spoke with all talked of being lifelong learners. As such, leaders proactively participated in diversity conferences and institutes, developed independent reading programs, and proactively sought out roles to serve as thought leaders in their chosen fields. They regularly write articles, maintain blogs, and give presentations at meetings around the world. In higher education in particular, this also has translated into writing about their experience as CDOs, producing blogs, refereed articles, and books in the area of strategic diversity leadership.[3] CDOs must be able to guide their institutions in this way, offering counsel to senior leadership on diversity best practices while also providing an informed perspective about diversity issues when they arise.

An Innovator's DNA

In *The Innovator's DNA: Mastering the Five Skills of Disruptive Innovation,* Jeff Dyer, Hal Gregersen, and Clayton Christensen (2011) address the five key characteristics of innovative leaders. For our purposes, these skills include the ability to associate, question, observe, network, and experiment in the interest of accomplishing diversity-themed change. This work has added significantly to our ability to frame the final competency of the most capable CDOs. Again, because their role is focused on change management, CDOs must be innovators. They are never satisfied with the status quo, even during times when it may not be possible to move their organizations in new directions.

The first skill of innovation is an ability to *associate* meaning and draw connections among questions, problems, or ideas from unrelated fields. CDOs must think differently from their peers and seek out new ways of engaging on diversity. Because they are unsatisfied with the status quo, CDOs develop strategies that catalyze profound new possibilities, even if surface results appear superficial. For example, consider the previous chapter's discussion of the importance of publishing a high-profile CDO transition plan. Although the surface goal is to communicate a new CDO's desire to make certain changes on campus, the deeper benefit includes helping others to associate leadership, formality, and strategic focus with the work of the CDO.

An additional skill that CDOs must possess is a persistent ability to *question* common wisdom about issues of diversity. For example, in Chapter 7 we investigated the need to question the common misperception that the lack of minority faculty in a particular field reflects a lack of minority candidates. Or in the case of the corporate sector, CDOs must be willing to question a decision to ignore Latino consumers when developing a targeted multicultural marketing campaign, especially considering their growing economic power as consumers. CDOs must have the courage to question and persuade their colleagues to more proactively pursue their strategic diversity goals.

Because the strategic diversity leadership field is evolving so rapidly, CDOs must *observe* the behaviors of those around them and look for ways to build promising strategies into their efforts. CDOs must be masters of "searching and reapplying" successful ideas in the service of diversity. For example, CDOs are working to develop new diversity-themed training programs that mirror the look, feel, and implementation approach of more traditional leadership categories like project management. By searching out promising practices in other areas, CDOs can leverage the overlay of non-diversity-themed training efforts to enhance a diversity-themed change strategy.

To truly innovate, CDOs must *network* with leaders both within and outside their normal sphere of relationships. Clearly, it is critical for CDOs to be plugged into the national strategic diversity leadership movement. Only by engaging with these and other leaders can CDOs be inspired to bring new approaches and technologies into their organizations. The most innovative CDOs will also network with leaders who do not focus on diversity issues, looking for ways to learn and build new strategies that they can take back to their organizations. For example, by spending time with chief information officers and learning how they create organization-wide alignment around technology goals, CDOs can generate and implement new techniques for enhancing diversity in their organizations. By participating in other networks, CDOs are able to extend their knowledge, test ideas, and gain new perspective about what is possible.

The skills of questioning, observing, and networking are foundational to the last skill of innovators, namely *experimentation.* The capacity to experiment is the most important skill for leading innovation, and in many ways can spark disruptive and productive change. This means developing a hypothesis about how to enhance diversity and developing an organizational initiative that can effectively drive change. Experimentation is the process of demonstrating that a model or an approach is viable, feasible, and capable of solving an issue. Again, experimentation is often what results from the other skills as change leaders must be willing to reexamine their efforts to show that they are successful, cost-effective, and sustainable. Without constantly experimenting and trying new approaches to diversity training, recruitment, leadership development, and retention, CDOs will not effect change.

Piloting new or reframed initiatives is key to accelerating the process of change. This is such a valuable skill for CDOs because many will face resistance and piloting allows CDOs to develop a convincing rationale, or business case, for a new initiative. Moreover, a pilot project allows leaders to make a provisional commitment, testing the waters on a promising effort without the fear of being locked into the effort forever. Experimentation is key to gaining buy-in and overcoming resistance to change because it allows the CDO to prove a concept that he or she believes will ultimately enhance the organization's ability to accomplish its diversity goals.

CDOs must be dexterous, moving gracefully in and out of conversations with leaders in different functional areas who may not view diversity as important. Relational abilities and political aptitude, absent an understanding of the core mission, will produce little in the way of results. Similarly, knowledge of diversity issues without a fundamental ability to innovate and engage in a process of change management is unlikely to truly advance diversity and inclusion efforts organizationally. Today's most competent CDOs have the ability to apply these skills daily and on multiple levels. The challenge for potential diversity leaders is to design a career arc not just centered on diversity, but on a wide range of experiences that provide the leadership with competencies necessary to succeed in an academic or corporate setting increasingly shaped by a diverse, global economy. There is no one set path, which is why many of today's diversity leaders emerge not only from human resources and student affairs, but from a variety of different pathways.

Pathways to the Chief Diversity Officer Role

CDO roles, although requiring many of the same skills as other executive positions, often require a degree of experience that cannot be acquired through a linear leadership trajectory. CDOs come from a variety of backgrounds, including human resources, marketing, and purchasing in the corporate sector, and professional schools, graduate training, human resources, administration, student affairs, and academic disciplines in higher education.

Our review of the CDO literature and the biographies of dozens of officers has informed our elaboration of four major themes that we believe capture the major trajectories, or pathways, into the CDO role. These are the *line leadership trajectory*, the *traditional diversity leadership trajectory*, the *affirmative action and EEO trajectory*, and the *strategic diversity leadership trajectory*. Each of these trajectories has several unique characteristics depending on whether they take place in higher education or the corporate sector; however, for the benefit of this discussion we maintain an integrated focus, describing some of the key characteristics associated with leaders who have navigated each of these pathways into the CDO leadership role. Table 9.5 explores the associated key characteristics of all four trajectories.

Line Leadership Track

The line leadership track is associated with those CDOs who have navigated through the core-business or mission function of their organization, as well as the leadership ranks. These individuals often have proven backgrounds, whether as a successful investment banker at a financial services company, a successful attorney at a law firm, a tenured faculty member, or an effective college or university administrator.

Leaders on this trajectory possess a strong understanding of the core mission of the organization and have a strong sense of the institution's history and culture, which facilitates their efforts to enhance diversity. It is common for the officer to have been with the organization for a long time, leading diversity initiatives on behalf of senior leadership, chairing committees, and serving as a vocal citizen in support of diversity. However, like faculty members who focus primarily on diversity research, these individuals may *not* have the greatest personal competency in the field of strategic diversity leadership. They may have personal experience in these areas resulting from their personal identity characteristics and service to the organization, but they are not necessarily experts in all areas of diversity leadership. As a result, the challenge for these officers is to get up to speed on the promising practices in the field of strategic diversity leadership and become acclimated to the political dynamics of diversity and inclusion leadership.

Traditional Diversity Leadership Track

The second CDO track that we have uncovered is the traditional trajectory. We refer to it as the *traditional diversity leadership trajectory* because student affairs, human resources, and procurement are the traditional ways that higher education and the corporate sector have defined diversity work. The student affairs trajectory is associated with higher education CDOs, whereas the human resources and procurement trajectories more closely align with the corporate sector. It is possible for someone to rise to an executive-level

TABLE 9.5
Career Trajectories in the CDO Leadership Role

Trajectory	*Description*	*Key Characteristics*
Line Leadership Trajectory	The line leadership trajectory is associated with CDOs who have navigated through the core-business or mission function of their organization. It is not uncommon for these individuals to lead in a hybrid CDO role, providing leadership to a number of general administrative or business functional areas as well.	• Success in a nondiversity-themed leadership role of the organization • Success as a faculty member with a diversity-themed research agenda • A long history of championing diversity issues within the organization • Limited experience with diversity best practices and the challenge of leading in a dedicated diversity leadership role • Limited experience leading change in an area that may not be completely understood or valued by the organization
Traditional Diversity Leadership Trajectory	The traditional diversity leadership trajectory refers to leaders coming out of student affairs, human resources, and procurement, the traditional areas that have often housed much of the diversity work outside of affirmative action and equal opportunity roles.	• Diversity-themed leadership role in either student affairs, human resources, or procurement • Experienced leaders on diversity issues defined in terms of student or human resources • Limited experience with academic or core-business functions of the organization • Limited experience with emerging areas of strategic diversity leadership
Affirmative Action and Equal Employment Opportunity Trajectory	The affirmative action and equal employment opportunity track is occupied by individuals who are classically trained in issues of workforce compliance, employment law, equal opportunity legislation, disability laws, gender equity, and other related areas.	• Extensive experience on classic affirmative action and equal employment opportunity issues • Limited experience with academic or core-business functions of the organization • Limited experience with emerging areas of strategic diversity leadership • May not possess the necessary credentials required of contemporary executive-level chief diversity officers
Strategic Diversity Leadership Trajectory	Whereas leaders on other trajectories may have to learn what the CDO role means in all of its complexity, these individuals have been intentionally grooming themselves for leadership as a CDO. Hence, their previous educational experience and professional development training have focused on knowing and understanding every dimension of strategic diversity leadership work.	• Intentional focus on becoming a CDO and pursuing a career as a strategic diversity leader • High-level experience with the complete range of diversity issues, having been groomed to serve as a CDO • A well-developed skill set and credentials that allow them to lead in a number of different areas, but have chosen to remain in diversity work as a preferred area of practice • May have received special training and professional development around diversity and inclusion management, as either part of their graduate degree program or other professional development experiences • Criticized at times for viewing diversity leadership as a career trajectory, rather than as a temporary leadership role that should exist for a limited time

CDO in higher education through the human resources department, but it is uncommon. The higher education human resources function is generally not involved in student issues, matters of academic affairs, or faculty hiring decisions.

Leaders on this trajectory are often very experienced with issues of diversity, having been involved in diversity-related roles within human resources, procurement, or student affairs. For example, one CDO we interviewed had served in a division of student life as the assistant vice president of multicultural student affairs. Another CDO on the corporate side had served as the diversity recruitment specialist within human resources at a packaged goods company. In each of these instances, the CDO's role was anchored in a core functional area of his or her organization, but the majority of the duties were tied to advancing the diversity mission of that particular area of responsibility. These individuals are very experienced with issues of diversity, but may not have the general organizational leadership experience that is necessary to serve as an effective CDO. These leaders may have opportunity areas when it comes to moving between functional areas and adding value in emerging areas of diversity responsibility, like multicultural marketing in the corporate sector, and teaching, research, and scholarship in higher education.

Affirmative Action and Equal Employment Opportunity Track

The affirmative action and EEO track is occupied by individuals who are classically trained in issues of workforce compliance, employment law, equal opportunity legislation, disability laws, gender equity, and other related areas. It is not uncommon for these leaders to have a legal background, particularly if they are in higher education and serve as the affirmative action officer for their institution.

As a general rule, leaders on this trajectory are very experienced with legal and compliance issues, having been involved with these issues for many years. The challenge for these officers is to illustrate a strong understanding of the core organizational mission and to embrace not only classic issues of diversity, equity, and inclusion, but newer topics such as infusing diversity into the curriculum, and expanding STEM success for students, and other academic areas. There is no reason that these officers cannot be incredibly effective on a wide range of diversity fronts; the challenge for them is to gain an understanding of the core-business function, as well as the key areas of diversity leadership, including complex historical and cultural dynamics that affect the workplace environment and campus community.

Strategic Diversity Leadership Track

The strategic diversity leadership trajectory is fairly new and is evolving along a track that parallels the emergence of the field of strategic diversity leadership. Individuals on this trajectory have often worked as a senior diversity leader in the office or division of the CDO at an established organization. Whereas leaders on other trajectories are often self-taught when it comes to the complexity of the CDO role, these individuals have been consciously groomed for diversity leadership. Hence, their previous educational and professional development training has focused on understanding every dimension of strategic diversity leadership, whether dealing with recruitment and talent development, multicultural marketing, supplier diversity, corporate responsibility, training, or the development of an inclusive organizational culture. On the higher education side, these individuals have intentionally developed their background in areas of access and equity, teaching and learning, climate and inclusion, and diversity-themed research and scholarship.

These leaders view themselves as twenty-first-century diversity professionals, although many may have spent time on one or more of the other tracks as they worked toward their long-term goal of becoming a CDO. These officers have been professionally trained to focus on multiple areas of strategic diversity leadership, having learned through various training and professional development experiences how to engage issues of organizational diversity. They may also enjoy an eclectic background that may include prior diversity leadership roles, line leadership roles, faculty appointments, and other unique experiences. For example, we encountered a CDO with a doctorate in organizational behavior and management who focused her coursework on managing diversity and inclusion, and conducted original research on workplace culture and climate. It is also common for these individuals to have received further professional development training through their participation in several national diversity conferences like those hosted by the Conference Board, the National Association of Diversity Officers in Higher Education, and others.

This section has highlighted the line leadership, traditional diversity leadership, affirmative action and EEO, and strategic diversity leadership track. Inevitably, some individuals will navigate a pathway to the CDO role that does not easily fit into this typography at all. These individuals are unique in their path to the CDO role and may have a package of experiences and leadership skills drawn from a range of different backgrounds, including public service and consulting.

Personal and Educational Characteristics

Our research into the demographic and educational characteristics of CDOs uncovered several important differences between higher education and corporate leaders (Figure 9.2). In both sectors, African American CDOs predominated; they constituted 74 percent of higher education CDOs and 37 percent corporate CDOs, making them the most clearly identifiable racial group of CDOs across both sectors.

In higher education, this trend is no doubt related to the early involvement of African Americans as leaders in helping colleges and universities to desegregate and accommodate the presence of the first large groups of African American students. As a result of federal laws, state-supported institutions in particular began working to increase the numbers of Black students, faculty, and staff. One approach was to create the administrative support positions dedicated to these incoming students and faculty. No doubt, these early roots inevitably helped shape the leadership roles that would ultimately emerge over the years, even as the definition of diversity has continued to expand and evolve.

Given the rapid population growth of Latinos, it comes as a surprise that our survey found so few members of this group serving as CDOs in either higher education (10 percent) or the corporate sector (4 percent). We expect that these numbers will increase as the demographic, educational, and economic influence of Latinos continues to grow. Asian American CDOs were also few in number in both the higher education and corporate sectors, at 3 and 2 percent, respectively. Although the lion's share of CDOs are members of minority groups, our study found that a substantial percentage of corporate officers (19 percent) and academic officers (13 percent) were White. For reasons that are beyond the scope of this book, a large number of corporate CDOs (39 percent) did not report their identity in the survey by Diversity Best Practices (2005).

Gender Differences

As Figure 9.3 demonstrates, the majority of CDOs in both the higher education (58 percent) and the corporate sector (65 percent) were women. Given the dearth of women in senior leadership roles across both academic and corporate sectors, this trend is encouraging.

That women have embraced the CDO role across sectors should come as little surprise, because as members of a historically disadvantaged group, they bring a nuanced perspective to diversity issues. At the same time, as our

FIGURE 9.2
Race and Ethnicity of Chief Diversity Officers in Higher Education and the Corporate Sector

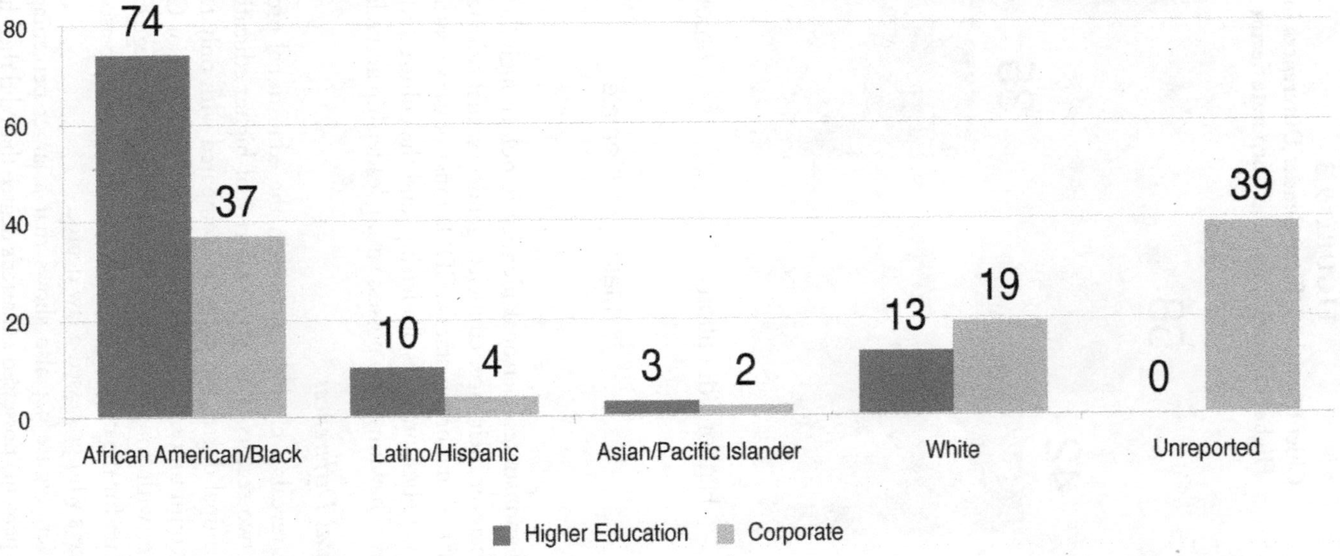

FIGURE 9.3
Chief Diversity Officer Gender Differences in Higher Education and the Corporate Sector

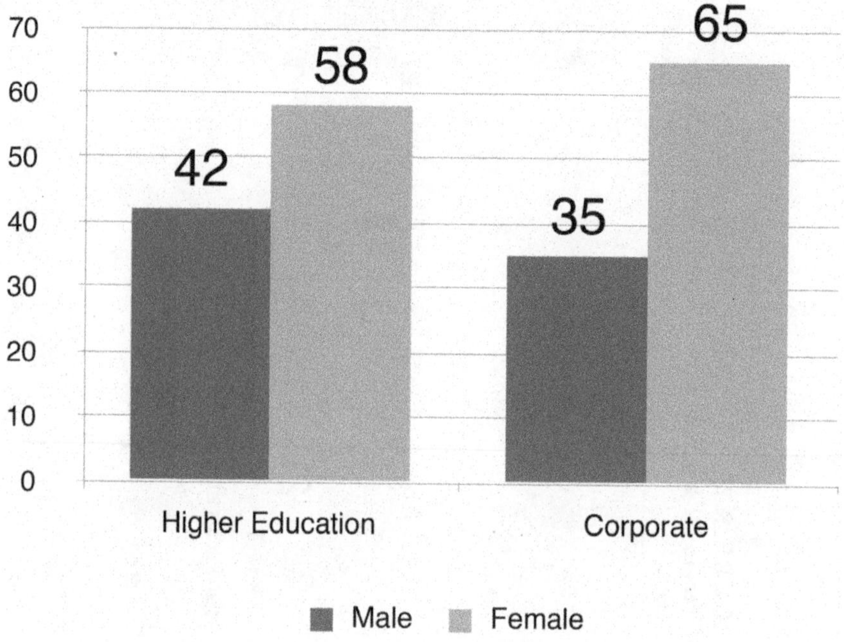

research demonstrates, personal identity is not enough to be a successful CDO. Whatever their race, ethnicity, gender, sexual orientation, disability, veteran, or national origin status, CDOs must possess a strong understanding of diversity best practices, leadership, and the culture and history of their institutions. They must also possess strong leadership and relational abilities.

Educational Differences

Figure 9.4 reveals a clear distinction in the educational profiles of officers across the two sectors. The large majority of higher education CDOs possessed a terminal degree (76 percent), compared with only 12 percent in the corporate community. In higher education, 67 percent of CDOs possessed a doctorate, with roughly 9 percent holding a law degree. Based on the available data for the corporate sector, we were unable to ascertain the number of officers who possessed a law degree.

However, Figure 9.4 also shows that a larger percentage of corporate CDOs (48 percent) possessed a master's degree than did their higher education

FIGURE 9.4
Educational Backgrounds of Chief Diversity Officers in Higher Education and the Corporate Sector

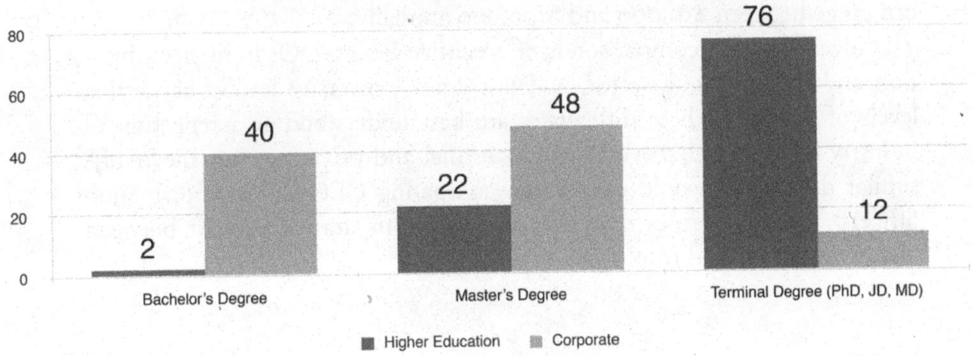

counterparts (22 percent), no doubt reflecting the importance of an MBA as a gateway to opportunity in the corporate sector. Fully 40 percent of corporate CDOs possessed only a bachelor's degree, compared with only 2 percent of higher education CDOs. Our research indicates that a bachelor's degree is insufficient for anyone hoping to emerge as a CDO in the academy.

Compensation Packages

Not surprisingly, corporate CDOs are compensated at a much greater level than higher education CDOs (Table 9.6). Although the comparison data are not perfectly matched between the two categories of diversity leaders, 69 percent of corporate CDOs made more than $200,000, whereas only 12

TABLE 9.6
Comparison of Personal Compensation of Higher Education and Corporate Sector CDOs

	Higher Education	*Corporate*
Personal Compensation	Over \$200,000: 12 percent \$100,000–\$200,000: 57 percent \$50,000–\$100,000: 30 percent Under \$50,000: 2 percent	Over \$300,000 and bonus of more than \$100,000: 23 percent \$200,000–\$300,000, with a bonus in the \$75,000 range: 46 percent \$100,000–\$200,000 with a bonus in the \$50,000 range: 30 percent

percent of higher education CDOs were compensated at this level. The difference in compensation is even more pronounced when we take into account the performance bonuses that corporate CDOs often receive, which can range between $50,000 and $100,000 annually.

Given that this comparison is of executive-level CDOs in higher education and the corporate sector, and not among diversity leaders at varying levels of seniority, these differences are best understood as a reflection of industry differences between the educational and private sector. Inevitably, similar differences would exist when comparing CEOs, chief information officers, and other roles that have a direct comparative context between higher education and the corporate sector.

Summary

Working across multiple studies, reports, and databases, we used this chapter as a means to introduce a quantitative and qualitative comparison of CDO roles in higher education and the corporate sector. If this preliminary analysis teaches us anything, it is that in both sectors the modern CDO is more strategic and mission focused than his or her earlier precursors. The role of the CDO in America is evolving, and at a rapid pace.

As diversity and inclusion efforts have become more than a matter of workforce compliance (in the corporate sector) or enrolling diverse students (in the higher education sector), the status of the diversity practitioner has risen to the "CEO" or "C Suite" level in many organizations. In higher education, early positions focused narrowly on recruiting and retaining diverse students, enforcing affirmative action policies, and creating policies and programs to enhance multiculturalism. Today's CDO, by contrast, is focused not only on these lofty goals, but on making diversity a strategic priority both internally and externally, whether to help drive a company's bottom line, or to tap into the rich educational benefits of a diverse classroom. Not all of these efforts can be quantified easily. In the corporate sector, for example, CDOs are still in the beginning stages of developing tools that measure the financial effects of diversity efforts. In academia, CDOs can no longer rely on student graduation rates or faculty promotion rates as the only adequate measures of their progress. With an emerging body of research exploring the broader educational and social benefits of a diverse campus community, CDOs in higher education have a broad new set of tools to explain and promote the value of diversity. It is only fitting that, as diversity becomes an increasingly valuable "commodity" in the global marketplace, the status and responsibilities of CDOs will continue to grow.

As this chapter also illustrated, there are important differences between the higher education and corporate CDO role. Although corporate CDOs focus on meeting the diversity needs of their companies' senior leaders and employees, the higher education CDO must meet the diversity needs of a broader mix of constituencies. The stakeholders in higher education include administrators, faculty, staff, students, alumni, donors, potential students, and even the parents of potential students. The corporate CDO works to bridge the gap between diversity challenges and opportunities and business management needs and opportunities to establish a competitive advantage. The higher education CDO must not only bridge that gap but also the gap of understanding that sometimes exists over why diversity matters within the broader campus constituency.

The strategic diversity leadership movement is a second-wave movement that builds on and extends the affirmative action and equal opportunity efforts of the 1960s and 1970s. It embodies a complicated relationship to its predecessor, by turns extending and discontinuing aspects of the earlier movement. For example, the strategic diversity leadership movement has largely replaced the moral imperatives of social justice and equity as the drivers for racial integration. In their place is a more robust assertion arguing that diversity serves as an educational and business catalyst for driving organizational success. Unquestionably, the social justice rationale continues to have currency in some communities, as it should. However, thanks in part to the maturation of the strategic diversity leadership movement, there is a new layer of understanding recognizing that diversity offers positive benefits for both academic institutions and the corporate sector. This approach can frustrate individuals who have a long and justifiable commitment to civil rights and helping vulnerable communities. In some ways, it is a central role of the CDO to thread the needle between these overlapping and in some ways competing rationales for why diversity matters. By mediating between these tendencies, and finding common ground between the social justice and diversity opportunity camps, CDOs can promote the best of both approaches.

Similarly, CDOs in both the corporate and academic sectors have much to gain from each other. Just as corporate CDOs have gained from an appreciation of the need to bring together diverse and disparate constituencies to find common ground—a matter of standard practice for higher education CDOs—college and university CDOs are gaining a new appreciation of marketing and customer service—a matter of standard practice for corporate CDOs. As our movement progresses, it would be in the best interests of both higher education and corporate CDOs to find more frequent and structured opportunities to meet and share ideas. Academia has a reputation of being slow to change, and could learn from the fast-paced world of business, where companies must adapt quickly if they are to remain competitive. On the other hand, businesses have a less explicit focus on the public welfare and are often faulted for putting private profits over the common good. Meanwhile, in both arenas, technological change continues to accelerate at the speed of light. Making best use of new online social media tools, as well as the most advanced marketing and financial analysis software, can help both sectors gain a better understanding of how to make their respective sectors, and American society generally, more welcoming, inclusive, and dynamic.

Notes

1. This CDO role is a joint appointment across the Democratic National Committee, the Democratic Congressional Campaign Committee, and the Democratic National Convention Committee. To learn more, visit www.politico.com/news/stories/1011/66169.html#ixzz1dW1osuoZ.

2. The Taking the Pulse: Global Diversity survey was conducted by i4cp, in conjunction with HR.com, in August 2008. The total number of respondents was 176. Approximately 51 percent of responding organizations reported an employee base of greater than 10,000. This information was downloaded from www.i4cp.com/news/2008/09/24/diversity-programs-now-essential-in-corporations. Also see www.workforcediversitynetwork.com/res_articles_4lessons.aspx.

3. See, for example, Arnold and Kowalski-Braun (2011).

REFERENCES

Abbott, A. (1988). *The system of professions: An essay on the division of expert labor.* Chicago: University of Chicago Press.

Alfred, R. (2006). *Managing the big picture in colleges and universities: From tactics to strategy.* Washington, DC: American Council on Education.

Alger, J. (2009). *Diversity in the age of Obama: New directions or status quo? (Employment context).* Paper presented at the 49th Annual Conference of the National Association of College and University Attorneys, Toronto, Ontario, Canada.

American Association for the Advancement of Science. (2010). *Handbook on diversity and the law: Navigating a complex landscape to foster greater faculty and student diversity.* Washington, DC: Author.

American Association of State Colleges and Universities and the National Association of State Universities and Land-Grant Colleges Task Force on Diversity. (2005). *Now is the time: Meeting the challenge for a diverse academy.* Washington, DC: Author.

American Federation of Teachers Higher Education (2010). *Promoting racial and ethnic diversity in the faculty: What higher education unions can do.* Washington, DC: American Federation of Teachers.

Ang, S., Van Dyne, L., & Koh, C. S. K. (2005). Personality correlates of the four-factor model of cultural intelligence. *Group and Organization Management, 31*(1), 100–123.

Antonio, L. (2004). When does race matter in college friendships? Exploring men's diverse and homogeneous friendship groups. *The Review of Higher Education, 27*(4), 553–575.

Arnold, J., & Kowalski-Braun, M. (2011). The journey to an inaugural chief diversity officer: Preparation, implementation and beyond. *Innovative Higher Education, 37*(1), 27–37.

Ashkenas, R., Ulrich, D., Jick, T., & Kerr, S. (2002). *The boundaryless organization: Breaking the chains of organizational structure.* San Francisco: Jossey-Bass.

Athens News Staff. (2007, April 12). OU prez announces plan to consolidate diversity programs. *The Athens News.* Retrieved from http://www.athensnews.com/ohio/article-14226-ou-prez-announces-plan-to-consolidate-diversity-programs.html.

Bartlett, C. A., & Ghoshal, S. (1990). Matrix management: Not a structure, a frame of mind. *Harvard Business Review, 68*(4), 138–145.

Bauman, G. L., Bustillos, L. T., Bensimon, E. M., Brown, M. C., II, & Bartee, R. D. (2005). *Achieving equitable educational outcomes with all students: The institution's roles and responsibilities*. Washington, DC: Association of American Colleges and Universities. Retrieved from http://www.aacu.org/compass/publications.cfm

Bensimon, E., Hao, L., & Bustillos, L. (2003, October). *Measuring the state of equity in public higher education*. Paper presented at the Harvard Civil Rights and UC Conference on Expanding Opportunity in Higher Education: California and the Nation, Sacramento, CA.

Bensimon, E. M. (2004). The diversity scorecard: A learning approach to institutional change. *Change, 36*(1), 45–52.

Bensimon, E., & Malcom, L. (2012). *Confronting equity issues on campus: Implementing the equity scorecard in theory and practice*. Sterling, VA: Stylus.

Bilimoria, D., & Buch, K. K. (2010). The search is on: Engendering faculty diversity through more effective search and recruitment. *Change, 42*(4), 27–32.

Birnbaum, R. (1988). *How colleges work: The cybernetics of academic organization and leadership*. San Francisco: Jossey-Bass.

Bolman, L., & Deal, T. (2003). *Reframing change: Training, realigning, negotiating, grieving, and moving on*. San Francisco: Jossey-Bass.

Bridges, B., Eckel, P., Cordova, D., & White, B. (2008). *Broadening the leadership spectrum: Advancing diversity in the American college presidency*. Washington, DC: American Council on Education.

Brown v. Board of Education, 347 U.S. 483 (1954).

Brown-Glaude, W. (2009). *Doing diversity in higher education: Faculty leaders share challenges and strategies*. New Brunswick, NJ: Rutgers University Press.

Bowen, W., & Bok, D. (1998). *Shape of the river: Long-term consequences of considering race in college and university admissions*. Princeton, NJ: Princeton University Press.

Chaffee, E. (1985). Three modes of strategy. *Academy of Management Review, 10*, 89–98.

Chandler, A. (1962). *Strategy and structure: Chapters in the history of American industrial enterprise*. Cambridge, MA: The MIT Press.

Clayton-Pedersen, A., O'Neill, N., & Musil, C. M. (2009). *Making excellence inclusive: A framework for embedding diversity and inclusion into colleges' and universities' academic excellence mission*. Retrieved from http://www.aacu.org/inclusive_excellence/documents/MEIPaperUpdate8.09Revised8.13.09.pdf

Clayton-Pedersen, A. R., Parker, S., Smith, D. G., Moreno, J. F., & Teraguchi, D. H. (2006). *Making a real difference with diversity: A guide to institutional change*. Washington, DC: AAC&U.

Coleman, A. L., & Palmer, S. R. (2004). *Diversity in higher education: A strategic planning and policy model regarding federal law in admissions, financial aid and outreach* (2nd ed.). New York: The College Board.

Collins, J. (2001). *Good to great: Why some companies make the leap and others don't.* New York: HarperCollins.

Collins, J. (2005). *Good to great and the social sectors: A monograph to accompany good to great.* San Francisco: Jim Collins.

Cox, T. (1991). The multicultural organization. *Executive, 5*(2), 34–47.

Cox, T. (2001). *Creating the multicultural organization: A strategy for capturing the power of diversity.* San Francisco: Jossey-Bass.

Davenport, T., Leibold, M., & Voelpel, S. (2006). *Strategic management in the innovation economy: Strategic approaches and tools for dynamic innovation capabilities.* Hoboken, NJ: Wiley.

Dexter, B. (2010). *The chief diversity officer today: Diversity gets down to business.* Chicago: Heidrick & Struggles.

DiMaggio, P., & Powell, W. (1983). The iron cage revisited: Institutional isomorphism and collective rationality in organizational fields. *American Sociological Review, 48,* 147–160.

Diversity Best Practices. (2005). *The chief diversity officer report.* Washington, DC: Author.

Dovidio, J. F., Glick, P., & Rudman, L. A. (2005). Reflecting on the nature of prejudice: Fifty years after Allport. In J. F. Dovidio, P. Glick, & L. A. Rudman (Eds.), *On the nature of prejudice: 50 years after Allport* (pp. 1–15). Malden, MA: Blackwell.

Dyer, J., Gregersen, H., & Christensen, C. (2011). *The innovators DNA: Mastering the five skills of disruptive innovators.* Boston: Harvard Business Review Press.

Earley, P. C., & Ang, S. (2003). *Cultural intelligence: An analysis of individual interactions across cultures.* Palo Alto, CA: Stanford University Press.

Ellström, P. E. (1983). Four faces of educational organizations. *Higher Education Journal, 12*(2), 231–241.

Farmer v. University of Nevada, 930 P.2d 730 (Nev. S. Ct. 1997), cert. denied, 523 U.S. 1004 (1998).

Fisher v. University of Texas, 631 F.3d. (2012)

Fleming, J. (1984). *Blacks in college.* San Francisco: Jossey-Bass.

Freudenberger, W., Howard, J., Jauregui, E., & Sturm, S. (2009). Linking mobilization to institutional power: The faculty-led diversity initiative at Columbia University. In W. Brown-Glaude (Ed.), *Doing diversity in higher education: Faculty leaders share challenges and strategies* (pp. 249–276). New Brunswick, NJ: Rutgers University Press.

Galbraith, J. (2002). *Designing organizations: An executive guide to strategy, structure, and process.* San Francisco: Jossey-Bass.

Galbraith, J., Downey, D., & Kates, A. (2002). *Designing dynamic organizations.* New York: AMACOM.

Gioia, G., & Chittipeddi, K. (1991). Sensemaking and sensegiving in strategic change initiation, *Strategic Management Journal, 12*(6), 443–448.

Goleman, D. (2006). *Social intelligence: The new science of human relationships.* New York: Bantam Dell.

Gratz v. Bollinger, 539 U.S. 244 (2003).

Greenwald, H. P. (2008). *Organizations: Management without control.* San Francisco: Sage.

Grutter v. Bollinger, 539 U.S. 306 (2003).

Gurin, P., Dey, E., Hurtado, S., & Gurin, G. (2002). Diversity and higher education: Theory and impact on educational outcomes. *Harvard Educational Review, 72*(3), 330–366.

Gurin, P., & Epps, E. (1975). *Black consciousness, identity, and achievement.* New York: John Wiley & Sons.

Hale, F. (2004). *What makes racial diversity work in higher education.* Sterling, VA: Stylus.

Hargrove, R. (2011). *Your first 100 days in a new executive job: Powerful first steps on the path to greatness.* Boston: Masterful Coaching Press.

Harper, S. R., Patton, L. D., & Wooden, O. S. (2009). Access and equity for African American students in higher education: A critical race historical analysis of policy efforts. *The Journal of Higher Education, 80*(4), 389–414.

Hollander, E. P. (2006). Influence processes in leadership-followership: Inclusion and the idiosyncrasy credit model. In D. A. Hantula (Ed.), *Advances in social and organizational psychology: A tribute to Ralph Rosnow* (pp. 293–312). Mahwah, NJ: Lawrence Erlbaum Associates.

Horn, C. L., & Flores, S. M. (2003). *Percent plans in college admissions: A comparative analyses of three states' experiences.* Cambridge, MA: Harvard Civil Rights Project.

Humphreys, D. (1997). *General education and American commitments: A national report on diversity courses and requirements.* Washington, DC: Association of American Colleges and Universities.

Humphreys, D. (2000). National survey finds diversity requirements common around the country. *Diversity Digest.* Washington, DC: Association of American Colleges and Universities. Retrieved from www.diversityweb.org/digest/Foo/survey.html

Hurtado, S., & Carter, D. (1997). Effects of college transition and perceptions of the campus racial climate on Latino students: Sense of belonging. *Sociology of Education, 70*(4), 324–345.

Hurtado, S., & Dey, E. (1997). Achieving the goals of multiculturalism and diversity. In M. W. Peterson, D. D. Dill, & L. A. Mets (Eds.), *Planning and management for a changing environment: A handbook on redesigning postsecondary institutions.* San Francisco: Jossey-Bass.

Hurtado, S., Milem, J., Clayton-Pedersen, A., & Allen, W. (1998). Enhancing campus climates for racial/ethnic diversity: Educational policy and practice. *The Review of Higher Education, 21*(3), 279–302.

Jackson, J. F. L. (2006, February). Hiring practices of African-American males in academic leadership positions at American colleges and universities: An employment trends and disparate impact analysis. *Teachers College Record, 108*(2), 316–338.

Jackson, J. F. L., & O'Callaghan, E. M. (2009). *Ethnic and racial administrative diversity: Understanding work life realities and experiences in higher education.* San Francisco: Jossey-Bass.

Jasper, M. (2006). *Professional development, reflection and decision-making.* Oxford, UK: Blackwell.

June, A. (2010, February 28). A drive to diversify the faculty yields results in Rochester: Innovative recruiting has helped the Rochester Institute of Technology hire more minority professors. *The Chronicle of Higher Education,* Faculty News Section. Retrieved from http://chronicle.com/article/A-Drive-to-Diversify-the/64384/

Kaplan, R. S., & Norton, D. (1992). The balanced scorecard—Measures that drive performance. *Harvard Business Review, 70*(1), 71–79.

Kaplan, W. A. & Lee, A. (2007). *The law of higher education.* San Francisco: Jossey-Bass.

Kates, A., & Galbraith, J. (2007). *Designing your organization: Using the STAR model to solve 5 critical design challenges.* San Francisco: Jossey-Bass.

Kezar, A. (2009). *Rethinking leadership in complex, multicultural, and global environments: New concepts and models for higher education.* Sterling, VA: Stylus.

Kezar, A., & Eckel, P. (2005). *Leadership strategies for advancing campus diversity: Advice from experienced presidents.* Washington, DC: American Council on Education.

Kezar, A., & Eckel, P. (2008). Advancing diversity agendas on campus: Examining transactional and transformational presidential leadership styles. *International Journal of Leadership in Education, 4*(11), 379–405.

Knapp, L. G., Kelly-Reid, J. E., & Ginder, S. A. (2012). *Postsecondary institutions and price of attendance in 2011–12, degrees and other awards conferred: 2010–11, and 12-month enrollment: 2010–11* (NCES 2012289 REV). Washington, DC: National Center for Education Statistics. Retrieved from http://nces.ed.gov/pubsearch/pubsinfo.asp?pubid=2012289rev

Knowles, M. F., & Harleston, B. W. (1997). *Achieving diversity in the professoriate: Challenges and opportunities.* Washington, DC: American Council on Education.

Kuh, G. D., Cruce, T. M., Shoup, R., Kinzie, J., & Gonyea, R. M. (2008). Unmasking the effects of student engagement on first-year college grades and persistence. *The Journal of Higher Education, 79*(5), 540–563.

Laird, T., Engberg, M., & Hurtado, S. (2005). Modeling accentuation effects: Enrolling in a diversity course and the importance of social action engagement. *The Journal of Higher Education, 76*(4), 448–476.

Lapchick, R., Benoit, D., & Morris, L. (2010). Hiring report card for NCAA FBS and FCS football head coaching positions. In *Protecting their turf: The Black coaches and administrators (BCA).* Orlando, FL: The Institute for Diversity and Ethics in Sport (TIDES). Retrieved from http://bcasports.cstv.com/about/bca-about.html#

Larson, M. S. (1977). *The rise of professionalism: A sociological analysis.* Berkeley: University of California Press.

Lawrence, P., & Lorsch, J. (1967). Differentiation and integration in complex organizations. *Administrative Science Quarterly, 12*(1), 1–30.

Leon, R. (2010). *Strategies for institutional transformation: A multi-case study of the chief diversity officer.* (Doctoral dissertation). Available from ProQuest Dissertations and Theses database. (UMI no. 3424043)

Loden, M. (1996). *Implementing diversity.* Chicago: Irwin Professional.

Maltbia, T., & Power, A. (2009). *A leader's guide to leveraging diversity: Strategic learning capabilities for breakthrough performance.* Jordan Hill, Oxford, UK: Butterworth-Heinemann Business.

Martin, J., Samels, J., & Associates. (1997). *First among equals: The role of the chief academic officer.* Baltimore: The Johns Hopkins University Press.

Matlock, J., Wade-Golden, K., & Gurin, G. (2002). *The Michigan student study: Students' expectations of and experiences with racial/ethnic diversity.* Ann Arbor: University of Michigan Office of Academic Multicultural Initiatives. Retrieved from www.oami.umich.edu/mss/downloads/synopsis0103.pdf

Matlock, J., Wade-Golden, K., & Gurin, G. (2010). The Michigan student study guidebook. *Ann Arbor: University of Michigan Office of Academic Multicultural Initiatives.*

Metzler, C. (2008). *Defining key emerging competencies of the chief diversity officer (CDO): Historical, analytical, and situational perspectives of a promising leadership role and its organizational significance.* Fairfax, VA: Stylus.

Meyer, J., & Rowan, B. (1977). Institutional organizations: Formal structure as myth and ceremony. *American Journal of Sociology, 83*(2), 340–363.

Michaelson, M., Meers, E., & Drier, A. (2006). *Race-conscious financial aid and other diversity-enhancing programs: Legal developments for colleges and universities.* Washington, DC: American Council on Education.

Milem, J., Chang, M., & Antonio, A. (2005). *Making diversity work on campus: A research-based perspective.* Washington, DC: Association of American Colleges and Universities.

Mintzberg, H. (1979). *The structure of organizations.* Englewood Cliffs, NJ: Prentice-Hall.

Modena, I. (2008). *Contingency in corporate communications: Risk perception in organisational change.* Retrieved from www.kent.ac.uk/scar/events/beijingpapers/Modenappr.pdf

Moody, J. (2004). *Faculty diversity: Problems and solutions.* New York: Routledge Press.

Moreno, J. F., Smith, D. G., Clayton-Pedersen, A. R., Parker, S., & Teraguchi, D. H. (2006). *The revolving door for underrepresented minority faculty in higher education: An analysis from the campus diversity initiative.* San Francisco: The James Irvine Foundation.

Musil, C., Garcia, M., Moses, Y., & Smith, D. (1995). *Diversity in higher education: A work in progress.* Washington, DC: Association of American Colleges and Universities.

Nagda, B. A., & Gurin, P. (2007). Intergroup dialogue: A critical-dialogic approach to learning about difference, inequality and social justice. *New Directions for Teaching and Learning, 111,* 35–45.

Nagda, B., Gurin, P., Sorensen, N., & Zúñiga, X. (2009). Evaluating intergroup dialogue: Engaging diversity for personal and social responsibility. *Diversity & Democracy, 12*(1), 4–6.

Oakes, K. (2008). *Taking the pulse: Diversity & inclusion.* Seattle: Institute for Corporate Productivity.

Ogbar, J. (2005). *Black power: Radical politics and African American identity.* Baltimore: The Johns Hopkins University Press.

Olson, C. L., Evans, R., & Shoenberg, R. F. (2007). *At home in the world: Bridging the gap between internationalization and multicultural education.* Washington, DC: American Council on Education.

Olson, G. A. (2007). Don't just search, recruit. *The Chronicle of Higher Education.* Retrieved from http://chronicle.com/article/Dont-Just-Search-Recruit/46546/

Paige, S. (2007). *The difference: How the power of diversity creates better groups, firms, schools, and societies.* Princeton, NJ: Princeton University Press.

Patton, L. (Ed.). (2010). *Culture centers in higher education perspectives on identity, theory, and practice.* Fairfax, VA: Stylus.

Peterson, M. W., Blackburn, R., Gamson, C., Arce, R., Davenport, W., & Mingle, J. (1978). *Black students on White campuses: The impacts of increased Black enrollments.* Ann Arbor, MI: Institute for Social Research.

Petit v. City of Chicago, 352 F.3d 1111, 1115 (7th Cir. 2003).

Pfeffer, J. (1992). *Managing with power: Politics and influence in organizations.* Boston: Harvard Business School Press.

Pittard, L. (2011). *Select higher education chief diversity officers: Roles, realities, and reflections* (Doctoral dissertation). Retrieved from ProQuest Dissertations and Theses database. (UMI no. 3446403).

Prahalad, C. K., & Hamel, G. (1994). Strategy as a field of study: Why search for a new paradigm? *Strategic Management Journal, 15,* 5–16.

Rasiel, E. (1999). *The McKinsey way.* New York: McGraw-Hill.

Regents of the University of California v. Bakke, 438 U.S. 312, 98 S. Ct. 2760 (1978).

Roberts, J. (2004). *Alliances, coalitions, and partnerships: Building collaborative organizations.* Gabriola Island, BC: New Society.

Rowley, D. J., & Sherman, H. (2001). *From strategy to change: Implementing the plan in higher education.* San Francisco: Jossey-Bass.

Schein, E. H. (1985). *Organizational culture and leadership: A dynamic view.* San Francisco: Jossey-Bass.

Schreiber, A., & Lenson, B. (2001). *Multicultural marketing: Selling to the new America*. Lincolnwood, IL: NTC Business Books.

Sellers, R. M., Smith, M., Shelton, J. N., Rowley, S., & Chavous, T. M. (1998). The multidimensional model of racial identity: A reconceptualization of African American racial identity. *Personality and Social Psychology Review, 2*(1), 18–39.

Simons, R. (2005). *Levers of organization design: How managers use accountability systems for greater performance and commitment.* Boston: Harvard Business Review Press.

Smith, D. (2005). The challenge of diversity. *Association for the Study of Higher Education Higher Education Report, 31*(1), 1–90.

Smith, D. (2009). *Diversity's promise for higher education: Making it work.* Baltimore: The Johns Hopkins University Press.

Smith, D. G., Turner, C. S. V., Osei-Kofi, N., & Richards, S. (2004). Interrupting the usual: Successful strategies for diversifying the faculty. *The Journal of Higher Education, 75*(2), 133–160.

Smith, D., & Wolf-Wendel, L. (2005). The challenge of diversity: Involvement or alienation in the academy? *Association for the Study of Higher Education Report, 31*(1). San Francisco, CA: Jossey-Bass.

Sorensen, N., Nagda, B., Gurin, P., & Maxwell, K. (2009). Taking a "hands on" approach to diversity in higher education: A critical-dialogic model for effective intergroup interaction. *Analyses of Social Issues and Public Policy, 9*(1), 3–35.

Springer, A. (2006). *How to diversify the faculty.* Washington, DC: American Association of University Professors. Retrieved from http://www.aaup.org/issues/diversity-affirmative-action/diversify-faculty

Stern, S., & Williams, D. (2009). *Faculty diversity and excellence: A compelling university interest.* Madison: University of Wisconsin–Madison Office of the Provost.

Stewart, D. L. (Ed.). (2011). *Multicultural student services: Building bridges, re-visioning community.* ACPA Books and Media. Sterling, VA: Stylus.

Stewart, R. W. (2011). You support diversity, but are you ethical? Examining the interactive effects of diversity and ethical climate perceptions on turnover intentions. *Journal of Business Ethics, 99*(3), 453–465.

Thomas, D. A. (2004). Diversity as strategy. *Harvard Business Review, 82*(9), 1–11.

Thomas, D. C., & Inkson, K. C. (2003). *Cultural intelligence: People skills for global business.* San Francisco: Berrett-Koehler.

Thomas, R. (1991). *Beyond race and gender: Unleashing the power of your total workforce by managing diversity.* New York: AMACOM.

Tierney, W. G., & Bensimon, E. M. (1996). *Promotion and tenure: Community and socialization in academe.* Albany, NY: SUNY Press.

Tierney, W. G., & Sallee, M. W. (2008). Do organizational structures and strategies increase faculty diversity? A cultural analysis. *American Academic, 4*(1), 159–184.

Turner, C. (2002). *Diversifying the faculty: A guidebook for search committees.* Washington, DC: Association of American Colleges and Universities.

Turner, C., & Myers, S. L., Jr. (2000). *Faculty of color in academe: Bittersweet success.* Upper Saddle River, NJ: Allyn and Bacon.

University and Community College System of Nevada v. Farmer, 930 P.2d 730 (1997).

University of Minnesota. (2006, March 2). University Senate Minutes: No. 3, Faculty Senate Minutes No. 3, Student Senate Minutes No. 4. Retrieved from www1.umn.edu/usenate/usen/060302sen.html.

Villalpando, O., Harvey, W., Moses, Y., Barcelo, N., & Williams, D. (2009). *How institutional chief diversity officers use our research.* Panel discussion at the Annual Meeting of the Association for the Study of Higher Education, Vancouver, British Columbia, Canada.

Washington, V., & Harvey, W. (1989). *Affirmative rhetoric, negative action: African-American and Hispanic faculty at predominantly White institutions.* Washington, DC: School of Education and Human Development, George Washington University.

Watkins, M. (2003). *The first 90 days: Critical success strategies for new leaders at all levels.* Cambridge, MA: Harvard Business School Press.

Wilensky, H. L. (1964). The professionalization of everyone? *American Journal of Sociology, 70*(2), 37–58.

Williams, D. (2006). Overcoming the brutal facts: Implementing a relentless campus diversity change process. *The Diversity Factor, 14*(4), 1–9.

Williams, D. (2008). *Strategic transition framework: Learning, relationship building, and prioritizing.* Madison, WI: University of Wisconsin Office of the Vice Provost for Diversity and Climate.

Williams, D. (2012). *The role of the chief diversity officer in academic health centers.* Washington, DC: American Association of Medical Colleges. Retrieved from https://members.aamc.org/eweb/upload/The%20Role%20of%20the%20Chief%20Diversity%20Officer%20in%20Academic%20Health%20Centers.pdf

Williams, D. A., & Clowney, C. (2007). Strategic planning for diversity and organizational change: A primer for higher education leadership. *Effective Practices for Academic Leaders, 2*(3), 1–16.

Williams, D., Berger, J., & McClendon, S. (2005). *Toward a model of inclusive excellence in postsecondary institutions.* Washington, DC: Association of American Colleges and Universities. Retrieved from http://www.aacu.org/inclusive_excellence/papers.cfm

Williams, D., & Wade-Golden, K. (2007). The chief diversity officer: A structural analysis. *CUPA-HR Journal, 58*(1), 38–48.

Williams, D., & Wade-Golden, K. (2008). *The chief diversity officer: A primer for presidential leadership.* Washington, DC: American Council on Education.

Wilson, R. (2005). Past their prime? After 35 years on campuses, Black-studies programs struggle to survive. *The Chronicle of Higher Education, 51*(33), A9.

Wolfle, D. (1950). A national science foundation: 1950 prospects. *Science, 111,* 79–81.

Wolf-Wendel, L., & Ward, K. (2006). Academic life and motherhood: Variations by institutional type. *Higher Education, 52*(3), 487–521.

Zúñiga, X., Nagda, B. A., Chesler, M., & Cytron-Walker, A. (2007). *Intergroup dialogues in higher education: Meaningful learning about social justice.* San Francisco: Jossey-Bass.

INDEX